Active Learning

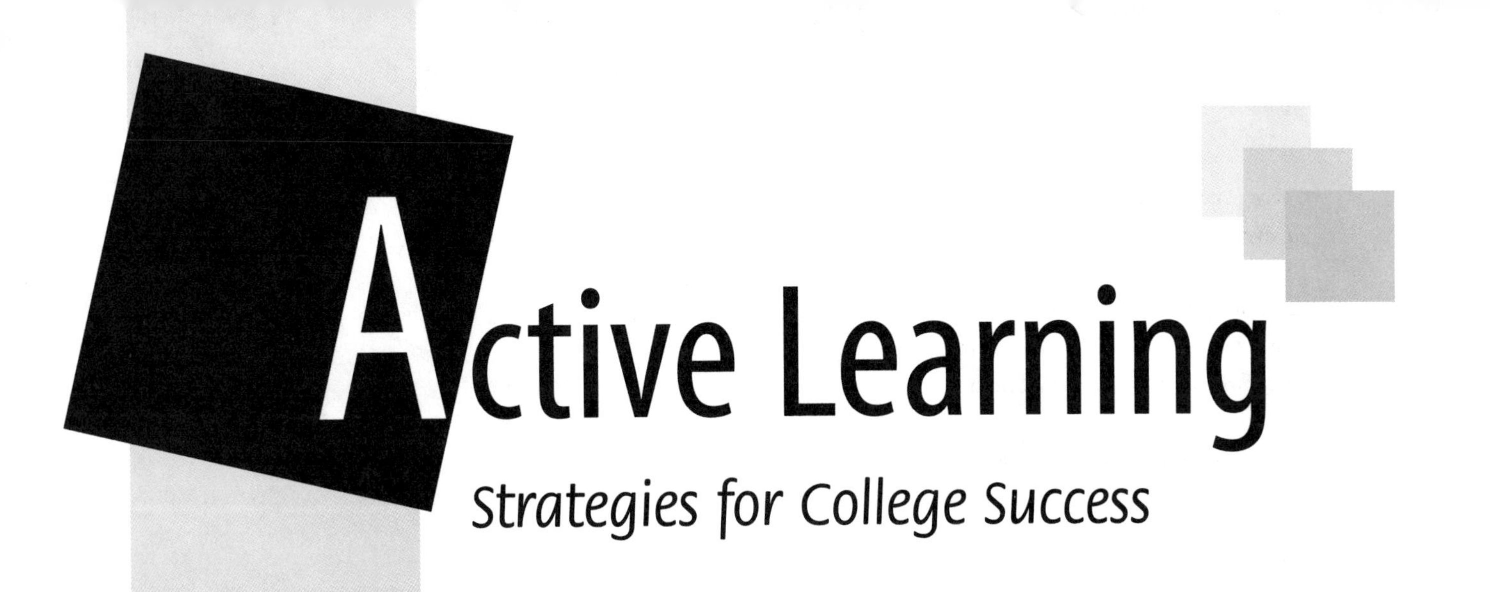

Active Learning

Strategies for College Success

Sherrie L. Nist
The University of Georgia

Jodi Patrick Holschuh
The University of Georgia

ALLYN AND BACON
Boston London Toronto Sydney Tokyo Singapore

Vice President: Joseph Opiela
Development Editor: Linda Bieze
Production Administrator: Susan Brown
Editorial-Production Service: Kathleen Deselle
Text Designer and Compositor: Boynton Hue Studio
Photo Researcher: Martha Shethar
Composition Buyer: Linda Cox
Cover Administrator: Linda Knowles
Manufacturing Buyer: Suzanne Lareau

A Pearson Education Company
160 Gould Street
Needham Heights, MA 02494
www.abacon.com

Library of Congress Cataloging-in-Publication Data
Nist, Sherrie L. (Sherrie Lee)
Active Learning : strategies for college success / Sherrie L. Nist, Jodi Patrick Holschuh.
p. cm.
Includes index.
ISBN 0-205-28856-1 (pbk.)
1. Study skills—United States. 2. Active learning—United States. 3. College student orientation—United States.
I. Holschuh, Jodi. II. Title.
LB2395.N54 2000
378.1'70281--dc21
99-31659
CIP

Photo Credits
p. 6, Robert Harbison; p. 10, Gary Conner/PhotoEdit; p. 29, Gary Conner/PhotoEdit; p. 45, Jean-Claude Lejeune/Stock Boston; p. 60, Will Hart; p. 62, Michael Dwyer/Stock Boston; p. 84, Will Faller; p. 98, Robert Harbison; p. 109, Will Hart; p. 130, Jean-Claude Lejeune/Stock Boston p. 145, Addison Geary/Stock Boston; p. 156, Gary Conner/PhotoEdit; p. 162, Sepp Seitz/Woodfin Camp & Associates; p. 167, Peter Menzel/Stock Boston; p. 193, Rudi Von Briel/PhotoEdit; p. 211, Robert Harbison; p. 227, Bill Aron/PhotoEdit; p. 253, David Young-Wolff/PhotoEdit; p. 270, Will Hart; p. 288, Elena Rooraid/PhotoEdit; p. 301, Will Hart; p. 309, Jean-Claude Lejeune/Stock Boston; p. 319, Robert Harbison; p. 337, Judy Gelles/Stock Boston.

Printed in the United States of America
10 9 8 7 6 5 4 3 2 1 04 03 02 01 00 99

Contents

Preface

The idea for *Active Learning: Strategies for College Success* came from our many interactions with both students and professors, as well as from our own and others' research focusing on what it takes to succeed in college. From our students we have learned that they often enter college unprepared to meet the learning and studying demands placed on them, even if they have been successful in high school. We have learned that students are sometimes overwhelmed with the reading and studying demands of college, and sometimes they become frustrated when they believe they are "working hard" but aren't seeing their efforts pay off. We learned that beginning students tend to be "one-trick ponies" who know only one way to study, often one that focuses on passive rather than active learning. We learned that it takes more than knowledge of a few strategies for students to achieve academically. It takes motivation, a belief that one can be successful, the ability to manage oneself and one's time, and the ability to prioritize responsibilities. But perhaps the most important thing we learned from our students is that they can be taught how to become active learners, and in most cases, they are eager to learn new skills that will help them succeed in college.

Student input was critical to the focus of *Active Learning,* but we also learned a lot from the professors who teach large numbers of first-year students. We learned that most college professors are more than willing to help students succeed in their courses. We learned that professors believe that when students walk into their classes on the first day it is the students' responsibility to be active learners—to have the skills to do whatever it takes to be successful in each particular class and discipline. We learned that professors and students don't always see eye to eye on what a discipline entails or even on what should be expected of students. The most important thing we learned from professors, however, may have been that, regardless of the particular discipline in which they teach, they view the overall purpose of college as much more than memorizing a bunch of facts. Rather, they see the purpose of a college education as to provide students with the skills to learn on their own in the future.

Finally, we learned from our own research efforts as well as those of others in our field. To prepare for writing this book, we reread some of the studies that influenced our own work and influenced the field of college learning in general. It became very clear to us that being an active learner includes many factors that all have to interact in order for learning to be maximized. In different kinds of ways, we learned this from our students and from professors as well.

The major premise of *Active Learning,* then, is the importance of academics. While other academic success books have only a chapter or two specifically devoted to the academic side of studying and learning in college, every chapter of *Active Learning* has this focus. It takes you on an academic journey and helps you to understand yourself as a learner and what it takes to be successful. The majority of this text focuses on four key factors of learning that all must interact: (1) your own characteristics as a learner; (2) the tasks you must complete in each of your classes; (3) the strategies that will help you read, understand, and remember what it is your professor expects you to learn; and finally (4) the texts with which you interact.

When we outlined this text and the approach we would take in writing it, we agreed on the importance of building the book on a strong research-based foundation. Many first-year and study skills books tout study methods that have conventional wisdom as their basis but are not necessarily grounded in research. *Active Learning,* however, is based on what research on college learning has found to be important to success. You will note as you go through the book that each chapter contains a *Research into Practice* reading that discusses a research study related to that particular chapter.

Using Active Learning

Active Learning: Strategies for College Success was designed not only to get you to read about what it takes to become an active learner but also to start thinking and talking about it. Thus, many of the activities ask you to discuss important questions with classmates, to critically think about issues, and to write your own reflections. We believe that active learners use many means to go about learning in college. They read, they write, they discuss, and they visualize. Interacting with information in a variety of ways encourages active processing, and active processing leads to academic success.

We have divided the text into six parts:

- **Part I, Introduction to Active Learning** helps you understand how college differs from high school and how active learning benefits you.
- **Part II, Characteristics of the Learner** helps you organize yourself and your time, motivate yourself, develop and maintain a positive attitude towards college, analyze your beliefs about learning, and deal with stress.
- **Part III, Identifying the Task** gives you advice on interacting with your professors, pinpointing the specific tasks you need to accomplish, and taking good lecture notes.
- **Part IV, Identifying the Strategies** offers you surefire strategies for prereading, reading, rehearsing after reading, and reviewing your texts.

- **Part V, Characteristics of Texts** helps you modify the basic strategies for every course you may take, from anthropology to zoology, and shows you how to vary your reading rate for efficient reading.
- **Part VI, Pulling Everything Together** offers strategies to study for and take both objective and essay exams and summarizes the factors that influence learning to help you put together your own action plan.

These parts present research-based strategies that you can learn and then apply to the excerpts from college texts in Appendixes A–C. We have included text excerpts from three disciplines—psychology, biology, and history—so that you can also practice modifying strategies according to the type of text you are reading.

Special Features of Active Learning

Active Learning offers a number of features to help you understand and apply the concepts and strategies presented in each chapter:

- **Research into Practice** Found in each chapter, this feature focuses on an important research article and how it translates into practice for college students.
- **Thinking Critically** These activities, found throughout each chapter, encourage you to think on higher levels.
- **Self-Evaluation** Each chapter offers you an opportunity to evaluate where you stand now in your use of study strategies in order to see where you want to go.
- **Real College** These scenarios, found at the end of each chapter, give you opportunities to evaluate the study practices of other college students by responding to real-life situations.
- **Networking** This resource, found at the end of each chapter, helps you get the most out of the vast amount of study assistance available on the World Wide Web.

Acknowledgments

When we were beginning to write *Active Learning,* Dr. Lee Schulman, President of the Carnegie Foundation for the Advancement of Teaching, spoke to the faculty at the University of Georgia. Among the many significant things he said, one idea—"Everyone here stands on the shoulders of those researchers and teachers who came before them"—stayed with us as we wrote this book. We believe it's important, then, to acknowledge all those researchers who came before us, those who conducted research that made breakthroughs in the understanding of what it takes to be an active learner. If it weren't for the work of those who came before us, we would not have found it possible to write *Active Learning.*

In addition, we want to acknowledge the students we have had the privilege to teach and the professors from a variety of disciplines who have shared their views on what it takes to be successful students in their respective areas. Our students have helped us ground this book in reality—the reality of what it takes to succeed in college, as well as the reality of the many pressures that face college students today. Professors, some of whom are friends of ours—Dr. Bill Barstow and Dr. Marshall Darley from the Botany Department at the University of Georgia and Dr. Bill Stueck and Dr. Bill Leary from the History Department at the University of Georgia, for example—have given many hours of their time to discussing learning and studying issues in their disciplines. This text would have not been nearly as effective without their valuable insights.

Certainly, we acknowledge our respective families—our spouses, parents, siblings, and children—who always offered their continuous support, and sometimes even additional insights, as we worked to turn this book from a concept into reality. We appreciate their understanding, support, and advice as this text seemed to take over our lives at times.

We acknowledge the major contributions of reviewers of early versions of this manuscript. Our utmost thanks go to Jerry Bouchie, St. Cloud State University; Carol R. Lyon, St. Ambrose University; Kimberly A. McDonald, Saginaw Valley State University; Candace Ready, Piedmont Technical College; Carolyn S. Smith, University of Southern Indiana; Jane Snyder, Fontbonne College; Sharon Silverman, Loyola University Chicago; Linda Spaeth, University of Wisconsin–Eau Claire; Joan Stottlemeyer, Carroll College; Joyce Stumpe, Purdue University North Central; and Susan S. Tully, Aiken Technical College. They often made us look at ideas from a different perspective and provided valuable suggestions that made this book move from good to great! In addition, the reviewers viewed this book from the perspective of their respective institutions, which helped us present the information in ways that will serve a variety of college curricula and college learners.

Finally, we would be remiss if we failed to acknowledge all of the assistance we received from those we have worked with at Allyn and Bacon—Virginia Lanigan, Joe Opiela, Linda Bieze, Bridget Keane, and Susan Brown. An especially loud THANK YOU to Linda Bieze who helped us so much and who probably now knows more about active learning than she ever wanted. We would also like to acknowledge Nancy Forsyth, Senior Vice President and Editorial Director at Allyn and Bacon. She read the initial prospectus and encouraged us to move forward. We are grateful for Nancy's belief in this project. It may not have come to fruition without her encouragement.

About the Authors

Sherrie L. Nist is Director of the Division of Academic Assistance at the University of Georgia, where she also holds the rank of Professor. Before becoming Director, she taught reading and studying courses to college students in the same Division. Dr. Nist received both her master's and doctoral degrees from the University of Florida. It was as a graduate student that she first became interested in how students learn, particularly in the factors that seem to influence a smooth transition from high school to college, and the academic struggles that first-year students seem to face. Sherrie has published over 80 articles, textbooks, textbook chapters, and other professional pieces all related to how college students learn and study. She has presented the results of her research in more than 100 national and international professional meetings. She has received many honors and awards for her contributions to both teaching and research.

Sherrie is married to Steve Olejnik, who is also a professor at the University of Georgia. They have one daughter, Kama, who lives in Los Angles, California, and a relatively new addition to the family, Mollie, a Jack Russell Terrier, who, by the way, is a very active learner! When not working, Sherrie loves traveling, cooking, and, of course, reading and learning new things.

Jodi Patrick Holschuh is an Assistant Professor in the Division of Academic Assistance at the University of Georgia. As a volunteer instructor for the Reading and Writing for Critical Thinking project, she teaches strategies for active learning to teachers in Estonia. Before returning to the University of Georgia, where she received her doctoral degree, Dr. Holschuh was an Assistant Professor at Texas A&M University. Jodi became interested in learning more about strategies for academic success while working as a Tutorial Coordinator at the Philadelphia College of Textiles and Science. It was there that she realized that students could be "studying hard" yet still struggling to pass their courses. Her research interests include students' beliefs about learning, learning in content-area courses, strategies for academic success, and motivation.

Jodi is married to Doug Holschuh, who never lost faith in her ability to complete this project. She has two cats, Puddin' and Amelia, who loved to nap on draft after draft of this book. When she is not teaching, researching, or writing, Jodi loves reading good books, traveling to new places, and fixing up her new house.

Dedications

For Sherrie: To my family—my husband Steve Olejnik, my daughter Kama, and my parents, Roy and Charlene Miller.

For Jodi: To the memory of my father, Stanley Erwin Patrick, who taught me the love of learning and the desire for teaching.

Active Learning

Introduction to Active Learning

College learning is very different from high school learning. Even if this is your first term in college, you may already have noticed many of those differences. In Chapter 1, we discuss the differences between college and high school and describe several special situations you will eventually encounter in college.

Chapter 2 introduces the concept of active learning. You will find out what active learning is and why becoming an active learner can help you succeed in college.

You will learn about the four factors that influence learning in Chapter 3: (1) the charactersitics of the learner, (2) the tasks, (3) the learning strategies, and (4) the texts. We explain how the factors work together to influence student learning. These four factors will guide the organization of the remainder of this book.

Before you read the chapters in Part I, please respond to the following statements. Read each statement and decide whether you agree or disagree with it.

Keep your responses in mind as you read the chapters in Part I. When you have finished reading Part I, revisit this page. How are your responses similar to or different from what is introduced in the chapters?

Chapter 1 Now That You're Here

Chapter 2 Active Learning: What's in It for You?

Chapter 3 Factors That Impact Learning

BEFORE			AFTER	
Agree	Disagree		Agree	Disagree
☐	☐	*1. The main difference between high school and college is that attendance in college classes is not required.*	☐	☐
☐	☐	*2. The methods I used for learning in high school are appropriate for college learning.*	☐	☐
☐	☐	*3. College professors don't care whether students learn or not.*	☐	☐
☐	☐	*4. Learning involves absorbing all of the information presented in class.*	☐	☐
☐	☐	*5. As long as I put in enough time, I should do just fine in college.*	☐	☐
☐	☐	*6. I study the same way for every course.*	☐	☐
☐	☐	*7. I will not do well in a course if I am not interested in the topic.*	☐	☐
☐	☐	*8. Given the right strategies, I can learn just about anything.*	☐	☐

Now That You're Here

Read this chapter to answer the following questions:

How does studying in college differ from studying in high school?

What special situations can you expect to encounter in college, sooner or later?

Starting college! You may feel as if you have been preparing for this day forever. You've taken a college preparatory curriculum in high school, you've talked with friends or siblings who are already in college, and you may have even visited several campuses before deciding which school to attend. Or you may be returning to college after several years of working. Regardless of your situation, you are probably excited about what the next years have in store for you. And you may even be a little wary and unsure of yourself as you begin down the college path. You may be particularly concerned about what awaits you if you don't have friends or relatives already in college.

In this chapter, we will discuss some of the concerns new college students have and some of the adjustments they must make, especially in their first term or year. These concerns and adjustments will be discussed in two sections. First, we will discuss some of the ways in which college differs from high school. Second, we will present eight situations that you are sure to encounter in college sooner or later, and we will offer suggestions about how you might deal with them. (Each of these issues will be discussed in greater depth later in this text.) Some of the factors presented here will focus on academics and others will focus on basic survival tactics. Keep in mind as you

STUDY TIP

Don't cram! Pay attention to every class every day.

read this chapter that campuses differ in size and in the expectations they have of students. For these reasons, some of the generalizations and solutions offered here might not apply exactly to your particular situation.

How Does College Differ from High School?

How many times since high school graduation have you heard one of your relatives say something like this: "Oh _______ (insert your name)! Enjoy these college years. They will be the best of your life." Although this statement is probably true—college is enjoyable and memorable—it is also demanding and, in many instances, just plain different from high school. It's a time in your life when you will go through many changes as you prepare for the world of work that follows. In this section, we will discuss some of the ways in which high school and college differ. Before you read this section, however, read *Research into Practice,* which focuses on a research study that scientifically examined some of the academic differences between high school and college. At the end of this section, you will be asked to brainstorm some additional differences.

Each chapter in this text will include a *Research into Practice* segment to help you think about how research influences what we know about studying and learning in college. Each one will include a research citation. Each citation tells you the authors (last name first), the year (in parentheses) the article was published, the title of the article, the journal or book in which it was published, and if appropriate, the volume number of the journal article and the pages on which the article can be found. The main text of *Research into Practice* is a brief description of the research and a summary of the practical implications of this piece of research.

Research Into Practice

Differences between High School and College*

In this study, Drs. Thomas, Bol, and Warkentin make the case that beginning college students often lack the skills necessary to be active, independent learners who know how to select and use appropriate strategies on their own. They suggest that at least part of this is because in high school, students are not given adequate opportunities to develop their

* Source: Thomas, J. W., Bol, L., & Warkentin, R. W. (1991). Antecedents of college students' study deficiencies: The relationship between course features and students' study activities. *Higher Education* 22: 275–296.

academic studying abilities. In other words, high school courses may demand considerably less of students than comparable college courses. For example, in high school students may be able to make high grades without using active study strategies or without taking adequate lecture notes. Moreover, their study found that in general, high school tests were considerably less demanding, thus not encouraging students to use study practices that are so necessary for success at the college level. A large percentage of high school tests focused on lower-level memorization items, primarily using multiple-choice formats.

This study is important because it was one of the first scientific investigations that actually pinpointed why first-year college students often have difficulty earning grades comparable to what they made in high school. Although it's probably safe to assume that your college history or biochemistry professor doesn't know about this study, the findings can help you to understand some of the reasons why making the adjustment from studying in high school to studying in college can be challenging.

☐ College requires greater independent learning.

In high school, you probably had teachers who wanted to help you succeed in the courses they taught, and so they were willing to give you lots of help in learning the information. They may have prepared study guides for you to use before a test or reviewed course material in such a way that they actually told you the exact questions that would be on their exams. Although college instructors also want you to succeed—we have

never met a professor who wants students to fail—they don't give students as much study help. Most college professors believe that it is their job to present information in a clear manner and that it is your job to learn both text and lecture information without much assistance. Sure, most professors will answer questions about course content and things you don't understand, but they will not provide you with a variety of supplementary learning materials, and they certainly will not give you test questions! They expect that you know effective and efficient study strategies that will enable you to learn the course information independently. Professors have little patience with students who claim that tests are not fair or that they have too heavy a workload. If you don't know how to study for their courses, they expect you to learn how, and to learn how quickly. Learning how to learn may be one of the most important benefits of going to college, because after you graduate, most employers will also expect you to do a considerable amount of learning on your own.

☐ College classes move at a faster pace.

If you ask first-year college students about the differences between high school and college, one of the most common responses will be that college courses move much faster and cover more ground than high school classes. What it might have taken you a year to cover in world history in high school will probably be covered in a semester in college. In addition, more topics are generally covered and in greater detail. However, most college professors expect you to fill in many of the details on your own. For instance, a typical lecture may cover the main points in a college biology chapter, but most professors expect you to fill in the gaps in the lectures by reading your text, viewing films or documentaries, attending special lectures, doing lab work, or engaging in computer-assisted learning modules. And most or all of this is done on your time, not on class time. It's not uncommon for college professors to move through three, four, or more chapters in a week and expect you to keep up.

☐ College classes require you to think critically.

What does it mean to think critically? Thinking critically involves reasoning, making and seeing connections between and among ideas, and problem solving. It's being able to analyze, synthesize, and critique. It's questioning what you see, hear, and read—not necessarily everything—but not accepting everything as truth either. Critical thinking involves not only understanding the information presented but also thinking about how this information fits into your own scheme of interpreting your environment.

In your high school classes, perhaps you were required to memorize a lot of facts and then give those facts back to your teachers on tests. Perhaps you were discouraged from questioning either your high school textbooks or your high school teacher. But as you proceed through college, you will find yourself in more and more classes in which your professor actually wants you to do more than memorize. You might have to critique an essay on gun control, read and respond to a historian's view of the Vietnam conflict, or compare and contrast conflicting theories. All of these tasks require you to think critically. Thinking critically certainly requires you to know some facts and to understand your texts, but that's not the be-all and end-all. You have to take the next step by applying what you've learned to new situations. As a way of encouraging you to think critically, you will find activities titled *Thinking Critically* throughout the chapters of this text.

☐ College classes have few safety nets.

Usually on the first day of a college class, your professor will give you a syllabus. The syllabus outlines the course requirements and also generally tells you how your grade will be determined. Something that will become clear as you read your syllabus is that many of the safety nets you had in high school have all but disappeared in college. By "safety nets" we mean ways to receive extra credit or other ways to improve your grade if you did poorly on an assignment or on an exam. For example, in high school you may have been able to take a math test several times until you received a passing grade. Or you may have been permitted to resubmit homework that was completed incorrectly. Such is not the case in most college classes, however. In fact, in college classes you'll be faced with fewer testing situations and many college professors neither assign nor collect homework. What this all boils down to is that your course grade will be determined by the grade you earn on a limited number of tests or papers. There's little chance for extra credit or redoing a test or paper on which you did poorly. Once you realize that the safety nets are no longer present, you can make sure that you have done things to the best of your ability right from the start.

☐ College requires you to study longer and more effectively.

You will probably find out pretty quickly that both the amount of time you put into studying and the way you study in college will have to change if you want to continue to earn high grades. During their first term, students often have "college shock"— an abrupt awakening to what it takes to be successful in college. When we talk with the students in our own classes about the way they approached studying in high school and how they must study in college in order to earn comparable grades, most have plenty to say! For the most part, students tell us that they really did not have to study in high school. Studying meant reading over a teacher-constructed study guide or going over their class notes for about a half hour. Few students ever had to read their texts, and many began college never having taken essay exams.

Furthermore, the thought of putting in two hours out of class for every hour in class only brings a laugh! The point we want to make is that it is important to realize early on that studying in college requires not only more time but also a variety of study strategies to have at your disposal. Later in this book we'll present numerous strategies and we'll discuss how to manage your time. For now, just latch onto the idea that in order to do well in college you'll need to be a student about forty hours per week (if you are taking a full load), and you'll have to experiment with new and perhaps different strategies if you want to be competitive.

☐ College provides fewer chances for evaluation.

In high school, it may have seemed as though you were always taking tests or writing papers. You were probably tested rather frequently, so there was only a small amount of information for you to learn from test to test. In addition, because you had numerous chances for evaluation, if you did poorly on any one test, you could usually make it up on the next test and it wouldn't influence your grade too much. In college, on the other hand, you will probably have fewer chances to be evaluated.

At first, many students find the idea of preparing for and taking only three tests per course in a term appealing. But think about the big picture for a moment. What does fewer chances for evaluation really mean? What if you do poorly on one of those three exams? What will happen to your course average? Additionally, think about the amount of information that you must learn for each test. If you have only three exams, you are going to be held responsible for much more information at one time than you were in high school. Finally, as we mentioned earlier, because you're faced with little chance for extra credit and because homework is generally not graded (it's assumed that you will keep up with the reading and homework assignments without someone checking up on you), you must rely on your tests and/or paper grades alone to get you through the course. What at first seems to be an advantage—fewer tests, homework that goes unchecked, a longer period of time between exams—may actually work against you. The message is this: Know what the course demands are and then budget your time so that you can stay on top of the workload and be ready when it's time to take those few exams.

☐ College gives you greater freedom and greater responsibility.

Legally you become an adult at age 18, which just happens to be at about the same time you graduate from high school. So whether you are living in a residence hall away from home or living at home and attending college, you are seen as an adult, at least in the eyes of college officials. In college, no one is there to be sure that you are keeping on top of your schoolwork. No one keeps track of what time you go out or is going to punish you if you come home past curfew. No one is going to ask you if you have done all of your reading and studying before heading out for a night on the town. This is particularly true if you are living away from your parents' watchful eyes. It is easy to see, then, that college gives you a lot of opportunities to succeed, but it also gives you greater freedom to make mistakes.

The flip side of this freedom is that it comes with a tremendous amount of responsibility. This means that you are more or less responsible for yourself. It is your responsibility to prioritize the tasks you *have* to do against the things you *want* to do. It is this responsibility part that students often forget about—the fact that making bad decisions can lead to disastrous effects in the long run. It is important to remember that although you have a tremendous amount of freedom in college, you also have the responsibility that goes with it. You're responsible for your successes, but it's also your responsibility if you mess up.

☐ College provides greater anonymity.

If you attend a medium-size to large-size college or university, you will be faced with being somewhat anonymous, and in some cases, very anonymous. By "anonymous" we mean that you can become another face in the crowd to your professors and can get lost in a sea of student faces on campus. Most of you probably attended high schools where you got to know your teachers and your classmates fairly well. Your teachers not only knew your name, but were also concerned about whether or not you were learning and understanding the information presented in their classes.

For the most part, in college, your professor has few opportunities to get to know you well. On larger campuses, class size in introductory courses can run into the hundreds, making class discussion next to impossible. You're reduced to being a number rather than a person with a name, and if you're having problems with the class, you may be sent to a graduate student or peer tutor for assistance. Even on smaller campuses, you may have problems getting to know your professor well because he or she may have several courses to teach. If a professor is required to teach five courses with an enrollment of around thirty students each, his or her teaching load is 150 students.

All is not lost, however. Most of the time, students are anonymous only if they want to be, regardless of the size of their campus. You can become a "face" to your professors by making appointments to talk with them. You can join clubs that have faculty sponsors. You can take part in a variety of campus activities in which other students share your interests. These are just some of the numerous ways in which you can make connections with both faculty and other students even on very large campuses.

☐ College requires you to be proactive.

When we say that college requires you to be proactive, we mean that it's your responsibility to take the initiative in a variety of situations. In high school, either your teachers or your parents may have insisted that you get help if you were having problems with a particular course. And you may have followed their advice reluctantly. In addition, since others guided you in getting help or in making choices, you may not have realized what help was available in your school and community.

In college, however, it becomes your responsibility to know the resources that are available on your campus, so that if you do run into difficulties or need the services of some office, you'll know how to find the information you need or where to go to get assistance. What follows is a listing of some of the more important resources that you should seek out on campus. If you are proactive and find out a little about them before you need their services, it will save you time in the long run. The other point is that you don't want to wait until you are in dire need of these resources before seeking them out.

- ***The library.*** Although this may sound strange, we have had sophomores in our classes who have never been in the library! Let's face it, at some point you will have to write a research paper, and unless you live in a big city, your public library probably won't have all the resources you need. Thus, it's important to not only know the location of the library, but also to become familiar with it. Most campuses have library orientations that help students learn to navigate large and complex systems. In addition to providing resources, however, the library is a great place to study, to do research on-line, or to meet your study group.

- ***The Learning Center.*** Most campuses have a Learning Center, often located in the middle of campus where access is easy. A Learning Center can be an excellent source of assistance because most offer a variety of services, from academic counseling to assistance with writing, studying, and mathematics problems. Currently many Learning Centers are equipped with state-of-the-art computers that can assist you in everything from word processing to reading-rate instruction. Individuals who work in Learning Centers are generally highly trained and enjoy working with students, either one-on-one or in small groups.

- ***Tutorial Services.*** Like Learning Centers, most campuses offer tutorial services for a broad range of courses. Generally, tutoring is provided by undergraduate students who earn top grades in the areas that they tutor. Tutoring is often free, but usually you must make an appointment. Being proactive and getting tutoring as soon as you begin to experience problems will help you get back on track.

- ***Health Services.*** Everyone gets ill, especially when they're under stress, when seasons change, or when a particular "bug" is making the rounds on campus and in the residence halls. Because getting sick enough to need the services of a doctor is probably inevitable, know where your campus health facility is and what the rules are to be able to see a medical professional. Again, don't wait until you feel as if you're on your deathbed. Find out where to go and what to do early in your first term.

- ***Student Center or Student Union.*** The Student Center is usually the hub of the campus. On most campuses you can meet friends there for food and conversation, but most Student Centers also offer a wealth of resources. Sometimes campus organizations and clubs have offices in the center. Social event and concert tickets can be purchased there. General information such as bus schedules, campus maps, and event schedules can be obtained. Often, the campus bookstore is located in or near the Student Center. In fact, on the University of Georgia campus, the Student Center also has a post office, a game room, a movie theater, a copy center, meeting rooms, and many other services. It's important to know what resources and services your Student Center provides. When you don't know where else to turn, the Student Center is a good place to start if you need information about your campus.

Although campuses differ dramatically, most provide numerous resources for students. The important thing for you to remember is to find out what those resources are, where they are located, and how to avail yourself of them *before you actually need to use them.* You should think of locating resources as part of your overall orientation to campus. Be proactive! Don't wait until two days before a paper is due to find out the library hours, or until you have a severe case of the flu before you stagger out of bed and try to locate the health center.

As you have just read, college is different from high school in many ways. You must think differently about the expectations, learning conditions, level of responsibility, and studying methods than you thought about them in high school. This is not bad. It simply means you will have to make some transitions in the way you learn and study in order to be successful.

How High School Differs from College

	High School		College
Independence	Less independence	⟷	Greater independence
Pacing	Slow pace	⟷	Fast pace
Level of critical thinking	Less critical thinking	⟷	Greater critical thinking
Safety nets	Teachers provide many	⟷	Professors provide few
Study effort	Little and sporadic	⟷	Greater and effective
Evaluation	Many opportunities	⟷	Limited opportunities
Responsibility	Rests on others	⟷	Rests on you
Anonymity	Little	⟷	A lot
Importance of proactivity	Low	⟷	High

1.1 SOMETHING TO WRITE ABOUT AND DISCUSS

Listed below are the services that we just discussed. For each service, write down the location, phone number, and hours. Use it as a convenient way to have access to important information.

Library

Location: ______________________________

Telephone number: ______________________________

Hours: ______________________________

Learning Center

Location: ______________________________

Telephone number: ______________________________

Hours: ______________________________

Tutorial Services

Location: ______________________________

Telephone number: ______________________________

Hours: ______________________________

Health Services

Location: ______________________________

Telephone number: ______________________________

Hours: ______________________________

Student Center or Student Union

Location: ______________________________

Telephone number: ______________________________

Hours: ______________________________

Bookstore

Location: ______________________________

Telephone number: ______________________________

Hours: ______________________________

Other Important Services

____

____

____

1.2

SOMETHING TO WRITE ABOUT AND DISCUSS

Thinking Critically

Now that you have read about some of the differences between high school and college, analyze your own experiences and respond to the following questions. Write your responses on the lines that follow each question. Then compare your responses with those of one or more of your peers.

1. *What do you think is the biggest difference between high school and college?*

___

___

___

2. *Have you changed the way you study since you have been in college? If so, why did you change? What made you realize that change was necessary?*

___

___

___

3. *What do you think your high school teachers should have taught you in order to better prepare you for a positive college experience?*

___

___

___

4. *What kinds of problems are your friends or your roommate having in making the transition from high school to college?*

___

___

___

What Special Situations Can You Expect to Encounter in College, Sooner or Later?

Now that you have seen some of the ways in which high school and college differ, let's examine this transition from another perspective. We'll briefly tell you about eight situations that most college students will encounter sooner or later. We'll also examine how you might cope with or handle each situation and leave you with some questions to think about. All of these situations will be addressed again throughout this text, so you will be able to explore these ideas in greater detail later.

In a perfect world, none of the following situations would occur. All students would go to class every day, distribute their study time over a period of days, stay on top of their reading, and make the Dean's List every term. No one would become ill, have problems with relationships, or worry about how he or she will pay next term's tuition. We all know, however, that the world is not perfect and that the world of college is an imperfect place as well. So, right up front, let's discuss some of the situations that you might encounter in college, some of which you might not be prepared for. As you read each section, think about how you might handle the situation and what additional information might help you cope better.

Professors Who Take Roll

Someone may have told you that the only time you really *have to* show up in college classes is on test days. Someone also may have suggested that if you can get the information on your own, professors don't really care whether you are in class. Although many professors don't take attendance, eventually you will run across one who does, and in reality, most actually do want you present in class. Some professors know what the research says about class attendance in college, that is, students who attend class regularly perform better than those who attend only sporadically. Thus, you will eventually come across a professor who truly believes that learning takes place in class as well as out of it. Of course, even if your professor does not take roll, it's still a good idea to attend class. But when you come across a statement on the syllabus that clearly states that attendance is required, take your professor at his or her word.

1.3 SOMETHING TO THINK ABOUT AND DISCUSS

- What are the advantages of going to class each day?
  For students?
  For the professor?
- Do you think that class attendance should ever be required?
  Why or why not?

An Early Morning Class

Let's face it. Most college students are not morning people. In fact there's even scientific evidence to suggest that college-age biological clocks are set differently than those of older adults. This research indicates that students' biological clocks are preset to stay up late at night and to sleep late in the morning. However, the college officials who determine the times of class periods evidently are unaware of this research! To be realistic, classrooms do have to be used throughout the day. However, certainly no one in his or her right mind would expect you to be awake and ready to think by 8:00 A.M.! Unfortunately (for most college students), a time will come when you will have to take an early morning class, or at least register for a class at a time you hate. That's the bad news. The good news is that you usually can arrange your schedule in such a way that this doesn't happen every term. Thus, you can think about it as a temporary situation. If you have that early class, try to juggle the rest of your schedule so that you can go to bed earlier than usual the night before. Additionally, if you are forced to take an early class, try to take one that meets only two or three days a week, thus allowing you a little more flexibility on other days. Who knows, you may even discover that taking an 8:00 A.M. class allows you to be more organized and on top of things. It can also give you the excuse you need to take a nap sometime during the day.

1.4

SOMETHING TO THINK ABOUT AND DISCUSS

- How might your personal biological clock influence your studying effectiveness?
- What are some other ways in which you might cope with an early morning class? A class that is at a time when you are not at your best?

A Course or Professor You Don't Particularly Care For

It's perhaps sad but true—there will be courses you don't like and professors with whom you fail to connect. Even if you have a wide range of interests and you tend to get along well with almost everyone, at some point you'll have to make it through a rough class. You can take one of two routes when this happens.

ROUTE A: You can have an "attitude" and think of every excuse imaginable not to do the work or go to class. You can blame your attitude on the professor or the boring material that you are expected to learn.

Consequences of Route A: A poor course grade, feeling bad about yourself, and having to work doubly hard in another course to bring up your overall grade point average.

ROUTE B: Acknowledge that you really don't care much for the course or the professor. It's one course, however, and you can make it through. Study with someone who seems to like the course. Try to motivate yourself with small rewards. Tell yourself that this is temporary and the course will soon be over.

Consequences of Route B: Perhaps you will not earn an A in the class, but you will emerge with your ego and your grade point average intact.

1.5 SOMETHING TO THINK ABOUT AND DISCUSS

- Have you been in a situation yet in which you were enrolled in a course or had a professor that you did not like?
- How did you deal with this situation?
- How would you deal with it if you haven't already experienced it?
- What suggestions do you have for others who might be in the same predicament?

Cramming for a Test

We firmly believe that most college students have good intentions. Few students head off to college wanting to do poorly or believing that they can earn good grades without studying. But sometimes good intentions aren't enough and you find yourself in a time management nightmare: A big test in a couple of days (or, worse yet, tomorrow), and you've done very little preparing. Now it's cram time! Personally, we've never met a student who didn't have to cram at some time. Students get sick and lose study time. They have family concerns or problems with friends that take up the energy so necessary to prepare for tests. A host of reasons can explain why cramming happens, even when students have good intentions. And cramming occasionally probably isn't a horrible thing, but it shouldn't become the way you live your academic life. If you have to cram now and then, try to use what time you have left to study to your advantage. If you haven't read the text, at least read the text summaries, questions at the end of the chapter, chapter outlines, and so on, so that you have some idea of what the chapter is about. Concentrate study time on your lecture notes, and study with another person or group, hopefully classmates who know considerably more than you. Cover as much territory as you can by using small pockets of time to rehearse the information. Fifteen minutes here and there can have a big payoff. If you can avoid it, don't stay up all night. Get some sleep; don't skip another class to study for this test or get behind in other classes while you're trying to cram. And as soon as possible, regroup. Plan ahead so that you don't have to cram again.

1.6 SOMETHING TO THINK ABOUT AND DISCUSS

- Have you been in a situation in which you had to cram? If so, think back to how you felt. What influence did cramming have on your test performance?
- What are some things that you can do so that you can avoid having to cram?

Maintaining Motivation for Academics

Most college students experience motivation problems at some time or another. Some students have problems maintaining motivation for an entire term. They begin on the right foot and are doing an excellent job of staying on top of things. Then they just get "tired." For many students this tiredness occurs just after the midpoint of the semester or quarter. It usually doesn't last long, but for some students the decline in motivation is long enough and severe enough to interfere with their schoolwork. Other students experience a lull in motivation in just one class, generally a class with which they may be experiencing difficulty. Still others begin the term with good intentions, yet quickly develop general motivation problems in every class. It's not that these students lack motivation for everything. It's just that they have lost their motivation for academic-related things. What can you do if you feel unmotivated? We'll explore this topic in depth in Chapter 4; but for now, if you are having motivation problems, try setting some specific, reachable goals. Whether your lack of motivation is concentrated in one particular course, occurs at a specific period of time, or is generalized across all your academic courses, goal setting can help you stay focused and improve your motivation to learn.

1.7

SOMETHING TO THINK ABOUT AND DISCUSS

- Next to procrastination, maintaining motivation may be the second biggest problem faced by college students. Why do you think students have motivation problems?
- Think about a time when your motivation to learn was low. What caused you to lose motivation? What did you do to restore it?
- What are some things you can do when you feel that you are losing your motivational edge?

Personal Problems and/or Illness

No one plans on getting ill or having personal problems. But few students are illness-free for their entire college stay. And all students at some point face personal dilemmas. These dilemmas can be anything from problems with relationships, roommates, and family to substance abuse. In a room of a hundred college students, you would probably be hard-pressed to find two students facing exactly the same set of problems. Knowing that you may become ill or run into personal problems does little to solve the entire problem. But there are some things you can do to salvage even a bad situation. First, as you plan your schedule for the term (planning is discussed in detail in Chapter 4) build in some flexibility, just in case. If everything goes according to plan, the worst thing that can happen is you'll have some extra time to study, work, or play. Second, as mentioned earlier, know what services are available on your campus. What services does the health center offer? Is there free counseling available? If so, where? Many students believe that asking for assistance, particularly in situations that might involve counseling, is a sign of weakness. Nothing could be further from the truth. Counseling, whether it focuses on academic problems such as time management or test anxiety, or personal problems such as dealing with the breakup of a relationship, can be healing and positive. It has been our experience that students who seek assistance early rebound the fastest. Third, develop a set of reliable peers who can be there for you in times of illness or other problems. Often knowing that some other person can help you out makes all the difference in the world.

1.8

SOMETHING TO THINK ABOUT AND DISCUSS

- What is your track record for dealing with personal problems? Illness?
- What generally happens to your grades when you have personal problems or an illness?
- What resources are available on your campus to help you? For example, where might you be able to receive counseling services?

Frustration

College often seems to be one long roll of red tape! Where you find red tape, you also find frustration. You can become frustrated at any number of things: Sometimes registration can be a nightmare, especially if you are in the last group to register, if the phone lines are constantly busy, or if the computers "go down." Likewise, most colleges have an add/drop period during which students can try to add classes that other students have dropped. We've seen many a student frustrated because they could not get in a course they needed because it was cancelled or because it was full. Buying books can also be frustrating—long lines and sold-out texts are the biggest complaints here. Then there's navigating the financial aid office, trying to get an appointment to see your adviser before registration, and a host of other obstacles that can wear on you to the point at which frustration sets in. Put all of these incidents on top of the studying demands and personal baggage that you carry around and you can see why at some point or another you're going to feel this frustration. Frustration often leads to stress, which further complicates the problem.

You will experience frustrations and stressful situations, but it's how you deal with them that makes the difference. Here are a couple of pointers: Try not to let things build up to the point where you can't emotionally cope. As much as possible, deal with frustrations as they come along, and try not to procrastinate. Evaluate all the alternatives. Try not to become stressed by things you have no control over. For example, if the entire computer system crashes just when it's your turn to register, there is nothing you can do about it. So take a walk. Go work out. Spend a few minutes venting to a friend. In time it will work out. We'll talk more about dealing with frustration and stress later in this text, but know that it is a natural thing.

1.9 SOMETHING TO THINK ABOUT AND DISCUSS

- How do you currently deal with frustration?
- How do you physically feel when you become frustrated?
- Why do you think it is particularly difficult to manage stress and frustration when you have little or no control over a situation?

Juggling Too Many Responsibilities

College students are like jugglers. Most jugglers have numerous balls in the air at once. As long as they concentrate on keeping all the balls moving the way they should, they're fine. But if one of the balls falls, all of the others can follow. Responsibilities and commitments in college are similar: If you drop the ball on one thing, all the others can come tumbling down.

College students tend to be busy people: going to class, studying, attending meetings, working, working out, taking part in athletics, and the list goes on. Add to all of this family responsibilities, social interactions, and some time to play, and you can easily become overcommitted. Although you certainly want to get the most out of your college experience, try to think about how new responsibilities will affect you. Remember that your major job in college is to be a student. That should come first. Then you can ask yourself: "What other kinds of responsibilities can I take on?" Try to think about the long-term consequences of taking on too much. Visualize yourself a month from now. Will you have so much to do that you will constantly feel stressed out and frustrated? What would happen if you became ill or if one of your professors tacked on an additional assignment around midterm? If you can think about this in advance and learn to say "No" when you find yourself maxing out, you will be able to keep all those balls in the air and be a much happier student.

1.10 SOMETHING TO THINK ABOUT AND DISCUSS

- List some of the reasons why students tend to be overcommitted.
- What are the advantages and disadvantages of being busy all the time?
- If you are currently overcommitted, how might you go about cutting back on some of your obligations?

1.11 SELF-EVALUATION

On a scale of 1 to 5, with 1 being "strongly disagree" and 5 being "strongly agree," respond to each of the statements below. This should give you a good idea about how much your high school experience differed from what you now are experiencing in college.

	STRONGLY DISAGREE	DISAGREE	NEUTRAL	AGREE	STRONGLY AGREE
My college professors seem to expect much more of me.	1	2	3	4	5
My college classes move at a faster pace.	1	2	3	4	5
My college classes require more than just memorization.	1	2	3	4	5
My college classes give me few chances to earn extra credit.	1	2	3	4	5

My college classes require me to spend more time studying.	1	2	3	4	5
My college professors give less frequent exams.	1	2	3	4	5
I have more freedom in college.	1	2	3	4	5
I often feel like just a number in college.	1	2	3	4	5
I have experienced motivation problems in college.	1	2	3	4	5
I have trouble managing my time effectively in college.	1	2	3	4	5
Column totals:	_____	_____	_____	_____	_____
Total of columns:	__________				

Now add up your score. The higher your score, the more differences you are experiencing in making the transition from high school to college. The more differences you experience, the more time it may take you to make the adjustment. The important thing to realize is that college, like high school, will become routine, and those things that initially seemed so new and different will soon become second nature.

Each chapter in this book contains a *Real College* exercise that focuses on the learning and studying problems that college students encounter. This scenario will, in some way, be related to the chapter you just read. Sometimes the problems portrayed in *Real College* are small and easily fixed. At other times, however, the students get themselves into real jams, and they often need the advice of an expert. Because you are taking a course in which you are learning how to be an active and effective learner, we consider *you* the expert! Your task is to suggest solutions to the students in the scenarios as a way of seeing how well you understand the concepts presented in the chapter and in previous chapters. Responding to the situation by explaining what the student did wrong as well as explaining how the student could do better will help you monitor your own understanding.

REAL COLLEGE: *Wanda's Woes*

Read the following scenario and then respond to the questions based on what you learned in this chapter.

Wanda was a pretty good student in high school. She earned good grades and "studied as much as she needed" to make As and Bs. She just naturally assumed that she would earn similar grades in college. But here it is, only three weeks into the fall semester, and things aren't going as planned. She didn't do well on her first chemistry test because she had to cram, so she asked the professor what she might do for extra credit. Her professor just smiled and shook his head. Then there's the pace. Things seem to be moving so fast. She's having a difficult time keeping up. From her perspective, she's studying about the same amount of time as she did in high school, but her efforts don't seem to be paying off. In addition to these academic problems, she feels alone and isolated. She likes her roommate, and would like to get to know her better, but her roommate knows a lot of people already so she's not around much. It seems so hard to make new friends.

What advice do you have for Wanda?

____

____

____

What could she do to help herself academically? Socially?

____

____

____

Have you experienced similar problems adjusting to college life? If so, how are you dealing with them? If not, why do you think that your adjustment has been going smoothly?

____

____

____

FOLLOW-UP ACTIVITIES

1. Sometimes professors can seem intimidating—especially when you first begin college—but most college teachers are personable people who enjoy interacting with students. In order to get to know one of your professors a little better, make an appointment to talk to him or her. You might discuss course expectations, ask for studying pointers, or discuss your past successes or problems with similar courses.
2. Find out where you can get help with academic problems. Is there a Learning Center on your campus? If so, what kinds of services does it offer? Can you receive free tutoring? If so, for which courses is

tutoring available ? Can you receive assistance with studying-related problems? How do you go about making an appointment in the Learning Center?

3. Find out where you can get counseling assistance. Is there a Counseling Center that can help you make the adjustment to college? What if you just need someone to talk to? How do you go about making an appointment to see someone?

4. Social life is a big part of being a college student, but it is often difficult to meet people with like interests. Therefore, think about the hobbies and activities that you enjoy. Then find a listing of campus- or community-sponsored organizations. Find one or two that interest you and gather additional information about them. Joining campus organizations is a great way to meet other students with like interests and to become involved at the same time.

Networking

- Access the web site of the college or university you are currently attending. Search the web site for information about some of the services discussed in this chapter such as the Learning Center, Health Center, or Counseling Center. What did you find out about these services that you didn't know before? What other services did you find?

- Check your syllabi to see if any of your professors listed their e-mail address. If they did, write a brief e-mail to introduce yourself or to ask a question. Also, some professors have their own web pages. If any of your professors has a web page, check it out.

Active Learning
What's In It for You?

Read this chapter to answer the following questions:

How do active learners differ from passive learners?

Why does active learning depend on a combination of both skill and will?

What is the holistic nature of active learning?

STUDY TIP

Be an active and involved learner in all of your classes by reflecting on and thinking about the information you are expected to learn.

You hear it all the time, read about it in magazines and newspapers, and even watch television programs dedicated to one theme: ACTIVITY! Be active, exercise. It's good for your heart. Children are becoming heavier these days because they are couch potatoes who watch too much TV. They need to become more active. Run. Play. Good for the body and the spirit! It seems as though everywhere you turn there's another piece of research or another claim about the importance of being active. So, let's take the premise that you are tired of being out of shape. You've decided that a healthy body promotes a healthy mind. You take the big step and join a fitness club or gym, especially so that you can take aerobics and work yourself back into shape. Such good intentions! But what if you went to the gym and merely watched other people exercise? Would you become fit? Would you lose any weight? Probably not because you would not be an active participant. Learning is much the same as exercising: If you are not an active participant in exercising, you won't become physically fit. If you are not an active participant in learning, you won't become mentally fit, nor will you maximize your performance in the classroom.

Before reading the remainder of this chapter, read the *Research into Practice* segment. Researchers Paul Pintrich and

Teresa Garcia discuss the importance of being an active learner, or what they refer to as a self-regulated learner.

Research Into Practice

Learning Involves Many Pieces*

Dr. Paul Pintrich of the University of Michigan and Dr. Teresa Garcia of the University of Texas at Austin have been involved in examining student motivation and learning for a number of years. Their research, which is based on a general model of learning suggested by Weinstein and Mayer,† looks at how rehearsal and organizational strategies (discussed in Chapter 14) and other factors impact student learning. In general, they have found that students who process information deeply (by using the appropriate organizational and rehearsal strategies) tend to perform better in their courses. Other factors, such as the ability to plan and monitor learning, also contributed to better academic performance. Pintrich and Garcia focus on the importance of students using strategies that they can control and modify.

Pintrich and Garcia have also examined the role that motivation plays in active learning. Their findings suggest that students who are intrinsically motivated (meaning that they are motivated by their own learning goals), rather than extrinsically motivated (motivated by some outside force), are more successful learners. They are more active learners, or what Pintrich and Garcia call "self-regulated."

This and other research by Pintrich, Garcia, and their colleagues is important because it shows that active learners participate in the learning situation by being both cognitively engaged and motivated to learn. This idea is tied very closely to the "skill versus will" idea that we will discuss later in the chapter.

What Do Active Learners Do?

As a way of defining active learning, we'll discuss the differences between active and passive learning by examining seven characteristics of active learners and contrasting them with the characteristics of passive learners. Active learners use the following strategies.

* Source: Pintrich, P. R., & Garcia, T. (1994). Self-regulated learning in college students: Knowledge, strategies, and motivation. In P. Pintrich, D. R. Brown, & C. E. Weinstein (eds.), *Student motivation, cognition, and learning* (pp. 113–134). Hillsdale, N.J.: Erlbaum.

† Weinstein, C. E., & Mayer, R. F. (1986). The teaching of learning strategies. In M. C. Wittrock (ed.), *Handbook of research on teaching,* 3rd edition, N.Y.: Macmillan Publishing Co.

Read with the purpose of understanding and remembering. You might ask "Who doesn't read with the purpose of understanding and remembering?" After all, no one deliberately sits down to read with the purpose of *not* understanding the text. However, we would be willing to bet that you have been in a situation, probably more than once, where you read an assignment, closed the text, and thought, "What in the world was that all about?" When you interact with a text in this manner, you are reading passively. Active readers, on the other hand, check their understanding as they are reading and realize that they are accomplishing more than just completing an assignment. When they finish their reading, they can talk about the main points covered and walk away knowing that they have understood what they have read. One way to be an active reader is to write summary notes or annotations in the margins of your text. Annotation will be discussed in Chapter 13.

Reflect on information and think critically. Being reflective is an important part of active learning. By reflecting on what you are learning, we mean that you are thinking about it. In other words, the information is being processed in some way: You are making connections between the new information and what you already know, you are identifying concepts that you may not understand very well, you are evaluating the importance of what you are reading as you go along. An active learner reflects constantly: As she is reading text, listening to lectures, and studying with her peers. Contrast this with a passive learner. A passive learner may read her text and listen to lectures, and she may even understand most of what she reads and hears, but she doesn't take that crucial next step of actually thinking about it. We will discuss more about reflection and critical thinking in several other chapters in this book.

Listen actively by taking comprehensive notes in an organized fashion. As part of the research we have conducted, we have sat in numerous college classrooms and observed the behaviors of students. While this is always an interesting exercise, we never cease to be amazed at the number of students engaged in activities other than listening and note taking. Students are reading the campus newspaper, reading an assignment for another class, working on crossword puzzles, chatting with a classmate, and even napping! Perhaps the all-time winner, however, was a student who regularly came to class with a pillow and blanket and fell asleep on his girlfriend's shoulder. The class was at 7:50 A.M. and it was very cold in the auditorium where this class was held—but talk about inappropriate and passive behavior! The point that we want to make here is that active learners are engaged learners. They are actively listening to the professor for the entire period, and they are writing down as much information as possible. Passive learners, on the other hand, may connect with only part of, or on an extremely bad day, little of the lecture. To be an active note taker, you must be more than simply present. You have to connect by letting the information go through your brain before it comes out your pen, and you need to take notes in as organized and comprehensive a fashion as possible. We will discuss active note taking in detail in Chapter 16.

Know that learning involves more than simply putting in time. Every student at least acknowledges the importance of having good time-management skills and expects to invest time in studying in order to be successful. Only a rare student is able to say that they put little time into their courses and still make good grades. But just putting time into studying is not enough. It is the quality of that time—what you actually do with it—that makes the difference. Two students can put in equal amounts of time studying for a test, yet one can do poorly and the other very well. Why? There are any number of reasons, but using improper strategies—thus using time ineffectively—tops the list. If you find yourself putting in a reasonable amount of study time and yet not doing as well as you think you should be, take a close look at how you are spending your time. Are you using organizing and rehearsing strategies appropriate for the task at hand?

Get assistance when experiencing problems. Because active learners are constantly monitoring their understanding and know when their comprehension breaks down, they ask for help and clarification before they become so lost that they cannot regroup and move on. In addition, active learners often can predict, with a fair degree of accuracy, the courses or even particular concepts within courses that may give them trouble. As such, active learners have a plan in mind for getting assistance should they need it. For example, we have interacted with students who know that mathematics is difficult for them. As active learners, some hire individual tutors, others take advantage of free peer tutoring, while still others seek assistance from their professor or from the Learning Center. It does not matter how they get the assistance; of greater importance is that they realize that they need help, and they get that help early in the game—and continue to receive help if they need it. Although passive learners may seek help at some point, it is often too little too late. In addition, because passive learners do not reflect and think critically as they read and listen, they often don't know, or don't want to acknowledge, that they even need help. Active learners, on the other hand, are in touch with themselves and can identify their strengths and weaknesses with a high degree of accuracy.

Accept much of the responsibility for learning. Active learners understand that the responsibility for learning must come from within, while passive learners often want to blame others for their lack of motivation, poor performance, time management problems, and other difficulties that they might experience. Remember what Pintrich and Garcia said in the *Research into Practice* segment: Students who are intrinsically motivated outperform their counterparts who rely on extrinsic motivation. Part of intrinsic motivation is accepting the responsibility for your own learning. When active learners fail to perform as well as they had hoped, they evaluate why they didn't do well and change those studying behaviors the next time around. Even if they have difficulty in connecting with the professor, they try to tailor the way they approach the course to what the professor expects. Passive learners, on the other hand, often approach every course in the same manner and then get angry with the professor when their performance is poor. It is only when students accept the responsibility for their own learning that they truly can be called active learners.

Question information. Active learners question information that they read and hear, while passive learners accept both the printed page and the words of their professors as "truth." It's not that active learners question *everything;* it's simply that because active learners are reflective and critical thinkers, they evaluate what they read and hear. When new information isn't in accord with what they already know, they may differ in the conclusions they draw or in the inferences they make. For example, a student whose uncle, grandfather, or aunt served in Vietnam may have a differing view of the conflict than a history textbook author who protested against the war. It's not that either of them is right or wrong; it's simply that they have different perspectives. Active learners who don't necessarily believe or agree with everything in print are those who grow intellectually during their stay in college.

TABLE 2.1 *Differences between Active and Passive Learners*

	Active Learners	Passive Learners
Reading	Read to understand and remember.	Read but may not understand or remember.
Reflecting and thinking critically	Make connections between what they already know and new information gathered from texts, lectures, and studying with peers.	Don't think about and process information that they read and hear.
Listening	Are engaged during lectures and take organized notes.	Are not attentive during lectures and take unorganized or incomplete notes.
Managing time	Put in quality study time.	May put in a lot of study time, but it isn't quality time.
Getting assistance	Realize when they need help and seek it early.	Seek too little help too late.
Accepting responsibility	Understand they are responsible for their own learning; analyze weak performance if it occurs and change their study habits accordingly.	Blame others for poor performance; approach every course in the same way and fail to learn from their mistakes.
Questioning information	Question new information that is not in accord with what they already know.	Accept without question what they read and hear in lectures as true.

2.1

SOMETHING TO WRITE ABOUT AND DISCUSS

Thinking Critically

Think about the seven characteristics of active learning outlined in Table 2.1. Now think about yourself as a learner and answer the following questions:

1. *Would you consider yourself an active learner? Why or why not?*

   ____

   ____

   ____

2. *Describe two ways in which you can change so that you can become a more active learner.*

   ____

   ____

   ____

   ____

3. *Why do you believe that many students are passive rather than active learners?*

   ____

   ____

   ____

   ____

   ____

Benefits of Active Learning

As you can probably tell by reading the last section, being an active learner involves having both *skill* and *will.* By "skill" we mean that you have the tools to handle the studying and learning demands placed on you. You have a variety of study strategies that you consciously employ, and these strategies change depending on the text, the task, and your own personal characteristics as a learner, as we will further discuss in Chapter 3. In addition, you know how to manage your time, when and where to get assistance if you are having difficulty, and you can monitor and evaluate your learning. This book can teach you the skills you need to be an active learner.

By "will" we mean that you have the desire and motivation to follow through. Skill is nothing without will. As an example, you may have a friend, relative, or peer who is knowledgeable but not motivated in the classroom. Even though he reads widely and can intelligently discuss a variety of issues, he does little work associated with school and rarely studies. Teachers may say that this person is "bright but lazy," or "... isn't working up to his potential." In other words, students such as these may have the skills to do well, yet for some reason they simply do not have the will. And because skill and will go hand-in-hand, unmotivated students—those who do not have the will—may experience difficulty in college and end up dropping out or being asked to leave by their college or university.

It should be apparent from this discussion that it's easier to teach someone the skills to be an active learner than it is to give them the will. Skill is something that can be developed only if one has the will to do so. Think about the example pertaining to the exercise used earlier in the chapter: If you go to the gym to develop a skill, and you have the will to put in the effort to persist in developing your athletic skill, you'll be successful. But if you work out for two weeks, then only sporadically, then not at all, you might lack the will to be successful, even though you might have the skill to do so. No one can force you to go to the gym, just as no one can force you to study effectively, to plan your time, or to go to class. That all is a matter of will, no matter how much skill you have.

Active learning, then, has numerous benefits in terms of both academic and psychological payoffs. In terms of academic payoffs, active learning leads to higher grades, increased time to pursue extracurricular and social activities, and most importantly, gained knowledge. Active learners tend to earn higher grade point averages, seek more involvement with their professors, and like to learn new things. And while all active learners certainly don't believe that they are studying simply for the love of learning, they are more apt to find learning new things more of a challenge than a chore or a bore.

But there are also psychological benefits to active learning that perhaps outweigh the academic benefits. Have you ever heard the saying, "Success begets success"? This saying means that being successful motivates you to do what it takes to have greater success. In other words, once active learners experience academic success, they want to continue along this path. Being successful makes them feel good about themselves, prompts positive feedback from family, and often increases future aspirations. We all know that it's much easier to continue to use the skills you have acquired if you get positive feedback as a result of using them. For example, one of the authors of this text had a student in her class who was a business major and was experiencing a considerable amount of difficulty in an economics course she was taking. As an active learner, this student tried different study strategies, invested a significant amount of time interacting with the course material, and went to the professor for help when she didn't understand the concepts. But she still wasn't doing well, and she was losing her will to persist with this class. She was losing confidence in herself as a learner and said things such as "Maybe I should just drop this course," and "Maybe I'm just not cut out to major in business." After talking with her about how she was studying for the class, it became very evident that she was using skills and strategies that were inappropriate for learning the material. Once she understood that she needed to be able to understand and explain examples—to go beyond simply memorizing economic principles—and she changed her studying accordingly, her grade improved, she felt better about herself, and she was encouraged to continue this change in her studying.

2.2 SELF-EVALUATION

On a scale of 1 to 5, with 1 being rarely and 5 being most of the time, evaluate how active you are as a learner.

	RARELY		SOMETIMES		MOST OF THE TIME
1. When I read my texts, I can make connections with what I have read earlier in the course.	1	2	3	4	5
2. After I read my texts, I can restate the key ideas in my own words.	1	2	3	4	5
3. After lectures and when I am finished reading my texts, I can clearly articulate what it is I don't understand.	1	2	3	4	5
4. I can take meaningful and organized notes for a full class period without losing concentration.	1	2	3	4	5
5. When I prepare for tests I use my time wisely.	1	2	3	4	5
6. I seek out help when I am having problems understanding the material presented in a course.	1	2	3	4	5
7. I reflect on my studying behavior if I am not succeeding in a course, and I develop a plan to change my approach.	1	2	3	4	5
8. If information I hear or read is not in accord with what I already know, I try to examine the issue from a variety of viewpoints.	1	2	3	4	5
9. When I go in to take a test, I have a good idea of how I will do.	1	2	3	4	5
10. I am motivated to learn in all or most of my classes.	1	2	3	4	5
11. I feel confident about myself as a learner.	1	2	3	4	5

After you have completed this self-evaluation, add up your score. The higher your score, the more active you are as a learner. The lowest score you can receive is 11; the highest score you can receive is 55. Your score gives you an overall picture of how much work you have to do and also lets you know which areas of active learning you need to work on.

The Holistic Nature of Active Learning

As Paris, Lipson, and Wixson* pointed out, active learners have three different kinds of knowledge about the strategies they use during learning. First, they have *declarative knowledge.* Declarative knowledge is knowing what—what you need to do and what strategy you need to use. For example, if you were in a history class and the task was to get ready for an essay exam in which you would need to synthesize information, you would be able to select the proper study strategy to match the task. You might say to yourself, "I need to begin by predicting some questions, and then I need to practice answering those questions." This is having declarative knowledge.

But it is not enough to know what you should do; you also have to know how to do it. This is having *procedural knowledge*—knowing how. Returning to our history example, you would have to know how to go about predicting questions that are likely to be on your test. You might search your lecture notes for hints your professor gave about important ideas, look to see what she spent a lot of time on in class, or look for

FIGURE 2.1 *The Three Kinds of Knowledge*

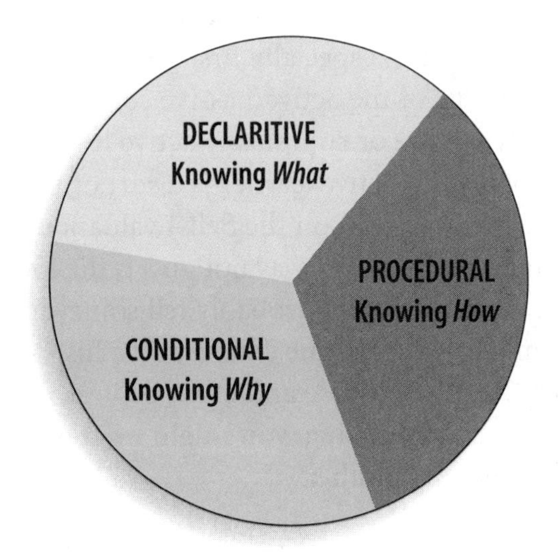

* Paris, S. G., Lipson, M. Y., & Wixson, K. K. (1983). Becoming a strategic reader. *Contemporary Educational Psychology* 8: 293–316.

overlap between your lecture notes and your text. Once you have predicted your questions, then comes the practice. You need to have a plan: Sketch out an outline of the key points you want to include in your answer, say those points to yourself, and practice writing out the answers to one of the questions you predicted. You might even show it to your professor if she is willing to give you feedback. As the name suggests, you have procedures to follow once you have identified the appropriate strategies.

The final type of knowledge possessed by active learners is *conditional knowledge*—knowing why. As the name implies, you also need to know why you should use certain strategies under certain conditions. Using our history example again, you would know to use an approach that will prepare you to synthesize information, because that is what you will be asked to do on the test. Therefore, you would not want to use a strategy that encourages memorization. In other words, you would not want to simply memorize names, dates, and facts. Under certain conditions, memorization strategies alone would work, but this history professor expects her students to do much more than memorize.

As you can see, active learners know a variety of strategies, and they pick and choose which strategies to use according to the task and their professors' expectations. Active learning is not as simple as sitting down, opening a book, and reading the words. It involves engagement, reflection, and monitoring. Active learners walk away from each learning session with an understanding of what it was they heard or read. They think about what it is they are learning, and the information makes sense to them. They monitor their learning by knowing when their comprehension is breaking down and whether they are ready for a test.

Becoming an active learner, especially if you have been a passive learner, does take some time and effort. It doesn't happen overnight. Most students, especially first-year students, are located somewhere in the middle of the active/passive continuum. That is, rarely are students totally passive or completely active learners when they begin college. Becoming an active learner is a sort of work in progress. Look back at the score you received on the Self-Evaluation (Activity 2.2 in this chapter). Your score probably was not an 11, the lowest possible score, nor was it a 55, the highest. You probably fell somewhere in between. Just try to keep in mind that everyone can improve his or her ability to learn. And because every course and every professor requires a slightly different approach to learning, you might even be a more active learner in one class than in another.

2.3 MONITORING YOUR LEARNING

In this chapter, we introduced the idea of monitoring your learning. Although we will discuss this topic in detail in later chapters, we believe that it is important to introduce this concept early on because much of your success in college will be influenced by your ability to monitor your learning. Remember that monitoring is being aware of your understanding, whether it's when you read, when you listen, or when you study. As a way of beginning to think about monitoring your learning, consider and then answer the following questions:

1. *Think about a class in which you are currently enrolled. Are you monitoring your learning in this class? If so, how?*

   ____

   ____

   ____

   ____

2. *How do you know when your understanding in this class is breaking down?*

   ____

   ____

   ____

   ____

3. *How do you know when and if you are prepared for a test in this class?*

   ____

   ____

   ____

   ____

REAL COLLEGE: *Roberto's Realization*

Read the following scenario and then respond to the questions based on what you learned in this chapter.

Roberto came to college with what he thought were active learning skills. When he was in high school, he set aside an hour or two for homework and studying every night, and he made sure he completed his schoolwork before watching TV, spending time with friends, or going to his part-time job. He was very systematic about studying, and he approached each class in the same way. He read over his texts, but concentrated primarily on the questions at the end of each chapter. He mostly studied the notes he took in class because that's what the teachers' tests focused on. Roberto rarely asked questions because he understood what the teachers were talking about, and after all, they were the experts. Although he rarely thought much about the material as he studied it, he still did pretty well on most of his high school tests and managed to stay motivated enough to earn a good grade in each class.

For some reason, things aren't going so well for Roberto in college. He follows the same basic plan that he used in high school, but it doesn't seem to be working very well. He has always considered himself to be a good student and an active learner (after all, he made high grades in high school), but in these first few weeks of college, he's been lucky to make Cs on his tests and quizzes. He has discovered that he can no longer ignore the reading assignments his professor gives because questions about text information not covered in class are on the test, but he's not sure how to go about this task. In addition, he realizes that he is lost in his geology class and doesn't even know where to begin to ask questions.

Give Roberto three pieces of advice based on what you have learned so far about active learning.

1. ______________________________

____

____

2. ______________________________

____

____

3. ______________________________

____

____

Evaluate Roberto's study habits in high school. Would you have done things differently? Why or why not?

____

____

____

____

____

FOLLOW-UP ACTIVITIES

1. Think about your general level of physical activity. Do you exercise regularly or are you a couch potato? Do you always seem to be on the go, or are you always in the process of either waking up or going to sleep? Generally, students whose level of activity is high also tend to be more active learners. Start to pay more attention to your level of activity. Remember that awareness is the first step to change.
2. Think of at least two things you can do right now to move toward becoming a more active learner. They can be small things, such as sitting closer to the front of the room in a class you don't like. Sitting closer might help you focus better and take better notes. Or you might try reading a section of one of your text assignments and then stopping to reflect on what you remember. Both are little changes, but if you make two small changes this week and two small changes the next, and so on, you will be well on your way to being an active learner.

Networking

- There is so much information available to you on the Internet that it takes an active learner to be able to sift through the information. To practice your skills as an active learner, go to your local newspaper, or *Time* or *Newsweek* magazine online, and use the search function to find a current article that interests you.

- Actively engage in the reading to find out the author's intent. Question the author as you read. Does any of the information seem suspect or unsupported? Does it agree or disagree with what you already know about the topic?

Factors That Impact Learning

Read this chapter to answer the following questions:

What are the four factors that influence learning?

How do your personal characteristics influence learning?

How do course tasks influence learning?

How do the characteristics of your texts influence learning?

How do you select the appropriate strategies for learning?

In college, you are constantly evaluated on what and how much you have learned. Performance checks in the form of tests, quizzes, papers, presentations, and projects are the way that professors evaluate how well you have learned. Some of the information is presented in class in the form of lectures, but professors also expect you to learn the information on your own—from a textbook, periodical, newspaper, computer program, or the like. Thus, because professors ask you to learn from different sources of information and to engage in a variety of tasks, it's easy to see why learning is often referred to as a complicated process. That is, ***real*** learning involves considerably more than reading over your text or notes. Real learning requires you to be an active participant in the learning process and to be a learner every day, not someone who has only occasional bursts of academic energy. In addition, as we stated in the last chapter, in order to do well in college you must not only have the skills to learn but you must also have the will to apply those skills. Skill and will go hand-in-hand.

Many of you using this text may have made good grades in high school without putting in much effort or by using only

STUDY TIP

When trying to change your study habits, be open-minded and try new approaches.

basic studying techniques like reading your texts and completing homework assignments. The ways you studied then were probably sufficient for the kinds of tests you had and the tasks your high school teachers asked you to do. And then there was always extra credit. If you weren't doing so well, you could do something more or something different to bring up your grade. In other words, you knew what you had to do in order to get a good grade, and you probably did what you needed to do. But in college, the rules seem to change and no one seems to inform you about these changes. You might think about these changes using the following analogy: Every evening you watch the game show "Jeopardy" on television. You're pretty good at playing the game, and you certainly know the rules. So when "Jeopardy" scouts are holding auditions near where you live, you try out and are selected to appear on the show. The day comes when you make your appearance with the two other contestants. But Alex Trebek has some bad news! The rules have all changed. No, he can't tell you what the new rules are. You just have to figure them out as you go along. Unfair you say? Probably, but for some students, that's how the studying rules go in college.

Think back to the *Real College* scenario in the last chapter. Remember Roberto? He was studying in college the same way that he had studied in high school, and it wasn't working very well. New college students encounter this situation all the time. Perhaps you go into college courses expecting the level of questions on tests to be very similar to those you encountered in high school. Then on the first test—SURPRISE! The rules have changed, and the questions ask you to think about the material in a very different way. Educational psychologist Richard Mayer (1996) refers to this as part of the "hidden curriculum."

Research Into Practice

Discovering the Hidden Curriculum*

In this article, Dr. Mayer, who teaches and researches many different aspects of learning, discusses a problem that many college students face: They read every word and study hard, but they still perform poorly on tests, particularly on tests that ask them to transfer information to a new situation. He discusses a variety of learning strategies that promote what he calls "meaningful learning," which is similar to what we call active learning. Mayer suggests that many students come to college unprepared

* Source: Mayer, R. E. (1996). Learning strategies for making sense out of expository text: The SOI model for guiding three cognitive processes in knowledge construction. *Educational Psychology Review* 8: 357–371.

to meet the demands placed on them because they have not been taught learning strategies. He goes on to state that

> Learning strategies are often part of the hidden curriculum, that is, knowledge we expect students to know without being taught. Indeed we expect students to use effective learning strategies but rarely do we provide instruction in how to use learning strategies in authentic academic tasks such as making sense out of … text. (p. 360)

Mayer's suggestion that students are not directly taught to be active or "meaningful" learners is an important one, especially for those of you enrolled in a course that focuses on improving your own learning. Many students who take such courses, either through choice or because their college mandates it, are often embarrassed. Like their former teachers, students often assume that they will know how to study in college. When they find themselves struggling, they may have feelings of inadequacy or that they aren't as smart as other students. If you feel like this, think about Mayer's point. If all of your high school teachers assumed that someone else taught you how to be an active learner, but no one ever really gave you any direct instruction, then you probably never learned how to study efficiently and effectively. So don't be so hard on yourself! Think of yourself as someone who is just now discovering the "hidden curriculum." In addition, students who take courses to improve their learning wind up having an edge over other students because they learn how to study effectively and efficiently.

3.1 SOMETHING TO WRITE ABOUT AND DISCUSS

1. *As we stated above, the studying and learning rules seem to change between high school and college. What rule changes have you observed so far?*

   ____

   ____

   ____

   ____

2. *How are you making adjustments to the new rules?*

   ____

   ____

   ____

   ____

Four Factors That Influence Learning

As shown in Figure 3.1, part of the complexity of learning is caused by the many factors that you have to consider. This complexity is often overlooked by students, resulting in academic difficulty. The problem is this: If you forget about or overlook one of the factors, it can influence all the others and thus, in the long run, influence your learning and test performance. Cognitive psychologists, those who study how individuals learn, suggest that there are four key factors that you need to think about if you want to be an efficient and effective learner:

1. Your own characteristics as a learner;
2. The tasks your professors ask you to do;
3. The texts with which you interact;

   and
4. The strategies you select.

We will briefly present each of these factors here and provide a "quick start" tip at the end of each section. We will then discuss each factor in greater detail in later chapters. In fact, you will notice that the remainder of the text is organized around each of these four factors.

FIGURE 3.1 Four Factors That Influence Learning

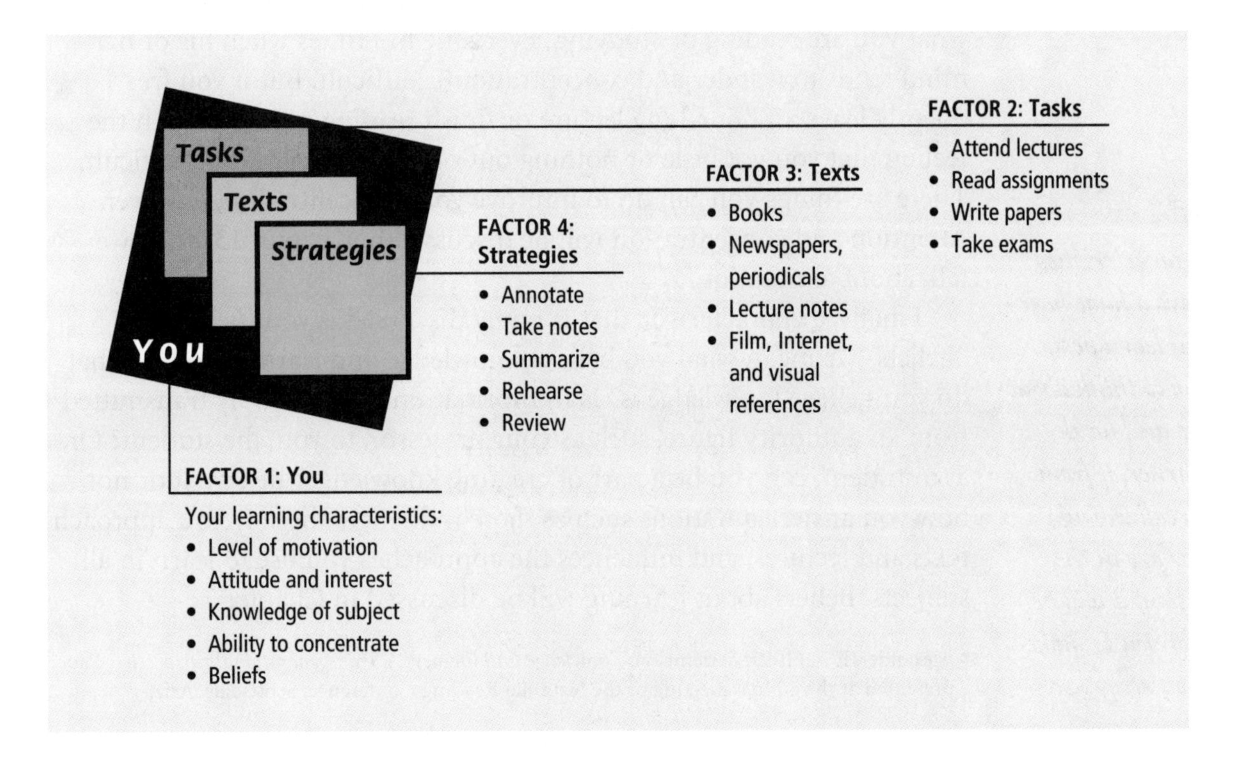

FACTOR 1: Characteristics of the Learner

As a student, you bring a variety of unique characteristics to each learning situation. These characteristics play a key role in how well you will perform, your interest in the material, and the strategies you will select to learn the course content. One of the most important characteristics is the *level of motivation* you have to learn and study the information. Motivation is the academic "glue" that holds everything else in place. Without motivation, you will probably experience frustration and failure as a student. Motivation will be discussed in Chapter 5.

A second characteristic is *attitude and interest.* Students who have a positive attitude about and interest in learning are going to be more motivated to study. General interest in the topic being studied helps, but if you are open to learning new things and expanding your interests, you will be more successful. Attitude and interests will be discussed in Chapter 6.

A third characteristic that you bring to the learning situation is your *knowledge about a particular domain,* such as history or biology, or about a particular topic such as the Vietnam conflict or genetics. Obviously the more background knowledge you have, the easier the material will be to learn. Research has consistently shown that the greater the amount of knowledge college students have about a topic, the better they perform.* Starting with subjects or courses that were particularly easy for you in high school because you knew a lot about them is a good beginning point for courses as a first-year student. Using the knowledge you already possess will be discussed in Chapter 12.

A fourth characteristic is your *ability to attend to and concentrate on* what you are reading or studying. Everyone has times when his or her mind tends to wander and concentration is difficult. But if you frequently leave an hour-long lecture or finish reading a chapter with the feeling that you got little or nothing out of it, learning may be difficult. There are things you can do to improve your concentration, however. Attention and concentration will be discussed in Chapter 13 when we talk about annotation.

QUICK START

Because the characteristics you possess have a huge bearing on how you learn best, take some time to think about your strengths and weaknesses as a learner. If from the start you realize how important YOU are in the learning equation, it will be much easier for you to make choices about strategy use.

Finally, a characteristic that is rarely discussed is your *beliefs.* By "beliefs" we mean what you believe knowledge and learning to be. What do you believe knowledge is? Is it information that is simply transmitted from an authority figure, such as your professor, to you, the student? Or, as a student, can you be a part of creating knowledge? Believe it or not, how you answer questions such as these influences the way you approach texts and lectures, and influences the approaches you use to learn in all subjects. Beliefs about learning will be discussed in Chapter 7.

* Alexander, P. A. (1997, December). *Knowledge and literacy: A Transgenerational perspective.* Paper presented at the annual meeting of the National Reading Conference. Scottsdale, Ariz.

These characteristics and others that you bring to each learning situation influence not only what you learn but also how you study course material. Active learners understand the importance of being aware of these characteristics as they approach learning tasks, whether these tasks are easy or difficult.

3.2 SOMETHING TO THINK ABOUT AND DISCUSS

Thinking Critically

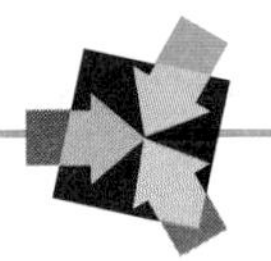

- Think about your current level of motivation. Why are you motivated to do well in college? When do you think you might have problems with motivation?
- Think about your current interest in and attitude toward getting a college degree. How do you think interests and attitudes influence college performance?
- In which courses were you particularly successful in high school? How do you think your success in high school will influence your success in college?
- Do you tend to have problems concentrating and paying attention? If so, what are some ways to deal with concentration problems?
- What do you believe your role in the learning process should be? Why?

FACTOR 2: The Tasks

Simply put, tasks are what your professors ask you to do. You can think of these as daily tasks, such as reading your text before you attend lectures, or larger tasks, such as preparing for various kinds of tests or writing papers. How you fare in these larger tasks is how you are generally evaluated—how you earn the dreaded grade! It is important, therefore, as part of being an active learner, to understand the tasks that professors set for their courses.

Most professors are clear about what the task is. They will let you know the number of tests you will have and the kind of tests they will be (e.g., essay, multiple choice, etc.), as well as their expectations about papers, lab participation, or library work. Some professors will even let you examine copies of old tests or examine student papers from previous terms so that you can see the kinds of questions they will ask or what their writing expectations are. Others will give you sample test questions so that you have an idea of question phrasing and the type of question he or she will ask: questions that test your ability to memorize, or questions that ask you to analyze, draw conclusions, synthesize, or provide examples.

But some professors aren't so clear in their definitions of the tasks they expect you to complete. Still others may give you conflicting messages. For example, a professor we know told students at the beginning of the term that a portion of each of their exams would consist of "objective questions." On the first three exams, this translated into multiple choice questions. When the professor told them that their final exam would also consist of objective questions, they assumed that this meant multiple choice items again. Imagine their surprise when they went into the final exam and found that the objective questions were of a fill-in-the-blank format. Many students complained that they had prepared for one kind of exam and were unfairly given something they didn't expect. The lesson here is to try to get the professor to be as clear as possible about the tasks you must undertake. If you don't know what is expected of you, then you can't select the proper learning strategies or the most effective way to approach your texts.

QUICK START

When you do not understand the task, ask your professor. Don't ask a classmate who may be as confused as you are. Go straight to the source.

It is difficult for many students to figure out the task when the professor is unclear or contradictory. These students' difficulties are more often than not reflected in their test grades and in the frustration they feel as they try different approaches to learning and still come up short. More about tasks and how to deal with this frustration will be discussed in Chapters 9 through 11.

3.3

SOMETHING TO THINK ABOUT AND DISCUSS

Thinking Critically

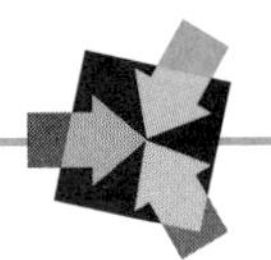

- Have you ever been in a class in which you were confused about the task? How did you handle your confusion?
- Why is it best to ask your professor rather than a classmate to clarify something?

FACTOR 3: The Texts

Texts are crucial to learning in college. In fact it has been estimated that 85 percent of all college learning involves text interaction. You can understand, then, why it's important to know something about the texts with which you are expected to interact and to understand the role they play in each of your courses.

Students often think of texts as simply textbooks. Certainly textbooks are a major source of information in many of your college classes. But texts also come in other forms. Periodicals, newspapers, and essays are printed texts. Another type of text that is being used more often on university campuses is computer text, sometimes called "nonlinear" or "hypertext." Computer text often uses printed material, but it can also use images and sound. Your professors will expect you to be able to evaluate and think critically about computer text as well as the more traditional textbooks. Sometimes you will view films or documentaries, which are visual texts.

In addition to textbooks, lecture notes are the other most frequent type of text with which college students must interact. Lecture notes as text differ from textbooks or other types of printed material for a number of reasons. First, unless they are tape-recorded, lectures are not permanent. Therefore, if you fail to write down an important point, it is gone forever. Second, lecture notes are your interpretation of what was important in a given lecture. Your interpretation may be similar to or different from your professor's. Third, your lecture notes may be much less organized than your textbooks or other printed material you read, perhaps because your professor lectures in an unorganized way or in a way that you have trouble following. Finally, although you can't change what's in your textbook, you do have control over the format of your notes and can learn to become a better note taker. Strategies for note taking will be discussed in Chapter 16.

Whatever types of text you are expected to interact with, it is important to know how the particular text is organized. In most textbooks, each chapter is usually organized in the same fashion. In addition, your professor's lectures probably use the same organization each day. Even visual text has organizational patterns. Once you have determined the organizational patterns of your texts, learning the material becomes a much easier task.

QUICK START
Familiarize yourself with each of your texts at the beginning of the term. Once you see how your texts are laid out, it will be easier to make connections between ideas.

Earlier in the chapter we talked about student beliefs and how they influence learning. Your beliefs about text are also part of your belief system. For example, when students believe that the text is always correct, they are much less likely to challenge ideas put forward by the text authors. They believe that such authorities have much more knowledge and understanding than they have, so who are they to challenge the author? Or students often run into problems when their own beliefs conflict with those put forth by a text author or their professor. Like learner characteristics and task, texts are an important part of the learning puzzle. Texts will be discussed in more detail in Chapters 16 and 17.

3.4 SOMETHING TO THINK ABOUT AND DISCUSS

Thinking Critically

- Examine the textbooks you are using this term. How are they organized? What similarities and differences do you see?
- How might these differences influence the approach you take to reading each text?
- Now think about how each of your professors lectures. How do their lecturing styles influence your note taking?
- What other types of texts—in addition to textbooks and lectures—do you have to engage with? How do you approach these different text types?

FACTOR 4: The Learning Strategies

The final, and perhaps the most complex, factor that influences learning is the strategies that you choose. Thus, a large portion of this text, Chapters 12 through 15, will be devoted to learning strategies. However, it is important to realize that the strategies you choose should be influenced by your characteristics as a learner, the tasks you have to do, and the texts with which you interact. Selecting strategies in isolation from these other factors is the reason why students sometimes use inappropriate strategies in a specific learning situation or try to use the same strategy in all situations.

In later chapters, we will present a variety of strategies that you can use before reading, during reading, after reading, and after studying in

QUICK START

Your first step in strategy selection should be to consider the other factors: your own characteristics as a learner, the tasks in which you are asked to engage, and the texts with which you interact. Your next step, then, is strategy selection.

order to review. These strategies for active learning have several features in common. First, once you learn them, you can use all of these strategies on your own. Because studying is mostly a solitary activity, it is important to be able to use strategies without guidance from someone else. Second, underlying these strategies are processes that research has consistently shown to lead to better performance. For example, all strategies have a self-testing component, which immediately tells you whether or not you are understanding the information. Third, strategies for active learning require participation on your part in the form of critical thinking and reasoning. If the task requires it, they help you to think beyond the text and to analyze, synthesize, and apply. Finally, the strategies are flexible. You can modify them according to your own learning preferences, the tasks, and the texts.

3.5 SOMETHING TO THINK ABOUT AND DISCUSS

Thinking Critically

- Currently, what kinds of study strategies are you using? Do you use the same strategies for every class?
- Why do you think that it is important to self-test?
- What do you think the differences are between memorizing and higher-level learning?

3.6 SELF-EVALUATION

Earlier in the chapter, in the *Research into Practice* section, we presented the idea of study strategies as part of a "hidden curriculum." As the term implies, the hidden curriculum is something that may not be explicitly taught, but that you are assumed to know. Or it could be that teachers and professors mention certain things about learning and studying but don't go into detail because they believe you already know the details. Think about what the *Research into Practice* section said (reread it if necessary), and then answer the following questions about yourself as a learner.

1. *Have you been a victim of the hidden curriculum? If so, in what way?*

____

____

____

2. *How much instruction did you receive about learning strategies from your teachers in high school? What strategies were you taught to help you learn?*

3. *How do you think this instruction (or lack of it) will influence your performance in college?*

4. *What learning strategies do you currently use?*

5. *How successful are these strategies?*

In our *Real College* scenario for this chapter, we meet Malcolm. Malcolm has a terrific attitude about being in college, but he's having a little trouble academically. Perhaps Malcolm doesn't understand that numerous factors must interact in order for him to be an active learner. Do you have any of Malcolm's characteristics?

REAL COLLEGE: *Malcolm's Malingering*

Read the following scenario and then respond to the questions based on what you learned in this chapter.

At the end of his first week on campus, Malcolm decided that he was made to be a college student. He has signed up for volunteer work, joined two campus clubs, and found several local "establishments" in which to hang out. He has discovered that he loves his freedom—he can come and go as he pleases. He never knew that a day could go by so quickly. Because he is often up late at night, trying to study while lying on his bed, he has trouble getting up for his 8:00 A.M. math class. Some days he is late; on other days, he never even hears his alarm. His other classes also present problems, although somewhat different ones. He hates his history class because there is so much to read, and English, well ... he's not very thrilled with that either. He is stressed out because he wants to do well, but he has already missed two math quizzes because of oversleeping, and he made a D on the first test. He thought he should have done much better because he did most of the homework, which is about as much as he did in high school, and he made As and Bs in those math classes. In English he made a C on his first writing assignment, which he felt was good for him. In history he has no grade yet because there is only a midterm and a final, but he is far behind on the reading assignments. Right now, things don't look promising for Malcolm.

Based on what you have read in this and other chapters in this book, what advice do you have for Malcolm? As you are thinking about this advice, remember what we said earlier about the four factors that you need to consider in order to maximize learning: (1) your characteristics as a learner; (2) the tasks you must complete, (3) the texts with which you interact; and (4) the strategies you select. How might Malcolm consider each of these factors in order to become a more active and effective learner?

___

___

___

___

___

___

___

FOLLOW-UP ACTIVITIES

Although we will come back to each of the four factors introduced in this chapter later in the text, it's important for you to begin thinking now about how they impact your learning. Thus, think about yourself as a learner—right now, today—and answer the following questions:

1. *What are two of your strengths as a learner?*

   ____

   ____

2. *What are two of your weaknesses as a learner?*

   ____

   ____

3. *What is one thing you can do today to become a more active learner?*

   ____

   ____

4. *In what course do you think you will experience the most problems this term? Why?*

   ____

   ____

5. *What is one thing you might do in this course to make yourself a more active learner?*

   ____

   ____

Networking

- Search the web for sites that deal with studying. You could use the search words "study skills" or "learning" as a start. Once you have found several web sites, compare the information provided on these sites with information provided in this text. For whom do you think these web sites were designed? Students? Teachers? Evaluate the usefulness of these sites.

Characteristics of the Learner

Part II discusses how your characteristics as a learner affect your success in college. In Chapter 4, you will learn strategies for managing yourself and your time. You will also create a schedule to help you keep track of your college and personal obligations.

Chapter 5 discusses motivation. You will learn what motivates people as well as discover some strategies for maintaining your own motivation for learning.

In Chapter 6, you will learn how your attitude toward college, your instructors, the topic, and yourself as a learner affect your learning. We also discuss ways to maintain a positive attitude.

Chapter 7 introduces five components of beliefs that influence learning. After we discuss these components, you will answer questions that assess your own beliefs about learning.

In Chapter 8, you will learn about sources of stress in college and how to control or reduce your stress levels. You will also learn about strategies for coping with specific types of academic stress such as writing, math, and test anxiety.

Before you read the chapters in Part II, please respond to the following statements. Read each statement and decide whether you agree or disagree with it. Keep your responses in mind as you read the chapters in Part II. When you have finished reading Part II, revisit this page. How are your responses similar to or different from what is introduced in the chapters?

BEFORE Agree	BEFORE Disagree		AFTER Agree	AFTER Disagree
☐	☐	*1. To manage my time effectively, I have to put schoolwork before my social life.*	☐	☐
☐	☐	*2. I treat college like a forty-hour-a-week job.*	☐	☐
☐	☐	*3. My motivation is usually more positive at the beginning of each term.*	☐	☐
☐	☐	*4. My attitude toward my instructors depends on my interest in the courses they are teaching.*	☐	☐
☐	☐	*5. I am confident in my ability to succeed in college.*	☐	☐
☐	☐	*6. I believe that some people are more able to learn math and science, whereas others are more able to learn literature and history.*	☐	☐
☐	☐	*7. I feel pressure from my family to do well in college.*	☐	☐
☐	☐	*8. I become stressed just thinking about taking an exam.*	☐	☐

Getting Organized
Managing Yourself and Your Time

Read this chapter to answer the following questions:

Why do you need to manage your time?

What is self-management?

How can you create a schedule you can live with?

How do you plan time to study for finals?

STUDY TIP

Make a studying schedule and follow it to help you reach your academic goals.

Managing yourself and your time may be one of the most difficult challenges for you as a college student. If you are a returning student who has been in the workforce for a while, or you are raising a family or holding a full-time job while attending college, you will face new challenges in juggling your many responsibilities. For example, you may take all of your courses at night or on the weekends. You may also find that you need to refocus your priorities to account for all of the work involved in college life.

If you are a recent high school graduate, you are probably used to having most of your time managed for you. Your teachers and parents were responsible for setting a good deal of your daily schedule; you were in classes most of the day, and after school you probably had some family obligations that were planned for you, or perhaps you had a part-time job in the afternoon. But in college, you are in class for fewer hours each day, which leaves you with big blocks of time to manage. And as we touched on in Chapter 1, you have the added responsibility of being in charge of managing yourself as well. You need to get to class on time, set your priorities, and plan your days.

For most students this new freedom is thrilling. You have a new social life, you may live in a new town or state, and you are experiencing new opportunities each day. However, some students become overwhelmed by the abundance of freedom they have and end up not managing themselves or their time at all. The trick is to start out with a plan and not have to scramble to make up for lost time once you are already behind. This chapter will present ways to create a plan that will help you maximize your time so you can get everything done without falling behind. Before reading the rest of the chapter, read the *Research into Practice* section, which discusses the relationship between time management and college grades.

Research Into Practice

Time Management and College Success*

In this article, Britton and Tesser examine how students' time-management habits affect their academic success in college. They suggest that how students learn new information is similar to how a computer processes information because both students and computers have limited resources. Students, like computers, have to deal with many different tasks of varying lengths and complexities (which usually have different deadlines), and they process many kinds of information. Just as a computer will run better if it has organized information-processing systems, they hypothesize that students learn better and achieve greater academic success if they use organized time-management systems.

To test their hypothesis, Britton and Tesser gave college students a questionnaire about their time-management practices. Examples of some questions are: "Do you have a clear idea of what you want to accomplish during the next week?" or "Do you make a schedule of activities you have to do on workdays?" The results of their study suggest that students who have effective time-management skills experience greater academic achievement in college. They also found that short-term planning is related to college grade point average. Students who make to do lists, plan their days, and set learning goals for themselves have higher GPAs than students who do not. Britton and Tesser conclude that it is important for college students to learn effective time-management skills to help them achieve greater academic success.

What does this research mean for students' everyday lives? It means that students who have a plan for managing both themselves and their

* Source: Britton, B. K., & Tesser, A. (1991). Effects of time-management practices on college grades. *Journal of Educational Psychology* 83: 405–410.

time each and every day should experience greater success in college than students who do not. In the rest of the chapter we will discuss strategies to help you achieve your academic goals through better time- and self-management.

4.1

SOMETHING TO THINK ABOUT AND DISCUSS

Read and discuss the following questions with a partner or small group.

- Do you agree with Britton and Tesser that when students learn new information it is similar to when a computer processes information? Why or why not?
- How do you think your current time-management system is affecting your grades in college?
- What do you think are the three most important things college students should think about when managing their time?

Managing Yourself

Before you can manage your time effectively, you have to be able to manage yourself. One aspect of self-management is being able to organize and keep track of all the things that you have to do. College life is very hectic; you have class assignments, roommates to deal with, tests to prepare for. You may also have a job to help pay your way through college, or you may have daily family obligations. The secret to getting organized is to create a balance between school, home, work, and social life. Sometimes people who give advice about time management seem to forget that an important part of the college experience is social. In the past you may have been taught about time management with an approach that suggested giving up your social life to focus only on studying. However, this is not our purpose in this chapter. We believe that you should have fun in college! We want you to be able to hang out with your friends, but we also want you to be able to get the work done for your classes so that you can be academically successful and STAY in college as well.

In order to create a balance between all the things you have to do and all the things you want to do, you should consider the following points.

☐ **Treat college like a full-time job.**

If you are a full-time student, academic work should take up about forty hours each week. So for the next several years, you should consider college your full-time job. You might be in class only fifteen hours per week, but the other twenty-five hours should be spent studying and preparing for class. If you break it down, you will see that it's not so bad. You will spend three to four hours in class and four to five hours reading, studying, and preparing for your assignments each day. The rest of the time is left for social activities and your part-time job (if you have one). If you already have a full-time job, you are most likely familiar with the pressures of a forty-hour workweek. However, your college obligations cannot be neglected. You might want to consider taking a reduced course load, or plan to do most of your studying in the evenings and on weekends in order to get everything done.

The good news is that unlike a full-time job, in college you have more control over when you want to schedule your classes and your study time. No one says that you must study between 9:00 A.M. and 5:00 P.M. Monday through Friday. You are free to study whenever you want—early in the morning or on weekends—which brings us to the next point.

☐ Schedule your classes for your most alert times.

Think about when you are at your peak mentally. Are you a morning person? A late afternoon person? An evening person? Are you the type who is up with the sun, or are you lucky to be awake by noon? If you know you will never make it to an 8:00 A.M. class, don't schedule a class for that time if possible. Likewise, if you are totally useless in the afternoon, try to schedule your courses so that they are over before lunchtime.

Many students don't consider their class times when making their course schedule, but because you have the luxury of creating your own schedule, you should try to tailor it to your alert times as much as possible. On the other hand, some students do consider class times when making their course schedule, but because classes fill up quickly, they may be able to register only for classes that meet during their least attentive times. If scheduling is a problem for you, try to schedule a course that you think you will really like for your least alert time, because you will be more likely to stay attentive and awake during the class if you find it interesting.

You also should plan to study during your alert times, and take frequent breaks if you find you are losing concentration. This topic will be discussed further in the next section.

☐ Go to class.

Although many professors don't take attendance in their courses, most still believe that going to class is a very important part of learning. Research shows that students who go to class do better in college. You wouldn't skip your full-time job just because you were up too late or

because there was a good afternoon movie on cable. Because college is your full-time job for the next few years, the same rules apply!

Students who skip a lot of classes miss out on the important information that they can get only from going to class. Some professors consider their syllabus a work in progress to which they make adjustments and additions during the term. For example, suppose a professor assigned a paper that was mentioned only in class and not on the syllabus. You would be responsible for turning in the paper, but the only way you would know it was assigned is if you went to class. Also, by going to class each day you will know what the professor emphasized, which will help you know what to focus on when you study. So do yourself a favor and go to class every day.

☐ Don't Procrastinate.

Procrastination is intentionally putting off work that should be done. This problem may actually be the toughest part of self-management for some students. Because you are in control of your own time, it is tempting to put off work until later. The trouble is that you can become quickly overwhelmed by the amount of work you need to do when you continually neglect your work. Almost everyone has a friend who procrastinated until the last minute and had to "read" an entire novel and write a five-page English paper all in one night. Procrastination tends to become a bad habit and a way of life for some students. Once you start procrastinating, it is difficult to get back on track. However, the strategies in the next section should help you avoid procrastination by helping you determine what you need to do each day.

4.2

SOMETHING TO THINK ABOUT AND DISCUSS

- How have you achieved a good balance between your school, social, and work obligations? How can you adjust your current situation to be more balanced?
- Do you find yourself with a lot of time during which you do not get anything accomplished? If so, how can you adjust your current schedule to account for this wasted time?
- What kinds of obstacles currently make it hard to manage yourself as a college learner?

Managing Your Time

In Chapter 5 we will discuss setting goals for learning. In this chapter you will find out how to manage time effectively in preparation for successfully achieving those goals. You will need to determine two important pieces of information to manage your time:

1. What do I need to accomplish?
2. How can I keep track of what I need to do?

The first step in managing your time is figuring out what you need to do. How many classes do you have to attend? What is your work schedule like? How many social commitments do you have? How many assignments do you have to do this week? This month? This term? How long will it take to complete everything? One of the hardest problems to figure out is how much time an assignment will take. For example, when writing a paper you have to know if it will take you one hour to find what you need in the library or if it will take several trips. Will you be able to write your paper in two days or will you need a full week? Some of the ability to know how long things will take comes with experience, but the following general rule may help you plan your time:

THINGS ALWAYS TAKE LONGER THAN YOU THINK THEY WILL.

Given this basic rule, try to plan more time than you think you need in most situations. When you rush to get an assignment completed, whether it is studying for an exam, writing a paper, or finishing a lab, you will probably be frustrated or angry when things take longer than planned. You may even give up without completing the assignment. It is much better to be left with some extra time than to be rushing to get an assignment completed at the last minute.

The second part of effective time management is creating some kind of system for keeping track of what you have to do. Most people who manage their time successfully say that they can't live without their schedule book or daily planner. Their schedule book keeps track of appointments, assignments, social commitments, and even important phone numbers. If you don't already use some kind of schedule book you should invest in one today. Carry your schedule book with you to class so you can be sure to mark down any changes to your assignments. By writing down when things are due, you will be better able to keep track of all of the things you need to accomplish each day. But writing it down is only half the battle—you have to make a habit of consulting your schedule book every day to see what you need to do. You can buy a schedule book for four dollars or forty dollars, depending on the features of the book. No matter how much you decide to spend, be sure to purchase one that fits your needs. For example, would you rather plan by the day, the week, or the month? Do you need to plan each hour, or would you rather just list your activities without including the time? Do you want a schedule book that is small enough to fit in your pocket so you can carry it with you, or would you rather have a larger book that gives you more space to write?

Keeping a schedule book is a good start to managing your time. But to be really effective you also need to schedule exactly when you will

study for your classes. You have so many things to juggle in college that sometimes it's hard to find the time to study. So you have to plan your study sessions along with the rest of your responsibilities. Some students are able to keep an hour-by-hour schedule in their schedule book, but many prefer to keep a separate daily or weekly study schedule. In the rest of this chapter we will discuss ways to keep a weekly schedule and follow it!

4.3

SELF-EVALUATION

On a scale of 1 to 5 with 1 being "not at all effective," 3 being "somewhat effective," and 5 being "very effective," respond to each of the statements below. This evaluation should give you a good idea of your current time management system.

	NOT AT ALL EFFECTIVE		SOMEWHAT EFFECTIVE		VERY EFFECTIVE
How effective is your current system for managing time?	1	2	3	4	5
How effective is your current system for balancing your school, work, and social obligations?	1	2	3	4	5
How effective is your ability to get things done in an organized way?	1	2	3	4	5
How effective is your use of short periods of time (such as the time between classes) to get things done?	1	2	3	4	5

What are your three biggest concerns regarding effective time management?

1. ______________________________

2. ______________________________

3. ______________________________

Creating a Schedule You Can Live With

Creating a schedule that works is a challenge. Many students start out with good intentions but ultimately end up with an unworkable schedule for a number of reasons. Some students create a schedule that is too rigid, so they don't have the flexibility they need. Others create a schedule that is not detailed enough to be of any use. Still others create a good schedule, but don't consult it daily, so they forget what they need to do. In order to avoid falling into one of the time management pitfalls, consider the following tips as you create you own schedule.

Timely Tips for Following Your Schedule

Plan to study when you are most awake. If you find that you are very tired or you are having trouble concentrating as soon as you sit down to study, you probably are not studying at your most alert time. Some students use caffeine to help them concentrate and stay awake when studying. Although a cup of coffee or tea or a glass of cola may give you a temporary burst of energy, too much caffeine can actually lower your ability to concentrate. So instead of relying on caffeine to keep you awake, try to find some blocks of time that are naturally best for you. Some students study best at night, others study best first thing in the morning. Try out several times of the day to find out when you are the most ready to study. Try times that you might not initially think are your best times of day—you just may surprise yourself and be a morning (or night) person after all!

Spend some time every day on each course you are taking. Even when you don't have an assignment due, plan some time each day to read the text, review your notes, and prepare for the next class. If you are taking classes that require problem solving such as math or chemistry, it's a good idea to work some problems each night. If you are taking a language class, plan to review new vocabulary or work on verb conjugation every day. By spending some time every day, you shouldn't have to cram for exams because you will always be caught up.

Be specific. The more specific you can be when planning your study schedule, the better, because you will know exactly what you need to do each time you study. When you create your schedule, don't just write down "study." It is much more effective to write "Read psychology text pgs. 219–230." By creating a schedule that lists specific tasks, you are more likely to accomplish all of your assignments in a timely fashion.

Make a reading schedule for each class. One of the simplest, yet most effective, ways to manage your time and stay on top of your reading assignments is to make a reading schedule for each class. To make a reading schedule, simply add up the number of pages you need to read in the next week (some students prefer to add the pages in between exams rather than weekly) and divide that number by five (or six or seven if you will read during the weekend). For example, Robert has the following reading assignments this week:

History	Read Chapters 3 through 6	65 pages
Statistics	Read Chapter 5 Complete fifteen practice problems	27 pages

Music	Read Chapters 4 through 7 Listen to two operas on reserve in library	39 pages
Literature	Read six chapters of novel	90 pages
Biology	Read Chapters 8 and 11	29 pages

That's 250 pages of text reading, which according to surveys of various colleges, is about average. If Robert falls behind on his reading this week and he has another 250 pages of reading next week, you can see how the work will snowball very quickly. Thinking about reading 250 pages is overwhelming, but when he divides the reading over five days he sees that he has only thirteen pages of history, six pages of statistics (and three practice problems), eight pages of music, eighteen pages of literature, and six pages of biology to read each day. And that sounds a lot more manageable. If he spreads it out over six or seven days, his daily reading load is cut even more.

To create your own reading schedule, survey the reading assignments (usually found on your syllabus) and divide up the reading in a way that makes sense. Use section breaks or headings to help you determine how to divide the readings so that you're not stopping in the middle of a concept.

Prioritize. When you make your schedule, it is helpful to prioritize what you have to do. You might want to label your assignments as high, medium, or low priority. For example, reading your biology text before the lab might be high priority, but starting on your history research paper that is due in three weeks might be a lower priority. In general, start with high-priority tasks first so that you are sure to get them done. But don't ignore the medium and low priorities. That history research paper may be low priority now, but if nothing gets done in the next three weeks it will become ultra super high priority—fast!

Make to do lists. Sometimes when students begin to study they start to think about all the other things they need to do—call home, get a haircut, cancel a dental appointment. All of these thoughts are very distracting. So to keep yourself on track and to avoid procrastination, keep a to do list next to you when you study. Write down all the things you think of including course work, household chores (such as laundry), phone calls, e-mails to answer, etc. Check items off as you complete them. Your to do list might look something like the one in Figure 4.1

Borrow time—don't steal it! If you decide to go out for a pizza instead of spending an hour reading your psychology chapter—great—as long as you don't steal that time! If you decide to go out instead of following

FIGURE 4.1
Example of a To Do List

Date: Thursday, 10/2/00		
What do I need to do?	**Priority**	**Completed?**
1. Finish revising English paper	high	✓
2. Do laundry	high	✓
3. Read math pp. 81-97 and do problems	medium	✓
4. Call home	medium	
5. Plan spring break trip	low	
6. Think about topic for final history paper	low	

your schedule, be sure to add the activity you missed (that is, reading your psychology chapter) to your schedule (or to do list) for the next day so that you can make up that time. By having a schedule that is very specific, you'll know exactly what you have to do to catch up, and you can easily make up for the lost time.

Use the time in between your classes. Oftentimes students don't know where all of their time goes—an hour in between classes, two hours between school and work, fifteen minutes before classes begin—all of this time adds up, and it's useful for getting your work done. You could read for one of your classes during hour breaks, review your notes while you are waiting for class to begin, use the time between lunch and class to review for class, or even study with a partner in the laundromat. Plan to use your short periods of time when making your schedule so that this time does not get lost.

Schedule breaks in your studying. If you plan to study for more than an hour at a time, schedule a ten- to fifteen-minute break for each hour of study. You should also plan short breaks when switching from one topic to another so you can give yourself some time to refocus. But be careful that your short breaks don't turn into long breaks!

Take some time off. Many students feel guilty when they take time off because they are always thinking about the things they "should be doing" such as working on that chemistry lab assignment. But when you have a good schedule, you will be able to reward yourself by taking time off without guilt, because you know that you have planned time to get all of your assignments done. So after you have completed your work, relax and enjoy yourself—you deserve it! In fact, we suggest that you plan some free time when creating your schedule.

Don't spin your wheels. Seek help from a tutor, a professor, or a friend if you are having problems with a course and you can't solve them. There is nothing that gets in the way of managing your time more than wasting it. If you find that your schedule is not working for you, find some help to get back on track before you fall behind.

4.4 CREATING A SCHEDULE

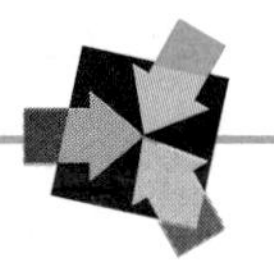

Thinking Critically

Consider the timely tips you just read as you create a schedule for the upcoming week. Before filling in the schedule in Figure 4.2, take a minute to jot down what you hope to accomplish this week. For example, what course assignments do you have to complete? What personal goals do you want to work on? Use this information to help you plan your schedule.

Fill in the schedule in the following order:

1. Enter your class and lab times.
2. If you commute, enter the time it takes to travel to and from campus.
3. Enter your work schedule.
4. Enter your meal times.
5. Enter all of your weekly personal activities (clubs, athletics, exercise).
6. Schedule your study times for each class. Include time for the following:
   - Reviewing your notes
   - Reading the text
   - Preparing for exams, writing papers, working on projects, etc.
7. Schedule study breaks of at least ten to fifteen minutes if you plan to study for longer than one hour.
8. Keep some time open so that you can be somewhat flexible with your schedule.
9. Add any other things that you have to do this week.

FIGURE 4.2 *Creating a Schedule*

	Monday	Tuesday	Wednesday	Thursday	Friday	Saturday	Sunday
7 A.M.							
8 A.M.							
9 A.M.							
10 A.M.							
11 A.M.							
12 P.M.							
1 P.M.							
2 P.M.							
3 P.M.							
4 P.M.							
5 P.M.							
6 P.M.							
7 P.M.							
8 P.M.							
9 P.M.							
10 P.M.							
11 P.M.							
12 A.M.							
1 A.M.							

Evaluating your schedule

1. *How many hours per week are scheduled for study time?* ____________________
2. *How many hours per week are scheduled for social obligations?* ____________________

3. *Is your schedule too tightly packed? Did you leave room to be flexible?* ____________________

4. *Is your schedule too free? Is there a lot of time when you do not have anything scheduled?*

   If so, that time will most likely be wasted. ____________________

Now, create a to do list of what you would like to accomplish today.

Date:		
What do I need to do?	**Priority**	**Completed?**
1.		
2.		
3.		
4.		
5.		
6.		

Planning for Midterms and Finals

Every principle of time management and self-management discussed in this chapter usually goes into warp speed when you are preparing for midterms and finals. Generally, you will need to rethink your entire schedule to cope with the added pressures of preparing for midterms and finals. At those two times during the academic year, you might even need to put in a few hours of overtime on your forty-hour workweek, but don't despair! By following the techniques outlined in this chapter you should get through it without going crazy. In addition to the strategies discussed in this chapter, we add the following points to help you cope with crunch exam time:

Plan ahead. Cut down on work or other commitments. If you work part-time, ask for some time off or fewer hours, and make sure that your friends understand that you will be extra busy. In addition, try to start to rehearse and review your notes and the texts before exam week so that you can cut down on your workload for that week. Starting early is especially important for classes in which you have cumulative exams that hold you responsible for everything you have covered through midpoint or during the entire term, because there is so much information to review.

Get enough sleep. Cramming all night for a big exam rarely pays off. Instead, try to create your schedule for exam week in a way that leaves you adequate sleep time. You won't do well on an exam if you are falling asleep while taking it!

Study with a partner. Misery loves company and this is never truer than during midterms and finals. Hopefully by the time midterms roll around you have found a study group that works. Study with your group or study partner to keep each other on schedule and motivated to work.

Don't panic. This point will be further discussed in Chapter 8, but to put it simply, midterms and finals are really just exams. The world will not stop and does not end because of midterms and finals. If you find that the pressure is getting to be too much, readjust your schedule to allow more break time and try to relax during those breaks. If you find that you have excessive anxiety, get some help before it becomes a stumbling block to doing well.

4.5

SOMETHING TO THINK ABOUT AND DISCUSS

Monitoring Your Learning

Respond to the following questions and then discuss your answers with a partner or small group.

- How do you think your schedule will change when you are preparing for midterms and finals?
- How do you plan to make those changes successfully?
- If you have taken midterms or finals in the past, what obstacles did you find to managing yourself and your time? What do you plan to do differently this term?

In this chapter you have learned some tips for managing yourself and your time. Try to make a schedule and follow it strictly for one week. Then make adjustments to suit your needs. Even if you don't consider yourself a "schedule person," you should find that keeping track of what you need to do really helps you organize and take control of your college career.

Read the *Real College* scenario and apply what you have learned about time management to help Janice organize her schedule.

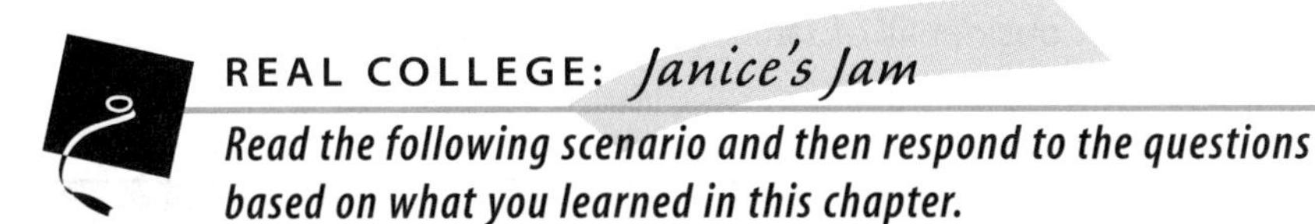

REAL COLLEGE: *Janice's Jam*

Read the following scenario and then respond to the questions based on what you learned in this chapter.

Janice is a freshman in college. She loves her new freedom—a new town, her own place, new friends, and a great social life. Gone is the 10:00 P.M. curfew that her parents had enforced in high school. Janice is living it up and having the time of her life. The problem is that she can't seem to make it to all of her classes, and she's falling way behind on her work.

Janice is taking five courses this term: American literature, accounting, sociology, history, and a chemistry course that involves lab projects. Her reading load is about 240 pages each week, and she has at least one exam every other week. She never seems to be able to keep up with her reading or to find time to study. In addition, Janice is having trouble making it to her 8:00 A.M. accounting class. In fact, she missed both class periods last week. She has even missed several of her chemistry classes—even though she really enjoys them—because she just could not seem to make it in time.

Another concern is Janice's part-time job at a local video store. Even though her hours are somewhat flexible, she always works at least two weeknights and one weekend day. She thinks that the fifteen hours spent at her job each week is really getting in the way of her studying, but she needs the money so she can't quit or cut back on hours.

She also finds her new social life to be a problem. It seems that no matter when she tries to study, someone is calling or stopping by to ask her to go out. Janice really has a hard time saying no and ends up procrastinating on her work. She never had trouble in school before, but now she is failing several courses including chemistry, which she wants to major in. She knows that she needs to do things differently, but she just can't seem to find the time to get everything done!

Using the strategies you learned about time management and self-management, what advice would you give Janice to help her manage her time?

____

____

____

____

____

____

____

____

Help Janice create a plan to stay organized. Consider all of Janice's obligations including class time, work, and her other commitments.

	Monday	Tuesday	Wednesday	Thursday	Friday	Saturday	Sunday
7 A.M.							
8 A.M.		*Accounting 140*		*Accounting 140*			
9 A.M.							
10 A.M.	*Chemistry 120*		*Chemistry 120*		*Chemistry 120*		
11 A.M.	*Sociology 130*	*History 100*	*Sociology 130*	*History 100*	*Sociology 130*		
12 P.M.							
1 P.M.	*American Lit. 160*		*American Lit. 160*		*American Lit. 160*		
2 P.M.							
3 P.M.							
4 P.M.							
5 P.M.	*Chemistry 120 Lab*						
6 P.M.	↓						
7 P.M.							
8 P.M.							
9 P.M.							
10 P.M.							
11 P.M.							
12 A.M.							
1 A.M.							

FOLLOW-UP ACTIVITY

Follow your schedule for one week and then evaluate it by asking yourself the following questions:

- Did you find that you accomplished more work?
- What adjustments would you make to your schedule?
- Have you left enough flexibility in your schedule for emergencies?
- Are you studying during your most alert times?
- Rework your schedule if necessary.

Networking

- There are many web pages devoted to helping people organize and manage their time. Find at least three such web sites. What kind of useful information did you find? How much overlap was there in the information about time management? What differences in time management advice did you find?

Academic Energy
Motivation and Goal Setting

Read this chapter to answer the following questions:

What is motivation?

How do you get motivated?

How can you stay motivated?

How can goal setting increase motivation?

In college, you may have already noticed that the term "motivation" is used in many different ways.

> "I really have to motivate myself to learn history."
>
> "Professor Jones is a lot more motivating than Professor Smith."
>
> "I am very motivated to make good grades this year."
>
> "I am more motivated to learn chemistry than literature."
>
> "I am always more motivated at the beginning of the term."
>
> "I am much less motivated to study on nice days."

These statements seem to say that motivation is something that drives you from within, something encouraged by a professor, something that depends on what you are learning, or something that depends on the time of year or the weather. How can the same word have so many meanings? Part of the reason is that people use the word "motivation" to stand for many different things. It could just be that motivation has so many definitions because it is complicated. Think about any class that you are currently taking. Even during a one-hour class period you may have several changes in motivation. As

STUDY TIP

Reward yourself for a job well done when you meet your goals.

the class begins, you may be motivated to take good notes, to listen attentively, and to make good grades, but as the hour wears on you might start looking at the clock and thinking about your next class or what to have for lunch, which lowers your motivation. Then the instructor might say something that piques your interest, which brings your motivation back up again. Your motivation is always changing depending on the situation.

Even though motivation may mean different things to different people, in general, students who are motivated are more successful in college. They approach each course with a positive attitude and are in college for more than just grades—they are there to learn. Think of motivation as "academic energy"—the more energy you have the more successful you will be. This chapter will discuss what motivation is, how to get motivated, and ways to stay motivated. Before we address these issues, however, read the *Research into Practice* section. Researchers Scott Paris and Julianne Turner talk about the factors involved in a person's motivation to learn.

Research Into Practice

Improving Motivation*

In this article, Paris and Turner talk about how motivation changes depending on the tasks and situations encountered in school. They say that a person's motivation depends on the four Cs of motivation: choice, challenge, control, and collaboration. That is, people are motivated when they have some ***choice*** about what they will learn. According to this theory, you will be more motivated to write a paper when given a choice of topics to write about than when you are assigned a topic. People are also more motivated to learn ***challenging*** things because there is a feeling of accomplishment about achieving a difficult task. If a person succeeds at a very easy task, he or she may not value that achievement as much as a more challenging one. Think about the classes you have liked the best. Chances are they challenged you more than those that you found very easy.

Once you are learning personally chosen and challenging tasks, it is also important to feel ***control*** in reaching your learning goals. This does not mean that the instructors need to give students total freedom all the time, but that students should be free to learn in the way that is best for them. For some students that means working with others; for others it means working alone. Some students like to work listening to soft music;

* Source: Paris, S. G., & Turner, J. C. (1994). Situated motivation. In P. R. Pintrich, D. R. Brown, & C. E. Weinstein (eds.), *Student motivation, cognition, and learning: Essays in honor of Wilbert J. McKeachie* (pp. 213–238). Hillsdale, N.J.: Erlbaum.

others need to work in total silence. Having control over your learning environment will help motivate you to learn.

Finally, Paris and Turner say that ***collaboration*** with other people is motivating because working with others helps to create interest in the topic and sharing ideas can bring out other perspectives. You're also more likely to persist with difficult tasks when working with other people. For example, when you work with a study group before an exam, your friends can help you figure out a confusing topic, you can quiz each other, and you can help each other learn successfully.

What does this research say to you as a college student? It should suggest that some situations and tasks might make you feel more motivated than others. This theory of motivation may explain why some students are motivated to learn in classes that are based on discussion, whereas other students are motivated in lecture classes. Some students are more motivated when asked to write essays, whereas other students are motivated by multiple-choice exams. Some courses are fascinating for some students, yet other students find them dull.

5.1

SOMETHING TO WRITE ABOUT AND DISCUSS

Thinking Critically

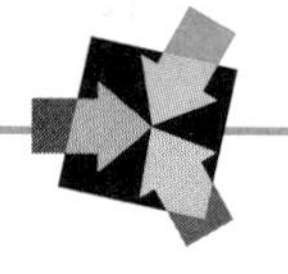

Paris and Turner have presented four factors that influence students' motivation to learn. Before reading the rest of the chapter, it's important to think about your own motivation to learn. Think about your learning experiences as you answer the following questions:

1. *In your experience as a learner, what kinds of choices have you been given in your classes? How have those choices affected your motivation to learn?*

____

____

____

____

2. *In your experience as a learner, what kinds of challenges have you experienced in your classes? How have these challenges affected your motivation to learn?*

____

____

____

____

3. *In your experience in school, how have you been in control of your learning? How has this control affected your motivation to learn?*

____

____

____

____

4. *In your experience in school, what role has collaboration played in your learning? How has collaborating with others affected your motivation to learn?*

____

____

____

____

Motivation Influences

Motivation is a combination of several factors including choice, desire for learning, and value of learning.*

1. Choice. Motivation is influenced by the *amount of choice* you have about what you are learning. Sometimes your professors will offer you several projects to choose from, or sometimes they will even ask you to choose what topics will be covered. Choices like these will help to increase your motivation. However, even if you are not given choices about the class content, college offers you many choices about what you will learn. You choose your major, and to a certain extent you choose the courses you will take and your course schedule.

2. Desire for Learning. Motivation is affected by your *desire to learn.* It's likely that because you are currently enrolled in college you do want to learn, but sometimes you might be required to take courses that you are not particularly interested in. (We will discuss more about interests in the next chapter.) For example, many colleges have a liberal arts requirement for all students, which means that regardless of their major, students

* McCombs, B. L. (1996). Alternative perspectives for motivation, In L. Baker, P. Afflerbach, & D. Reinking (eds.), *Developing engaged readers in school and home communities* (pp. 67–87). Mahwah, N.J.: Erlbaum.

must take courses in the humanities, mathematics, and the sciences. As you probably have already noticed, the more you want to learn in a particular course, the more motivated you will be. So because you do have some choice in the courses you take each term, it is a good idea to use these choices to maximize your motivation to learn. For example, it is a good idea to balance your course schedule by taking courses you feel motivated to take along with courses that you don't feel especially motivated about.

3. Value of Learning. Motivation depends on *how much you value the subject* to be learned. The more you believe the subject to be worthwhile, the easier it will be to become motivated. For example, many colleges require students to take at least one foreign language course. If you believe that it is valuable to learn another language, you will feel motivated—perhaps even enough to take a second course. However, if you do not, you may have a harder time motivating yourself to learn in your language course.

In an ideal setting you would have all of the components of motivation. However, you can learn successfully without choice, desire, and value, but learning will take a more conscious effort from you.

5.2 SOMETHING TO THINK ABOUT AND DISCUSS

Discuss the following questions about your motivation to learn in college with a partner or a small group. Summarize your answers to present to another group or the entire class.

- What do you want to get out of college?
- What do you want to get out of your courses this term (other than a good grade)?
- Why do you think you have to take courses that are outside your major?
- How would you describe your general level of motivation for learning in college?

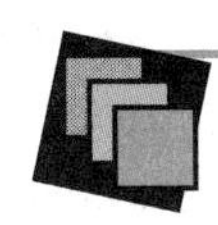

What Motivates People?

You may not realize it, but you are always motivated—you may not be motivated to learn, but you are motivated to do something. No matter where you are or what you are doing, *you are always motivated to do something* even if it's just sleeping! Focusing your motivation on learning, however, may be challenging sometimes.

You should also know that you are responsible for your own motivation. Even though an interesting instructor makes it easier for you to stay motivated, no one can directly motivate you to learn. But given that you are always motivated and that you are responsible for your motivation, there are some differences between students who are motivated to learn and students who are not.

You may have heard the terms *extrinsic* and *intrinsic* rewards. Usually extrinsic rewards are those that are given to you from someone else. For example, when you were younger, you may have received money for cleaning your room or getting good grades. On the other hand, intrinsic rewards are those that are internal. For example, you may have felt a sense of pride in completing a very difficult task like running a marathon or writing a short story or a poem just for fun. In general, people accomplish more when intrinsic rewards are at stake, even though the extrinsic rewards may seem appealing at first.

Motivation can also be considered intrinsic or extrinsic, because people can be intrinsically or extrinsically motivated. Intrinsic motivation occurs when the activity is its own reward. For example, some people read for the sheer enjoyment, others like to calculate numbers for the pleasure of it. Still others like to conduct experiments for the thrill of discovery. Think of intrinsic motivation as being curious about something or doing something you choose to do.

Extrinsic motivation, on the other hand, occurs when your incentive is a reward such as grades or praise. Think of extrinsic motivation as incentive to get something done rather than doing something for the sake of learning. For example, you may be failing organic chemistry, but when the professor offers an extra credit assignment you decide to do it even though you are not motivated to learn in the course. In this case, you are extrinsically motivated to earn extra credit points that can boost your course grade rather than to learn organic chemistry for the sheer pleasure of it!

The more you are intrinsically motivated to learn, the easier it will be for you to learn. The key to becoming intrinsically motivated, even in classes you don't particularly like, is to find something about the course that you find motivating and try to focus on the positives of the course rather than the negatives. It also helps to focus more on understanding the concepts to be learned rather than focusing solely on grades.

5.3

SOMETHING TO WRITE ABOUT AND DISCUSS

1. *As we stated above, your motivation depends on many different things. Think about the courses you are taking this term. What aspects of the courses do you find intrinsically motivating (e.g., type of exams, type of assignments, lecture style of professors, format of the courses)?*

___

___

___

2. *In the courses you are taking this term, what aspects of the course do you find unmotivating (e.g., type of exams, type of assignments, lecture style of professors, format of the courses)?*

___

___

___

3. *When you find that you are not motivated to learn in a class, what do you do to increase your motivation?*

___

___

___

___

Getting Motivated

Getting motivated is the first step to staying motivated. One of the best ways to become motivated is to set learning goals. Your goals should be more than just "I want to make an A in the course," because grades are an extrinsic motivator. In fact, students who focus only on grades to motivate themselves usually have a harder time maintaining their motivation as the term goes on. Students who set goals that focus on learning rather than grades tend to be more successful.

Goal Setting

You probably have set goals before without even realizing it. Think about some New Year's resolutions you have made—to exercise more, to stop smoking, or to increase your GPA. How many of your resolutions have you kept? If you are like most people, you forget your resolutions by Valentine's Day! That is because most people do not set themselves up for achieving their New Year's goals. People tend to be unrealistic when they make New Year's resolutions. For example, although a goal of exercising more and getting in shape is a good resolution to make, it is unrealistic to expect to get into great shape quickly if you have not been exercising regularly. Individuals who do not set short-term goals on their way to reaching long-term goals will soon find that their goals are not easily achievable and will give up on them.

FIGURE 5.1 *Characteristics of Achievable Goals*

Now think about your academic goals. Are your academic goals like those New Year's resolutions? What is important for you to achieve this year? How can you set yourself up for successful achievement of your goal? First, it's important to set realistic, achievable goals. If your goal is to maintain a 3.00 GPA to keep your academic scholarship, you should start out with some smaller goals to achieve this larger goal. Are you taking courses that you feel motivated to learn about? Do you believe that you can reach your goals?

As summarized in Figure 5.1, in order to set goals that can be achieved, your goals should be realistic, believable, desirable, and measurable.

Realistic: Can the goal be achieved? If not, how can the goal be divided into smaller goals? You should try to have short-term, intermediate, and long-term goals. In terms of academic goals, *a short-term goal* is one that you will achieve within the next few days. "I will read Chapter 10 of my biology book tonight" is an example of a short-term goal. *Intermediate goals* are ones that you will achieve within the next few weeks or months. An example of an intermediate goal is "I will compare my notes to the text material each night to prepare for my next psychology exam, which will be in three weeks." A *long-term goal* is one that will take longer still, perhaps a few months or even years to achieve. An example of a long-term goal is "I want to learn Spanish this year" or an even longer-term goal is "I want to graduate with a degree in marketing." Most people make the mistake of making only intermediate and long-term goals, but short-term goals are a necessary part of goal setting. Short-term goals help you keep track of the progress you are making, and they help you stay on track toward your larger goals.

Believable: Do you feel that you will be able to achieve your goal? Being confident in your ability to learn is crucial to motivation. If you feel that a task is too difficult for you to achieve, your motivation will decrease and you might give up before you even try. Some students believe that they can succeed only in certain topics. Students will say "I'm good at math, but I'm terrible at English" or "I can learn history really well, but not science." These statements tell us that the students are motivated to learn one topic, but not another. If you find yourself making these kinds of statements, take a minute to reflect on how it is negatively affecting your motivation to learn in those courses.

Desirable: How much do you want to reach your goal? In order to succeed in reaching your goals, they should be goals that you really desire. Then learning will be particularly rewarding or enjoyable to you, and it will be easier to achieve. Your goal may be to graduate from college within four years and land a good job in your field, but you must have the desire for success to reach that type of goal.

Measurable: How will you know whether or when your goal has been met? Some goals are easy to measure. For example, if your goal is to lose ten pounds you will know whether your goal has been met when you weigh yourself. But sometimes learning goals are not as easy to measure. Therefore, you need to set some standards to help you measure your progress toward your goal. This may be as simple as taking a few minutes to think about what you have learned after each study session, or it may include a more in-depth assessment such as the motivation checkpoints discussed in the next section. In general, you will need more checks of your progress for long-term goals than for short-term goals.

By taking the time to set and review your goals, you are on the way to becoming more motivated because you have an idea of what you would like to accomplish. In the next section we will discuss ways to stay motivated.

5.4 SELF-EVALUATION

This self-evaluation is a little different from those you took in Chapters 1 through 3 because this is an evaluation that you will continue to need to revisit. Consider this a pretest of your goals for this term. Be sure to check back to this evaluation periodically to be sure your goals are being met.

1. *List three to five short-term goals for this term.*

______________________ ______________________

______________________ ______________________

______________________ ______________________

Do you believe you can achieve these goals? ___________

How will you know when your goals have been achieved?

____

____

2. *List two to three intermediate goals for this term.*

____

____

____

Do you believe you can achieve these goals? ___________

How will you know when your goals have been achieved?

____

____

3. *List one or two long-term goals for this term.*

____

____

____

Do you believe you can achieve these goals? ___________

How will you know when your goals have been achieved?

____

____

4. *What is your long-term goal for your college career?*

____

____

____

Do you believe you can achieve this goal? ___________

How will you know when your goal has been achieved?

____

____

____

5. *Are your goals desirable to you? Why or why not?*

____

____

____

6. *Are your goals realistic? Why or why not?*

____

____

____

Staying Motivated

Getting motivated is one thing; staying motivated is another. One way to stay motivated is to give yourself some checkpoints on your way to reaching your goal. It is a good idea to monitor your motivation for learning just as you monitor your comprehension when you read (discussed in Chapter 3). Each time you sit down to study, ask yourself about your level of motivation for what you are doing. As discussed in Chapter 4, you have an internal "body clock," which means that you will find that certain times of the day are more conducive to learning than others. Listen to your body clock to find out when you are most motivated (first thing in the

morning, late afternoons, evenings) and try to plan your study sessions around those times.

It is also a good idea to begin by studying the subjects you find the most difficult, or are least motivated to learn. Then move to the subjects that are easier, or those that you enjoy more. In that way you will be more likely to stay motivated to study the subjects you find the most interesting. In addition, as discussed in Chapter 4, plan some breaks in your study time; don't try to study for more than one hour without a short break because you will find it difficult to maintain your motivation.

You should also have a strategy to follow if you find that you are losing motivation. You may want to take a break and come back to it, you may want to switch topics every hour, or you may find it helpful to work with a study group. If you find that your social life is interfering with studying because your friends are calling you or dropping by, plan to study in the library or another quiet place where you will be free from distraction and temptation. Anything you do to renew your motivation is great! Just try a few techniques to find out what works best for you instead of giving up entirely.

The motivation checkpoint chart in *Monitoring Your Learning* should help you monitor your motivation in many different situations in all of your courses to help you discover the kinds of tasks you find particularly motivating and the kinds of tasks that you find less motivating. Once you know what motivates you and what doesn't, you can be prepared with some of the techniques discussed above.

5.5 MONITORING YOUR LEARNING

One way to maintain your motivation is to figure out all of the tasks that you need to complete in your courses. By listing this information, you should be able to find something in the course that is motivating for you. You will also be able to determine the tasks you find unmotivating, which can help you psych yourself up to maintain your motivation in advance. Before each exam (or paper or project) for each of your courses this term, complete the chart in Figure 5.2 on page 86 to monitor your motivation.

Losing Motivation

Sometimes students find that they lose motivation as the term goes on. Some of this is natural—people are generally more motivated at the beginning and at the end of a term. So if you experience a slight dip in

FIGURE 5.2 Motivation Checkpoints

Checkpoints	Course 1	Course 2	Course 3	Course 4	Course 5
What do I need to learn? What is the task? (exam, paper, presentation, discussion, etc.)					
What sources will I need to use? (text, labs, lecture, discussion, etc.)					
What is my level of motivation for beginning the task? (high, medium, low) Why?					
What are my goals for completing this project? (Include short-term, intermediate, and long-term goals.)					
What is my level of motivation for completing the task? (high, medium, low) Why?					
What, if any, adjustments do I need to make to reach my learning goals?					

your motivation toward the middle of a term or during the first nice day of spring, you probably shouldn't be too concerned. Set some new goals to get back on track. However, sometimes losing motivation can be a sign of a bigger problem. If you think your loss of motivation may be a problem, reflect on the source of your lack of motivation. Can you pinpoint a reason for it? Or are you unsure why you are unmotivated? Sometimes students become unmotivated by poor grades in a particular course, or sometimes outside influences (e.g., family, roommates, social situations, or health concerns) may cause students to lose their motivation.

Usually once you identify the reason why you are losing motivation, you can use some of the strategies in this chapter—such as setting new goals or finding a study partner—to increase you motivation. However, if you find that you are losing so much motivation that it is interfering with your college success, you might want to get some help from a friend or counselor to try to regain your motivation for learning.

Now that you know how to get motivated and how to stay motivated, read the *Real College* scenario and use your knowledge to help Keisha maintain her motivation to learn.

REAL COLLEGE: *Keisha Knuckles Down*

Read the following scenario and then respond to the questions based on what you learned in this chapter.

Keisha attends a large college. She has had trouble staying motivated to learn in her classes because so far she has not been able to take courses in her major. Actually, she has not yet been accepted into her major—accounting—because the business school requires an overall 3.00 GPA. Currently Keisha has a 2.67 GPA; her goal is to raise her GPA to 3.00 so she can officially be accepted into the business school by next term. Keisha is planning to enroll in five courses this term: two business classes (introductory accounting and principles of economics), two classes that fulfill some general requirements (European history and physical science), and one elective class (art history), which her roommate said was interesting. In order to reach her goal, she needs to get As in all her courses this term.

She feels very motivated to make good grades this term, even though she typically begins every term feeling motivated and winds up totally unmotivated by finals week. This time she has already made a study schedule, and she plans to read and study for six hours every night, seven days a week. Even if she doesn't feel like studying, she will just push herself for the full six hours each night—no matter what! Although this schedule may interfere with her social life and her twenty-hour workweek at a local restaurant, she believes that she will just have to tough it out for fifteen weeks.

1. *What do you think may be Keisha's biggest obstacle in reaching her goal?*

____

____

____

____

2. *What advice would you give Keisha to help her maintain her motivation throughout the term?*

3. *How could she modify her study plan to make it more motivating?*

4. *Do you think Keisha's goals are realistic? Why or why not?*

FOLLOW-UP ACTIVITIES

1. In each of your courses, monitor your motivation throughout the term. What activities do you find particularly motivating? What do you find unmotivating? What strategies do you find helpful in regaining your motivation? How can you use these strategies in other situations to help you get or stay motivated?
2. Revisit your goals from the self-evaluation activity on page 82. How have you met your goals? Which goals are you continuing to work on? Are there any goals that need to be modified? Do you have any new goals to add?
3. As you plan your schedule for next term, consider your motivation to learn in each course you select. Remember to balance courses you don't feel particularly motivated about with those that greatly motivate you to learn.

Networking

- Many sites on the Internet feature tips for getting and staying motivated. Some good sources include college counseling centers or freshman-year experience sites. Try the following key words to find at least three motivation sites:

  motivation
  college motivation
  student motivation
  learning motivation

  What kind of information did you find that will help you become more motivated or to maintain your motivation?

Changing Attitudes and Interests

Read this chapter to answer the following questions:

How do interests and attitudes influence learning?

How can you change your attitude or maintain a positive attitude?

How can you develop an interest for topics you don't like?

STUDY TIP

Because attitudes are situational, you should retool often to adjust for differences in courses, professors, and your own level of motivation and interest.

How many times have you dealt with a clerk in the grocery store, a family member, your adviser, a server in a restaurant, or even your best friend and walked away thinking, "Now there's a person with a bad attitude"? Everyone probably has a bad attitude about something at some time, which suggests that attitude is situational. Rarely are people positive about everything, nor are they negative about everything. For most people, their attitude depends on a variety of situations and factors.

Likewise, interest is situational. Students generally aren't interested in everything. In general, individuals tend to show great interest in a limited number of areas, moderate interest in a greater number of topics, and low or no interest in many more. Everyone knows people who have a strong passion for something: computers, fly fishing, travel, photography, writing, history. More often than not, such passions are reflected in majors that students select. For example, students who are curious about the world and who love to travel often major in history. As they grow older, they may even plan their vacations to visit significant historic sites. By the same token, individuals who have no interest in mathematics probably won't pursue careers in statistics, chemistry, or architecture. Interests can't help but influence the academic decisions students make and how actively students pursue certain goals.

Like motivation, which was discussed in the last chapter, attitudes and interests help define who you are as a learner. Moreover, each of these factors is either directly or indirectly a part of your personality, thus making them a bit more difficult to change than basic study habits. However, although attitudes and interests are influential and are closely linked with motivation, we believe that they need to be discussed separately because they are not the same as motivation. Before beginning our discussion of attitudes and interests, however, complete Activity 6.1.

6.1 SELF-EVALUATION

Think about what you know about yourself as a learner. Part of this thought process should involve thinking about your attitudes and interests, particularly how they are related to your choice of college and your major. As you consider your attitudes and interests, answer the following questions:

1. *In general, what is your attitude about attending college?*

   ____

   ____

   ____

2. *What is your attitude about the college you are attending? Why do you have this particular attitude?*

   ____

   ____

   ____

3. *What is your attitude about the courses you have this term? List each course and explain why you have a particular attitude about it.*

   ____

   ____

   ____

4. *List at least three topics that are very interesting to you, three that are of moderate interest, and three in which you have little or no interest.*

   High Interest

   (a) ____________________

   (b) ____________________

   (c) ____________________

   Moderate Interest

   (a) ____________________

   (b) ____________________

   (c) ____________________

   Low Interest

   (a) ____________________

   (b) ____________________

   (c) ____________________

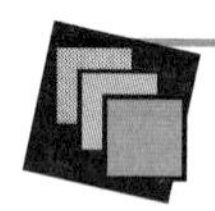

Attitudinal Directions

Although everyone seems to know someone who generally has an overall bad or good attitude, attitudes can actually be thought of as emotional reactions to specific situations. Attitudes are often reflexive, meaning you experience them without even thinking about it. For example, if your professor assigns you two extra chapters to read before a quiz on Friday, and you already have every minute of your schedule between now and Friday planned, you may have an immediate negative reaction. However, that attitude may not be permanent. Perhaps a professor in another class cancels a test that was scheduled for Friday, or a date that you really didn't want to go on in the first place begs off—both can cause your initial bad attitude to mellow. The bottom line is that most students' attitudes about things change like the weather. What you have a bad attitude about on Tuesday may be seen in another light by Wednesday.

In addition, your attitude affects your motivation. It makes sense that if you are motivated in a particular course, your attitude will be more positive than if you were unmotivated. Moreover, it's important to realize that your attitude matches your behavior. If you have a bad attitude toward learning a foreign language and feel that you can't succeed no matter what, your behavior will follow suit. You won't interact with the material on a daily basis, you won't say much in class, and you even may display a poor attitude toward your professor, even if she is a good teacher.

As shown in Figure 6.1, as a college student, you will often experience four attitudinal directions: (1) attitude toward college; (2) attitude toward your instructors; (3) attitude toward the subject and learning environment; and (4) attitude toward yourself as a learner. As you read about each one, think about yourself as a learner and the attitudes that you have.

Attitude toward College

When students enter college, they generally come with an overall attitude about what they will experience there. For some students, college selection takes a considerable amount of time and thought. They visit a variety of campuses, talk with college recruiters, and request numerous college catalogs. They spend hours thinking about the pros and cons of each college and finally narrow their choices to a few schools to which they apply. After they are accepted and make a final decision about where they will go, they are generally pleased with that decision and begin their first year with a positive attitude. Because they did their homework when selecting their college, they have a good idea of the social, emotional, and academic support that the campus has to offer.

On the other side of the scale, there are students who don't actively participate in the selection of the college they attend. Perhaps the reason is financial, or perhaps one or both parents attended "State U" and they expect their son or daughter to go there as well, even if it is not a particularly good fit. Perhaps the student just isn't ready for college but is under pressure to attend anyway. Whatever the reason, there are students who

FIGURE 6.1 *Attitudinal Directions*

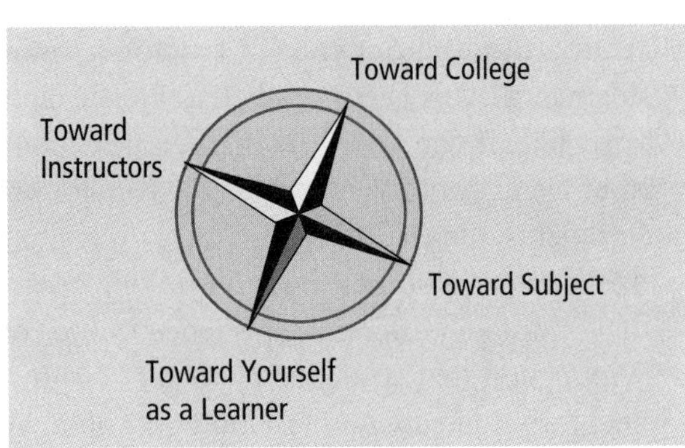

begin college with a less-than-positive attitude simply because they had little or no say in where they would attend.

As you can see from these examples, students begin college with different attitudes for many different reasons. Obviously it's better to begin on the right foot—with a positive attitude about the college you are attending—but also remember that attitudes change. We've known many students who started college having one perception about what they would experience only to be either disappointed or elated later on. For whatever reason you chose to attend your current college, know that your general attitude about being in college and your expectations of what that college experience will be strongly influence the attitudes you will have. In turn, these attitudes influence your academic performance. Sometimes college just isn't what students expect it to be. Factors such as large class sizes, classes that are difficult to get into, long lines, roommate problems, and homesickness are just a few of the many problems that can turn initially good attitudes sour. We might add that on the first day of a fall semester, as one of the authors looked out her window, the first thing she saw was a line of students that appeared to be about a mile long. This wall of students was attempting to get to a computer where they might be able to add or drop a class. She silently wondered what attitude these students, particularly the first year students, had toward college today.

6.2

SOMETHING TO THINK ABOUT AND DISCUSS

- Think about your first few days as a college student. Did anything happen to give you a bad attitude or that frustrated you? How did you deal with it?
- What caused your attitude to change?

Attitude toward Your Instructors

Your attitude about your instructors also influences your academic performance. This is especially true for disciplines that you don't particularly like. If you go into a mathematics course hating math, and project that feeling onto your professor, you are probably going to experience problems. On the other hand, if you try to have the attitude that each instructor has something unique to offer to your education, you may well have a totally different experience in the course and with that professor. We suggest that students try to get to know their professors and not to feel intimidated when talking with them. We know of a student who, at the beginning of every term, makes an appointment to see all of his professors. He takes only about fifteen minutes of their time introducing himself and talking with each of them about how to study in their courses. He says it helps him see his professors in a different light, and although he still has a better attitude toward some professors than others, the experience makes all his professors "human." Rarely does a professor turn down his request for an appointment, and in many cases, this initial contact makes it easier for him to approach a professor if he experiences problems with a course later on.

6.3

SOMETHING TO THINK ABOUT AND DISCUSS

Thinking Critically

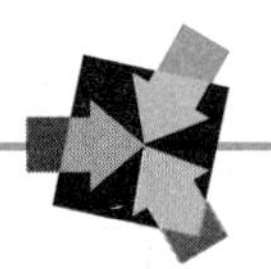

- Think about a teacher or professor who has made a difference in your developing a positive attitude about learning in a particular course. What characteristics does this teacher have that have helped you connect with him/her?
- Do you tend to make better grades in courses in which you like the professor? Why?

Attitude toward the Subject and Learning Environment

When we think about attitudes toward subject matter, it's difficult to separate attitude from interest because most students have a more negative attitude toward subjects in which they are not interested. The link between attitude and interest offen occurs to students during the registration process. Most programs have a designated number of credits that students must take in certain core areas. These areas are usually broken down into the humanities, social sciences, lab sciences, mathematics, and the like. If you are strong in mathematics and science and have been successful in those courses in the past, you will most likely enter into these courses in college with a positive attitude toward learning the material. However, if you have little interest in math and science and fail to see any relevance in these courses to your future career choice, then you are much more likely to have a bad attitude toward these classes. In fact, some students try to avoid subjects they dislike until the very end of their program. We know students who delayed taking their lab science or mathematics requirements until their senior year, only to find that the course wasn't as bad as they thought it would be.

The important thing to remember is to try not to have preconceived notions about a course. A personal example here might help to explain our viewpoint. One of the authors of this text was never much of a history buff until she sat in on an introductory American history course to help students learn how to write better essays. The professor in the class was dynamic and made history come alive. She looked forward to attending this class, read on her own, and was able to make connections between what she had relearned in this course and what she saw in her travels across the United States. Students in the course felt the same way. Many students who had entered the course with little interest in history left with a renewed curiosity, even though the demands of the course were rigorous. Thus, beginning a course with an open mind can go a long way in changing your attitude and helping you maintain motivation.

6.4 SOMETHING TO THINK ABOUT AND DISCUSS

Thinking Critically

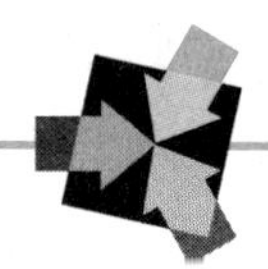

- Think of a course you have taken about which you had a negative attitude before you even started. What do you think led to those negative feelings? Did they change over the course of the term?
- What could you have done to approach this course more positively?

Attitude toward Yourself as a Learner

The attitude that you have toward yourself as a learner may be the most important of the four attitudinal directions. Your attitude about yourself as a learner is a sum total of the educational experiences you have accumulated in your 12+ years of schooling. If you have had teachers who encouraged you, if you were challenged in school, if you have experienced academic success, and if you have parents who have been actively involved in your learning at home, you probably have a positive view of yourself in learning situations. Students with positive views have confidence in themselves, know and use a variety of study strategies, are willing to take new challenges, and generally have an "I can do this" attitude. That's not to say that students who have a positive attitude never doubt themselves. They do. But they know themselves well enough to realize what they will have to change and how they will have to change it in order to improve things.

On the other hand, if school was not challenging, if you experienced only moderate academic success, and if your family had little involvement with your learning, you may have a more negative view of yourself and lack confidence academically. Students who fall into this category initially may have a more difficult time adjusting to college, but we have seen such students continue to gain confidence in themselves when they begin to experience academic successes.

6.5 SOMETHING TO THINK ABOUT AND DISCUSS

Thinking Critically

- What is your general attitude toward yourself as a learner? Do you have a general attitude toward learning or does your attitude depend on the situation?
- How do you think your attitude about learning influences how and to what extent you study for a class?

Maintaining a Positive Attitude

Few students begin college with a totally negative attitude. The majority of beginning students are positive about something. Thus, we suggest that your first step is to evaluate what it is you like about college. You may have a great roommate, you have at least one class and professor that seem to be enjoyable, or maybe you are simply positive about having a new beginning. Whatever excites you and makes you feel positive should be what you actually concentrate on, especially during those first few days of a new term. Yes, things will go wrong. The computer might crash just when you finally are making some progress in adding a class you want, the registrar may have lost proof that you actually paid your tuition, and the lines in the bookstore may go out the back door. But you have no control over these things. Take a deep breath, count to ten (or fifty, if need be), and try not to let all of these negative happenings get in the way of your excitement and positive attitude. We realize that this can be difficult, but it's important to learn early on that you have little or no control over many things in life. Don't let those things bring you down. Save your energy for staying on top of what you can control and do something about.

Another suggestion that students find helpful in maintaining a positive attitude is not to dwell on past mistakes. For example, if writing has always been a struggle for you, telling yourself "I'm a terrible writer" will do little to help. Rather, concentrate on the positives such as "I'm a good learner in general, so writing should not be impossible. I can get help at the Writing Center if I need it, so I know I can do it." Everyone has strong points and weak points. The secret is one of balancing. If you lack confidence in writing, for example, be sure to balance that writing course with another course that you will like and that will be less of a struggle for you. Try to avoid negative thinking. We have worked with students who convince themselves that they can't do something before they even

attempt it, and they are doomed before they begin. Try at least to give each course and each professor a chance, particularly each professor. Students who have had problems in a particular domain, such as math or writing, will often grow enormously if they click with their professor. Enter each course with the attitude that you will do your best. In some courses, this may mean that you will not earn the best grade. There's nothing wrong with earning a C in a course that is particularly difficult for you. There is something wrong, however, in settling for a C because your attitude in that course was negative and you simply did not put in the necessary effort.

Another suggestion is to expect to learn something valuable in every course you take. We know that's often a difficult suggestion to follow, but if you try to think that parts of a course might be interesting and valuable, both your attitude and your motivation will be better. It's particularly difficult to follow this suggestion when you are a first-year student because we know that first-year students often get stuck taking "leftover" courses or core courses in which they haven't developed much interest. Moreover, first-year students tend to be more oriented toward immediate gratification and find it difficult to think about how the content of a course might benefit them at some point in the future. But no matter how uninteresting or boring you might find a course, look toward the positive. Think how you might use some of the information at a later date or how it might be related to other areas that do interest you and for which you already possess a positive attitude. For example, if you are enrolled in an art history course that you find rather boring, think about trips that you have taken to museums in which you knew little about the art or the artists. Museums are much more exciting and appealing if you know something about why different artistic movements developed. Such knowledge enables you to tie together history, art, music, and even the sciences.

Developing Interests

As we mentioned earlier, attitudes and interests go hand in hand. Whatever you have an interest in, you also probably have a good attitude toward. Likewise, when you're not interested in a topic or course, you may not have a very good attitude about having to learn it. Before completing this section on interests, read the *Research Into Practice* section, which focuses on the importance of interests to learning.

Research Into Practice

Interests Are Important to Active Learning*

Dr. Hidi's research is actually a synthesis of numerous other research studies that have been conducted concerning the role that interest plays in learning. The focus of this study was to synthesize the body of research on the role that interests play as students select and process text information.

Hidi's synthesis revealed two interesting findings that have practical applications for college students. First, she concluded that students' interests were key not only in selecting information to process but also in how students persist as they are attempting to learn information. In other words, you will spend more time and work harder on processing information that you find interesting. Second, as the brain processes information that is interesting to a student, it processes that information differently. Thus, information that is interesting to you will be remembered and recalled more easily than information that is uninteresting.

But Hidi's synthesis also left many questions unanswered or at least unclear. It is still unclear how the kind of interest influences processing. For example, interest can be individual and have personal significance, or it simply can be a piece of text or information that most people would find interesting (such as information pertaining to sexual issues). Simi-

* Source: Hidi, S. (1990). Interest and its contribution as a mental resource for learning. *Review of Educational Research* 60: 549–571.

larly, questions remained unanswered about the differences in processing when an individual has a general interest in a topic—say World War II—versus interest that is generated simply due to the way a piece of text is written, not necessarily the subject matter that it covers. Researchers continue to grapple with these issues.

6.6

SOMETHING TO WRITE ABOUT AND DISCUSS

Thinking Critically

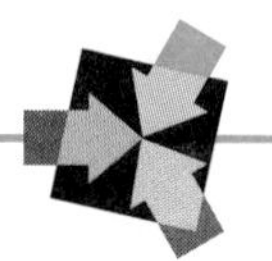

After reading the *Research into Practice* section, think about your own interests. Earlier (Activity 6.1) you jotted down a few things that both interested and did not interest you. Think about those interests a little more, particularly those areas that you identified as having moderate interest in. Those areas certainly have the potential for developing into high-interest areas. Respond to the following questions as a way of evaluating your interests:

1. *Do you agree with Hidi's conclusion that it is easier to remember and recall information that is interesting to you? Why or why not?*

   ____

   ____

   ____

2. *What about a text (and by "text" we mean anything you read, not just a textbook) makes it interesting? For example, why do millions of people every year continue to read books such as* The Diary of Anne Frank *or* Animal Farm*? What makes a text interesting to you?*

   ____

   ____

   ____

   ____

3. *What factors might contribute to your developing an interest in a course in which you currently have no interest?*

   ____

   ____

   ____

   ____

   ____

Dr. Hidi's research concerning how interest influences learning, as well as the synthesis that she conducted, helps us consider and clarify the importance that interests play in learning. It is easy to see from this synthesis why students who have a wide variety of interests may do better in college. Thus, it would help every college student to do better if he or she continued to develop interests so that learning would be easier in a broader number of courses.

We have found that many students lack interest in a wide variety of areas, which puts limitations on the courses that they want to take. But not having a wide variety of interests doesn't mean that you can't develop them. As we suggested above, every course has something interesting about it or people wouldn't study it. Students who have the most focused interests are usually those who have the most difficulty developing new interests. We have had conversations with students that go something like this:

STUDENT: Why do I have to take this stuff—history, sociology, and drama for goodness sakes! I'm a computer science major, and none of this is important to me. I just want to be able to work with computers.

PROFESSOR: Well, I understand that, but you also have to take a series of what are called "core courses"—courses that help you have a well-rounded education. Once you get the prerequisites out of the way, you'll be able to enroll in your major courses. Besides, it's important to develop other interests. One of the reasons for a college education is to give you a broader view of the world.

STUDENT: (rolling his or her eyes) Maybe so, but I don't care about any of this. I'll do it because I have to, but I'm not going to like it.

The student shuffles off, unhappy, determined to get nothing from any course, unless it is in some way computer related. Chances are that this student will get into academic trouble simply because he or she is already convinced that there is nothing about these courses that could possibly be of interest. How different the scenario might have been if this student thought about courses as a chance to develop new interests and learn new things.

There are also students who enter college with no overriding interest in any one particular area. Many of these students have not yet selected a major and hope to find something that interests them as a result of enrolling in general core courses. The best advice we can give to these students to develop interest is to keep up with assignments. Do the reading, participate in discussion groups, study with others, and seek assistance when the going gets rough. Often a class that starts out slowly turns into an interesting course if you keep on top of things. It particularly helps if you create study groups to talk about the information, and it helps even more if at least one person in the group has more than a superficial interest in the course. One of the authors remembers being in a biology study group as an undergraduate. She joined the group because she really didn't have much interest in biology but needed to do well in the course. Since she learned best by discussing the information with others, the study group was a natural way for her to study biology. Much to her surprise, one member of the group was a biology nut! Not only that, but he could make even the dullest topic interesting, and his images were often so vivid that it was difficult not to remember the information at test time. What started out as a way to try to earn a decent grade in a class turned into an experience that created an enormous amount of interest in biology. To this day, biology still interests her and, in fact, some of her research in studying has been conducted in college biology courses.

A final suggestion about developing and maintaining interest: Don't save up all the courses you think you'll hate (because you think they'll be uninteresting and boring) until the end of your college career. Intersperse the good with the bad. In other words, try to balance a course you know you'll be interested in with those that you think hold little interest for you. And for those less-interesting courses, try to select your instructors carefully. A good instructor can make or break your interest toward and attitude about a particular course.

REAL COLLEGE: *Martin's Misery*

Read the following scenario and then respond to the questions based on what you learned in this chapter.

Martin is a first-year student. Because Martin did very well in high school and also earned high entrance exam scores, he had his pick of colleges and was courted by some of the top schools in the country. Martin's parents, who were very proud of their son's accomplishments, persuaded him to attend a large prestigious eastern school. Martin wanted to go to a smaller school that had a good reputation in the sciences, because he has a strong interest in majoring in biology. In fact, although he had been successful in all of his courses in high school, he really doesn't want much to do with anything that isn't in some way related to science. His career goal is to become a veterinarian.

When Martin arrived on campus, he immediately felt overwhelmed. The campus was too big, he didn't know anyone, and his classes were extremely difficult. He had no choice in his courses for the first term because his schedule was set for him. He was enrolled in five courses:

World Literature I, Political Science, Calculus, Anthropology, and Computer Applications I. Martin became miserable—fast! For the first couple of days, he tried to maintain a positive attitude, but he kept asking himself "Why am I here? Why did I let my parents talk me into this?" Before he knew it, he found himself with a bad attitude about being in college, and he knew that if he didn't do something fast, he was going to dig himself into a hole he couldn't get out of.

Martin is obviously bright and has long-term career plans. But it is also obvious that his bad attitude about school and his classes might influence him negatively if he doesn't do something fast. Based on what you have read and what you know about the role that attitudes and interests play in learning, what advice would you give Martin?

My advice to Martin is:

____

____

____

____

____

____

FOLLOW-UP ACTIVITIES

1. It's always interesting to find out about how people become interested in things. Students ask us all the time: "How did you ever become interested in writing about and doing research in the area of studying?" or "How in the world could you be interested in cooking?" We usually have pretty long and detailed answers to these questions. Think about your own interests. How did those interests develop? Did you use to have interests in something that no longer interests you at all? Why did you lose interest?
2. Now interview one of your classmates about his or her interests. Find out how his or her interests developed and compare this to how your own developed.
3. Think about small steps you could take to improve your attitude in a course this term. Could you get help from a tutor if you are having problems with the class? Could you join a study group? Would it help to talk things over with the professor? If these suggestions won't work, think of some that will.

Networking

- Find at least three web sites on an area in which you are interested. For example, someone who is interested in travel could look at the Travelocity web site *(www.travelocity.com);* someone interested in cooking could examine the Epicurious web site *(www.epicurious.com)*. In many cases, all you have to do is direct your browser to the general name of whatever it is you are interested in, such as dinosaurs or Impressionist art.

7 Just What Do You Believe Anyway?

Read this chapter to answer the following questions:

How is what you learn affected by your beliefs?

What are the five components of beliefs that influence learning?

STUDY TIP

Take responsibility for your own learning by finding out about your beliefs about knowledge.

Many different kinds of beliefs affect your life every day. People have different religious beliefs, moral beliefs, political beliefs, and so on. You may have thought a lot about those kinds of beliefs, but have you ever considered your beliefs about learning? Have you ever thought about how you come to know something? Have you ever considered how you gain knowledge or what knowledge is? If you are like most students, you probably haven't thought much about where knowledge comes from, but believe it or not, your beliefs about knowledge impact what and how you learn.

In this chapter, you will learn about the types of beliefs that can affect your learning in college. You'll also answer some questions to find out about your personal beliefs about learning. In addition, you will learn some techniques for changing your current beliefs to ones that promote academic success. Before you read the rest of the chapter, read *Research into Practice,* which discusses the type of beliefs that shape a person's approach to learning. These beliefs are called "personal theories of beliefs" about learning, because no two people approach learning in exactly the same way.

Research into Practice

Personal Theories of Beliefs*

In this article, Schommer discusses research on beliefs about knowledge and how those beliefs affect how students learn. She suggests that beliefs about knowledge are personal theories. In other words, each person has his or her own unique beliefs about what knowledge is and where knowledge comes from. Students' personal theories have five basic components, which will be outlined briefly here and discussed in more detail later in this chapter.

The first component is the extent to which a person sees knowledge as fixed (set) or changeable. Some people strongly believe that all knowledge is set in stone and others believe that all knowledge is changeable. Still others hold a belief somewhere in between, believing that some knowledge is fixed and some knowledge is changeable. For example, in a history class one student believes that history consists of truths to be learned, but another student believes that history consists of stories that are only an interpretation of events and can be changed depending on who is telling the story. The first student holds a belief that knowledge is fixed; the second student sees knowledge as changeable.

The second component is the extent to which a person sees knowledge as a group of individual facts or as concepts that are related to each other. For example, two students are studying for their chemistry exam. One student believes that knowledge is a series of unrelated facts, so he tries to memorize all of the formulas and key terms to prepare for the exam. The other student believes that knowledge consists of ideas that are interrelated, so when studying for the exam, she tries to see how the chemistry concepts are related to each other.

The third component is the extent to which people believe that knowledge is external (and is given to an individual from an outside authority such as a teacher or a parent) or internal (and comes from within the individual). For example, two students are taking an engineering course. One student believes that the professor's role is to be the knowledge provider, so she only studies what the professor covered in class. The other student believes that knowledge comes from within, so when he studies he tries to make himself understand the information even if it means reading more than was assigned.

The fourth component deals with beliefs about the speed of learning. Some people believe that learning happens quickly or not at all, while other people believe that learning happens gradually. For example,

* Source: Schommer, M. (1994). An emerging conceptualization of epistemological beliefs and their role in learning. In R. Garner & P. A. Alexander (eds.), *Beliefs about text and instruction with text* (pp. 25–40). Hillsdale, N.J.: Erlbaum.

two students are enrolled in a French course. One student believes that learning should happen quickly, and she gets frustrated because learning French doesn't happen overnight. The other student believes that learning takes time, so he is not surprised that is takes a long time to learn a language.

The fifth component deals with beliefs about the control of learning. Some people believe that the ability to learn is fixed at birth, whereas others believe that people can learn how to learn. For example, two students are experiencing trouble learning in a calculus course. One student believes that he can't learn math because he wasn't born with that ability, and he gives up. The other student believes that people can learn how to learn, so when she has trouble, she finds a tutor to help her learn or she makes adjustments in her approach to studying.

Research has suggested that students' beliefs about knowledge are related to how they learn in college, because beliefs can actually affect how people interpret and comprehend information. You may have already noticed that people learn things differently. The differences in how people approach learning might be connected to their personal theories about learning.

7.1 SOMETHING TO THINK ABOUT AND DISCUSS

Think about the following questions and discuss your responses with a partner or small group.

- What have you observed about your own beliefs that may make learning easier for you?
- What have you observed about your own beliefs that may make learning harder for you?

Five Components of Beliefs That Influence Learning

As the belief components are discussed in the rest of the chapter, think about your own beliefs about learning. Where do your beliefs fall? How might these beliefs affect your learning in college courses? Remember that in order to get off on the right foot in college, you may need to reevaluate your beliefs and the role they play in your academic success. Table 7.1 summarizes the components of beliefs.

TABLE 7.1 The Five Belief Components

Component	Belief ranges from ...		to ...
COMPONENT 1: *Certainty of Knowledge*	Knowledge is fact.	or	Knowledge is continually changing.
COMPONENT 2: *Simple Knowledge*	Knowledge is made up of isolated bits of information.	or	Knowledge is complex.
COMPONENT 3: *Responsibility for Learning*	It is the professor's responsibility to ensure that students learn.	or	It is the individual's responsibility to learn.
COMPONENT 4: *Speed of Learning*	Learning happens fast or not at all.	or	Learning is a gradual process that takes time.
COMPONENT 5: *The Role of Ability*	The ability to learn is fixed.	or	People can learn how to learn.

COMPONENT 1: Certainty of Knowledge

One aspect of your beliefs about knowledge depends on your beliefs about the certainty of knowledge. Some students believe that knowledge is continually changing based on current information. When they are in class, they think about what they already know about the topic and may change their beliefs about the topic by adding new information to what they already know. For example, a student might enter a physics class believing that when a bullet is shot from a gun, it falls to the ground faster than a bullet that is simply dropped. However, that student might change her beliefs after learning new information about the laws of gravity. Other students believe that there are absolute answers and that there is a definite right or wrong solution to every problem. These students approach learning by trying to find the truth in all situations. In the same physics class, another student may have trouble understanding that scientists believe that physics is based on theories, not truth, and that these theories are in a constant state of change based on new research.

You may have been taught in your history classes when you were younger that "In 1492 Columbus sailed the ocean blue," and that he found an uncharted land. But when you got to college your history professor might have discussed the consequences of Columbus's actions on native culture. History has revisited its "truths" in light of new information and today's standards of conduct. This revisiting of "facts" is true of other disciplines as well. There was a time when people believed the

earth was flat, or that bleeding sick people with leeches would cure them. Such beliefs would be laughed at today by most people—although the Flat Earth Society still exists today!

However, even though experts are continually reassessing what they know, students are often encouraged only to look for the facts in their textbooks. Students may approach reading history texts by looking strictly for names, dates, and places because that was what was important in their previous experience. But most college courses expect you to do more than learn facts. Professors tend to view their disciplines as constantly changing. Therefore, to memorize only facts would be a waste of time. Instead, most professors want you to be able to understand concepts, and they want to prepare you to apply what you learn to future situations. This means that they expect students to question what they read and be willing to live with the notion that there may not be a solution or definite answer to every question. Even in everyday life we are constantly reassessing what we know to be true. In that sense, knowledge is viewed less as an absolute truth and more as an ever-changing uncertainty.

7.2

SOMETHING TO WRITE ABOUT AND DISCUSS

Thinking Critically

1. *List three concepts that you believe are "truths."*

___

___

___

2. *List three concepts that you believe are not certain (there are no "truths").*

___

___

___

3. *How do these concepts differ? Do other people consider the concepts you regard as "truth" as uncertain?*

___

___

___

COMPONENT 2: Simple Knowledge

Your beliefs about knowledge are also based on how simple or complex you think knowledge is. Some students believe that knowledge consists of interconnected concepts, but other students believe that knowledge consists of a series of unrelated bits of information. Students who believe that knowledge is complex look for relationships between ideas as they learn. They try to see the "big picture." For example, when studying literature, a student might look for similar themes, or plots, or she may look for the historical significance between several stories or poems.

On the other hand, students who have a strong belief that knowledge is simple tend to break information down into very small isolated parts. Although breaking information into smaller chunks is a great strategy for some tasks (e.g., when learning vocabulary or something you must memorize, like the periodic table of the elements; or even when learning a completely new topic), a student who learns only isolated pieces of information will miss the big ideas. For example, a student in a chemistry class who believed that all knowledge consisted of isolated facts would memorize formulas and think he was learning the information properly, but he would not be prepared for an exam that asked him to apply chemistry concepts to new situations. Nor would he be able to see the interconnection between ideas in chemistry. The same is true in all content areas. If a student in history class only memorized dates and names, she would be unprepared for an essay question that asked her to compare and contrast ideas about the larger concepts. Because most of the assignments you will experience require you to apply what you have learned, you need to go beyond memorizing small bits of information and begin to see how the information is connected.

7.3

SOMETHING TO WRITE ABOUT AND DISCUSS

Thinking Critically

1. *As a general rule, why is trying to see the "big picture" more effective than memorization?*

____

____

____

2. *What strategies do you currently use to help you see how concepts are connected?*

____

____

____

COMPONENT 3: Responsibility for Learning

Beliefs about knowledge also depend on your beliefs about who is in charge of making sure you learn. Who is responsible for your learning in college? Are you in control of what you learn, or are your professors responsible for your learning? Some students believe that it's the professor's responsibility to be sure that all students learn the information. Other students believe that, although the professor guides their learning, they are ultimately responsible for their own learning.

In high school, your teacher probably took a lot of the responsibility for your learning in class. You most likely had little choice in the subjects you studied, what you learned, or the way you were assessed (e.g., tests, papers, labs, etc.). In fact, the teacher may have even gone over all of the relevant information in class, which left you little to learn on your own. You probably have already noticed, however, that college professors have different assumptions about who is responsible for learning.

Some students think that college professors don't care whether or not students learn. It's not that professors don't care. Rather, they expect students to take responsibility for their own learning. For example, often professors will ask test questions about information covered in the assigned readings, but not necessarily covered in lecture. They expect students to be able to figure out information on their own, and they also may expect students to be able to pull together information from a variety of sources. This is a good skill to learn, because when you enter the workforce you will be expected to draw on your ability to direct your own learning (look at the number of help-wanted ads looking for a self-starter), which includes making decisions and creating new solutions.

7.4 SOMETHING TO WRITE ABOUT AND DISCUSS

Thinking Critically

1. *What do I want to get out of each course this term?*

____

____

____

2. *What are my responsibilities as a learner in each course?*

____

____

____

3. *What are my professors' responsibilities to help me learn in each course?*

____

____

____

COMPONENT 4: Speed of Learning

Another aspect of your beliefs about knowledge deals with the speed of learning. Some students believe that learning is a gradual process, but other students believe that if learning is going to happen, it happens quickly or not at all. In other words, some people believe that you can learn how to learn, but other people think that if you don't "get it" right away, you never will. Students who believe that learning takes time are better prepared for college tasks. For example, in a meteorology lab, this type of student would try many different ways to solve a lab problem. On the other hand, students who believe that learning should happen quickly might give up after trying one or two solutions to the lab problem. Students who believe that learning should be quick are often frustrated in college when they are faced with complex information (like in physics or music theory) that cannot be grasped quickly.

Many college students may believe that learning should happen quickly because of their experiences in high school (and elementary and middle school, too). Learning may have come quickly and easily for some students in their high school classes. In fact, research has shown that in high school mathematics classes, most problems that students answered could be solved in less than two minutes. It's no wonder that many students are unprepared for more difficult tasks in college and why some students just give up when faced with more challenging problems.

Most things worth doing take time and lots of it. For example, your favorite athletes have invested years and years of practice in order to have the skills to make them exceptional players. If you have ever tried to play an instrument, you know about the hours of practice that are needed before playing music looks effortless. The same is true for learning in college. Your professor may appear to know her topic thoroughly, but rest assured that she spent years and years of continuous study in order to become so knowledgeable.

7.5 SOMETHING TO THINK ABOUT AND DISCUSS

- Discuss three activities that have taken you a long time to learn.
- How can you apply those learning experiences to your college learning?

COMPONENT 5: The Role of Ability

The final component concerns the role of ability. Some students believe that people can learn how to learn, but other students believe that the ability to learn is fixed and that people are naturally good at some things but will never be able to do other things. For example, a student may say, "I am good at math and science, but not history or English." What this student means is that she thinks she has the ability to learn math but does not have the ability to learn English. Everyone has natural talents or things that come easy to them, but when you believe that your ability determines everything you can and can't do you dramatically limit your academic challenges.

Students who believe that the ability to learn is fixed tend to talk to themselves in a negative way. For example, a student may say, "I will never be able to do this" or "I am too dumb to learn this" when in fact this student may be just giving up too easily. On the other hand, students who believe that people can learn how to learn tend to view difficult tasks as challenges that can be met. Instead of giving up, these students will try different strategies for learning and will ask for help from the professor or their friends if they need it. For example, if a student had trouble in a Japanese language class, she might try to find a native speaker to help her, or she might go to a tutor, or meet with the professor. She would certainly invest a good deal of effort in learning the language instead of telling herself that she lacked the ability to learn. There are probably students in your courses who make learning look easy, but students who appear to learn "naturally" probably spend time and effort in activities that promote academic success, such as reading and reflecting.

7.6 SELF-EVALUATION

Read the following scenario about learning in a biology class, and then respond to the fifteen questions honestly to find out your personal theory of beliefs. The purpose of this scenario is to get you to think about your beliefs. Remember that there are no right or wrong responses to the statements.

Chris is a student in introductory biology. He studies hard for the class, but he failed his first two exams. When he studies, he tries to focus on the material covered in the lectures. Because Chris believes that the professor always goes over the important information in class, he focuses on the notes, but really doesn't read the text. He does try to memorize almost all of the bold-faced terms in the text. He writes the terms on 3" x 5" notecards and flips through them until he has memorized the definitions. After the last exam, he tried studying with friends, but he didn't find it helpful. His friends were explaining the information in a different way than the professor, so he was not sure if they knew what they were talking about and didn't want to get confused. Because he usually runs out of time studying for the next exam, Chris plans to concentrate only on the topics that were covered on the computerized practice exams. He believes that science is really just memorization and that most science problems have only one answer, so if he looks at the material enough he should do fine. Even though he doesn't spend a lot of time studying, he feels that he puts in hard work and effort; therefore, he feels he should be receiving high grades, but this has not been the case.

Chris thinks his poor grades could be a result of the new professor teaching the course. Professor Smith wants to change the class format to have discussions, despite the fact that there are 250 students enrolled in the class. She told Chris that science is a process and that there are no "facts"—just theories. She told Chris to study hard, to look at the diagrams in the text, and to try to understand the science processes when he studies. Professor Smith also tries to tell the class about all sides of each issue. When there are competing scientific theories, she is sure to discuss each one because she wants to give an unbiased lecture each time. However, Chris knows that science is based on proven facts and finds all these theories confusing. When Chris went to Professor Smith's office hours asking which theory is the right one, or which one he needed to know for the exam, she told him that all of the theories have some merit and that he must decide for himself what to believe. Chris believes that it is the professor's responsibility to make sure that the students learn in class. However, this professor often asks exam questions about topics that were covered in the text but not during the lectures. Chris is beginning to believe that he is failing the class because he is not able to learn science.

Please circle your response to each statement.

	STRONGLY DISAGREE	DISAGREE	NEUTRAL	AGREE	STRONGLY AGREE
1. I agree with Chris that science is based on proven facts.	1	2	3	4	5
2. I agree with Chris that the students should only be responsible for the scientific theories that the professor discusses in class.	1	2	3	4	5
3. Like Chris, I believe that there must be one theory that is more correct than others.	1	2	3	4	5
4. I agree with Chris that the professor is responsible for student learning.	1	2	3	4	5
5. I agree with Chris that if I don't do well on my biology exam it is because I am not able to learn science.	1	2	3	4	5
6. Like Chris, I believe that I don't have to read the text as long as I listen in class because the professor goes over all of the important information.	1	2	3	4	5
7. I agree with Chris that learning competing science theories is too confusing for students.	1	2	3	4	5
8. I agree with Chris that there is usually only one right answer to a science problem.	1	2	3	4	5
9. I believe that some people will do fine in Chris's class because they are good learners, but others have a limited ability to learn science.	1	2	3	4	5
10. Like Chris, I believe that I will only do well in this class if I can learn information quickly.	1	2	3	4	5
11. Chris's plan of taking good notes and trying to memorize facts should be all it takes to get a good grade in biology.	1	2	3	4	5
12. Chris will be able to understand the complex processes involved in biology if he memorizes definitions.	1	2	3	4	5
13. If Chris tried to understand every theory it would take him too much time to read a chapter.	1	2	3	4	5
14. Like Chris, I believe that no matter how much time and effort they spend, some people will never be able to learn biology.	1	2	3	4	5
15. I believe that if I am going to understand my biology text, it will make sense the first time I read it—rereading will not help me understand any better.	1	2	3	4	5

Source: Adapted from Holschuh, J. L. (1998). *Epistemological beliefs in introductory biology: Addressing measurement concerns and exploring the relationship with strategy use.* Unpublished doctoral dissertation, University of Georgia, Athens.

Scoring Directions:

To find out your personal theory, add your scores to the preceding questions together.

Component 1: *Certainty of Knowledge*

Question #1		*Question #3*		*Question #8*		*Total*
	+		+		=	

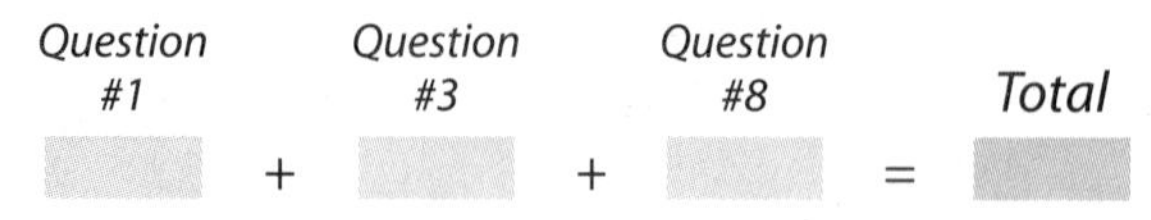

Component 2: *Simple Knowledge*

Question #7		*Question #11*		*Question #12*		*Total*
	+		+		=	

Component 3: *Responsibility for Learning*

Question #2		*Question #4*		*Question #6*		*Total*
	+		+		=	

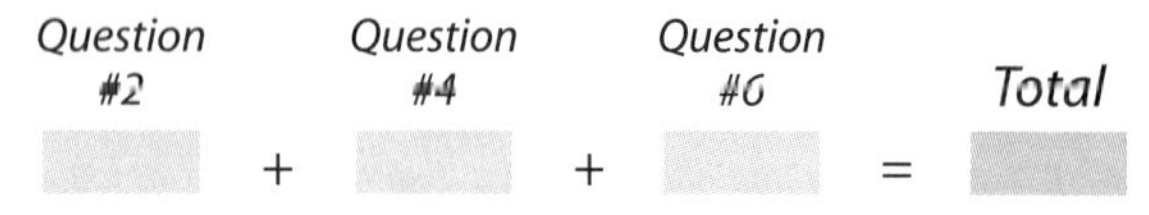

Component 4: *Speed of Learning*

Question #10		*Question #13*		*Question #15*		*Total*
	+		+		=	

Component 5: *The Role of Ability*

Question #5		*Question #9*		*Question #14*		*Total*
	+		+		=	

Assessing Your Personal Theory

Your score on each component could range from 3 if all of the responses were ones to 15 if all of your responses were fives. Take a look at where your scores fall on each component. The way the scale is structured, the higher your score on a component, the more strongly you hold a belief that may get in the way of your academic success. The lower your score on a component, the more strongly you hold a belief that research has been shown to lead to academic success. Because no person is completely consistent in his or her beliefs, chances are you hold strong beliefs on some components (as indicated by either high or low scores) but are more in the middle on other components.

Based on what you have read about beliefs, you probably have figured out that students who believe that knowledge is changeable, that knowledge consists of interrelated concepts, that learning is under the control of the student, and that learning may take time and effort will be expected to have more success in college than students who hold the opposite beliefs.

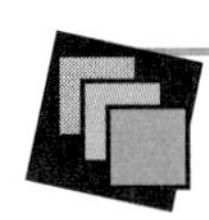

Changing Your Beliefs

After evaluating your personal belief theory using the above scale, you may have found that you have some beliefs that need to be changed because they may negatively affect your success in college. This section will present some strategies for promoting change.

Your beliefs about learning influence the strategies you use to study, which is part of the reason why beliefs are related to college performance. For example, if you believe that knowledge is simple, then you will select a strategy that reflects your belief, such as making flash cards to memorize definitions of key terms even when the task requires that you integrate ideas. Thus, when you have all of the terms memorized, you will feel that you have prepared enough for the exam. If you do not pass the exam, you may not understand what you did wrong, because according to your beliefs about learning, you were adequately prepared. The question, then, is: If you currently hold beliefs that may make academic success more difficult, how do you go about changing those beliefs?

Be aware of your beliefs. Do you have beliefs that are getting in the way of your learning? Those are the beliefs you should consider changing, but before you can change a belief, you must first be unsatisfied with your current beliefs about learning. Then when you find yourself giving up on a task too quickly or trying to merely memorize when you need to understand difficult concepts, you can rethink your approach and take the time to really learn the information.

Look for the "big picture." Instead of memorizing a lot of separate facts, make a conscious effort to relate ideas to what you already know and to other ideas discussed in class. Many of the strategies presented in Part III of this book will help you learn to integrate and synthesize ideas as you read.

Learn to live with uncertainty. This is sometimes difficult, but there are no right answers to some questions. For example, in a statistics class, you may want to know the right way to solve a problem, and although there are some ways that are better than others, chances are that if you ask three statisticians how to solve the problem you will get three different answers.

Don't compare your ability with others. Worrying that you are not as good as your roommate in math will not get you anywhere! Focus instead on how to improve your ability to learn in the subjects that you find most difficult. For example, find a tutor to work with or form a study group to help you learn.

Realize that learning takes time. If you begin your assignments with the expectation that they will take time to fully understand and complete, you are likely to experience less frustration and more understanding. For example, don't expect to learn complex biology concepts the first time that you encounter them. Plan to spread out your study time so you can review difficult material several times.

7.7 MONITORING YOUR LEARNING

The next time you encounter a difficult task or concept, think about your personal theory of beliefs.

- How are your beliefs affecting how you approach and carry out the task?
- Are your beliefs leading you toward academic success?
- Are you talking negatively to yourself and keeping yourself from learning successfully?
- Now that you know about how your beliefs affect your learning, you can begin to examine your beliefs in the many learning situations you encounter. Your beliefs about learning are continually changing based on experience, but by being aware of what those beliefs are you can help yourself learn more effectively by not letting your beliefs get in the way of your learning.

REAL COLLEGE: *College Knowledge*

Read the following scenario and then respond to the questions based on what you learned in this chapter.

In this section, you will read about the beliefs of four college students. Use what you know about beliefs about knowledge to consider the following students' beliefs.

Pat is taking history mostly because it is required. He believes that it is the professor's responsibility to make sure that the students learn in class. However, in this history class, he finds that the professor often asks exam questions about topics that were not covered in class. Pat doesn't think that is fair because he doesn't know how he is supposed to know what to study if the professor doesn't tell him what is important.

Amy believes that she will be successful in biology, because she knows that science is based on proven facts. She believes a scientist, if he or she tries hard enough, can find the truth to almost anything. One problem she has is that her professor tries to tell the class about many competing theories, which Amy finds confusing. She wishes her professor would just tell the class which one is the right theory.

David was a good English student in high school. He was always able to quickly understand the concepts and didn't need to spend a lot of time on homework. When he started his literature class the readings were familiar, and he didn't really spend much time outside of class reading or studying. However, he found that he did not do well on the first essay exam and that the new concepts were confusing. He still believes that he should be able to learn the information quickly and is unsure why he is having so much trouble.

Lisa believes that she is the type of person who can't do math. She sees that some students just seem to get it because they are naturally good at learning calculus. She wishes that the university would understand that some people just can't learn math and that it shouldn't be a requirement for all students.

Answer the following questions then discuss your responses with a partner or small group:

1. *How are these students' beliefs similar to yours? How do they differ?*

____

____

____

2. *How do you think these beliefs will affect the students' performance in their classes?*

____

____

____

3. *What advice would you give these students?*

____

____

____

____

____

FOLLOW-UP ACTIVITIES

1. As you read your texts, think about how the authors' beliefs are affecting how and what they write. For example, is your history text presenting the information as fact, or are you encouraged to think about multiple viewpoints? Does your science textbook try to point out connections between concepts, or are concepts presented as isolated bits of information?
2. At the end of this year retake the self-evaluation (found on page 113). How have your beliefs changed in the past year? What do you think you still need to work on in the future?

Networking

- You may have noticed that some of the information you find on the Internet seems to contradict other information. Your personal theory of beliefs will influence how you decide which information to believe. Find three sites that give you different perspectives about the same topic. For example, you might look at three reviews of the same movie, or three political essays from a democratic, republican, and independent perspective. Think about how you will decide which one to believe. How do your beliefs about knowledge affect your decision?

Dealing with Stress

Read this chapter to answer the following questions:

What are common sources of stress?

What is academic stress?

How do you control or reduce stress?

STUDY TIP

Keep your stress level under control by planning ahead.

When you are under a lot of pressure, you might tell your friends that you are "totally stressed." Usually we think of stress as something to be avoided, but actually that's not always true. Stress is a normal part of life, and much of the stress you experience in college is helpful and stimulating—without stress we would lead a rather boring existence. The problem comes when you experience too much stress.

Believe us when we say that as a college student you will experience many different types of stress, including social pressures, financial burdens, and academic competition. In fact, stress levels in college tend to ebb and flow—you might feel more stress at the beginning of a term when everything is new, less stress in the middle of the term (until midterms, of course), and more stress again at the end of the term when you have to take final exams. In this chapter, you will learn about the sources of stress you will experience in college, strategies for coping with and reducing stress, and four common types of academic stress. Before reading the rest of the chapter, read the *Research into Practice* section to find out what researchers are discovering about the effects of stress on college students.

Research Into Practice

Stress and College Life*

In this article, the researchers investigated the relationship between stress and quality of life in college students. Attending college is a major source of stress that may entail moving to a new area, leaving family for the first time, and developing new relationships. College students generally feel stress that stems from issues about

- family or parents
- accidents or illness
- sexuality
- independence
- peer relationships
- relocation

Because changes that come from attending college can cause a great deal of stress, the researchers wanted to see how stress factors affected students' overall well-being, or quality of life. They defined quality of life as consisting of eight levels: level of anxiety, level of belonging, level of memory and concentration, level of depression, level of current health, level of bodily pain, level of emotional well-being, and level of social activities.

The results indicated that students who reported greater levels of stress had a lower overall quality of life in almost all of the eight levels. Distressing events, such as thoughts about suicide, were most strongly related to a low quality of life, which the researchers found often resulted in poor general health and well-being. They also found that social support influenced how students perceive and handle stressful situations. Students who feel that they can count on their family or their peers in a time of need have less anxiety and a greater sense of general well-being.

These results are meaningful for college students, because by identifying the causes of stress and their effect on quality of life, students can begin to be aware of and manage stressful situations. The results also suggest that because social support was found to be an important aspect of stress management, students should seek out a support network to help them through stressful times.

* Source: Damusch, T. M., Hays, R. D., & DiMatteo, R. M. (1997). Stressful life events and health-related quality of life in college students. *Journal of College Student Development* 38: 181–189.

8.1

SOMETHING TO WRITE ABOUT AND DISCUSS

1. *What kinds of changes did you experience when you began to attend college?*

____

____

____

____

2. *How do you think these changes affected your quality of life as defined by the research summarized above?*

____

____

____

____

3. *Do you think your ability to cope with stressful situations has changed since you began college? If so, how?*

____

____

____

____

Sources of Stress

Although at times it may feel as if there are infinite sources of stress, generally college stress can be broken down into six categories: prior academic record, social influences, family, finances, career direction, and situational problems (such as illness or drug problems). Most students think that stress is caused by outside factors. They might say that a test, a professor, or a paper is "stressing them out." But stress is really an internal process. Suppose your friend fails her first mathematics exam. She may feel that she will flunk out of college, not be able to get a good job, or not find success in life. She may even consider dropping out. Obviously your friend is overreacting to the situation, but that is the way stress can work. Your friend needs some strategies for dealing with her stress in order to put her reaction into perspective. As you read about the six categories of stress, remember that stress is natural, it is internal, it is often an overreaction to a specific situation, and *it can be controlled.*

- ***Prior academic record.*** Your previous academic success can affect your current level of stress. Students who have a shaky academic past may feel that they can't succeed in college. On the other hand, students who maintained a 4.0 average in high school may feel pressure to keep their stellar grade point average. Either way, your past history as a learner affects your stress level.
- ***Social influences.*** You probably have realized that dealing with your friends can often be stressful. A fight with your roommate, breaking up with a boyfriend or girlfriend, meeting new people—all of these situations can be stressful. In fact, even situations we would consider to be positive social factors, such as falling in love or socializing with really good friends, can cause a stressful reaction. Overall, however, having good friends and social support actually reduces your stress levels because you have someone to confide in.
- ***Family.*** Your family relationships can cause you to feel stress in several ways. You may feel pressure to do well in college in order to make your family proud, you may feel stress because you have moved away from your family, or you may feel stress because of family crises that arise. Your family can also be a source of support to help you when you experience a lot of stress. Some students feel stress because they are away from family; others feel the pressure of being the first child or the last child in their family to attend college. Still others feel stress because they have families of their own and college work takes away from time with the family.
- ***Finances.*** Financial stress usually begins in college because students take out loans for tuition, get jobs to help pay for college, or have to maintain a certain grade point average to keep their scholarships. In addition, many college students get their own credit cards, which can lead to great financial stress if used excessively. We know numerous college students who have graduated college not only with a diploma but also with student loans and a substantial credit card debt! College students are also usually responsible for paying bills and are gaining responsibility for their financial security. Students returning to college after working for several years may feel the financial stress of paying tuition or making less money while taking college courses.
- ***Career direction.*** "So what's your major? Oh yeah, what are you going to do with that?" You may have heard similar questions or

comments from friends and relatives. Everyone (perhaps yourself included) wants to know what you will do with your life after college. More and more often college students are expected to know what their career will be as soon as they enter college. The less sure you are about your career direction, the more stress you might feel about it. You may even be concerned that you'll never find your direction. On the other hand, students who have already decided on a career might also feel stress about it. If you have already decided on your career path, you might be concerned about achieving your goals. For example, a student who has decided to go to veterinary school might feel anxious to do exceptionally well in college because she knows that very few applicants are accepted each year.

- ***Situational problems.*** Certain stresses are unexpected and sometimes devastating. You may become ill during the term, experience the death of someone close to you, realize you have a drug or alcohol problem, or you may have an eating disorder, and so on. As with all of the categories of stress, if you feel overwhelmed by situational problems, seek help from a counselor on campus or someone you can talk to about these concerns.

8.2 SELF-EVALUATION

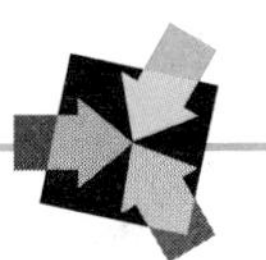

Take the following assessment of stressful situations to determine your current stress level. This assessment will help you determine whether you are currently experiencing an unhealthy amount of stress. Remember, some stress is necessary for everyday life, but if you are experiencing an overwhelming amount of stress, look for ways to reduce it and seek help if necessary.

Student Stress Scale

Check those events you have experienced in the past six months or are likely to experience in the next six months.

1. Death of a close family member	_______	_______	100
2. Death of a close friend	_______	_______	73
3. Divorce between parents	_______	_______	65
4. Jail term	_______	_______	63
5. Major personal injury or illness	_______	_______	63
6. Marriage	_______	_______	58
7. Fired from job	_______	_______	50

8. Failed important course	________	________	47
9. Change in health of a family member	________	________	45
10. Pregnancy	________	________	45
11. Sex problems	________	________	44
12. Serious argument with a close friend	________	________	40
13. Change in financial status	________	________	39
14. Change of major	________	________	39
15. Trouble with parents	________	________	39
16. New girlfriend or boyfriend	________	________	38
17. Increased workload	________	________	37
18. Outstanding personal achievement	________	________	36
19. First quarter/semester in college	________	________	35
20. Change in living conditions	________	________	31
21. Serious argument with instructor	________	________	30
22. Lower grades than expected	________	________	29
23. Change in sleeping habits	________	________	29
24. Change in social activities	________	________	29
25. Change in eating habits	________	________	28
26. Chronic car trouble	________	________	26
27. Change in number of family get-togethers	________	________	26
28. Too many missed classes	________	________	25
29. Change of college	________	________	24
20. Dropped more than one class	________	________	23
21. Minor traffic violations	________	________	20
TOTAL	________________		

A score of 300 or higher indicates an extremely high stress life;
a score of 200 to 299 indicates a high stress life;
a score between 100 to 199 indicates a moderate stress life;
and a score below 100 indicates a low stress life.

If you find that you are having a very high stress life, you might want to seek help from a counselor, friend, or family member.

Sources: DeMeuse, K. (1985). The relationship between life events and indices of classroom performance. *Teaching of Psychology* 12: 146–149. Holmes, T. H., & Rahe, R. H. (1967). *The social readjustment rating scale. Journal of Psychosomatic Research* 11: 213–218. Insel, P., & Roth, W. (1985). *Core concepts in health* (4th ed.). Palo Alto, Calif.: Mayfield Publishing.

Strategies for Reducing Stress

Now that you know what stress is and what causes stress for most students, you will be happy to know that there are many ways to control or reduce your stress levels (see Figure 8.1). Before you start feeling overwhelmed, consider the following strategies for reducing your stress:

Relax. You should make relaxation a regular part of your day. If you don't know anything about how to go about relaxing, there are numerous paperback self-help books available that actually offer some great techniques and advice. At the very least, try deep breathing or meditation for a few minutes each day to help you unwind. If you find yourself "stressing out," stop whatever you are doing, close your eyes, and focus on your breathing for a few minutes. This should help you relax so that you can return to what you were doing and feel more in control of the situation.

Exercise. A great way to reduce stress is to work out. Physical activity helps take your mind off of stress, and the chemicals your body releases during exercise actually boost your ability to handle stressful situations. Try to make time to exercise each day. If you are feeling especially stressed out, try taking a walk or a jog to clear your head.

Take charge. You are in control of your own situation, and you have to accept that responsibility. By taking charge, you can control the amount of stress you feel by remembering that stress is an internal reaction to situations and it is often really an overreaction. However, when stress gets out of control, you can also take charge of the situation by seeking help.

Put problems in perspective. Sometimes it helps to talk to a good friend or a parent who has been in a similar situation to help you put your problems in a more realistic light. Don't allow yourself to get carried away imagining all the things that could go wrong in a situation; instead, focus on the positives. For example, if you fail an exam, instead of saying, "I'll never pass this course" tell yourself that "I can and will pass the course—it was only one test after all!"

Be flexible. Everyone makes mistakes, and learning from your mistakes will help reduce your stress level. But if you are too set in the way you do things or the way you view the world, you may end up causing yourself additional stress. For example, sometimes students are afraid to change the way they study, even if their methods are no longer working. By being inflexible about their study strategies, these students are putting themselves in a stressful situation come exam time.

FIGURE 8.1 *Strategies for Dealing with Stress*

Develop interests. Join a club on campus, meet with others who share similar interests, or find some new interests on your own. By having interests outside of schoolwork, you will be able to enjoy yourself and relax during your time off from studying. Developing new interests also helps you in the classroom, because you tend to do better in subjects that interest you.

Seek help. Find your support resources: friends, family, counseling centers. Seek out campus resources to help you through stressful times. In fact, it is a good idea to seek out the people and places that can support you before you need them. We touched on the idea of seeking out help if you need it back in Chapter 2, but it doesn't hurt to repeat that advice here. Often a problem can be solved easily if you ask for assistance before it balloons into a major problem.

Enjoy yourself. Take a walk, read a good book, see a movie, call a friend. Do something you like to do before you start feeling overwhelmed.

8.3

SOMETHING TO WRITE ABOUT AND DISCUSS

Thinking Critically

1. *List three to five sources of stress that you are currently experiencing.*

_______________ _______________

_______________ _______________

_______________ _______________

2. *When you are feeling very stressed out, what do you generally do to reduce your stress level?*

____

____

____

3. *How can the strategies for reducing stress discussed in this section help you reduce your current stress level?*

____

____

____

____

4. *How effective are you in dealing with friends who are stressed out? What do you do to help? How might some of these same strategies work for you?*

____

____

____

____

Academic Stress

The stress students feel in college, or academic stress, is due to many different factors and is a part of the general stress you feel every day. You want to do well in your classes, you want to gain valuable experience, and you want to be a success in life. However, four common types of academic stress that some students experience can actually get in the way of their goals—public speaking anxiety, writing anxiety, mathematics anxiety, and test anxiety. If you have experienced one of these stresses, you know how harmful it can be. In this section we will discuss the four types of academic stress and strategies for coping with each of them.

Public Speaking Anxiety

Public speaking causes people to react in strange ways. They may find that their hands get sweaty, that their mouth gets dry, or that they forget what they were going to say. These reactions might occur because public speaking can cause a high degree of anxiety. In fact, research has found that some people fear public speaking more than death! In college, there will be times when you are required to speak in public, whether it is making a comment in a large lecture class or giving a presentation or speech. In order to cope with the stress that can result from public speaking, you need some strategies to help you prepare for the task.

Coping with Public Speaking Anxiety. The best way to cope with a fear of public speaking is to be prepared. Practice your presentation out loud several times before presenting it to your class. Practice in front of a mirror, or better yet, recruit some friends to listen to your speech. Have them record your time to be sure that you are on track, and ask them to critique your speaking style using the following questions:

- *Are you speaking too fast?* Sometimes when people are nervous they talk very fast, which makes it difficult for the audience to follow. Don't rush through your talk. Instead, try to use a conversational tone.
- *Are you using good inflection?* Again, when people are nervous they sometimes speak in monotone, which is difficult to listen to for an extended period of time. Try to speak confidently and with enthusiasm!
- *Are you jittery?* You may find yourself moving from side to side or wringing your hands when you are nervous. It is good to move around a little, such as using hand gestures or walking around to include the audience, but too much nervous movement can be distracting to your audience.

- *Are you making eye contact?* When you are giving your presentation, it may help to focus on one or two friendly faces in the room and present to them. You should be sure to make eye contact with the other people in the room, of course. But concentrate mostly on those two people. This strategy should help calm your fear of speaking in front of a large group.

Another strategy for coping with the fear of public speaking is to make some notes to follow during your presentation. Even though you have rehearsed your talk and have a good idea of what you will cover, you should have notes of your presentation with you just in case you need a reminder of what you are going to say.

Writing Anxiety

Many students experience a great deal of stress when asked to write something for class, especially if they are asked to write during class under the added pressure of time limitations. It might be an essay exam in history, a paper for English, or a research paper in political science. Students might be anxious about having to think of a good idea, flesh the idea out, and then have their writing evaluated by their instructor. They sit staring at a blank page waiting for the words to come. This is sometimes called writer's block, and it is a very frustrating experience that can happen to anyone. Just about every writer, the authors of this book included, has had difficulty finding the right words to write. But writing anxiety becomes harmful when students experience writer's block almost every time they try to write. When students are anxious about writing, they try to avoid it as much as possible because they find it so stressful. The problem is that in college (and in most careers after college) you are often asked to express your ideas in writing.

Coping with Writing Anxiety. One way to keep your writing anxiety under control is to write often. Yes, write often! Like any skill, your ability to write will improve with practice. You may want to keep a daily journal in which you record your experiences. Or you might want to do some freewriting, when you give yourself a fixed amount of time (five to ten minutes) to write about whatever you want. Or sit on a bus or in a coffee shop and write some character sketches about the people you see. What do you imagine their lives are like? Where are they going and what are they doing? No matter what you choose to write about, if you write each day you will be more confident about your ability to write for your classes.

Another way to cope with writing anxiety is to have a plan of what you will write before you begin your paper. It's helpful to make a list of the points you want to make and then use your list to guide you when you are writing your paper. If you are having trouble organizing the points you want to make, talk to a classmate or a tutor about your ideas. Most campuses have a writing center or a place where students can talk to a tutor about their papers at any stage—from choosing a paper topic, to reading rough drafts, to critiquing final drafts.

If you are preparing for an essay exam, try to predict the questions you will be asked. This will be covered in detail in Chapter 18, but in brief, use your class notes and topics emphasized in the text to predict the kinds of questions that might be asked. You might want to look at some of the professor's old exams to help you predict good essay questions.

Above all, start early. Because students who experience writing anxiety try to avoid writing, they often procrastinate until the last minute, which only adds to their stress. Sometimes these students believe that they can write only under pressure, but they are fooling themselves because they are actually making their stress level greater by waiting until the last minute. If they do not make a good grade on the paper, they blame it on the fact that they have trouble writing instead of the fact that they churned it out quickly. If this sounds like you, the next time you have a paper to write, start early. Work on the paper a little each day. If you have trouble in the beginning, you'll still have enough time to get some help and finish your paper on time.

Mathematics Anxiety

As with writing, some students feel stress when they encounter anything that has to do with numbers. Students who experience mathematics anxiety usually try to avoid taking math or math-related courses. The problem is that most colleges require students to take at least one (and sometimes several) mathematics and mathematics-related courses as part of the general degree requirements.

For most students, mathematics anxiety usually results from previous experiences in math classes. You may have had some trouble with a particular topic (say, word problems in algebra) and have told yourself "I can't do math" ever since. Students have bad experiences with almost any school subject you can think of, but for some reason mathematics anxiety seems to be the most traumatic and widespread. But just like any other type of stress, mathematics anxiety is an overreaction to a situation, and therefore, you can change your response to mathematics.

Coping with Mathematics Anxiety. One way to cope with mathematics anxiety is to face it head-on. Don't wait until your senior year to take your math courses; take them early and overcome your fears. However, be sure that you are taking a class that is at an appropriate level for you. For example, don't try to get into calculus if you have never had a precalculus course.

Once you have registered for a course that is at a good level for you, spend some time each day reading the textbook and doing the practice problems. Going to class is not enough because you must be able to apply what you have learned to new situations. In addition, one of the best strategies for learning math is to solve problems with words. That is, explain in words how to solve the problem rather than just trying to plug in numbers.

If you find that you are having trouble learning math concepts, don't give up! Seek help from a classmate, the instructor, or a tutor. Don't wait until the last minute—seek help as soon as you need it. Plan to work with a tutor weekly if necessary. In math classes, the information you are learning usually builds on itself, so if you don't understand what you learned in Chapter 2 you will have even more trouble learning the material in Chapter 6. You will find that there is a snowball effect to math trouble: If you don't get help early, you may need to do a lot of catching up later on; or it may be impossible to catch up, which will only cause you to feel more anxious.

Finally, speak positively to yourself when working on math problems. Don't say "I can't" or "I'll never" to yourself because these thoughts can be self-defeating. Instead, try to focus on the positives. Reward yourself for figuring out a tough problem, and keep trying to do your best.

Test Anxiety

Test anxiety is a feeling of stress when studying for or taking an exam regardless of the subject. You might worry about the types of questions that will be on the test, forgetting about and missing the test, studying the wrong material, and so on. Some students experience test anxiety only in specific situations. For example, some students do well on classroom tests that they can prepare for, but perform badly on standardized tests (such as the SAT or ACT) where there is a lot at stake. Students who experience test anxiety are often paralyzed with fear when faced with a test situation, and they end up missing questions that they know the answers to. If you have test anxiety, you might have trouble reading and understanding test questions, organizing your ideas, or worse yet, remembering information that you spent hours studying.

Many different experiences can lead to test anxiety. It might be caused by past test-taking experiences, such as blanking out on answers or failing an exam. It could also be caused by inadequate test preparation. If you know that you are not really prepared to take an exam, it's natural to be anxious about it. Test anxiety can also be caused by competition with your friends or classmates. If you are focusing on how others are doing, you might cause yourself undue stress.

Finally, test anxiety can be caused by a lack of confidence in yourself as a learner. When students feel that they are not good learners, they tend to become more anxious about testing situations. If you find that you are talking negatively to yourself about your ability to learn, you may actually be causing yourself greater anxiety. Try to maintain a positive attitude. After all, you were successful enough to make it to college; have confidence that you will remain successful.

Coping with Test Anxiety. One way to overcome test anxiety is to be prepared. If you monitor your learning to the point where you know which concepts you understand and which concepts are giving you problems, you will feel more confident. Allow enough time for studying, but also have all of the things you need ready for the test. Do you need a pencil, calculator, notes, or anything else? You don't want to be tracking these things down right before the test, so be ready to go the night before.

Another way to cope with test anxiety is to know what you are getting into. Talk to the professor about what the exams will be like. Even better, try to look at some of the professor's old exams. Examining retired tests will give you an idea of what kinds of questions the professor asks and will also help you become familiar with the professor's questioning style. It is also a good idea to talk to the professor, or to students who have taken the class, about the content and format of the exams.

Arrive early on test day to get yourself organized, and practice some deep-breathing techniques to relax yourself. Take a few deep breaths, think of something you find relaxing, and concentrate on and relax each of your muscles.

If you find that you blank out on exams because you get so nervous, try to make a list as soon as you get to the test. Read each question and jot down everything you know about it in the margin of the test. If it is a multiple-choice-type test, don't look at the possible answers—just write everything you know before you blank out. More tips for taking exams will be discussed in Chapter 18.

Another way to cope with test anxiety is to focus only on what *you* are doing. Ignore other students who finish the exam before you. Just because they finish before you does not mean that they know more than you do. It might be that they finish early because they *don't* know the answers. But either way, don't worry about what other students are doing.

If you find that your test anxiety is getting in the way of your academic success in college, get some help! There are usually several resource areas on campus that can help you. You might need tutoring on course content, or counseling to deal with your anxiety, or you might be eligible for alternate testing situations such as increased time for tests.

Finally, visualize your success on the exam. Think about how well you will do before you walk into the test, and remind yourself as the test is being handed out that you are well prepared and ready to go. The more positive you are, the less anxiety you'll feel.

8.4

SOMETHING TO THINK ABOUT AND DISCUSS

Monitoring Your Learning

- What kinds of academic tasks (e.g., essays, mathematics, standardized tests) cause you to feel the most stress? Why do you think you experience anxiety when faced with those tasks? What can you do to reduce your anxiety in those situations?
- How can you tell the difference between being really stressed out and having normal, productive stress?

Tips for Reducing Academic Stress

In addition to ways of coping with math, writing, and text anxiety, here are some tips for coping with the general academic pressures that you experience every day.

Don't procrastinate. This sounds simple enough, but probably most of the academic stress students experience comes from waiting until the last minute to get their assignments done. As we discussed in Chapter 4, you are much better off starting early and doing some work each night rather than letting it wait until it is due.

Don't listen to other students cram right before the test. If your classmates are discussing something you have forgotten, it will just make you more nervous. Simply take your seat, gather your thoughts, take a few deep breaths, and wait for the test to begin. Many students who experience academic stress madly rush through their notes as they are waiting for the exams to be passed out, but this too can make you more stressed if you find a topic that you forgot to study. It is much better to use this time to relax.

Learn to say no. Many students experience academic stress because they have too much to do. Don't take on too much responsibility beyond your classes. Even though you might be offered some interesting opportunities, if you wind up with too much to do, your grades and your health could suffer. So learn to say no to some things if you find you already have enough to handle.

Now that you know about the different types of academic stress and how stress affects college learning, read the *Real College* scenario to help Andrea reduce her stress level.

REAL COLLEGE: *Andrea's Anxiety*

Read the following scenario and then respond to the questions based on what you learned in this chapter.

Andrea is a first-year college student. She is the first person in her family to attend college, and she is trying hard to make her parents proud, but she is worried that she won't make it in college. Every day she wakes up with a pounding headache, and sometimes she even has trouble sleeping because she is so stressed out. Part of the problem is that she is homesick for her family and friends. She is also worried about her relationship with her boyfriend who still lives at home—six hours away. He gets angry when she doesn't come home every weekend, and it seems likely that they will break up soon. In addition, although Andrea is starting to meet new friends in college, they are not like her old friends from high school; she just doesn't have anyone she can really confide in yet.

Another problem is that Andrea was forced to register for a math class because it was the only course open. She hates math! Every time she studies for an exam, she gets so nervous that her palms get sweaty and she can't really concentrate on what she is doing. She just knows that she will fail the course, but she doesn't know what to do about it because she believes that there is no way she will ever be able to learn math. She is thinking about dropping out of school because she's afraid that she is not smart enough to make it.

Use what you have learned about coping with and reducing stress to help Andrea figure out what to do.

1. *List three to five strategies Andrea should use to reduce her general stress about her social and family relationships.*

___________________________ ___________________________

___________________________ ___________________________

___________________________ ___________________________

2. *How do you think these strategies will help Andrea's situation?*

____

____

____

____

3. *List three to five strategies Andrea should use to reduce her math anxiety.*

_______________ _______________

_______________ _______________

_______________ _______________

_______________ _______________

4. *How do you think these strategies will help Andrea's situation?*

____

____

____

____

FOLLOW-UP ACTIVITIES

1. Think about your general stress level. Are you stressed out all the time? Or do you find yourself stressed out in specific situations? Keep a stress diary in which you record your reactions to stressful events. Use the strategies presented in this chapter to help you cope with those stressful situations.
2. Find someone you know who seems to handle stress well. Interview that person about the ways he or she deals with stress. What strategies does that person use? How does that person plan for stressful situations ahead of time? What advice can he or she give you about dealing with the stresses of college life?

Networking

- Many colleges and universities offer advice for stressed-out college students. Use the following key words to search for at least three web sites dealing with stress management: stress, stress management, college stress, student stress, test anxiety, math anxiety, and writing anxiety. What kind of useful information did you find about the causes of stress or about stress management? How will this information help you cope with your own stress?

Identifying the Task

The chapters in Part III discuss the different tasks you will perform in college. Chapter 9 presents effective ways to interact with your professors. It gives you some tips for approaching and talking with professors, as well as general information about why it is important to get to know your professor.

Chapter 10 introduces the concept of task. We define the term *task* and offer strategies to help you figure out what professors expect from you.

One of the major tasks you will have to accomplish in college is taking effective lecture notes. In Chapter 11, you will learn about the importance and characteristics of good lecture notes. You will also learn strategies for taking more effective lecture notes.

Before you read the chapters in Part III, please respond to the following statements. Read each statement and decide whether you agree or disagree with it.

Keep your responses in mind as you read the chapters in Part III. When you have finished reading Part III, revisit this page. How are your responses similar to or different from what is covered in these chapters?

BEFORE			AFTER	
Agree	Disagree		Agree	Disagree
☐	☐	***1. My professor is the person who determines my grade.***	☐	☐
☐	☐	***2. A professor's main responsibility is teaching classes.***	☐	☐
☐	☐	***3. I try to visit my professors during their office hours at least one time each term.***	☐	☐
☐	☐	***4. I study for a multiple-choice exam differently than I study for an essay exam.***	☐	☐
☐	☐	***5. It is impossible to figure out what professors expect from students.***	☐	☐
☐	☐	***6. The key to taking good notes is writing down everything the professor says.***	☐	☐
☐	☐	***7. I take notes in outline form.***	☐	☐
☐	☐	***8. I use my notes to test myself on important information.***	☐	☐

Interacting with Your Professors

Read this chapter to answer the following questions:

How are professors ranked?

How can you make a positive impression on your professors?

How can you approach a professor to ask for help?

STUDY TIP

See your professors during their office hours. Making personal contact is especially important for courses in which you are having problems or in courses that require writing.

As we stated in Chapter 1, college can at times be intimidating. Sometimes it's easy to find yourself in situations where you want to initiate conversations with classmates or professors but are simply just too scared to follow through. This uncomfortable feeling can be especially painful if you are overly shy or feel like the new kid on the block. One situation that seems to make many college students uneasy, particularly first-year students, is approaching professors. Whether it's to ask for assistance, to clarify a reading assignment, or to discuss a grade on a paper or an exam, talking with your professor doesn't have to be so threatening.

The purpose of this chapter is to try to demystify the professorate. We will first discuss the different ranks that college or university teachers hold and then explain the variety of tasks a professor engages in. Finally, we will discuss how to make a good impression on your professors and how to talk with them in a more comfortable way.

What Is a Professor?

Take thirty seconds to jot down the characteristics that you believe define a professor.

Did you write down words or phrases such as smart, well-educated, reads a lot, well-informed? When college students are asked to complete this task, they generally write down descriptors that have to do more with the education a professor has rather than terms that focus on other traits. For example, when we carry out this activity with our students at the beginning of the term, we rarely get comments such as fair-minded, cares about students, helpful, or energetic, nor do we get comments such as mean, unapproachable, distant, or unfair. The point we want to make here is that most students seem to lump all professors in the same bag ... professors are smart, they have a considerable amount of education, and they are *the* source of knowledge in the classroom. After all, students think, the professor is the one with all the education and expertise; who are they to question what she says? Yet often it is important to be able to talk with your professor about ideas you may disagree with or about points on which you need clarification. In the *Research into Practice* section that follows, consider the premise that males and females may even view professors in different lights and interpret what they say differently.

Research into Practice

Making Sense of College*

Knowing and Reasoning in College by Marcia Baxter-Magolda is a book that tells the stories of 101 college students, 75 of whom she followed for a period of five years, from the time they began college as first-year students until a year after they graduated. Much of the discussion in Dr. Baxter-Magolda's book examines the differences in how male and female students go about the task of understanding and making sense of things in the world of college. Throughout the book, Dr. Baxter-Magolda examines how students at different stages of knowing and reasoning interact with and respond to their professors.

Baxter-Magolda suggests that there are four different "ways of knowing": absolute, transitional, independent, and contextual. Students who are ***absolute knowers*** tend not to question what their professor says and

* Source: Baxter-Magolda, M. B. (1992). *Knowing and reasoning in college.* San Francisco, Calif.: Jossey-Bass.

believe that knowledge resides in authority. They believe that it is the job of professors to communicate knowledge to students. ***Transitional knowers*** realize that there can be two different sides to a story and that the role of the professor is to guide students. Professors are still seen as authority figures whose opinions supercede those of classmates, and transitional learners still look at professors as the ones giving grades. They may argue with their classmates but rarely argue with their professors. ***Independent knowers*** believe that knowledge is open to a variety of interpretations and that the professor should both promote the sharing of opinions and allow students to define learning goals. Independent knowers like to discuss issues with their professors, not just look to them for answers. Finally, as the name suggests, ***contextual knowers*** believe professors should promote the application of knowledge in a specific context and that student and professor should critique each other. Contextual knowers believe that knowledge is a shared experience and that they are on more or less equal footing with the professor.

According to Dr. Baxter-Magolda, both the male and female college students experienced all four different ways of knowing. It was the movement from one way of knowing to the next that differed between men and women.

Dr. Baxter-Magolda's research is important because it indicates that how students view the professor's role in the classroom is based on where they are on the knowing continuum. Interesting, and perhaps not very surprising, was her finding that first-year students are primarily absolute knowers; as students progress through college, they move toward being independent and contextual knowers. It is also important to think about how absolute knowers would interact with their professors versus how contextual learners would interact with theirs.

9.1

SOMETHING TO WRITE ABOUT AND DISCUSS

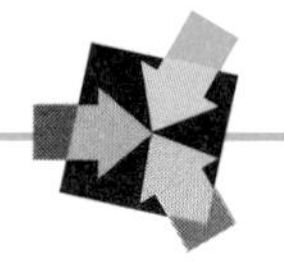

Thinking Critically

Think about the *Research into Practice* section and where you fit in as a learner. From the brief description given, would you consider yourself an absolute knower, a transitional knower, an independent knower, or a contextual knower? Then think about how each type of learner would interact with a professor if he or she went in to talk with the professor about a grade on an essay exam.

1. *What kind of a learner are you?* ______________________________

2. *Why did you classify yourself as this type?* ______________________________

3. *An absolute knower might say this to a professor:* ______________________________

____

____

4. *A transitional knower might say this to a professor:* ______________________________

____

____

5. *An independent knower might say this to a professor:* ______________________________

____

____

6. *A contextual knower might say this to a professor:* ______________________________

____

____

Students are often unsettled when talking with professors because they believe that the professor is the one who determines their grade. Many students fail to acknowledge that grades are earned, not given; therefore, they see the professor as the power person in the classroom. Because they view the professor as having all the control, they see little they can do in the way of talking to professors as being very influential on their grade. What students don't realize is that knowing how to interact in a positive way with their professor can go a long way toward helping them *earn* a better grade. Notice that we didn't say that just because the professor knows who you are and gets the impression you are trying, he will *give* you a better grade. No professor we know gives a student a grade just because the student has gotten to know him. But knowing how to talk with your professor can go a long way toward making a positive impression and helping you feel more relaxed with that professor and other professors in the future.

Most professors have what are called advanced degrees. The degree required generally depends on the type of postsecondary institution in which an individual teaches. For example, a community college may require each of their teachers to have a master's degree while a large college or university would expect a doctorate. It is becoming more and more common for colleges to prefer or require the professors they hire to have a terminal degree—a Doctor of Philosophy, or Ph.D. for short. (A similar degree specifically for individuals who major in education is called a Doctorate of Education, or an Ed.D.) A person can have a

TABLE 9.1 Rankings of College Professors

Title	Degree Held*	Years in Rank
Assistant Professor	Master's or doctorate	4 to 7
Associate Professor	Master's or doctorate	5 to 7
Full Professor	Master's or doctorate	Until retirement

* The level of degree professors must hold depends on the type of college at which they teach. For example, universities would require professors at all ranks to hold a doctorate, but at a community college, a master's degree might be sufficient.

Doctor of Philosophy in botany, English literature, history, or just about any other discipline you can think of. Usually it takes an individual three or more years after he or she has completed a master's degree to earn a doctorate.

When a professor who has a brand-new Ph.D. under her belt is hired, she will normally begin at the Assistant Professor level. Each new Assistant Professor receives guidelines from her institution that outline what she must do in order to get promoted to the next level, which is an Associate Professor. Depending on the type of postsecondary institution, the criteria for promotion may be weighted heavily on the professor's ability to teach, but it might also be based on the research she publishes, the committees she serves on, and the service projects in which she participates. Often, faculty must be evaluated as having superior accomplishments in two of these areas—teaching, research, service—in order to get promoted. It takes anywhere from four to seven years to reach the Associate Professor level.

The next rank, Full Professor, is reserved for those who are able to sustain exemplary teaching, research, and/or service records for another several years, since college teachers must usually hold the rank of Associate Professor at least five years before being promoted to Full Professor. Full Professors generally have high status because they have an extended track record (see Table 9.1). A personal note may illustrate how ranking systems used to be viewed by undergraduates. When one of the authors was an undergraduate at a medium-sized college in the Northeast, the amount of time you had to wait for a professor before you were allowed to consider that class was cancelled was based on the professor's rank. It was actually written down that students had to wait ten minutes for an Assistant Professor, fifteen minutes for an Associate, and twenty l-o-n-g minutes for a Full Professor. This meant that students found out early in

the term what specific rank their professor held. Before you rush to determine your professor's rank, we assure you that few schools state a policy such as this one today!

The ranking system of professors is quite complex and unlike that of any other profession. One of the more interesting aspects of the promotion system that college faculty go through is that at every level they are judged by their own peers. That is, a committee of faculty who already have been promoted to the Associate Professor level examine the credentials of those who are trying to advance to this level. Those of us who are part of this unique system often wonder how and why it has become that complicated.

We believe that it is important for students to be somewhat familiar with this ranking system so that they can better appreciate how much work their college professors must invest in order to be promoted. Some college students believe that all professors have to do is to sit in their offices and wait for students to come and ask them questions. Nothing could be further from the truth. Certainly, most professors enjoy interacting with students and enjoy teaching, but the majority has other expectations and responsibilities that extend beyond the classroom. Even professors who are at colleges where they are not expected to conduct research, publish in professional journals, or write books usually have a heavy teaching load, serve on numerous committees, advise students, and are expected to stay abreast of developments in their discipline. The point here is that college professors, regardless of what kind of college they teach at, are busy people who can't afford to waste time.

9.2 SOMETHING TO WRITE ABOUT AND DISCUSS

In an attempt to get to know one of your professors a little better, make an appointment to talk with him or her about some specific concerns you have about the class. You could also modify these guidelines and introduce yourself via e-mail. Use the following format to guide your discussion:

1. *Introduce yourself. Tell the professor your name, the course in which you are enrolled, and the period you are taking the course.*
2. *Tell the professor why you are there (to try to get some hints on studying for the course, to find out a little more about your professor, to find out how you might get tutoring or some other assistance for the course, etc.).*
3. *Take your text and lecture notes along with you.*
4. *If you have already had an exam, take the exam along with you as well.*
5. *Ask specific questions and write down the responses. The following questions may help you focus the discussion:*

   Do you have any suggestions about ways I should study for this class?

   ____

   ____

   ____

   How should I pace my studying?

   ____

   ____

   ____

   What should I do if I run into problems with the material in your class? Are there tutors available? Should I make an appointment to see you?

   ____

   ____

   ____

Would you look at my lecture notes to see if I'm on the right track?

____

____

____

What other information would be helpful to keep me on track in this class?

____

____

____

General Tips about Interacting with Professors

"The first impression is a lasting one" holds true when interacting with professors as much as it does with others with whom you come in contact. Recall the first time you met someone whom you eventually became friends with. What was your first impression of him or her? Chances are that you liked that person right from the beginning. You didn't become best friends overnight, but there was something about the person that made a good impression on you and made you want to get to know him or her better. Because first impressions don't change dramatically, it's important to make a good impression on your professor right from day one. How can you do that? Several general tips may help you out:

Sit up front in class. When you are up front, you are more likely to stay alert and focused on the lecture, especially if you are in a class with lots of other students. If you can't get a seat up front, at least try to sit in the professor's line of vision. If you have to sit in the back, sit in the center, not off to one side where it's more difficult to focus on the professor.

Ask questions. Professors may begin or end each class with a question/answer period. Some professors use the first few minutes to answer questions about the previous lecture or reading assignments. Others will take questions near the end of the lecture period. Still others will tell students to raise their hands at any time during the lecture if they have a question. And more and more professors are taking questions on e-mail. When you ask *well-thought-out questions,* you make a good impression because professors sense that you are interested and that you are keeping up with the course material. These questions should be phrased in such a way that the professor understands the clarification you need and that she isn't being asked to repeat something she just said a minute ago.

Ask for help sooner rather than later. Nothing makes a worse impression than waiting until the day before the test—or worse yet, five minutes before the test—to ask a question about course material that was presented a week earlier. This is especially true if it's a rather large chunk of material that is giving you trouble. As soon as you realize that you're having trouble, make an appointment to see your professor, a tutor, or some other person designated to provide assistance.

Read the syllabus. Be sure not to waste time by asking questions whose answers are outlined on the syllabus. For example, if your professor has not discussed in class how your course grade is determined, before you ask him to explain it, check your syllabus. Most professors explain how your grade will be determined right on the syllabus. If it's not there and he hasn't explained it in class, then ask. The syllabus contains a wealth of information and should always be your first source when you have questions about grading, course pacing, or expectations.

Know and follow the class rules. Most professors have pet peeves about something. Both of the authors of this text, for example, get quite upset when students habitually come to class late. Although we make this clear both orally and in writing on the syllabus, and explain what the consequences will be, there is always a student who regularly marches into class late. This does not make a good impression at all! It's important for students to know what rules are in place and to follow them. Don't be the student in the class that the professor uses as an example of inappropriate behavior.

Talk with your professors via e-mail. As we briefly mentioned above, more and more professors are encouraging students to communicate with them through e-mail. In fact, we know of some professors who require students to interact with them using e-mail at several points over the term. In addition, more professors have web pages where you can view the syllabus, download class notes, and obtain additional information about both the course and the professor.

Talking with Your Professors

Like it or not, at some time in your college career, you will probably have to interact with one of your professors. It can be a positive experience if you follow a few simple guidelines. In this section, we will outline those guidelines and offer some suggestions about how to make talking with your professors a more enjoyable experience. Of course not all professors are easy to talk with and some can make you more ill at ease than others, but if you can answer a few questions and use some common sense, you should be able to get through the situation thinking, "Gee, that wasn't so bad! Professor Jones really isn't so unapproachable after all."

1. ***Why am I going to see my professor?***
This question should be an easy one to answer. Do you need clarification about a project that is due? Are you having trouble understanding how to do the chemistry problems? Do you have to explain to your professor about a specific learning disability that you have? Are you trying to get clarification on why you received a low grade on your essay test? Did your professor request to talk to you? Whatever your reason for seeing your professor, the answer to this question should be very evident to you. You may be going to see your professor just to get to know him a little better, as did the student we mentioned in Chapter 1. That's fine. Just make sure you have a reason in mind and that you begin your conversation with something such as, "Good morning, Professor Carter. I am here to see you this morning because...." Beginning on this note shows your professor that you do have an overarching reason for showing up in his office. We realize that this advice is basic and that you might be reading this asking yourself, "Why would anyone go to see a professor without having a clear purpose in mind?" But you would be surprised at the number of students who have sat in our offices without a clear notion of why they were there.

2. ***What are the logistics of this meeting?***
We assume that if you need to see your professor, you have approached her either before or after class about setting up a time that would be convenient for both of you. Some professors list office hours on their syllabi and announce that you can drop by during those hours without an appointment. In our opinion, however, it never hurts to check out a time with your professor. When professors post office hours at the beginning of the term, they often don't realize that there will be days and times when conflicting meetings, conferences, or personal obligations necessitate their not being available during their normal office hours. It is never inappropriate to ask the professor something such as the following: "I noticed on the syllabus that your office hours on Friday are from 9:00 to 10:30. I just wanted to check with you to be sure that you would be in around 9:30 so that I could ask you a couple of questions."

After you know what time your appointment is, find out where the meeting will take place. We have often assumed that students would know to meet us in our offices only to find out that they went to the classroom instead! If there is any question at all in your mind about where you are supposed to meet your professor, be sure to get clarification. Once you know the building and room number, make certain you know the location. This is especially important on larger campuses where getting across campus for an appointment can take 15 or 20 minutes, and it might take another 10 minutes to find the office once you have found the building. Whatever you do, don't show up late! If you have made an appointment for 9:30, get there at least 5 minutes early rather than 5 minutes late. Showing up late indicates that you don't think your professor's time is worth much, and that's not the impression you want to make.

3. ***How do I talk with my professor?***
Before you go to see your professor for the first time, it's important to think about the approach you are going to take and what you are going to say. Depending on why you are going to see your professor, this can be an easy task or one that is a bit more difficult. In the two examples that follow, John goes to see Professor Thomas knowing full well that writing has always been a problem for him. Harry, however, usually did well in high school English, but he did poorly on his first college composition paper and goes to see Professor Thomas with somewhat of an attitude.

John's approach: John has made an appointment to see his composition professor, Professor Thomas, because he did not do well on his first paper. Writing has always been difficult for John, but with the help of his past teachers, he managed to do fairly well. Professor Thomas seems like a fair-minded person and said he was willing to talk with students about their writing problems. During his appointment with Professor Thomas, John acknowledges that he has weaknesses in writing and states that he feels his low evaluation on the first paper was pretty accurate. He takes out his paper and begins to ask the professor questions about the comments written on his paper. He takes notes on the suggestions that Professor Thomas gives and asks for clarification if necessary. At the end of the appointment, he thanks Professor Thomas and tells him that those suggestions should help him do better on the next assignment. John leaves feeling positive about the conference. Professor Thomas has similar feelings and enjoys having students like John in his class. Although John isn't the best writer, he's far from the worst. In addition, he's working hard and taking advantage of the available assistance. Professor

Thomas is sure John will improve on the next paper if he follows the suggestions they discussed.

Harry's approach: Harry is also in Professor Thomas's composition class. Harry made good grades in English in high school, but he has somehow forgotten that he actually did very little writing in those English classes. He really doesn't like to write that much, but he always thought he was pretty good at it. So, he was quite surprised and, in fact, downright upset when he got his first paper back with such a low score. "Doesn't Professor Thomas know that I made excellent grades in English and that my teachers rarely commented on any problems I might have had writing? What's up with this guy?" thought Harry. Harry talked with the professor after class and made an appointment to find out if Professor Thomas made a mistake in grading his paper. Harry arrives about ten minutes late for his appointment with the excuse that he had trouble finding the office. He sits down, puts his paper down on Professor Thomas's desk, and says, "So, can you fill me in here? I have never gotten a grade like this on an English paper! My high school teachers never gave me less than a B and I even worked on the school newspaper for a while." Professor Thomas reads through Harry's paper, pointing out some of the more apparent problems. Harry only tries to justify his writing and does not seem to be paying attention to Professor Thomas's suggestions for improvement. Professor Thomas asks Harry if he has any questions. "Not really," mutters Harry as he picks up his paper and leaves.

9.3

SOMETHING TO THINK ABOUT AND DISCUSS

Thinking Critically

Think about the approaches used by both John and Harry. Then with a classmate, compare and contrast how they interacted with Professor Thomas. How much of someone's individual personality do you think enters into the picture when thinking about how students interact with professors? How about past experience? For example, if Harry had had more writing experiences in high school where he received feedback that his writing was problematic, might he have approached Professor Thomas differently?

It's obvious which of these students used the right approach. Even if you *feel* the same as Harry did—that there must be some mistake, that you've never been evaluated this low—it is very inappropriate to attempt to interact with a professor as Harry did. In the *Thinking Critically* activity above, you and your partner should have discussed why Harry's behavior was inappropriate. Although students have been rewarded for trying hard ever since kindergarten, college professors rarely award students higher grades simply because they are giving it all they've got. However, they do remember students who have been respectful and those who have not. There's no excuse for lack of respect.

In addition, let's say that John and Harry had similar grades on all of their papers and John's average was a 79.2 and Harry's a 79.3. On his syllabus, Dr. Thomas stated that his grading scale was the traditional 90–100 = A, 80–89 = B, and so forth. But he also stated that he had the right to raise someone's grade but would never give a lower grade than he or she had earned. Although some might view grading such as this as subjective, Dr. Thomas could ethically award John a B and Harry a C.

Perhaps the biggest problem students have when they go to talk to their professors about concerns they are having with the course material is that they don't go in with specific questions prepared. For example, if you are in a mathematics or chemistry course and find yourself totally lost, it's often difficult to know the questions to ask. You may sit in class and have no idea what the professor is talking about. But when you go to see your professor, you need to be prepared to ask specific questions. Going in and stating "I don't understand the material" is only going to get you the response, "Okay. So what concepts are unclear?" Thus, it's important to try to articulate your questions as clearly as possible. Go back to your notes or your homework problems and see where your understanding broke down. Show the notes or homework to your professor so that she can try to get an idea of what happened. Try to talk through how you have been thinking about the information as well. Say something such as "I understood everything up to this point, but then when we had to add this step, I became lost. Now I don't even have the slightest idea of how to solve these types of problems. This is what I know...." If you open your conversation with your professor with a general statement such as "I don't understand any of this," you're probably going to get a response such as "Are you reading the text? Are you coming to class? Are you doing all the homework problems? Well, you'll just have to work harder (or more)." None of these suggestions will be very helpful to you. When you can state as specifically as possible what your problems are, you and your professor will walk away from the meeting with a much better feeling.

In this chapter, we have tried to give you a better understanding of how to interact with your professors. It's often not an easy thing to do, especially if you are frustrated about your performance in the course, if the professor is distant and seems not to want to have to deal with students, or if you believe that you are being treated unfairly. On the other hand, most students find it enjoyable to talk with their professors and find that getting to know them better helps when they need recommendations for jobs, scholarships, or even admission to graduate or professional schools.

REAL COLLEGE: *Marsha's Mistake*

Read the following scenario and then respond to the questions based on what you learned in this chapter.

Marsha rolled over, opened her eyes, and saw the bright sun streaming in her window. She jolted straight up like a bolt of lightning. "What time is it? What time is it?" she yelled jumping out of bed. She looked at her digital clock only to see 12:00 flashing over and over. She knew she was in trouble. She was supposed to be in class for a mid-term exam at 8:00 and knew that it wasn't anywhere near this light when she usually got up. She grabbed her wristwatch off the dresser … it was 9:30. The test was already over. "What am I going to do?" she thought. She liked her professor, Dr. Luther, but she also knew that he was a stickler for rules and that if you missed a test without some sort of major documentation as to why, you couldn't make up the exam.

Marsha's intentions were good. She had been studying for the test for several days, but she still felt that she wasn't ready. So she made the mistake lots of students make—she studied until 3:30 A.M. and set her clock for 5:30, thinking that would give her time to have an hour more to review. She was really tired when she finally went to sleep but thought her alarm would wake her up. She didn't count on a power failure at 4:30! Now she was in real hot water. Dr. Luther would never let her make up the test with a lame excuse such as "My alarm didn't go off."

She knew she would have to make an appointment to talk with Dr. Luther. But how should she handle this situation?

Think about what you would do if you were in Marsha's shoes. Explain how you would handle the problem and why you would handle it that way. Then, discuss solutions with your classmates. Are some solutions better than others? What are some factors you think Marsha should consider before she goes in to talk with Dr. Luther?

____

____

____

____

____

____

____

____

____

FOLLOW-UP ACTIVITY

From the information we have presented in this chapter and from your own interactions so far with professors, which of the following do you think are positive things to do when interacting with a professor and which are negative? Check those that are positive. Discuss your responses with your classmates.

- ☐ You call two weeks in advance for an appointment to see your professor so you can be sure you have an appointment with him the day after the second exam.
- ☐ You go ask the professor if you missed anything important during the three days in a row you were out sick.
- ☐ You are having a hard time taking notes from your professor so you raise your hand during a lecture and ask her to slow down.
- ☐ You send an e-mail to your professor to try to set up an appointment time.
- ☐ You made an appointment to talk to your professor about a couple of concepts that were giving you trouble. You ask him, "Is this important to know for the test?"

Networking

- As a way of learning a little more about one of your professors, check to see if he or she has a web page. You can begin by looking at the professor's department web page. For example, if you want to see if your botany professor has a web page, you could first find the web page for the botany department. Department web pages generally list every faculty member with links to their individual web pages. At smaller colleges, which may not be large enough to have a botany department, look for the science department instead, or perhaps life sciences.
- Once you have found the web page for your professor, look to see the information that is included. For example, does your professor include a syllabus, additional information about tests and assignments, or other material that would be helpful to you in the class? Some professors even include their notes on the web or post example test questions. After you have checked out the web page, consider sending your professor an e-mail if you have any questions about the syllabus or course.

What Is It I'm Supposed to Do, Anyhow?

Read this chapter to answer the following questions:

What do we mean by task?

How can you figure out what your professor expects?

STUDY TIP

Be sure you understand what your professor expects from you. Knowing the task right from the start enables you to select the appropriate strategies.

In Chapter 3, when we introduced the idea that there are four factors that impact learning, we briefly discussed the role that task understanding plays in being an active learner. Because much of your success as a college student rests on your ability to interpret the task, we will talk about it here in greater detail. As we have tried to suggest, there's more to studying and being a successful student than meets the eye and that "studying hard" is not always "studying good." Your ability to understand what it is your professor wants you to do and the way you are supposed to do it goes a long way in making you a more efficient and effective student. Why? To answer this question, we'll explore two important aspects of task: What do we mean by *task*? How can you, as a student, go about figuring out what the task is?

What Is a Task?

The task for any course consists of two parts: the type of activity in which you engage and the level of thinking required as you engage in the activity. The activity is usually a test, a paper, or a project by which your instructor will evaluate you.

Knowing that you have to take a test is not enough information to be able to carefully select an appropriate approach to studying. You need to know the *type* of test you will take. Is it an objective exam, which includes multiple-choice, true/false, or matching items? Is it a more subjective exam that requires answering essay, short-answer, or identification questions? Is it a combination of both types? Because you should not approach studying for multiple-choice tests in the same way you approach studying for essay tests, it's very important to know right from the beginning the basic type of test you will have. As we will discuss in greater detail later in the book, the kind of reading you do, the way you think about the material, and the strategies you select all have a bearing on the kinds of tasks you are asked to complete in a course.

It is important to reiterate and alert you to the importance of precisely knowing the task by describing a situation that occurred to students enrolled in a large-lecture history course. For each test, students were told that they would have objective items and two essay questions. On the first four exams, these objective items were always multiple-choice. Thus when it came time for the final exam and the professor told students that they would have a test that was part objective and part essay, they assumed that they would once again have multiple-choice questions. Imagine their surprise when the tests were distributed and the objective items were fill-in-the-blanks! Many students were outraged and went to see the professor when they discovered that they had done poorly on the test. But the professor wouldn't budge. His definition of task for objective items included fill-in-the-blank as well as multiple-choice. The point here is clear: Get as much information as possible about the test. Ask the right questions. Just knowing that you will have an objective test is obviously insufficient information.

Likewise, if the task in a course consists of papers or projects rather than exams, the same advice holds true. Talk with your professor about specific aspects of the paper, especially if you are unclear. In political science courses on our campus, for example, students must do a project that involves several pieces. First, they select a political issue to follow all term.

They must subscribe to and read the *New York Times* daily and find a minimum of thirty articles concerning their issue. For each article, they must write a summary. At the end of the term, they complete two additional tasks. First, they write a policy statement about the issue; then, they write a memo to an influential political figure about this issue. Students who fail to understand how to carry out the numerous pieces involved in this task have severe problems doing well on a long-term project that is 30 percent of their grade. Or students who wait until the last minute and have stacks of newspapers all over their room with little else accomplished rightfully panic.

Once you have identified the specific activities your professor expects, you're about halfway there. The other part of task identification, and perhaps even the more important part, is knowing what level of thinking is required to carry out that task. There are many types of thinking that a professor may want you to engage in. For example, if your exams consist mostly of factual questions, your professor is expecting you to memorize information:

- When did "black Thursday" occur?
- What is the role of gray matter?
- What is the definition of *artificial concepts*?
  Or you may be asked example questions:
- Which of the following is an example of *everyday formal reasoning*?
- Which of the following illustrates an example of Theory X in operation?
- All of the following are examples of *exponential population growth* except....

The professor assumes that you have to know the definition in order to answer the example question, so example questions require higher levels of thinking.

Your exams may ask you to apply and or synthesize, as do the following questions:

- During the 1960s, the United States was plagued with high levels of domestic unrest and violence. Discuss the sources of this unrest and the political decisions that were made as a result of it.
- If a plant with the genotype of BbCcDd was crossed with a plant that was BBCcdd, what are the chances of producing a plant with the genotype of BbCcDd?

Here your professor is asking you to understand the course material on a much higher level.

Many students fail to think about this part of the task, which often results in lower test grades and frustration. Another mistake that students, primarily first-year students, often make is that they believe that objective exams don't involve higher-level thinking. That is, they think that multiple-choice and true/false tests are basically memorization tasks. This is a false assumption and one that can get unsuspecting students into academic hot water.

10.1

MONITORING YOUR LEARNING

Most college students do not consciously sit down at the beginning of the term and say to themselves, "Gee, before I start doing my reading and studying for this class, I'd better figure out the task!" For students who intuitively understand that it is important to figure out the course demands, it's more of an unconscious task. Think about yourself as a learner and then respond to the following questions:

- Have you taken time this term to figure out the task in each of your classes? If not, how might you begin to gather that information this term and in future terms?
- Have you ever been in a class where you had a very difficult time understanding what the professor's expectations were? How did you handle that situation? What might you do differently now?

In the *Research into Practice* section that follows, we describe a study conducted by Dr. Michele Simpson and Dr. Sherrie Nist, one of the authors of this book. Their findings in this study strongly support the importance of knowing and understanding the task.

Research into Practice

A Case Study of How Students Figure Out Task*

In this article, Dr. Simpson and Dr. Nist followed and interviewed ten students enrolled in a large-lecture introductory history course over an entire term. Some of these students performed very well, some were average, and some were below average in their test scores. The researchers were interested in determining the factors that enabled some of the

* Source: Simpson, M. L., & Nist, S. L. (1997). Perspectives on learning history: A case study. *Journal of Literacy Research* 29: 363–395.

students to earn As and Bs while others failed. Although they found that the high-performing students used more efficient and effective study strategies, the more important finding was that they understood what their professor expected from them. They correctly interpreted the task, which was to write essay answers that called for synthesis and analysis in a well-structured format, and selected their strategies for studying *after* they had determined the task. In other words, their task definition drove their strategy choice, not vice versa. Dr. Simpson and Dr. Nist concluded that:

> When we reflected on the congruency between the professor's and students' perceptions of task, we concluded that Dr. Stack [the professor] did communicate the task to students in a variety of explicit and implicit ways.... The HPG [high-performing group] had little problem in determining what it was that Dr. Stack wanted them to do.... However, the LPG [low-performing group] ... failed to "accommodate" Dr. Stack and his communication about the task.

Dr. Simpson and Dr. Nist's finding about the importance that task interpretation plays in learning and studying in college is an important one. If you don't know precisely what it is your professor expects from you, you are doomed to struggle, at best becoming frustrated and at worst making low grades. Simpson and Nist found that students in history, for example, often defined the task as memorizing names, dates, and facts, much as they had done in high school. But their college professors looked at history as more analysis and synthesis. Students who held fast to their high school model of studying history, continuing to memorize, struggled all term with the course. Some, who never figured out the task, actually failed. The implications of this study for you, the student, are clear: Figure out the task and figure it out early in the term. Then select the strategies that will best fit your professor's expectations.

The point we have tried to make in this section is that task definition involves two parts (see Figure 10.1). First, you need to find out the type

FIGURE 10.1 *Task Definition*

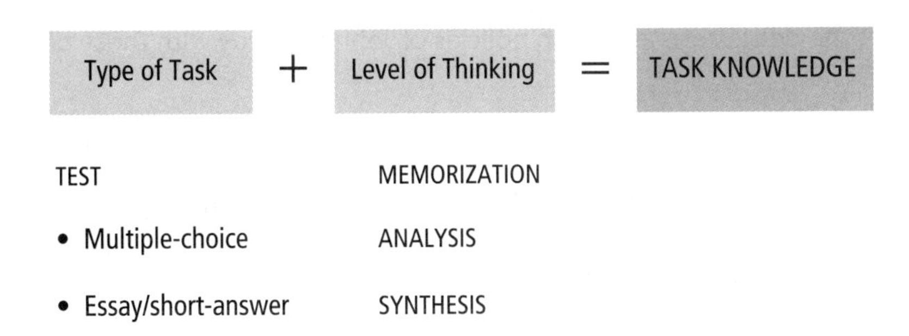

of test you will have to take or paper you will have to write. Then, you also need to know the level of thinking required. Most objective exams will require a little of everything. Some of the questions will be factual in nature, some will ask for examples, and some will require you to synthesize and analyze. Most essay questions require the highest level of thinking, but other subjective exams, such as identification items, could ask for just factual information. The bottom line is *be able to state the task.* Know it precisely and accurately. If you are unsure, ask questions. And remember, unless you know the task, you will have a difficult time selecting the appropriate study strategies. In the next section, we will give you some hints about how to get more information about the task.

10.2 SOMETHING TO WRITE ABOUT AND DISCUSS

Thinking Critically

1. *Think about the courses in which you are currently enrolled. For each course, state as accurately and precisely as possible what you think the task is. Then talk your answers over with a classmate.*

   Course 1: ______________________________

   ____

   Course 2: ______________________________

   ____

   Course 3: ______________________________

   ____

   Course 4: ______________________________

   ____

2. *For each of the following questions, decide the level of thinking in which you will have to engage. Put M for memory-level tasks, E for example tasks, and A for application or synthesis tasks. After you have completed this exercise, discuss your responses with a classmate.*

   _____ (a) Compare and contrast the domestic and foreign policies of John Kennedy with those of Lyndon Johnson.

   _____ (b) Which of the following diagrams indicates the telephase stage of meiosis?

   _____ (c) When a male and female reproductive cell fuse, what is formed is called a(n) ________.

   _____ (d) Why would a scientist want to do a cross test?

_____ (e) Which of the following best illustrates the principle of cognitive dissonance?

_____ (f) Identify each of the following as either an *ecosystem,* a *community,* or a *population.*

_____ (g) How has twentieth-century technology influenced domestic life?

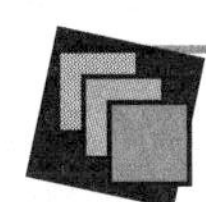

How Can You Get Information about the Task?

Now that you understand how important it is to know the task for each of your classes, you might ask the obvious question: How do I figure out how to carry out the task? Because few professors will state the task precisely and completely, it becomes important for you to be able to piece together bits of information from a variety of sources in order to paint the picture for yourself.

The best place to begin, of course, is with what your professor says in class, especially in the early part of the term. Some professors spell out the task very neatly and clearly on the first day when they go over the syllabus. That's why it's important *to be in class from day one.* Others will give you a big picture of the task early in the term and then spell out the details as the course moves along. Still others, and perhaps most college professors fall into this category, give you a combination of implicit and explicit cues and expect you to pick up on those cues. In whatever way your professor gives you information about the task, it's important to remember to *write it down.* It's just as important to take notes concerning what's expected of you as it is to take content notes. Students often think that they will remember how to structure an essay, or the types of questions that will be on their exams, only to discover two or three weeks later that there's only a faint recollection (or worse, no recollection at all) of some important piece of information that the professor had discussed in class. Your best source of task information, then, is your professor. Go to class, listen carefully, and write down what your professor says about the task right in your lecture notes.

A second source of task information, and one that is easily overlooked, is your syllabus. As we said in an earlier chapter, your syllabus contains a wealth of information. Read your syllabus carefully at the beginning of the course, looking for any statements that tell you about course expectations. Most professors spell out, at least in broad terms, how many tests you will have or papers you will have to write and the approximate dates tests will be given or papers will be due. Certainly, your professor will tell you where her office is located and when her office hours are so that if you are having problems determining what the task is, you can make an appointment to talk with her. In addition, most

syllabi provide information about a professor's policies on makeup work or the consequences of missing an exam or another deadline, as well as attendance policies. All of these factors either directly or indirectly relate to task. Thus it is important not only to read your syllabus carefully at the beginning of the term but also to refer to it often as the term progresses. What you learn from your syllabus, plus what your professor says in class, should help you to have a solid understanding of class expectations.

A third source of information about the task is copies of old exams for the course in which you are enrolled. Even if you think you have a clear understanding of what the task is, it's always a good idea to look over old exams as a way of confirming course requirements. Many professors routinely make old exams available to students, while others will provide example questions only when asked. Looking at old exams gives you lots of information, especially about the level of thinking required. You want to use these exams as a way of gathering information about the level of thinking, not about the actual content that you should study. Few professors give exactly the same tests from term to term, but most professors do write questions that require similar levels of thinking. For example, if the old exams your professor let you look at had questions that asked for examples, synthesis of information, and abstraction, chances are that the test she will give you won't be a memorization task. She will probably write the same *types* of questions on future exams. We know a biology professor who puts copies of old test questions on the web site for the course. Students who use these questions to see whether they are able to think about the course content in the right way, not to see what specific questions the professor asks, tend to do well in the course. Again, old exams add another piece that helps you figure out the task puzzle.

One final way to gather task information is to ask students who have already taken the class and done well in it. Former students will be able to give you quite a lot of details about a course and a professor, details that can often make the difference between doing very well and only average in a course. Just make sure that you ask former students the right questions. For example, asking someone "Are Professor Smith's tests difficult?" is not the best way to pose the question because what is a difficult test for one person may not be difficult for another. Better questions would be: "What kind of tests does Professor Smith give?" "Can you remember examples of some questions?" "What kinds of structure does he expect for essay questions?" "Does he give you much guidance?" Questions such as these give you answers about the task.

10.3

SOMETHING TO THINK ABOUT AND DISCUSS

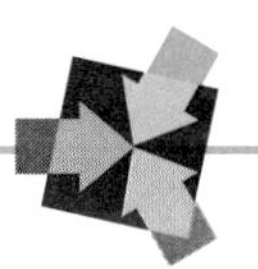

Thinking Critically

- Can you think of any other sources that might be able to give you task information? We have mentioned your professor, the syllabus, copies of old exams, and students who have already taken the course.
- Why do you think it is important to write down any information that your professor gives you about task? What might you do if you got conflicting information?
- How might you organize your notes to draw attention to task information that your professor gives you?

REAL COLLEGE: *Tina's Task*

Read the following scenario and then respond to the questions based on what you learned in this chapter.

Tina decided that she could no longer put off taking a required history class, even though she "hates history with a passion," so she reluctantly registered for the course. It's not that she hasn't done well in history. On the contrary, her grades in high school history classes were quite good. She sees herself as a good memorizer and since her high school history experience involved lots of memorization of names, dates, events, and the like, she tended to make good grades. She just doesn't like history, plain and simple. In addition, she is terribly anxious about thc upcoming experience because she has heard horror stories about the course expectations.

As Tina looks over her class schedule for the term, she thinks about skipping the first class or two because, from her perspective, two less history classes to go to is a good thing. But her roommate, who has already taken this course, advises her to attend every class—even the first one! Tina reluctantly takes her advice and actually thought that the professor was engaging and humorous.

Obviously, in order to earn a good grade in this course, Tina is going to have to figure out what the tasks are. On the first day, the professor said that there would be three essay exams as well as a cumulative final, but he didn't say much else about the tasks. Think about Tina's situation and respond to the following questions:

1. *What additional information do you think Tina needs so that she can have a clearer idea of the task?*

____

____

____

____

____

2. *How should she go about gathering the necessary information?*

____

____

____

____

____

FOLLOW-UP ACTIVITIES

1. *Think about the model of the four factors that influence learning introduced in Chapter 3. How does task definition fit into this model?*

___

___

___

2. *What influence does task definition have on the study strategies you might select in a particular course?*

___

___

___

Networking

- Find the web page of one of your professors and look for information concerning task. For example, if you have multiple-choice exams, look to see whether your professor has put any example test items on the site. Also check out on-line information about the course. Sometimes, rather than putting material concerning tests and other course requirements on their own personal web page, professors will have a separate page for each course they teach. These pages can provide a wealth of information to help you better understand the task.

Take Note! Lectures
A Different Kind of Text

Read this chapter to answer the following questions:

Why is it important to take good lecture notes?

What should you do before class, during class, and after class to take good notes?

How can you use your notes to self-test?

STUDY TIP

Stay actively involved during lectures by writing for the full period. Take notes in an organized fashion and review your notes as soon after class as possible.

Whether you are attending a large four-year university or a small community college, a large percentage of information will be transmitted to you through lecture. In the traditional lecture format, the professor explains information that he or she feels is important for you to learn in the class. Usually, some of what the professor covers in lecture overlaps with what is presented in your text, but this isn't always the case. Some professors lecture on exactly what the textbook says; others have very little overlap. Most fall somewhere in the middle. Whatever method your professor uses, you can be sure of one thing: The professor expects you to take notes in an organized fashion so that you can study and review the notes throughout the course.

Although much of the time you spend in college classes will be spent taking notes, many students come to college unprepared for the demands that this type of note taking puts on them. Note taking isn't too difficult if you have a professor who speaks slowly and clearly and who lectures in an organized fashion. Some professors like that are roaming around college campuses ... maybe a few are even on your own campus! But perhaps many more professors aren't top-notch, engaging lecturers. In this case, it's important for students to be able to sup-

ply their own organization, to get down the important points, and to fill in the gaps when necessary.

Before continuing, however, read the *Research into Practice* section that follows. Dr. Alison King has conducted numerous studies in approaches to taking and studying lecture notes. In the following study, she examines the effects of self-questioning.

Research into Practice

Questioning Classmates Improves Lecture Understanding*

"Improving Lecture Comprehension: Effects of a Metacognitive Strategy" focused on whether self-testing enhanced students' understanding of a lecture. Two groups of students were taught to ask themselves questions during the lecture. After the lecture, some students used only self-questioning and then answered their own questions. Another group of students used self-questioning and reciprocal questioning with their peers. (Reciprocal questioning is similar to reciprocal teaching, which we will discuss in Chapter 14.) A third group of students simply reviewed the lecture material without any self-questioning or peer interactions. The

* Source: King, A. (1991). Improving lecture comprehension: Effects of a metacognitive strategy. *Applied Cognitive Psychology* 5: 331–340.

results indicated that the two groups of students who were taught to self-question (either with or without peer interaction) significantly outperformed those who only reviewed. The author maintains that a self-questioning strategy can improve students' lecture comprehension and that this strategy can be easily taught to students.

Dr. King's study is important because it shows the importance of self-questioning. When students are forced to think about the lecture by forming questions and then proceed to answer those questions either by themselves or with a peer, their performance can improve. Self-questioning works because it is an active strategy that allows you to monitor what is important and what is not. It also encourages you to think about the information in different ways for each lecture rather than waiting to review your notes right before an exam. In addition, this study is good news for students who prefer studying alone since the results indicate that it was the self-questioning, not the peer interaction, that made the difference.

11.1 SOMETHING TO THINK ABOUT AND DISCUSS

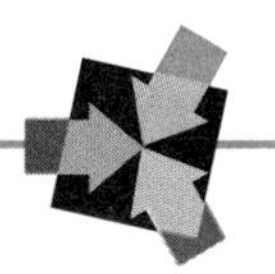

Thinking Critically

We have offered some reasons why self-questioning works in practice here and in other chapters in this book. Discuss these questions with a partner.

- From what you have learned so far, why do you think self-questioning works in a variety of situations?
- How important do you think it is to share and discuss your questions with a classmate?
- What are the benefits and drawbacks to working with another student?

The Importance and Characteristics of Good Lecture Notes

It's important to be able to take good lecture notes for a variety of reasons. First, good lecture notes serve as a complete record of what goes on in class each day. Without a complete record, it's difficult to have all the information you need to prepare for subsequent classes or exams. Second, if you can take notes in an organized fashion, it is easier for you to see patterns in your professor's lectures. Once you see patterns, you get a better idea of what your professor feels is important. Third, good lecture notes will not only enable you to see patterns, but they will also help you to spot overlap between your text and the professor's lecture. Good students look for these overlaps as fertile ground for test questions as they prepare for examinations.

Have you ever borrowed notes from classmates? If you have, or even if you have just observed the students around you taking notes, you have probably noticed that not everyone takes notes the same way. Student A, who sits on your right, may have notes that are well organized and legible. Student B, who sits on your left, may have notes that are incomprehensible. The way one person takes notes may differ dramatically from the next. You would probably agree, however, that it's much easier to study and learn from notes such as Student A's.

We have already discussed the reasons for taking good notes, but what distinguishes good notes from poor notes? As you will see, good notes are more than just legible. As you read about the characteristics of good notes below, look at the examples in Figures 11.1, 11.2, and 11.3. These figures show examples of both good and bad notes related to the text excerpt entitled "Cognition: Thinking, Deciding, Communicating" found in Appendix A. We will refer to these figures throughout the chapter.

Good notes are organized. When you look at the three examples of notes provided in Figures 11.1, 11.2, and 11.3, it is easy to see which one is best organized. Notice that the notes in Figure 11.1 use organizational strategies such as underlining the main points, indenting details, noting examples, and numbering reasons. This figure differs dramatically from the notes in the second and third figures. In Figure 11.2, it's difficult to tell where one idea stops and another begins or what is a main point and what is a detail. Much of the information written in the notes in the second example is lost or difficult to link together. And what can we say about the notes in Figure 11.3 except that some students actually have notes that are this bad! Scant notes—those that are incomplete as well as imprecise—occur most frequently in courses that students finding uninteresting or when they have not yet mastered the art of active learning.

Good notes distinguish main points from details. Every lecture has both main points and details. The main points might be reasons, characteristics, or theories, to name a few. Details include information that supports or explains the main points. It's important to write your notes in such a way that the main points are distinguishable from the details. If the information all runs together or if you have only written down the main points and excluded the details, you will have difficulty studying your notes.

FIGURE 11.1 *An Example of Good Lecture Notes*

Questions for self-testing

What is a concept?

Give an ex. of a concept.

Define the 2 types of concepts.

Give an example.

What is diff. between the 2?

what is a prototype?

Give an ex.

Cognition Nov. 10

Simple paragraph form

concepts

DEF.– a mental category used to rep. a class or grp. of things; share common char. or attributes; units of thought

EX: furniture, college, flowers
EX: dog = a concept for a class of animals sharing similar char., even though they may differ in impt. ways

Use abbreviations

Can be abstract & tangible
EX: love dog
beauty flower
democracy book

Leave space between key points

Underline key points

2 types

Number lists

1. formal concepts – "artificial" con.; clearly defined by a set of rules or class system; often found in sciences or other academic discp. Rouche: not related to real experiences

2. natural concepts – "fuzzy" con.; get by everyday experiences; not clear-cut + systematic; after experiences with +'s and –'s of a concept kids gain understanding.

Have prototypes – DEF: an example that has typical features.
EX: a prototype of "bird" might be a robin, not a penguin or a stork.

Process notes

EXAM NEXT THURS. (Nov. 17) = 50 multiple-choice = 2 essay . . .
HINT: Think about exs & applications. KNOW THEORIES.

FIGURE 11.2 *An Example of Weak Lecture Notes*

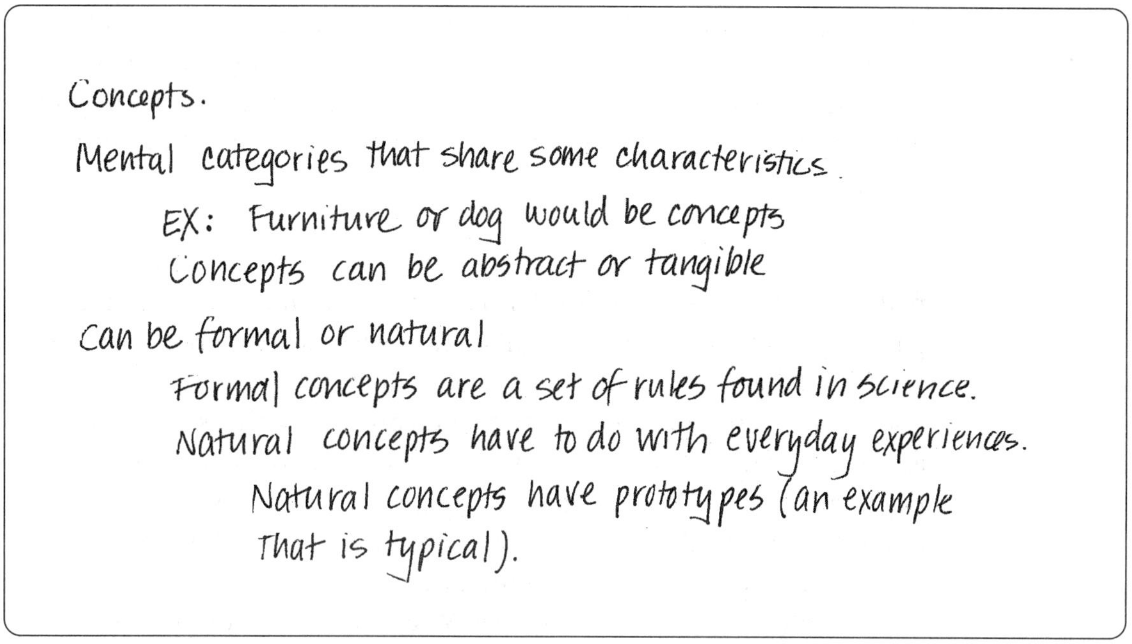

Concepts.

Mental categories that share some characteristics.

EX: Furniture or dog would be concepts
Concepts can be abstract or tangible

Can be formal or natural

Formal concepts are a set of rules found in science.
Natural concepts have to do with everyday experiences.
Natural concepts have prototypes (an example
That is typical).

FIGURE 11.3 *Notes of a Very Inactive Listener (Note the Doodles!)*

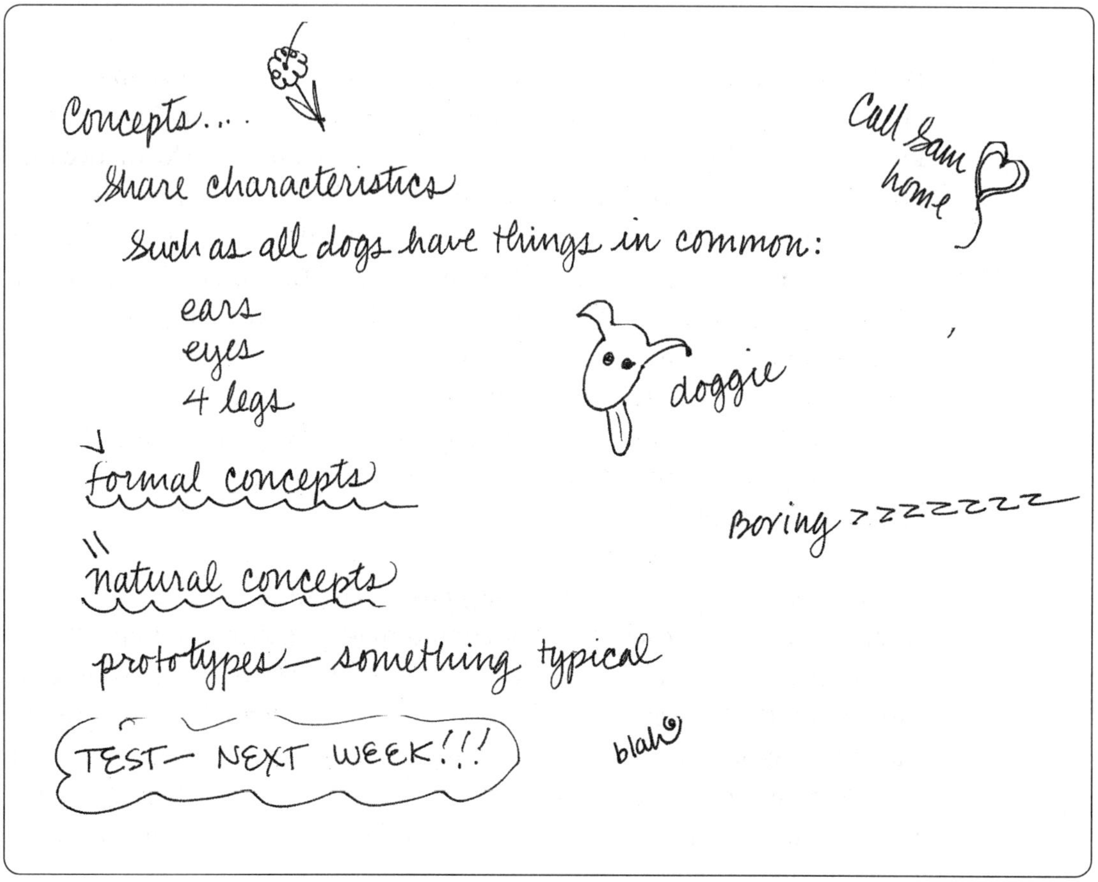

Concepts...

Call Sam home

Share characteristics

Such as all dogs have things in common:

ears
eyes
4 legs

doggie

formal concepts

Boring zzzzzzz

natural concepts

prototypes—something typical

TEST—NEXT WEEK!!!

blah

Good notes include examples. Often when professors get to the point in the lecture at which they are giving examples, students are nodding off or thinking about what they plan to have for lunch. Since examples often surface on exams, it's crucial to write down every example of a particular main point that the professor provides. These examples should, in some way, stand out so that as you study, you know what concept the example illustrates.

Good notes clearly indicate lecture patterns. Most professors use the same pattern in all of their lectures. The two most common are the inductive pattern and the deductive pattern. *Inductive* lectures progress from the specific to the general. For example, an inductive lecturer would provide a series of reasons or characteristics and conclude with a statement such as, "So, all of this means. . . ." This concluding statement is the generalization that helps make sense of the lecture. *Deductive* lecturers are the opposite. They begin with the generalization and then fill in the reasons, details, and examples. It is generally easier to follow lectures when they are presented in a deductive manner. Whatever style your professor uses should become apparent to you after the first few class sessions. Your notes should reflect this lecture pattern.

Good notes allow for self-testing. When students take notes, rarely do they think about how the way they take notes will influence the way they study. Most students merely read through their notes rather than doing any self-testing. Reading through your notes often gives you a sense of knowing the information well enough to turn in a high performance on an exam when, in fact, you do not. Writing questions or key words, called annotations, in the margin of your notes can help you test yourself. Note the difference among the notes in Figures 11.1, 11.2, and 11.3 once again. The notes in Figure 11.1 have questions in the margins that you can ask yourself and then answer in your head, checking your notes to see whether you were correct. Remember what Dr. Alison King found in her study about self-questioning over lecture notes. (We will discuss self-questioning of lecture notes, or what we call self-testing, in more detail later in the chapter.)

Good notes stand the test of time. Because your notes are a record of what is said in class each day, they should make sense to you long after class is over. You should be able to study your notes two days, two weeks, or two months later and they should still be understandable. Because of the way memory works, you will be unable to remember everything your professor says in class every day. That's why you take notes to begin with. It's important, then, to be sure that your notes are organized in such a way that they will make sense down the line and that they include as much detail as you can reasonably get on paper.

Good notes use abbreviations. Because most professors talk faster than you can write, it's important to use abbreviations that make sense to you. For example, if your professor is lecturing on the Industrial Revolution, it would be too time consuming to write out both words every time they were mentioned. Rather, using *Ind. Rev.* or even *IR* saves a considerable amount of time. Likewise, it's efficient to develop a series of abbreviations for common and high-use words. Some suggestions are provided in Figure 11.4.

FIGURE 11.4 *Examples of Abbreviations for Common or Frequently Used Words*

&	and
b/c	because
∴	therefore
/	the
=	means, definition, is equal to
w/i	within
+	in addition to/positives
–	negatives
$	money
<	less than
>	greater than/more
↑	increased
↓	decreased
☆	very important
#	number

11.2

SELF-EVALUATION

Examining Your Notes

Examine the notes from one of your classes and evaluate them on a scale of 1 to 5, with 1 being "Hardly ever" to 5 being "Almost always."

	HARDLY EVER		SOMETIMES		ALMOST ALWAYS
My notes are organized.	1	2	3	4	5
My notes distinguish main points from details.	1	2	3	4	5
My notes include examples.	1	2	3	4	5
My notes indicate lecture patterns.	1	2	3	4	5
My notes allow for self-testing.	1	2	3	4	5
My notes can stand the test of time.	1	2	3	4	5
My notes contain abbreviations.	1	2	3	4	5

Now describe what you believe are your note taking strengths and weaknesses. What three specific improvements would you like to make?

Strengths: ______________________________

____

Weaknesses: ______________________________

____

Improvements:

1. ______________________________
2. ______________________________
3. ______________________________

Taking Good Lecture Notes

Taking good notes involves much more than being a warm body in a classroom. It involves active listening, attentiveness, and the ability to synthesize and condense a considerable amount of information on the spot. Effective note takers know that a good deal of thinking goes on during the entire period of note taking. Information needs to flow through your mind before it flows out of your pen. Without this important active listening and thinking going on during note taking, you are likely to leave class with an inadequate or even an incorrect representation of what took place.

We have watched students take notes many times; it can be an illuminating experience. Most students probably enter the lecture situation with every intention of staying alert, paying attention, and taking good notes. But for a variety of reasons, many students cannot prevail. From our observations, it seems that several factors enter into students' abilities to take good notes. First, the larger the class size, the easier it is not to pay attention and stay connected with what the professor is saying. And the farther back or to the side that students sit in a lecture hall, the worse the problem tends to become. In large-lecture classes, we have seen students reading the campus paper, chatting among themselves, listening to music with headsets on, studying for another class, doing crossword puzzles, and of course sleeping, to name a few activities.

The second reason students have problems taking good notes is the way a professor lectures. If a professor is not entertaining or tends to speak in a monotone, students tune out rather than tune in. Similarly, professors who are difficult to follow or those who talk too fast will cause students' minds to wander rather than to stay actively involved in listening.

Third, the level of students' preparation also makes a difference. Students who come to class prepared—they have read the text assignment, reviewed their notes, and have everything ready to be an active listener—are usually more engaged than students who lack preparation. In most classes, professors recommend that you read the text before coming to class because they believe that knowing something about the information that will be lectured on makes a big difference in students' abilities to make sense of the lecture.

Fourth, the time of day seems to have a big influence on taking good notes. Interestingly, students seem to be most inattentive and most likely to fall asleep in an early morning class, presumably after they have had several hours of uninterrupted sleep. Granted, many students would consider themselves to be "night people," whose body clocks resist going to bed before the wee hours of the morning and who resist getting up prior to noon. And we know some students who do manage to get eight hours of sleep on most nights and still don't function very well much before 10:00 A.M. If you count yourself in these numbers, try as hard as you can not to schedule an early morning class. We can almost guarantee you that your notes will suffer.

Students also seem to have trouble attending right after lunch or during the late afternoon hours for opposite reasons. Right after lunch, you may be full and somewhat sluggish. Late in the afternoon, as dinnertime approaches, you may feel hungry and lack energy. We recommend that if you have a class immediately after lunch that you try to eat a light meal rather than wolfing down several pieces of pizza. If a late afternoon class is on your schedule, try eating a snack before class to help keep the hunger pangs at bay and to keep your energy level up.

Finally, your ability to concentrate on the lecture and to take good notes also seems to depend on your health, both emotional and physical. Breaking up with your friend, family problems, sick children, illness, and taking prescription medication all can influence your attentiveness in class. Everyone experiences problems at one time or another and no one can expect to be perfectly attentive all the time. But when emotional or physical problems become constant barriers to learning, it's time to think about a course of action to get back to health.

General Guidelines

Let's begin our discussion of how to take good lecture notes with some general guidelines. These guidelines tend to work for every type of lecture, regardless of class size.

Sit up front and within the professor's line of vision. As we mentioned above, students who sit in the front of the classroom (or at the very least, in the professor's line of vision) tend to be more attentive and listen more actively than those who sit in the back. This generalization holds true both in larger classes and in smaller classes. In small classes, students who sit in the front tend to ask questions with greater frequency and get to know their professors better. In addition, research indicates that there is a significant relationship between students' grades and where they sit in the room. That is, the closer they sit to the front, the higher their grade tends to be.

Adjust your note taking to the professor. Don't expect the professor to adjust to you. Every professor lectures a bit differently. Some are well organized; taking notes from them is a breeze. Others are unorganized, provide few transitional cues, and get off the topic very easily. Whatever your professor's lecturing habits seem to be, you need to figure them out early in the term and make the appropriate adjustments in your note taking. Don't expect lecturers who talk quickly to slow down because you can't write down every word they say.

Listen, think, and write. Students who try to copy down everything the professor says are doomed to write only partial ideas in their notes and have notes that will not stand the test of time. Rather than trying to write down every word, listen first, think about what the professor is saying, and then write that thought, as much as possible, in your own words. Because professors tend to repeat information or say it a couple of times in different ways, it's important to listen and think before you write. Your intent should be to understand, not to be someone who copies down only about a quarter of the important ideas.

Paraphrase. This advice is similar to what we said above about listening first, thinking, and then writing. But sometimes professors talk so quickly and try to cram so much into a lecture that it is virtually impossible to get down all of the key points. If you find yourself getting more half-thoughts than complete thoughts in your notes, or if you read over your notes and find that you can't piece together the important parts of the lecture, then you probably need to begin to do some serious paraphrasing. Paraphrasing, in this case, means getting down key concepts in your own words and then filling in the details with information from the text. Figure 11.5 gives you an example of the notes a professor might use for a lecture on the topic of memory. Then, in the same figure, you will see how a student's paraphrased notes might look.

FIGURE 11.5 *Example of a Professor's Notes and a Student's Paraphrased Notes*

Professor's Lecture Notes	Student's Paraphrased Notes
There are 3 major parts to the memory system: the sensory store, short-term memory, and long-term memory. Each has certain properties, and forgetting occurs in the 3 memory parts in a variety of ways. Keep in mind that these 3 "parts" are not compartmentalized; one really "flows into the other."	MEMORY SYSTEM = 3 parts 1. Sensory store (SS) 2. Short-term memory (STM) 3. Long-term memory (LTM) Each has properties; not really separate pieces
The visual sensory store, for example, has 5 major characteristics. First, we are not aware of it. Second, it lasts less than a second. It's fleeting. How long it lasts depends on viewing conditions. Third, it's more a kind of persistence than it is a real form of memory. Fourth, forgetting occurs through decay because this is basically unattended information. Finally, sensory store is unlimited in capacity. An example of when the sensory store is used is when you turn off the TV, but the image still persists for a split second.	Visual Sensory Store (5 Char.) 1. unaware of it 2. lasts < 1 sec. (length depends on viewing cond.) 3. more of a persistence 4. forgetting = decay b/c it is unattended to 5. capacity = unlimited Example: When you still "see" an image after it is gone.

Learning how to take good lecture notes is an integral part of being a successful college student and an active learner. Like approaching text, taking good notes and using them as a successful study aid involve preparing to take notes, being an active listener during the lecture, and then annotating and self-testing after the lecture.

Getting Ready to Take Notes

Just as you preread before beginning to read a text (prereading will be discussed in the next chapter), you need to do some preparation before you begin to take notes. Engaging in pre–note-taking activities can make the difference between being an active and a passive listener. In order to get ready to take notes, you should:

Do the assigned reading. Most professors expect you to be somewhat familiar with the topics they will lecture on. Reading before you attend the lecture gives you the advantage of being able to make better connections between the text and lecture. But perhaps even more importantly, you will also be able to follow the "listen, think, and write rule" better. That is, being somewhat familiar with the topic of the lecture will allow you to take down the key points in the lecture in a more organized fashion. If you run out of time and can't read the text in its entirety, at least skim the chapter(s) using the techniques described in Chapter 12. That will give you some idea of the key points that will be lectured on.

Review your notes from the previous lecture. Take five or ten minutes before class to read through your notes from the previous lecture. By reviewing, you are refreshing your memory and getting your mind ready to become actively involved in what will be said in the current class. In addition, when you review, you can be sure that you understand the information that has been presented. Because many professors begin each class by asking if anyone has questions, you can get unclear information explained before you become totally lost. Finally, reviewing your notes has a big payoff given the small amount of extra time you are interacting with the material. Just by spending ten minutes each weekday reviewing your notes, you have added fifty extra minutes of study time to the class without even realizing it.

Have the extra edge. Try to get to class with plenty of time to spare. You can actually use this time to review. Get out your notebook, get your paper ready (we'll talk more about this later), and, if possible, sit in the front. Always be sure that you have more than one pen or pencil, just in case.

Staying Active during Note Taking

In this section, we will discuss not only the format and organization of good notes but also the kinds of information that you should include in your notes. By following these suggestions, you will be able to remain alert and active throughout the class.

Format and Organization of Your Notes If you were to examine the notes of five different college students, you would probably see five different formats. Perhaps none of these formats would match up with the method we recommend—the split-page method. We will concentrate on this particular method because it allows for self-testing, which we believe is important if you want to be an active learner who monitors his or her learning.

Look again at the example in Figure 11.1. You can see that a line has been drawn down the left-hand side of the paper, creating a two- to three-inch margin. During note taking, you do not write in this margin. Rather, you take your notes on the wider right-hand side of the paper. You should have your lines drawn on several sheets of paper, your paper dated, and several pages numbered before your professor begins to lecture.

As you read the following guidelines, look at Figure 11.1 to see what your notes might look like:

- Use a three-ring binder rather than spiral-bound notebook. A binder allows you to include class handouts, easily remove your notes, and easily insert notes if you are absent from class.
- Take notes on the front of the paper only. It is easier to self-test this way, and you can use the other side to add information later on.
- Take notes in simple paragraph form rather than in a tightly structured outline. Outlining causes many students to get hung up on the outline itself rather than the content of the lecture.
- Leave spaces between and underline key points. This enables you to see where one idea stops and another begins; it helps to distinguish between the key points and the details.
- Indent and mark details and examples. Indenting helps you know what information is related. If your notes all run together, it's difficult to tell what is a key point and what information supports that key point.
- Number lists of reasons, characteristics, types, etc. Numbering lists enables you to know at a glance how many factors on the list you need to remember.

- Use abbreviations whenever possible. We mentioned this idea earlier. Abbreviating saves time. Also use abbreviations to distinguish certain kinds of information, such as indicating an example by "ex." and a definition by "def." A sample of possible abbreviations is shown in Figure 11.4. You can think of others and add them to the list.

Although we believe that the split-page method of note taking promotes higher academic achievement, we also know that active learners modify strategies to match the learning situation and their individuality as learners. Feel free, then, to modify exactly how you take your notes. For example, if you have always taken notes in outline form and have had success with that method, we would probably advise you to continue, with perhaps some minor adjustments. We do, however, feel strongly about the importance of including a two- to three-inch margin on the left-hand side for self-testing.

11.3 SOMETHING TO WRITE ABOUT AND DISCUSS

In the space that follows, rewrite a page or two of lecture notes from one of your classes in the split-page method. Note that the vertical line has already been drawn for you. Remember to write your notes on the wider right-hand side and then annotate or write questions on the smaller left-hand side. After you have completed this activity, share the two versions of notes with a classmate and discuss the advantages and disadvantages of the split-page method.

Active Listening It's important to know not only how you should take and organize your notes but also what kinds of information you should listen for. Of course, the kinds of information you should include in your notes vary from class to class. For example, although you may include names, dates, and events in your history notes, your psychology notes will probably be more focused on research and theories than on key events. Given that the specific type of information may differ from class to class, listen for the following cues that your professor may give as a way of knowing what to put in your notes:

- **Lists.** Lists of things begin with cues such as: "There were three major reasons why President Johnson committed more troops in Vietnam," "Short-term memory has five characteristics," or "Mitosis progresses through eight stages." Anytime you hear a number followed by several factors, stages, characteristics, etc., make sure you write the number of factors, stages, characteristics, etc., and the explanation. In other words, just don't write the stages of mitosis in your notes; write down what happens in each stage as well.

- **Cause/effect.** When you hear your professor discuss causes and effects, be sure to write them down. Cause/effect cues are common in history. For example, there might be an event that caused a president to make a certain decision and this decision, in turn, had numerous effects on other events and decisions. In science, cause/effect can deal with drug reactions, diseases, or the food chain.

- **Definitions.** Perhaps one of the most frequent types of information your professor will give in a lecture is definitions. Your professor might cue you by saying something as basic as "The definition of *prototype* is ..." or "*Prototype* can be defined as...." It's a good idea to get definitions written in your notes precisely, especially in science. If you write down only a portion of a definition or aren't sure that you have it exactly right, check in your text or with your professor as soon after class as possible.

- **Examples.** Definitions are quite frequently followed by examples, yet it's easy for students to neglect putting the examples in their notes. Often, students will see example time as an occasion to tune out, doodle, or think about what they are going to do after class. But examples discussed in class make prime test questions. When professors write questions about examples, they are actually finding out whether you know definitions as well. Thus, if you have to choose, we believe that it's more important to get examples in your notes than definitions.

- **Extended comments.** Another cue that information is important is when the professor spends a considerable amount of time explaining something. However, there are two sides to this coin. First, if your professor is an inductive lecturer, it may be difficult to stay tuned in because it may take a while to get to the really important piece of information—the generalization. In such cases, students often get so mired in the details that by the time the professor gets to the key point, they are doodling, snoozing, or daydreaming. It's important during extended comments to try to stay connected with the lecturer and to take down as much of the information as possible. Essay, short-answer, and higher-level multiple-choice items often have extended comments as their source.

- **Superlatives.** Anytime a professor uses words such as "most important," "best explanation," "least influential," or "greatest significance," be sure to write them down and underline them in your notes. For example, there may be many explanations for how memory works, but your psychology professor might believe that one explanation is the "best." Or in history, there are numerous reasons why the world chose to ignore what was going on in concentration camps during World War II, but some reasons were more influential and had a greater impact than others.

- **Voice or volume change.** When individuals think something is important or they want to stress it, they generally speak more loudly and slowly. That's why it's important to tune in to your professor's voice patterns. Most of the time, when your professor is saying something that she thinks is important, her voice will change. Sometimes the pitch gets higher, but in most cases the voice gets louder and slower. A change in voice can be a clear indication that something important is being said.

Becoming an active listener takes time, especially for classes in which you have little interest. It's not too difficult to stay connected with the lecturer in classes that you like or in classes where you have a professor who is dynamic. It's much more difficult in those courses that are, in some way, less appealing. If you try to think about the bigger picture, however, studying and learning the course material will be a much easier task if you are an active listener and take organized notes for the entire class period.

One final suggestion about information to listen for in a lecture: Certainly it is important to take good notes over the content presented in class, but don't ignore the process notes. Process notes (see Figure 11.1) consist of information the professor gives about tests, how to study, when study or review sessions are held, how to think about the information, or how he wants an essay structured. Such comments can also include clues, in the form of off-the-cuff remarks, about what information might be on the exam. Process notes often come right at the beginning of class, before some students are ready to take notes, or at the end of class, when some students have already closed their binder and are impatiently waiting for the professor to end it! Sometimes professors will even comment after a particular lecture something to the effect "Hmmm ... Wouldn't this make an interesting essay question?" Students who fail to write the process notes down risk losing valuable points on exams.

11.4

SOMETHING TO THINK AND WRITE ABOUT

Thinking Critically

Evaluate the lecturing style and patterns of one of your current professors by answering the following questions. Then think about how you can use this information to help you take better notes in this professor's class.

1. *What class is this?* ______________________________
2. *What kind of lecturer is your professor (inductive or deductive)?* ______________________________
3. *How do you know?* ______________________________
4. *What kind of cues does your professor give?* ______________________________
5. *How does your professor organize the lectures?* ______________________________
6. *How much overlap is there between your professor's lectures and the textbook used in the class?* ______________________________
7. *What kinds of adjustments might you have to make to this professor's lecturing style?* ______________________________

Annotating and Self-Testing after Note Taking

You have gotten ready to take notes prior to the lecture, you have remained active and taken notes in an organized way during the lecture, but you still aren't finished! Interacting with your notes after the lecture is perhaps the most important phase of note taking. As soon as possible after the lecture, it's important to read over your notes to be sure you understand all the major concepts presented. This is when you use the two- to three-inch margin on the left-hand side of your paper. As shown in Figure 11.6, you can use this margin to write notes that indicate the key points. We refer to this as annotation. You can use the margin to pose questions (as shown in the lecture notes in Figure 11.1). Either way, use the annotations or questions to self-test as you study the course material. Good annotations or questions have several features:

- They focus on the major points or broad topics.
- They get at higher-level thinking by asking how or why or by asking for examples.
- They are brief.

Annotating your lecture notes as soon after the lecture as possible helps you get the information moving through your memory and, in the long run, helps you remember it better. In addition, when you go through your notes, you can determine whether you have questions about what was presented in class. If you have problems annotating or writing good questions, you probably didn't understand that portion of the lecture, or you were not actively listening at that point. Whatever the reason, writing questions or annotating gives you immediate feedback about what you understand and when your understanding has broken down.

When you prepare for the exam, use your annotations or questions to self-test. Actively read through your notes, trying to get the information fixed in your memory. Then fold your paper, exposing only the annotations or questions you have written in the left-hand column. Ask yourself the question or explain the concept. Flip your notes over to see how much of the material you have remembered. If you knew it completely and accurately, go on to the next concept. If you had problems, read it over another time or two and try again. As you learn the concepts, check them off in the margin. Then when you begin the next study session, review what you know, but concentrate your efforts on what you don't know.

Self-testing by using annotations or questions in the margin of your notes should give you confidence as you enter a testing situation. Students who do not self-test often have a false sense of knowing the infor-

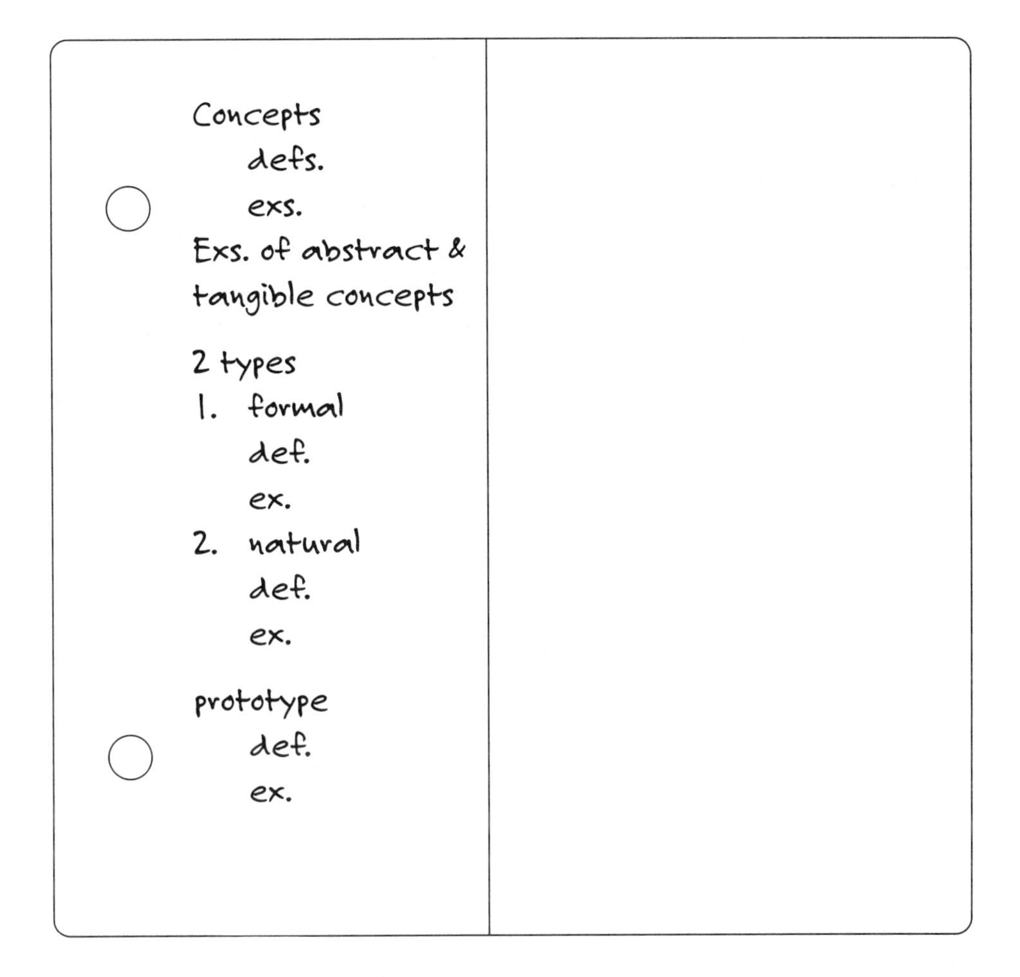

FIGURE 11.6
Annotations for Lecture Notes Pictured in Figure 11.1

mation because they have only read over their notes. As we have stressed several times already, when you self-test, you get a fairly accurate idea of the concepts you know and understand very well and those that may still be somewhat unclear or fuzzy. As with other rehearsal strategies, self-testing of lecture notes has a tremendous payoff.

Note-Taking Myths

We end this chapter by briefly touching on some myths—information that students tend to believe about note taking that isn't necessarily so!

Myth 1:

If you can't keep up with professor, tape-record the lectures.

Tape-recording in classes that are difficult for you probably isn't a bad idea *if and only if* it doesn't take the place of taking notes during the lecture and *if* you will actually listen to the lecture and take the notes once the lecture is over. The truth is that when students tape lectures, they generally don't go back and listen to the tapes. It's easy to understand why. If you are taking five classes, you hardly have time to do all your reading, studying, and other learning activities, let alone sit and listen to lectures for a second time. In addition, students who tape lectures find it much easier to tune out what the professor is saying and will miss information written on the chalkboard or overhead. Our advice to you is to go to class, take the best notes you can, and supplement those notes either with information from the text or by forming a study group that has as one of its goals to share notes with everyone. Unless you have a disability that necessitates recording class lectures, tape-recording in your courses simply is not an efficient and active way to learn.

Myth 2:

Copying a classmate's notes who is a better note taker than you is better than struggling with it yourself.

Copying someone else's notes, no matter how good a note taker he or she is, is about as passive as you can get! Think back to some time in your distant past when you may have actually copied someone's homework. How much did you learn from that experience? We would guess not much. You won't learn much from copying someone else's lecture notes either. We're not saying that you shouldn't compare your lecture notes with a classmate's. That can be a very positive and active strategy. And we're not suggesting that if you have to miss class because you're ill that you shouldn't borrow a classmate's notes. Copying someone's notes simply should not be something that happens frequently.

Myth 3:

It's impossible to take notes in a class that involves a considerable amount of class discussion.

When we have observed students in classes that involve a lot of discussion, it seems that we see very little note taking going on. Students seem to think that only information presented by the professor has any merit and fail to write down any comments made by their peers. However, if you think for a minute about the purpose of classes that involve discussion, you'll realize that the professor's role is generally just to initiate the discussion. It's the students who actually generate the ideas, and these ideas often find their way to the exam. We recommend that for a discussion class, you modify the note-taking process somewhat. Rather than dividing your paper into a narrow and a wide margin, divide it into thirds. In the first column, write the question that is being posed or the theory that is being debated. In the second column, take notes on what the professor has to say about it. In the last column, take notes on what your classmates say. Then when you are studying, you can evaluate your classmates' comments and evaluate which ones are worth studying and which ones can be ignored.

REAL COLLEGE: *Chad's Challenge*

Read the following scenario and then respond to the questions based on what you learned in this chapter.

"Why did I ever sign up for this 8:00 class?" Chad wondered as he dragged himself out of bed around 7:30. It was like this every morning: Drag out of bed, throw on a pair of jeans and a T-shirt, gather up the books, and try to get to Professor Wilson's anthropology class *on time*! Every day it was a real challenge ... and he even liked Professor Wilson. He was experiencing some problems, however.

Chad never had problems taking notes in high school. His teachers talked slowly and would repeat information if students asked. So everyone's notes really looked and read pretty much the same. If you didn't feel like taking notes, you could always borrow a friend's and copy them. Plus, most of his high school teachers gave him study guides to prepare for the tests, so all he had to do was look up the answers that came mostly from the teacher's lectures. But Professor Wilson. WOW! She talked so fast and tried to get so much in one lecture that Chad usually got only a small portion of the key ideas that were presented. Then, because he was late to class a lot, he would arrive in the middle of an extended comment and have no idea what she was talking about. His notes were full of doodles, he almost fell out of his seat some mornings when he nodded off, and his notes were a disorganized mess. Chad tried two different solutions prior to the first exam. First, he gave up taking notes altogether and brought a tape recorder to class. Second, he borrowed a classmate's notes and copied them. He made a very low D.

After this poor performance, he decided that he had greater problems than just getting up. He really didn't know how to take notes from Professor Wilson. But he really wanted to make a concerted effort to do better. The information was interesting and, in spite of talking fast, Professor Wilson was a pretty good lecturer. He decided to take the note-taking challenge once again.

What advice would you give to Chad so that he can improve? (Hint: You may *not* advise him to drop the class and take it later in the day next term. Remember, time isn't his only problem!)

____

____

____

____

____

____

____

____

____

FOLLOW-UP ACTIVITIES

1. Try taking notes in all of your classes using the split-page method for one week. Be sure to use the left-hand margin for questions or annotations. Then evaluate what you like and don't like about this method.
2. How might you modify this method to suit your own note-taking preferences? When you modify, you should keep the left-hand margin, but what other adjustments could you make?
3. For each of your current classes, try to determine how much overlap there is between the text and the lecture. Do your professors' test questions come primarily from the lectures or the text?

Networking

- Some professors are putting their lecture notes on the web daily. If any of your professors is doing this, check out his web site. What are the advantages and disadvantages of simply copying these notes off the web?

Identifying the Strategies

Part IV introduces a wide variety of strategies for active learning. In Chapter 12, you will learn strategies for gearing up, which you can use before reading or studying. In this chapter, you will also learn about the importance of creating a good environment for learning.

Chapter 13 introduces you to strategies for staying active while reading. In this chapter, you will learn an effective system for marking your texts.

In Chapter 14, you will learn about the importance of rehearsal strategies. We discuss strategies for both written and verbal rehearsal to help you remember what you have studied.

Chapter 15 discusses strategies for reviewing. In this chapter, you will learn strategies to help you organize information to review as you prepare for exams.

Before you read the chapters in Part IV, please respond to the following statements. Read each statement and decide whether you agree or disagree with it.

Keep your responses in mind as you read the chapters in Part IV. When you have finished reading Part IV, revisit this page. How are your responses similar to or different from what is introduced in the chapters?

BEFORE Agree	BEFORE Disagree		AFTER Agree	AFTER Disagree
☐	☐	*1. Before I read my textbooks, I look through each chapter.*	☐	☐
☐	☐	*2. Having a good place to study is important to doing well in college.*	☐	☐
☐	☐	*3. When I read, I use a highlighter to identify important points.*	☐	☐
☐	☐	*4. After reading my text, I am sure I understand all of the key ideas.*	☐	☐
☐	☐	*5. One good way to be sure I understand important concepts is to say the information to myself.*	☐	☐
☐	☐	*6. When I study, my main goal is to memorize terms.*	☐	☐
☐	☐	*7. Working with a study group is usually a waste of time.*	☐	☐
☐	☐	*8. I am never sure whether I am completely prepared before an exam.*	☐	☐

Gearing Up
Prereading Strategies

Read this chapter to answer the following questions:

Why do you need to gear up before reading and studying?

What are some strategies for gearing up?

Sitting down to read or study is something every college student needs to do every day. But when you study, are you wasting time when you start to read? Do you find that your first half-hour is unproductive because you are not concentrating on what you are doing? Maybe the reason is that you have not geared up for studying.

Picture a track meet at a local college. The athletes pile out of a van just as the first race begins. They throw off their sweats and start running. Would that ever happen? Of course not. Just as an athlete would never run a race or even practice "cold," you should not expect to start reading or studying without warming up in some way. Athletes warm up to get their muscles ready to perform. If they don't warm up, their bodies are not as efficient or prepared. The runners described above would have warmed up for at least a half-hour before running a race. A student who attempts to simply start reading is like a runner who has not warmed up. When you begin to read or study, you need to warm up your brain so that you will be more efficient and productive when you read or study.

STUDY TIP

To make the most of your study sessions, take some time to warm up before reading or studying.

In this chapter, we will present strategies to help you gear up for reading, studying, and listening in class. The purpose for using these strategies is not only to increase your efficiency and productivity but also to increase your interest and motivation for studying. Before reading the rest of the chapter, read the *Research into Practice* section. Dr. Wade and Dr. Trathen discuss how prereading strategies help students learn important information from texts.

Research into Practice

Prereading Questions*

In this article, Wade and Trathen hypothesized that students who read questions about the main idea of a text before reading it would remember more important information than students who did not. In their study, they gave 160 college students a science text about the sea. Some students were asked five prereading questions, such as: What causes the tides? How have living things on earth adapted to the tides? Other students read the passage without the prereading questions.

Wade and Trathen found that students who were given prereading questions remembered more important information and less unimportant information than students who did not receive the questions. They concluded that the prereading questions helped students learn by focusing their attention on important information.

* Source: Wade, S. E., & Trathen, W. (1989). Effect of self-selected study methods on learning. *Journal of Educational Psychology* 81: 40–47.

This study is important for college students because although you are rarely given questions before reading, you *can* ask yourself some questions before reading. These questions could come from chapter headings, subheadings, diagrams, or bold-faced words. By asking yourself some questions about the reading, you will be helping to focus your attention on the important information contained in a text.

Strategies for Gearing Up

Create a Learning Environment

Before you can gear up for reading and studying, you must first create an environment that promotes learning. Think about the place where you currently study. Do you study in a setting that allows you to concentrate and study effectively, or are you constantly distracted by people, noise, or other diversions? Your learning environment can help your progress when reading or studying, but if you do not have a good setting, it can actually hinder your progress. You need to create a place that is free from distractions and that allows you to maximize your studying time.

Some students say they need complete quiet to study. Even hearing a clock ticking in the background is enough to distract them. Other students say they study best in a crowded, noisy room because the noise actually helps them concentrate. Some students study most successfully when they are in familiar surroundings, such as their bedroom; for others, familiar surroundings do not make a difference. Some students like quiet music playing; others do not. However, one general rule for all students is that the television seems to be more of a distraction than music or other background noise. So even if you are the type of person who studies best with some background noise—leave the TV off when you are reading or studying. Also don't let yourself become distracted by computer games or Internet surfing when you are trying to study.

You will also concentrate better when you read or study in a straight-backed chair, such as a desk or kitchen chair, than in your bed. Students will often tell us that reading in bed leads to more napping than studying! Your ideal learning environment is one where the only thing you do in that place is study. If you have a desk, set it up so that you are ready to study. Have at hand pens and pencils, a tablet of paper, a calculator, or anything else you need to study. If you do not have a desk, you can transform your kitchen table into your learning environment by removing anything that does not have to do with studying (dishes, food, etc.) and replacing it with the tools you need for studying.

If you find that you cannot create an effective learning environment in your home because there are too many distractions, try to find a quiet place on campus to study, such as the library or the student union.

12.1

SELF-EVALUATION

Something to Write About

Think about your current learning environment when responding to these questions.

1. *Where do you currently study? Check all that apply.*

   ☐ Bedroom
   ☐ Living room
   ☐ Bed
   ☐ No set studying place
   ☐ Library
   ☐ Desk
   ☐ Kitchen table
   ☐ Other ______________________

2. *Which of these best describes your learning environment? Check all that apply.*

   ☐ *TV on*
   ☐ *Complete quiet*
   ☐ *Roommates/others studying*
   ☐ *Music playing*
   ☐ *Roommates/others talking*
   ☐ *Other* ______________________

3. *What are the greatest distractors to your studying?*

   ____

   ____

   ____

4. *What changes do you need to make to create a more effective learning environment?*

   ____

   ____

   ____

Survey Your Textbooks

Now that you have set up a learning environment to meet your needs, the next step in gearing up is examining your textbooks. All textbooks are not created equal. Some textbooks are written and presented in a way that is very reader-friendly. These texts are called *considerate texts.* Considerate texts are those that usually have some preview questions or an organizer at the beginning of each chapter to help readers focus on what they are about to learn. These texts make good use of diagrams, pictures, and figures to give readers a better picture of the topic. Considerate texts often use **bold-faced** or *italicized* words to emphasize key terms. They also usually have summary or review questions at the end of each chapter. Often, considerate texts have large margins so readers have room to write notes as they read. On the other hand, some textbooks are *inconsiderate texts.* These texts are usually not written in a way that helps readers focus on key ideas and do not contain the features, such as preview questions or chapter summaries, that are found in considerate texts. Inconsiderate texts are usually more difficult to read because the topics are not presented in an organized reader-friendly way.

One way to determine the level of considerateness is to examine the way your textbooks are arranged. This will help you prepare to study in several ways. For example, in Chapter 2 we discussed the importance of connecting what you know to your prior knowledge; by examining the chapters before you start to read, you will know all of the topics that will be covered and can begin to activate your knowledge about those topics. In addition, because you will know what topics to expect, you may find that your interest in reading the chapters is increased. By examining your textbooks, you will also be giving yourself the time you need to gear up for reading effectively.

12.2

SOMETHING TO WRITE ABOUT AND DISCUSS

Thinking Critically

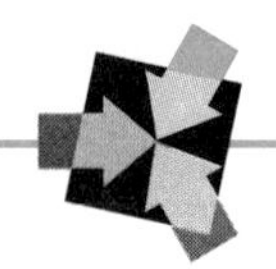

Use this text feature checklist to examine your textbooks. Which of the following features do they contain?

	Textbook 1 Course:	Textbook 2 Course:	Textbook 3 Course:	Textbook 4 Course:	Textbook 5 Course:
Preview questions					
Bold-faced terms					
Summaries					
Diagrams					
Formulas					
Glossaries					
Application activities					
Large margins					
Review questions					
Text boxes					

1. *How do you think these text features can help you learn?*

____

____

____

2. *Now examine the table of contents page of at least one of your textbooks. With which topics are you already familiar? Which topics are completely new to you?*

____

____

____

Preview the Reading

You have found a quiet place to study and have all of your studying tools at your fingertips. Now you're ready to gear up for the day's reading by previewing what you will be reading. Previewing the chapter doesn't take very long, but just as surveying your entire textbook helped you gear up for the class, previewing what you will read today will help to activate your prior knowledge and build your interest in the topic. Previewing consists of the following steps:

- ***Read the chapter title.*** The title tells you about the overall topic of the chapter and may clue you in to the author's intent.
- ***Read the headings and subheadings.*** The headings and subheadings will tell you about the specific focus in the chapter and may suggest the author's approach to the topic. For example, a subheading in your history text called "The Horrors of War" would introduce very different material from a subheading called "War: Benefits and Advances."
- ***Read the bold-faced or italicized terms.*** These terms will clue you in to ideas that will be emphasized in the text and will point out new vocabulary or content-specific terms that will be discussed in the chapter.
- ***Note the typographical aids.*** Besides bold-faced or italicized words, many texts use graphs, charts, tables, or illustrations to emphasize key ideas. Read these sections to find out what is important in the chapter.
- ***Read the introduction.*** If your textbook offers chapter introductions, it is a good idea to read this section when you preview the chapter to get an idea of what the topic is about and the scope of information that will be covered in the chapter.

- ***Read the summary.*** If your textbook contains chapter summaries, it is a good idea to read this section *before* you actually read the chapter. The summary section outlines the key information you should have learned when you have finished reading the chapter. By reading it before reading the chapter, you will be able to identify the key points in the chapter.
- ***Read the end-of-chapter material.*** This may include study questions, vocabulary lists, or application exercises. These will also tell you what is important in the chapter.

Although this might sound like a lot to do before reading, previewing actually takes a only few minutes to accomplish because you are not getting bogged down in the details of the chapter. Your purpose in prereading is to get a general idea of the concepts that will be covered in the chapter.

12.3 SOMETHING TO WRITE ABOUT AND DISCUSS

Preview the excerpt titled "Technologies of Mass-Production and Destruction" found in Appendix C for the following information. Discuss your responses with a partner or small group.

1. *What do the headings and subheadings tell you this chapter will be about?*

____

____

____

2. *List and define the bold-faced terms.*

____

____

____

____

____

____

____

____

3. *What kinds of typographical aids—such as pictures, figures, tables, or diagrams— are contained in the chapter? What do they tell you about the focus of the chapter? Which typographical aids will be the most important to study?*

___

___

___

4. *How will the bulleted list at the beginning of the chapter help you focus your reading?*

___

___

___

Determine Your Reading Purpose

As you preview a chapter, you should begin to think of some questions about the key topics. For example, in previewing the chapter on technological systems, you might ask yourself how demographic shifts affect technology, how the economy affects technological advances, or how technology affects warfare. By asking questions, you are starting to think about the key ideas contained in the text, which will make your reading more effective. Jot down your questions and try to answer them as you read.

It is always a good idea to read with a purpose in mind. When you are reading your textbooks for a class, your primary purpose is to learn the information contained in each chapter. However, this is a tall order. If you tried to learn every idea contained in every chapter, you probably would have a difficult time. So what you need to do is figure out and focus on learning the key ideas contained in each chapter. One good way to help you determine what is important is to use your class syllabus and lecture notes as a guide. (See Chapter 11 for discussion on using your lecture notes to guide your reading.)

Gearing Up for Class

Just as it is important to gear up before reading or studying, it is also important to get yourself ready to take notes in class. Gearing up for class means that you are getting yourself ready to listen, take notes, or discuss the day's topic. Once you have done the reading for class, you may feel that you are ready for the lecture, but you still need to gear yourself up right before class begins.

As discussed in Chapter 11, one way to get ready is to review your notes from the last class session. Reviewing your notes will help you remember what was discussed and where the class was headed. It may also remind you of questions you want to ask. Another way to gear up for class is to review the headings of the textbook chapter you read for that lecture. This will help you recall the important text points that will be discussed in class.

Gearing up for class is something that doesn't take much time. In fact, if you arrive five to ten minutes before the class begins, you should have enough time to get prepared. You should find that a boring class becomes more interesting and a difficult class becomes less confusing when you gear up for taking notes and listening to the lecture because you are preparing yourself in advance for what you are about to learn.

REAL COLLEGE: *Stan's Strategies*

Read the following scenario and then respond to the questions based on what you learned in this chapter.

Stan is a student at a local college. He is currently taking five courses that all have heavy reading loads. In fact, he averages over 300 pages of reading each week. The problem is that when he starts to read for class, he finds he gets bored very quickly and really doesn't pay attention to what he is doing. He always studies in his bedroom and usually props himself up in bed to read his texts; however, this term he seems to be napping more than reading. Another problem is that his housemates are always playing the stereo, which he finds very distracting. He thinks it is funny that he has no trouble sleeping with music blaring but can't even focus on one paragraph with music on. In order to get his reading done, Stan tries to read as fast as he can, just to get it over with quickly. However, he is not getting much done.

Knowing what you know about the importance of gearing up, what would your advice be for Stan?

____

____

____

____

____

____

FOLLOW-UP ACTIVITIES

1. This week, preview each chapter before you start to read for each of your classes. Remember to look at headings, subheadings, bold-faced words, and typographical aids.
2. Ask yourself questions as you preview. Write down the questions and see whether you can answer them as you read.

Networking

- Another way to gear up is to build your background knowledge. You have already previewed "Technologies of Mass-Production and Destruction" in Appendix C; in the next section, you will begin to read that chapter. To help build some greater knowledge of the topic of technology and society, find at least three web sites using the following key words: technology and society, technological advances, and role of technology. What questions do you have about the role of technology, based on the information you found?

Staying Active during Reading

Read this chapter to answer the following questions:

What is the difference between active and passive reading?

What are some strategies for concentrating on textbook reading?

STUDY TIP

Be sure you understand the concept you are reading before you move on to the next one.

Have you ever finished reading a chapter of your text only to realize that you don't remember anything you just read? If so, chances are you were not reading actively. You may have had trouble concentrating on your reading, or you may not have understood some of the concepts presented in the chapter. But because reading textbooks rarely tops any student's list of favorite activities, and also because reading textbooks is one of the most common college tasks, it is important to learn strategies for concentrating while you read.

Students sometimes tell us that it doesn't matter if they don't really concentrate the first time they read a chapter because they will just reread it anyway when they study for the exam. But as we discussed in Chapter 4, college students average about 250 pages of reading each week. Thus, you'll find that you barely have enough time to get through that much reading one time, and you certainly won't want to read each chapter several times. In this chapter, you will learn strategies for increasing your concentration during reading and for remembering what you read without resorting to rereading entire chapters. Before going on to the rest of the chapter, read the *Research into Practice* section where Simpson and Nist discuss annotation, a text-marking strategy to improve students' concentration while reading.

Reasearch into Practice

Text Annotation Leads to Better Performance*

In this article, Simpson and Nist compared text annotation with prereading questions. Text annotation is a strategy by which students note important points, key ideas, definitions, and examples in the margins of their texts. (We introduced the term *annotation* in Chapter 11 when we discussed taking lecture notes.) This research stems from the fact that many college students approach reading as memorizing or "looking over" the page. However, approaching reading this way leads to passive learning. In order to become active readers, students need strategies like annotation that will help them engage with the text.

In this study, students were separated into two groups. One group read and annotated a piece of text; the other group read some questions about the text before reading it but did not annotate it. Both groups were given time to study the material; then they completed a multiple-choice exam about the passage. The research indicated that students who annotated their text performed better on the exam than students who were given the prereading questions. In addition, the annotation group actually spent *less* time studying than the other group. Thus, Simpson and Nist concluded that annotation is an efficient and effective study strategy for learning from text.

This research is important for college students because it suggests that annotation not only increases academic performance but also results in more efficient use of study time. It also suggests that when prereading questions are not used in conjunction with other strategies, textbook understanding is not maximized. Although these results may seem contradictory to the results of the *Research into Practice* section in Chapter 12, remember that those results only addressed the value of using questions as a strategy for gearing up *before* reading. The current *Research into Practice* article stresses the importance of using strategies to promote comprehension *during* reading.

* Source: Simpson, M. L., & Nist, S. L. (1990). Textbook annotation: An effective and efficient study strategy for college students. *Journal of Reading* 34: 122–129.

Put Away Your Highlighters

When we ask students how they go about reading their textbooks, many students tell us they try to pull out key ideas from their texts by highlighting or underlining what they read. Although this appears to be a popular strategy, highlighting is often a very passive activity because students do not really understand the ideas they are highlighting. Many students actually put off reading for understanding until after they have highlighted the text. In other words, they skim the text looking for important information, highlight entire sections that seem important, and plan to return to those sections later when they study for the exam.

If you have ever seen a textbook that has been highlighted, you probably have noticed that the person was not very selective because sometimes entire pages are highlighted in bright pink or yellow or blue. What this person has done is select information but has not been very discriminating about what to mark. Students who highlight a lot of the text will have just as much information to cope with when they go to study … and they will have to go fishing in a pink or yellow or blue sea in order to pull out key points!

On the other hand, some college students don't highlight too much; they highlight too little. If these students tried to rely on their highlighting for their test review, they would not have adequate information so they would probably end up rereading the chapters. So put away your highlighters because you want to use strategies that promote greater active involvement in reading and learning.

13.1

SELF-EVALUATION

Something to Think and Write About

1. *Think about how you currently read your textbooks. What strategies do you use to help you concentrate and focus on your reading?*

____

____

2. *What do you do to improve your focus when you find you are having trouble concentrating on your reading?*

____

____

____

Make a Note of It

Becoming an active reader means that you are focusing on your reading. Sometimes students tell us that they have trouble concentrating when they read or that reading the text is usually a waste of time because they don't really get anything out of it. Other students tell us that they find they are often confused about the ideas when they read and have trouble figuring out which ideas are the most important to remember. One way to be sure that you are concentrating on and understanding what you read is to annotate your text.

In high school, you probably were not allowed to write in your textbooks so you couldn't annotate them, but in college you own your texts. In fact, you probably invested a considerable amount of money buying the texts for your classes, and you want to be sure to get your money's worth out of them. So annotate your texts!

What Is Annotation?

As presented in the *Research into Practice* section, annotation is one of the more effective strategies for marking your text. When you annotate, you sum up the information in your text by briefly marking the key ideas in the margin. Unlike highlighting (when you can passively mark ideas), annotation requires that you understand what you are reading and actively make decisions about what is important because you are putting the ideas in your own words. As shown in Figure 13.1, an annotated piece of text includes key ideas as well as examples, definitions, and other important details about the concepts. The annotations also include some predicted test questions.

In order to annotate properly, you need to think about what you read before you write. If you find that your mind is wandering or that you are not concentrating, you have to put yourself back on track so you are not wasting time. Because you stop reading after a few paragraphs to annotate what you have read, hopefully you will be able to reconnect with the reading without wasting too much time.

Why Annotate Your Text?

Annotating your text is an effective strategy because it helps you:

- ***Isolate information.*** By annotating your texts, you are selecting important information you want to remember.
- ***Reduce information.*** You reduce the information you need to study into more manageable amounts.

FIGURE 13.1 *Model Annotations of a Sociology Text*

Incorrect assumptions about poverty

1. to get rid of poverty, get children out of it.

2. Poor children lack basic skills (ex. Reading) so they continue to live in poverty.

Popular wisdom and sociological tradition have held a number of assumptions concerning poverty and inequality—assumptions upon which much federal policy-making has rested. First, the task of eliminating poverty is primarily a matter of helping children escape from it, for once people escape from poverty, they do not fall back into it (the belief that middle-class children rarely end up poor). Second, the basic reason poor children fail to escape from poverty is that they cannot read, write, calculate, or articulate, and lacking these skills, they cannot get or keep well-paying jobs.

Table from Simpson, Michele L., & Nist, Sherrie L. (1990. October). Textbook annotation: An effective and efficient study strategy for college students. *Journal of Reading* 34(2): 122–129. Reprinted with permission of the International Reading Association.Text excerpted from Zarden (1975). Poverty and inequality in America. In *Sociology.* New York: Ronald Press, pp. 215–217.

- ***Organize information.*** Sometimes your textbooks do not do a good job of organizing information. Through annotation, you can reorganize the material in a way that is meaningful for you. And that will make it easier for you to remember what you have read and to prepare for exams.
- ***Identify key concepts.*** Annotation also helps you tell the difference between major concepts and supporting ideas. Although (for most courses) you will have to know something about both major concepts and supporting details, by determining what is really important, you will know how to focus your studying.
- ***Monitor your learning.*** Annotation helps you determine what you do and do not know. Because you annotate in your own words, it helps you monitor your comprehension because you will be able to write the information in your own words only when you really understand what you are reading.

How Do You Annotate?

When you annotate, you have to read first, then annotate. Read one section at a time, think about it, and then write. You should also think about how your reading fits in with the concepts that the professor has been stressing in class. To help you decide what is important to mark, read a section and then think about what would be important information to remember if you were going to teach that section to someone else. Ask yourself, How would I summarize it for a friend? That is the information you should select to annotate. Sometimes students try to read and annotate at the same time, but they end up writing too much or too little because it's impossible to know what information is important or how it fits together until they have read at least a few paragraphs. Some textbooks make sections very clear by using a lot of headings and subheadings, but if you have a book that does not have clearly defined sections, read at least three or four paragraphs before stopping to annotate. Another alternative is to keep reading until the text seems to move to a new topic.

Remember, you want to put the information into your own words when you annotate. Don't copy directly from the book, unless you are annotating something that must be learned exactly as it is stated in the book. For example, a chemistry or statistics formula should be annotated verbatim. When you are annotating definitions, you will want to simply paraphrase the author's words so that you don't change the meaning of the definition. Otherwise, put all information into your own words. (See Figure 13.2 for examples of the difference between paraphrasing and writing in your own words.) This is a good way of knowing that you understand what you are annotating. If you don't understand the material you are reading, you won't be able to write it in your own words. So if you find that you cannot put the information into your own words because you don't fully understand the material, you should note that section and ask a friend or the professor about it. Don't just skip over it because that concept may turn out to be an important one.

What Type of Information Should You Annotate?

In Chapter 11, you were introduced to the concept of annotation with lecture notes. Annotating your textbooks is similar because you are isolating the information you need to learn. Regardless of the content area, you should always look for some specific kinds of information whenever you annotate your texts:

- ***Definitions*** are important to look for—especially content-specific terms and concepts. Content-specific terms are words you find in that particular subject. For example, *syllogistic reasoning* (p. 356) is a

FIGURE 13.2 *Difference between Paraphrasing and Writing in Your Own Words*

	Your text states ...	Your annotations ...
Paraphrasing	**Concepts** are mental categories for objects, events, experiences, or ideas that are similar to one another in one or more respects.	*Concepts—mental categories for objects or experiences that are similar to one another.*
Writing in your own words	Prototypes emerge from our experience with the external world, and new items that might potentially fit within their category are then compared with them. The more attributes new items share with an existing prototype, the more likely they are to be included within the concept.	*Prototypes—a system for organizing concepts into categories based on similar traits. Items with more traits in common are more likely to be included.*

content-specific term in the "Cognition" passage in Appendix A. However, you wouldn't need to annotate general vocabulary words such as *attribute,* also in the "Cognition" excerpt. If you didn't know the meaning of attribute, you should look it up in a dictionary, but you would not want to annotate the definition.

- ***Examples*** are also important to annotate because they depict specific instances, theories, experiments, cases, etc. In fact, examples in your texts often show up on your tests, so it is crucial to note them. You also should include personal examples when you can because relating the information to what you already know will help you better remember the information. If something you read reminds you of a personal experience, then note that experience in the margin. Or if the text does not provide an example but you think of one that helps you, add that information to your annotations.
- ***Predicted test questions*** are also an important consideration when you are annotating. When you read, try to predict some likely test questions about the material. Try to ask higher-level questions as well as questions that connect your reading to the class lecture. Higher-level questions are those that require more than just memorization of facts; they require application of the concept. For example, a higher-level question over the text in Figure 13.1 might be, How can the incorrect assumptions about poverty lead to inadequate federal policy regarding the elimination of poverty?

- ***People, dates, places, and events*** are important in certain types of courses like history, social science, and political science, but this should not be the only type of information you annotate. In college, you will rarely be asked to memorize dates because the professors assume that you learned the dates in your high school classes. Instead, the types of questions you will be asked will require you to think at a higher level about the significance of the names, dates, and events. The only reason you annotate this type of information is to get a chronology of events. So when you annotate names, dates, or events, be sure that you are thinking about their significance and how they fit into the larger context of the material.
- ***Numbered lists or characteristics*** contained in your text should also be annotated. If your text states that "there are 3 major causes of" or reasons for or factors that contribute to a certain idea, annotate these by numbering them in the margin. In this way, you are connecting and learning those ideas together. For example, in the "Cognition" excerpt, the text presents five basic sources of error in reasoning (p. 356). Even though the text heading does not point out that there are five, you should be aware of and note this list of reasons.
- ***Relationships between concepts,*** such as causes/effects or comparison/contrasts, are important to note. When you read your text, look for relationships between concepts, even if the text doesn't explicitly point out these relationships, because they will help you reorganize the information in a meaningful way. For example, in the "Cognition" passage, a comparison and contrast between formal and everyday reasoning is presented (p. 356). By noting this relationship, you are preparing yourself for questions about those topics.
- ***Graphs, charts, diagrams,*** and other graphical sources of information are important to annotate because they often contain information that is not anywhere else in the text. In addition, graphs and diagrams can also provide good examples of the concepts discussed in the text.

(One final helpful hint: It is best for you to read an entire section before annotating. In this way, you will avoid copying directly from the text or annotating too much or too little information.)

13.2 SOMETHING TO WRITE ABOUT

Practice annotating the excerpt titled "Cognition: Thinking, Deciding, Communicating" in Appendix A of this text. Remember to annotate definitions, examples, and other significant information. Compare your annotations with one of your classmates.

Predict at least two exam questions about the material contained in the passage:

___

___

___

___

Studying Your Annotations

Studying your annotations is an excellent way to test yourself on the material to find out what you know and what you still need to learn. To use your annotations to help you study, cover up the text with your hand or a piece of notebook paper. Read over your annotations a few times to be sure that you understand the concepts. You should probably try to review a little bit each day so that when you are ready to study for the test, you already know most of the information. You may want to review your annotations each time you sit down to read.

After you are sure that you understand the material and that your annotations are complete, look at the major points in your annotations and then look away from the text. Try to say the information to yourself without looking at the page. You should be able to talk about each topic that is annotated as well as give explanations, examples, and details. If you find there is a section you don't know, then you should reread your annotations. If you still don't understand, then reread that section in the text, ask a friend, refer to your lecture notes, or ask your professor.

13.3 SOMETHING TO THINK ABOUT AND DISCUSS

- Read over your annotations for the "Cognition" excerpt. If you were able to use only these annotations to prepare for an exam over the material, would they be sufficient? Why or why not? Compare and contrast your annotations with those of a classmate.

- Practice the studying technique described above using your annotations of the "Cognition" excerpt. Remember to read over your annotations, then cover up the text and try to say the information to yourself. You also might want to use your annotations to pose questions to a classmate.

Some Common Concerns about Annotation

Annotation is a strategy that many students find is one of the best ways to help them focus on their reading. However, many students have concerns and questions about their annotations:

- ***How do you know what is important to mark?*** Deciding what is important to annotate is sometimes tricky. You want to look for what is being stressed in class and what the text focuses on. You can often tell what is important by looking at the headings and subheadings in your book. You will probably find that the more you annotate in a textbook, the more familiar you will be with how the text is written and what the professor stresses in class. So even if you are having trouble organizing the information right now, eventually you should feel more confidant about it.
- ***Doesn't this take a lot of time?*** Yes. In the beginning, annotation does take more time than reading alone—maybe even twice as long. However, if you have annotated properly, you have already taken a big

step toward preparing for exams. When you annotate, you have pulled out all of the information you will need to study, so you should never have to reread the chapter unless you need some clarification of a specific concept. Most students say that they find the extra time spent annotating is worth it when they go back to study because they are sure they understand the material.

- ***How can you be sure that you are annotating the information that will be on the exam?*** By listening to class lectures and discussion, you should be able to determine most of the important information. However, the goal of annotation is to learn the concepts that are presented in the text, not to guess exactly what will be on the exam. If you understand all of the information in the text, you will be prepared for almost any exam question on that topic.

13.4

SOMETHING TO THINK AND WRITE ABOUT

Thinking Critically

1. *List three benefits you see to using annotation:*
   - ______________________________
   - ______________________________
   - ______________________________
2. *List three concerns you have about using annotation:*
   - ______________________________
   - ______________________________
   - ______________________________
3. *Discuss your responses in pairs.*

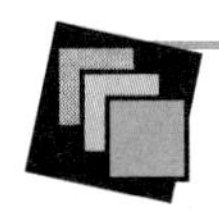

Annotation Pitfalls

Simpson and Nist (1990) discuss three types of problems students sometimes experience when they are learning to annotate. In order to help you avoid these pitfalls and to assess your own annotations, we will outline these pitfalls and offer some suggestions for overcoming them (see Figure 13.3).

The first pitfall students often encounter is called the "medieval monk" syndrome. This happens when a student annotates by copying the text almost word for word. Sometimes students fall into this trap because they are trying to memorize information instead of really learning it. But college professors rarely quote directly from texts on their exams, so you may feel that the exam questions are tricky or confusing if you tried to only memorize the information.

Students who write too much in the margins may be afraid they will leave out something important if they try to paraphrase. However, with practice, you should be able to tell the difference between key ideas and details that can be left behind. If you find yourself experiencing the medieval monk syndrome and your annotations are really just copying the author's words, preview the text before you read to familiarize yourself with what is going to be included in the chapter. Read one section at a time before you annotate to determine what is important to mark. After reading each section, think about what would be important information to tell someone about the material you just read. That should be the information you annotate. Check to be sure you are annotating in your own words by stopping after each section to read over your annotations.

The second major pitfall students often come across, the opposite of the medieval monk syndrome, is called the "nothin' here" syndrome. Here students do not annotate very much at all. They may just have random words annotated, or may just copy the heading or subheading in the margin. Often, these students will annotate bold-faced words but little else. This is a problem because if there is not enough information annotated in the margins, it is difficult to use the annotations to study.

Sometimes students don't annotate enough because they feel that the strategy takes too much time. If this is a concern you have, try annotation with one course this term. You will probably find that it actually *saves* you time when you go to study because you have already thought about the information and organized it in some way.

Occasionally, students do not annotate enough because the margins in the text are very small. If this is a problem for you, invest in some

FIGURE 13.3 *Annotation Examples: Pitfalls and Models*

Medieval Monk	Nothin' Here Syndrome	Rest of the Story	Model Annotations	Passage
Assumptions concerning poverty and inequality on which federal policy-making has rested *1. the task of eliminating poverty is primarily a matter of helping children to escape from it* *2. the basic reason poor children fail to escape from poverty is that they cannot read, write, calculate, or articulate*	*Once people escape poverty they do not fall back* *Middle-class children rarely end up poor* *The poor lack basic skills* *The poor cannot get or keep well-paying jobs*	*Why we have poverty —the assumptions* *Where?* *Who?*	*Incorrect assumptions about poverty* *1. to get rid of poverty, get children out of it.* *2. Poor children lack basic skills (ex. Reading) so they continue to live in poverty.*	Popular wisdom and sociological tradition have held a number of assumptions concerning poverty and inequality—assumptions upon which much federal policy-making has rested. First, the task of eliminating poverty is primarily a matter of helping children escape from it, for once people escape from poverty, they do not fall back into it (the belief that middle-class children rarely end up poor). Second, the basic reason poor children fail to escape from poverty is that they cannot read, write, calculate, or articulate, and lacking these skills, they cannot get or keep well-paying jobs.

Table from Simpson, Michele L., & Nist, Sherrie L. (1990. October). Textbook annotation: An effective and efficient study strategy for college students. *Journal of Reading* 34(2): 122–129. Reprinted with permission of the International Reading Association.Text excerpted from Zarden (1975). Poverty and inequality in America. In *Sociology.* New York: Ronald Press, pp. 215–217.

adhesive notes to stick in the margins to give you more room. One final reason students don't annotate enough may be due to laziness or procrastination. In college, you probably have found that you barely have enough time to get through the reading one time, so you surely won't have time to reread it. So even though annotation appears to take a lot more effort, you may find that it is worth it.

The third major pitfall is called the "rest of the story" syndrome in which students may identify the key topics but do not annotate complete ideas. Often students only partially mark ideas to save time, but if they do not pull out entire ideas, they will have trouble using their annotations to help them study. This is especially a problem in courses that give cumulative finals. You may be tested over information that you annotated three months ago. If you did not annotate in enough detail, you may have to resort to rereading just to make sense of the information. So in the long run, you are actually spending more time trying to relearn the material than if you had taken the time to make good annotations in the first place.

Sometimes students try to annotate only the information they don't know. In other words, when they come across a topic that they know a little bit about, they will only annotate the new information not the material they already knew. However, one of the benefits of annotation is that it helps you connect new ideas with prior knowledge, which helps you remember the new information. A student who doesn't link the information together will be less likely to remember it on an exam. To overcome this pitfall, write everything you think you will need to remember, even if this information seems commonsense now. You should also read over your annotations to be sure they are complete and make sense. One way to know whether they are complete is to ask yourself—and be honest about this—If I were allowed to use only my annotations to prepare for an exam over the material, would I be able to pass?

Practicing annotating your text will help you become better at locating the key information and pulling out complete ideas. By taking the time to create good-quality annotations, you will save yourself time when you go to study the information. However, doing a job halfway will not be much help come exam time.

13.5 SELF-ASSESSMENT

Assess your annotations for the "Cognition" excerpt in Appendix A by answering the following questions:

YES	NO	
☐	☐	Are my annotations complete?
☐	☐	Did I annotate all the major ideas?
☐	☐	Did I include examples presented in the text?
☐	☐	Did I include personal examples/experiences?
☐	☐	Did I paraphrase the information?
☐	☐	Did I annotate in my own words?
☐	☐	Did I annotate all key definitions?
☐	☐	Did I annotate tables, graphs, etc.?
☐	☐	Did I annotate relationships between ideas?
☐	☐	Did I annotate lists or characteristics?
☐	☐	Are my annotations a useful study aid?

REAL COLLEGE: *Hillary's Highlighter*

Read the following scenario and then respond to the questions based on what you learned in this chapter.

Hillary is a returning student. After twenty years, she has decided to quit her job and return to school full-time. Because she wants to get off to a good start, she bought herself all the supplies she thought she would need—pencils, notebooks, pens, and especially highlighters. Hillary does not see how she could study without her highlighter. Her daughter jokes that most of the pages in her books are now bright yellow!

For Hillary's sociology class this term, she must read her textbook and the local newspaper. When she reads the text, she tries to highlight everything that seems important. One problem is that it *all* seems important so she sometimes ends up highlighting whole pages. There are so many details in the textbook that she is not sure what the professor will focus on for the exam. She is especially careful to note every name and date discussed in the book, but she doesn't spend a lot of time reading the newspaper because the professor barely mentions the newspaper in class. Basically she just skims the articles for the facts. Hillary is surprised when she does not do well on the first essay exam even though she studied for hours. The exam seemed to focus on relating the sociology topics to the newspaper articles. She now knows that she needs a new approach to learning because when she studies, she finds that she rereads almost every chapter because it was all highlighted. She hardly has time to read all of her text once, much less twice.

Using what you know about annotations, give Hillary advice on switching from highlighting to annotation and some insights into how she should approach annotating her sociology readings.

____

____

____

____

____

____

____

____

____

FOLLOW-UP ACTIVITIES

1. Annotate the excerpt entitled "Technologies of Mass-Production and Destruction" in Appendix C. How does the information you need to annotate differ from the information you annotated in the "Cognition" excerpt?
2. Annotate the text for one of your classes for one week. Remember to annotate in your own words and to mark all of the important information contained in the text.
3. Reflect on your learning of the annotated material. Do you remember the concepts in the chapters you annotated better than the concepts in other chapters? How do you feel the strategy will benefit you when you begin to study for your exam?

Networking

- Many colleges and universities offer advice for learning from text on their web pages. First, try to locate these resources at your own institution by looking at an Academic Assistance or Learning Center page. Then, seek out advice from Learning Centers at other institutions using the following key words: learning center, tutoring center, study strategies, study skills, and textbook reading.

Rehearsing after Reading

The Actor in You

Read this chapter to answer the following questions:

What are rehearsal strategies?

Why is it important to know a variety of rehearsal strategies?

When is it appropriate to use CARDS*? concept mapping? concept charting? questions/answers? time lines?*

Why should you be flexible and modify strategies?

STUDY TIP

Don't be a one-trick pony! Use different rehearsal strategies for different content areas.

What comes to mind when you hear the word *rehearsal?* If you have ever acted in a play or play a musical instrument, you probably thought about the word *practice.* Rehearsal, like practice, means doing something over and over again so that you can get better at it. You might rehearse your part in a play with a friend by saying your lines several times out loud. Right before the play, you would go to dress rehearsal, where you would put on the play under almost the same conditions as opening night. Or if you are in a band, you would practice or rehearse your part so that the music you had to play became almost automatic. Even though on the night of your performance the old expression "Practice makes perfect" may not have exactly been the case, the fact is that it was only through rehearsal that you got better at the task at hand.

What is rehearsal? Why does rehearsal pay off? What are some of the rehearsal strategies that will help you learn concepts efficiently and effectively? It is to these questions that this chapter will speak.

Rehearsal

What Is Rehearsal?

Just as actors rehearse their lines, so students must rehearse what they want to learn. By rehearsal we mean engaging in activities, either written or spoken, that will help you learn information in a variety of courses. You might say the information out loud to a classmate, write down the information in an organized fashion, repeat the information to yourself "in your head," or even record information on a tape recorder and listen to it several times. There are numerous ways you can go about rehearsing, which we will present later in the chapter. What's important at this point is that you understand what rehearsal is and why it is important to your academic success.

Think back to what we said in Chapter 1 about the differences between high school and college. We suggested that it would probably be difficult to be successful in college if all you did was read the text without active involvement and critical thinking. Rehearsal strategies force you to be active because you must think as you organize the concepts that your professor expects you to learn. In the two previous chapters, we stressed the importance of engaging your mind even before you begin to read by previewing. This warm-up activity is getting the mind ready for mental exercise. Then you're ready to actively read and annotate. You're putting the information in your own words and beginning to see how the concepts relate. If everything goes well, you understand what you have read. Well ... sort of. You have comprehended it, but you just can't remember all of it. This is where the next step—rehearsal—enters the picture. Rehearsal helps you to actually learn and remember the material. You organize the information from your text and lectures, make it meaningful in some way, and then write it and say it to yourself. If you rehearse properly, you will be able to retrieve or have access to the information at exam time.

Why Is Rehearsal Important?

We already touched on why rehearsal is important, but let's think about this a little more by reviewing how memory works. Although no one really knows for sure exactly how memory works, there are two major theories. The first theory, called the Information Processing theory, says that there are actually three types of memory—sensory memory (SM), short-term memory (STM), and long-term memory (LTM). Each memory type serves a somewhat different purpose. SM screens information entering your mind, STM enables you to remember something for only a brief period of time (perhaps thirty seconds to a minute), and LTM stores things for an indefinite period of time. In fact, some researchers believe that once something is in LTM, it is stored permanently, even if you can't retrieve or get at the information.

The second theory, and the one that is currently the more popular of the two, is called the Levels of Processing theory. According to this theory, there aren't exactly three types of memory. Rather, the degree to which you remember something depends on the level at which you process the information. For example, if you looked up a number in the phone book, read the number, closed the phone book, walked to the phone, and could not remember the last two digits by the time you got to the phone, you would have processed the number at a "shallow" level. In other words, it was processed at a level at which you didn't remember the information very well. On the other hand, if you looked up the number, repeated it several times to yourself, related it to something familiar to you (maybe the first three digits of the number are your birthday—August 16, or 816), and then closed the phone book and dialed the number, you would be processing the information at a "deep" level. The theory purports that processing information deeply enables you to remember it.

It matters little which theory you believe more accurately reflects how memory actually works. What does matter, however, is that in order to get information into LTM or to process it deeply, you must rehearse in some way. Just reading over the material is not enough. At the rehearsal stage of learning, it's time to further organize by pulling out key ideas and supporting concepts and to personalize or *elaborate* the ideas to the point where you have not just memorized: You have conceptualized and you truly understand.

Written or Verbal Rehearsal Strategies?

Now that you have an idea of what rehearsal is and why it's important to use rehearsal strategies, let's think about two different types of rehearsal strategies: written strategies and verbal strategies. When you use written strategies, you write down the important information in an organized fashion. The way you organize this information depends on the task your professor expects from you (see chapter 10), the materials with which you are interacting (which will be discussed in Part V), and the particular way that you learn best. In other words, because the tasks and materials vary from course to course, the written strategies that work well for you in biology will probably be very different than those that work for you in political science. Likewise, what works well for you may not work for the person sitting next to you. Specific written strategies, which we will present and discuss in detail in the next section, include:

- CARDS (an acronym for **C**ognitive **A**ctivities for **R**ehearsing **D**ifficult **S**ubjects)
- Concept maps
- Concept charts
- Questions/answers
- Time lines

Verbal strategies are those rehearsal strategies that require "talking" rather than writing. They work best for students who are more auditory learners, meaning those who learn better through hearing information rather than by reading it or writing it. You can use verbal strategies in two ways. You can say the information to yourself or out loud and then check to see whether you are correct, or you can say the information to someone else and have her check your accuracy. Like written strategies, the verbal strategies you select depend on all the other factors that impact learning—your characteristics, the task, and the text—although we believe that talk-throughs seem to benefit all students. (See *Research Into Practice* later in this chapter.) The specific verbal rehearsal strategies that will be presented later in the chapter are:

- Reciprocal questioning
- Talk-throughs

It is important to understand that there is no one best strategy, either written or verbal. The best rehearsal strategy is the one that works for you in a particular situation. And the best students know and appropriately use a variety of strategies, both written and verbal.

Components of Good Rehearsal Strategies

When you were in high school, you may have used rehearsal strategies without even knowing it. You may have made outlines after you read your text or put vocabulary words or foreign language terms on index cards. You may have had a family member or friend ask you questions before a test. All of these are examples of rehearsal strategies, some of which are better than others.

The most important element of all good rehearsal strategies is that they allow for self-testing. When you self-test, you rehearse without actually looking at the answer. For example, if you need to learn the characteristics of short-term and long-term memory for a psychology exam, you would say those characteristics to yourself or out loud, and then immediately check your rehearsal strategy to see whether you are correct. This process differs greatly from looking over or reading through information and having no real idea of whether or not you know the material. In other words, good rehearsal strategies allow you to monitor what you know and allow for the element of self-testing. Going back to the example of using either outlines or index cards to learn information, you will find that an outline is not a particularly good rehearsal strategy; index cards, if completed in the right way, are because index cards help you test yourself. This will be explained further on page 225.

A second component of good rehearsal strategies is that they include complete and precise information. In fact, when you write or say information that is incomplete or inaccurate, it is just about as valuable as doing nothing. If you have ever taken a test, particularly a multiple-choice test, and the information has seemed familiar to you yet you had a difficult time selecting the correct answer, you probably didn't rehearse completely and precisely. Complete and precise rehearsal requires you to say or write all the information related to an important concept and to see connections and relationships between ideas.

A third component of good rehearsal strategies is clear organization. Just sitting down and writing information on a piece of paper or saying everything you know about a concept out loud as it pops into your head will not maximize your test performance. Rather, your strategy has to have some structure so that you isolate the information in a way that makes sense and helps you remember it.

Your brain files information very much like a computer. That is, there is a logic in the way concepts are stored. Likewise, your rehearsal strategies need to have a logical flow as well. Look at the difference between the information written on the two concept cards in Figure 14.1. Both are focused on the same term, *reticular formation,* taken from "The Human Nervous System" excerpt in Appendix B. Note that in card A, the information is organized around the properties of reticular formation, whereas in card B, the information is simply written down in unorganized phrases. In addition, some of those phrases on card B would be difficult to interpret at a future study date, and some of what is written is so imprecise that you would probably learn it incorrectly.

Finally, good rehearsal strategies synthesize information by helping you state the ideas in your own words. Trying to memorize material straight from the text or lecture in someone else's words will cause problems at test time when the exam questions are written in yet another voice. Few professors take information from their text or lectures verbatim. Rather, they paraphrase and synthesize concepts—professors put them in their own words—and expect you to do the same. After a test, if you find yourself thinking things such as "That test was tricky," or "The professor never talked about the information that way in class," you probably aren't trying to put the information in your own words as you're studying.

FIGURE 14.1 *Two Concept Cards for the Term* reticular formation.

Card A

- neurons extend fr. central medulla—pons—midbrain—lower forebrain
- receives into fr. all senses & parts of body & most areas of brain

ROLE:

- plays role in sleep, arousal, emotion, muscle tone & reflexes
- filters sensory info. & forwards impt. info. on for processing

EX: could awaken a sleeper to a noise of someone in house but not to a train

Card B

midbrain—a relay center for senses—select info. for processing

made of neurons that run through whole body

helps you sleep and controls emotions

14.1 MONITORING YOUR LEARNING

Think about yourself as a learner and the kinds of rehearsal strategies you currently use. Then answer the following questions. Answering these questions will help you see whether your current rehearsal strategies are helping you be an active learner.

1. *In the past, how have you rehearsed information?*

___

___

___

2. *Do the rehearsal strategies you currently use have the characteristics of good rehearsal strategies outlined above? What might you do to improve the quality of your rehearsal strategies?*

____

____

____

3. *Which theory of memory seems more plausible to you? Why?*

____

____

____

4. *From what you have read about rehearsal so far, what role do you think memory plays in rehearsing?*

____

____

____

We have discussed the general notion of rehearsal strategies as well as the general characteristics of good rehearsal strategies. Now we will present some specific strategies. Some can be used in a variety of learning situations, and others are very task-specific. We discuss both written and verbal strategies.

Written Rehearsal Strategies

CARDS—Cognitive Aids for Rehearsing Difficult Subjects

Of all the rehearsal strategies we will present in this chapter, you are probably most familiar with CARDS: Cognitive Aids for Rehearsing Difficult Subjects. CARDS is a strategy that uses 3 x 5 index cards. As shown in Figure 14.2, you write the key concept that you want to learn on the front of the card. Write another word or phrase, called an organizing term, in the top right-hand corner. The organizing term helps you group like concepts together. For example, look again at the CARDS for *concepts* in Figure 14.2 and note that the organizing term is *basic elements of thought.* This suggests that *concepts* is only one of the basic elements of thought and that it is linked to other ideas. Also write the source of the

FIGURE 14.2 *An Example of CARDS.*

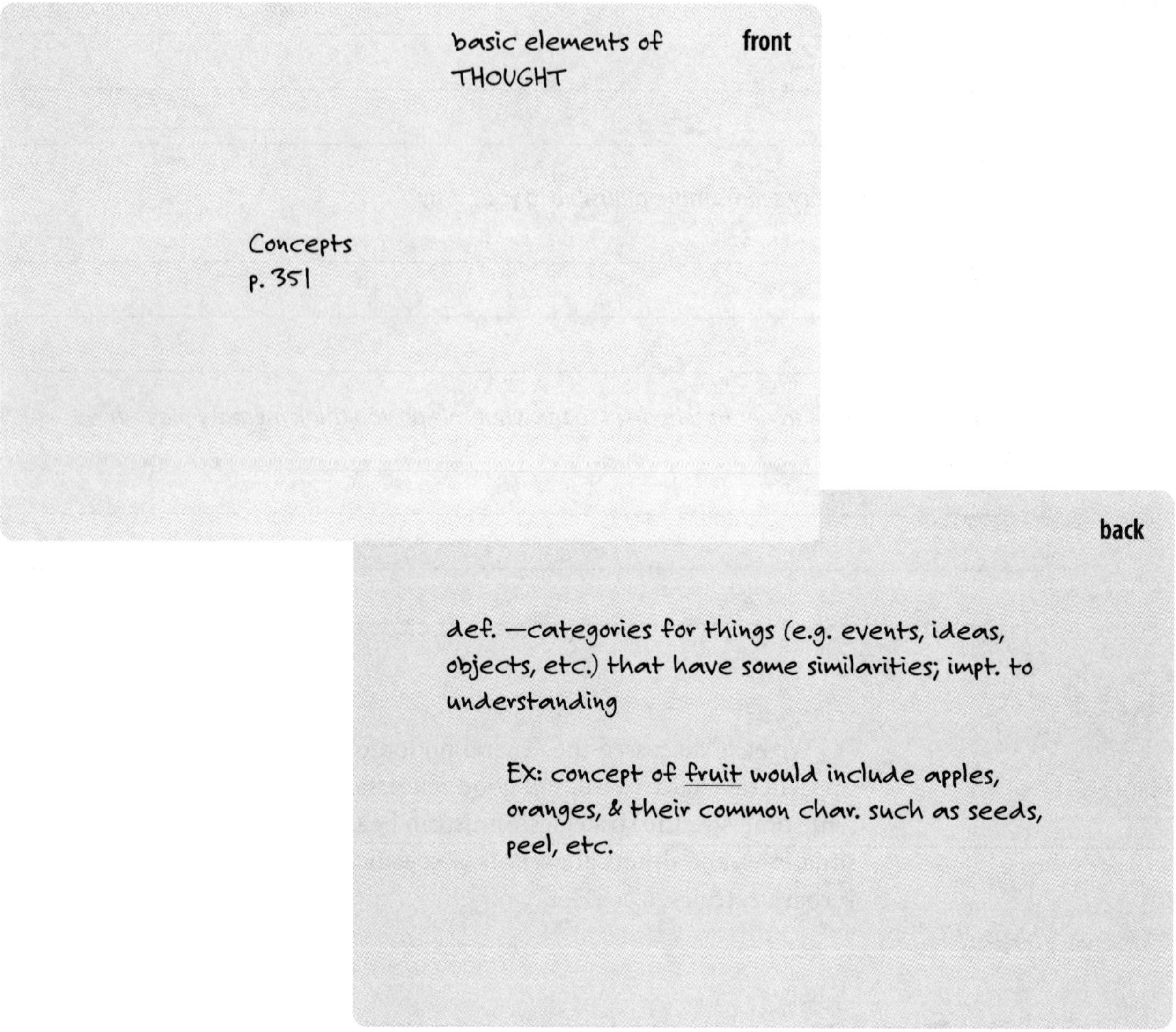

basic elements of THOUGHT — front

Concepts
p. 351

back

def. —categories for things (e.g. events, ideas, objects, etc.) that have some similarities; impt. to understanding

EX: concept of fruit would include apples, oranges, & their common char. such as seeds, peel, etc.

information—the text page or date of the lecture, documentary notes, and so forth—on the front of the card.

Look at Figure 14.2 once again, this time concentrating on what is written on the back of the CARDS. Here you write all of the material you want to learn about this particular concept in an organized fashion *and* in your own words. Notice that this CARDS has not only a definition of *concept* but also an example. If you were enrolled in a course that required just memorization of the definition, you would simply need to write the definition. However, most college professors expect you to go beyond memorization, so you would want to include examples, links to other concepts, and a general synthesis of the key points you need to remember about the concept.

CARDS has a couple of major advantages over other rehearsal strategies. First, index cards can be carried around easily. You can put a rubber band around the cards, stick them in your backpack or shirt pocket, and then easily pull them out when you have a few minutes to rehearse. Those few minutes while you are waiting for the bus, standing in line at the bookstore, or quickly eating lunch in the cafeteria can be small pockets of time in which you can rehearse information rather than waste time. When you rehearse ten minutes here or fifteen minutes there, the additional study time adds up quickly.

Second, the CARDS strategy is versatile and can be used in a variety of learning situations. Index cards work well in classes where you have to learn numerous terms, and if done correctly, you can even use your cards to see connections between ideas. For example, suppose you were in a biology course and you were reading a chapter on meiosis. Many terms go with this overriding concept. Rather than making just one card with a weak definition of meiosis, you would use meiosis as the organizing term and write it in the upper right-hand corner of all the cards relating to meiosis. Then you would clip all of your meiosis cards together so that you could see how the different terms relating to meiosis connect.

Although primarily used for courses in which you have to learn many new terms, the CARDS strategy is also beneficial in other situations. It works well for learning vocabulary, rules, conjugations, and so forth in foreign languages. Likewise, many students like to use index cards in mathematics, statistics, or chemistry—courses in which they have to learn and then apply formulas.

You have read and annotated your text, you have made a good set of CARDS, and you have an exam on the material at the end of the week. How do you go about studying your CARDS? The first thing you do is organize them. Use the organizing term in the upper right-hand corner to group all like terms together. You can hold the index cards together with a paperclip or rubber band so that you don't have to reorganize them every time you study. Next, start with one particular organizing term. Read the key concept on the front of the first card, flip it over to the back, and read the information through a couple of times. Flip the card back over to the front and see how much of the information you can say to yourself without actually looking at it. Turn the card to the back again, and see how much you remembered. Do that with each concept. Then return to the organizing term. Think about how all of the concepts you just learned are related not only to the organizing term but also to each other.

As you learn each set of concepts, separate out what you have learned and what you need to spend more time on. Review your CARDS each day, using those small pockets of time. Spend larger time slots interacting with the concepts that are giving you the most trouble. After you feel that you know most of the material on your CARDS, review with a classmate. (See the section on *Reciprocal Questioning* later in the chapter.) Have your classmate ask you the term, and then check to see how much of the material you are able to say accurately and precisely. Then exchange roles. Be sure each of you can clearly discuss how the smaller concepts relate to larger ones and how the larger concepts relate to each other.

SOMETHING TO THINK AND WRITE ABOUT

Thinking Critically

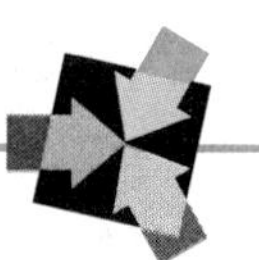

1. Select five other terms from the "Cognition" excerpt in Appendix A and make CARDS for each one. Then with a partner, evaluate your CARDS for strengths and weaknesses. As you make your CARDS, you should include information that would help you study for a test in which you might be asked to apply and synthesize information.

2. For a course that you are currently taking, try making a set of CARDS for a chapter that you need to study for an exam. Don't forget to use the organizing term to help you group like concepts together.

Concept Maps and Charts

As shown in Figures 14.3 through 14.7, concept maps and charts are visual representations of information, and thus, these strategies are very useful for students who tend to learn visually. On concept maps, the material is organized in such a way that it is easy to see the major concept that is being mapped as well as related concepts and even how everything is related. Look carefully at the map in Figure 14.3. This map came from the text excerpt titled "The Human Nervous System" located in Appendix B. From the map, you can easily tell that the human nervous system has two major parts—the central nervous system and the peripheral nervous system. This particular map provides a big picture of what this section of text is all about and enables you to see how the different parts of the nervous system are related, but other maps, such as the one in Figure 14.4, focus in detail on one particular concept.

Concept mapping works well when it is important to see the relationship between complex concepts, and it works particularly well in the sciences, where many ideas tend to be related and interact. For example, mapping is a good way to see the relationship between hormones of the

FIGURE 14.3 *Concept Map*

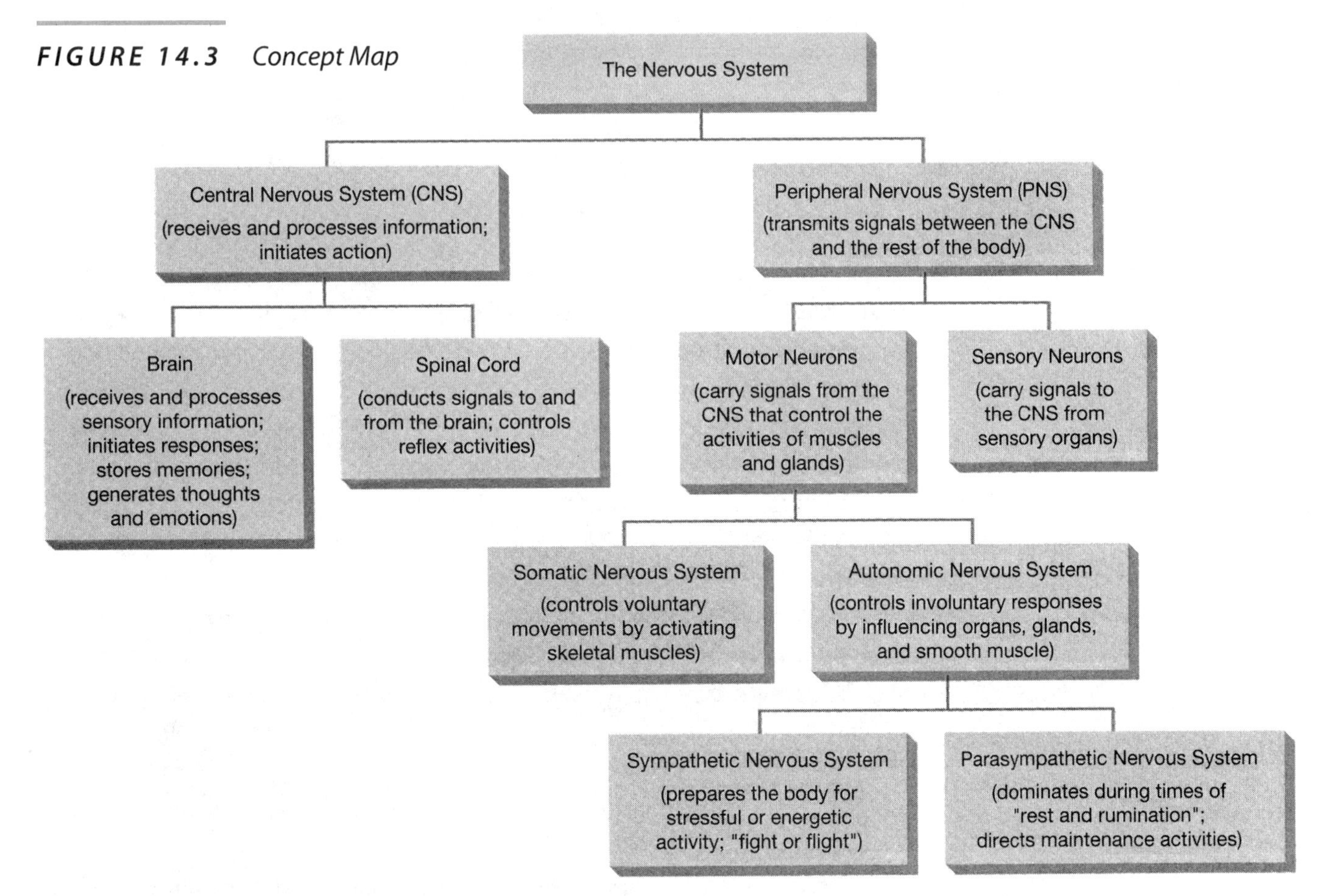

FIGURE 14.4 *An Example of a Detailed Concept Map of the Central Nervous System*

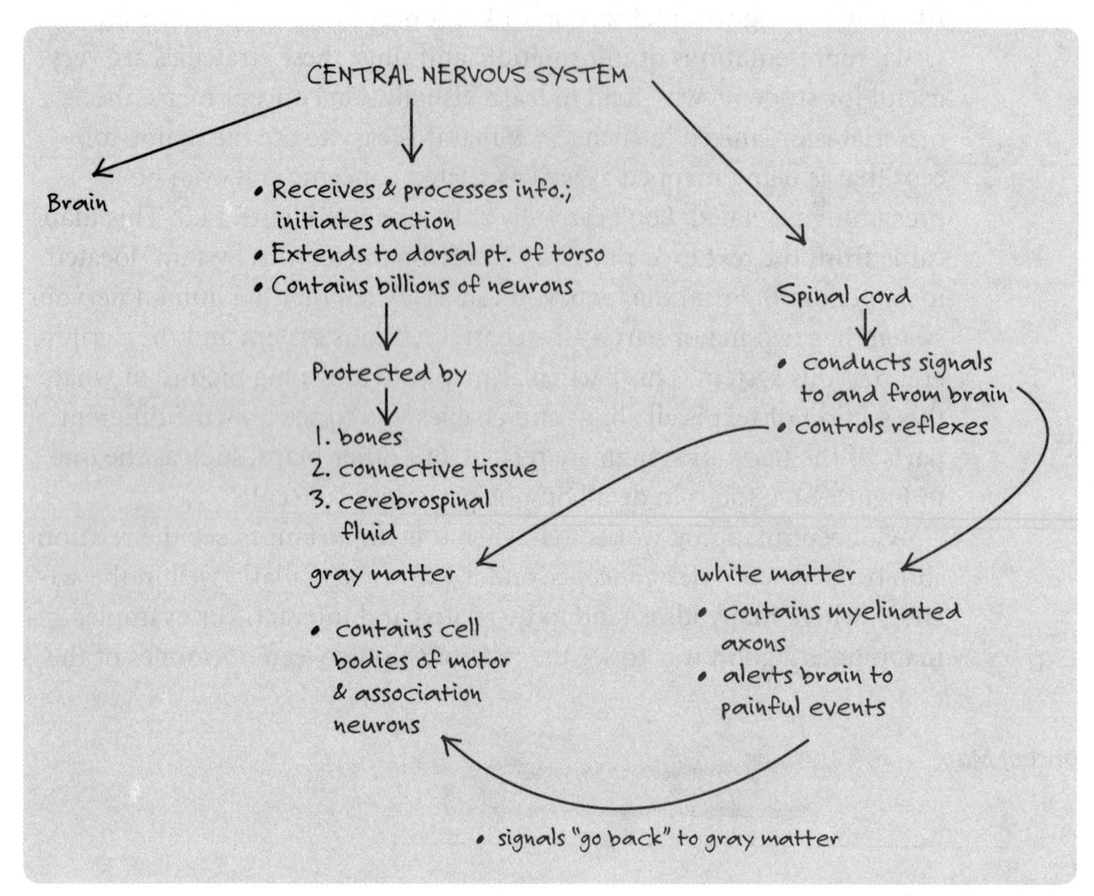

endocrine system or the different stages of meiosis and mitosis. Mapping is also a useful strategy for students who like to personalize strategies because there is no right or wrong way to map. The important thing is that the way ideas are linked together be clearly shown in your concept map. Figures 14.5, 14.6, and 14.7 show three ways you might construct a map containing information about the functions of the right and left hemispheres of the brain. Note that each is a bit different yet shows the functions of each hemisphere of the brain in an organized fashion.

When you study your map, rehearse one concept at a time. Then cover up everything except the main concept, and begin to talk the information through. Say the related material, and then check to see how accurate you are. Also be sure to learn how the concepts are related to each other since that is the major strength of mapping. Rather than viewing ideas one at a time, as is the case with CARDS, mapping enables you to understand how these ideas fit together.

Charting is similar to mapping but is useful in different kinds of situations. As Figures 14.8 and 14.9 show, charting helps you synthesize

FIGURE 14.5

Concept Map—Option 1

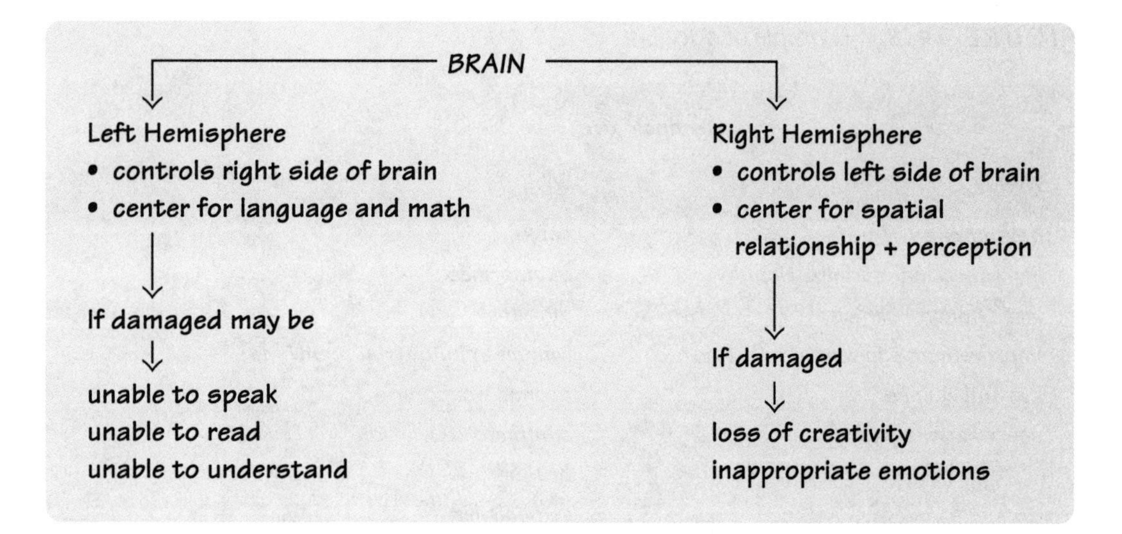

FIGURE 14.6

Concept Map—Option 2

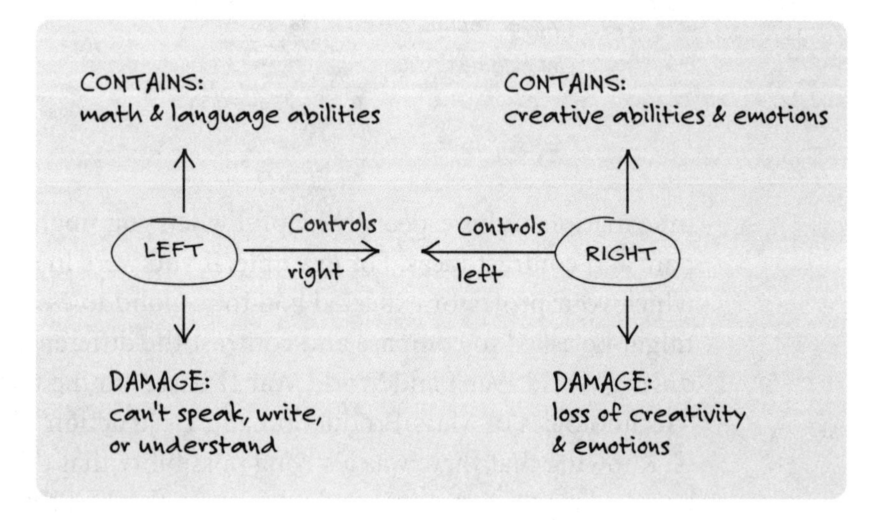

FIGURE 14.7

Concept Map—Option 3

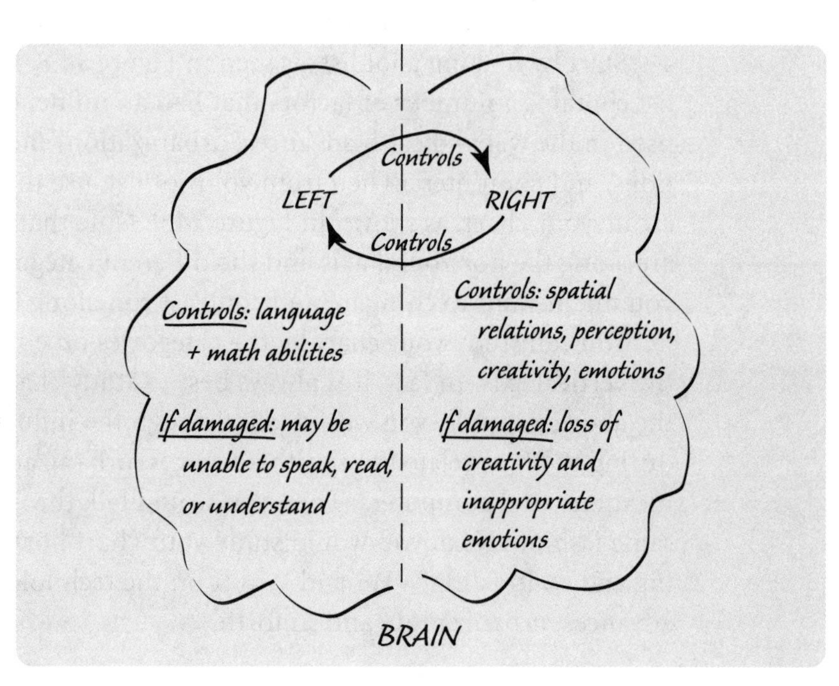

FIGURE 14.8 *Example of a Jot List*

Technologies

WWI	WWII
poison gas	tanks
increased industrialization	submarines
birth control clinics	aircraft
improvements in communication	women in industrial positions
assembly lines	atomic weapons
new weapons systems	commercial aviation
	drugs
	penicillin
	sulfa drugs
	bigger technological budgets
	jet engine

information and is especially helpful when you might be asked to compare and contrast ideas. For example, if you were in a history class in which your professor expected you to respond to essay questions, you might be asked to compare and contrast the differences in technology during World War I and World War II based on the text excerpt titled "Technologies of Mass-Production and Destruction" located in Appendix C. Knowing that there was a strong possibility that this question would be asked on the exam, you would want to think of several technology-related factors to use to compare and contrast the two wars.

Start by making a jot list, as seen in Figure 14.8. Notice that this jot list contains a number of factors that had an influence on the technology used in the wars—health advances, urbanization, energy, communications, and computers. Then from your jot list, use those categories to create your chart, as shown in Figure 14.9. Note that the two World Wars are along the horizontal axis and the different categories or factors that you might want to compare and contrast run along the vertical axis.

You can study your chart by the categories on either the horizontal or the vertical axis. In fact, it is always best to study charts both ways. Using the above example, you would talk through the influence of technology during WWI as related to health advances, urbanization, energy, communications, and computers. Then you would talk through WWII in the same fashion. Next, you would study your chart horizontally by comparing and contrasting WWI and WWII on the technologies of health advances, urbanization, and so forth.

FIGURE 14.9 *Example of a Chart*

	WWI	WWII
health advances		
urbanization		
energy		
communications		
computers		

14.3

SOMETHING TO THINK AND WRITE ABOUT

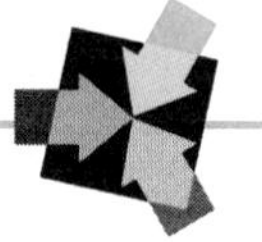

Thinking Critically

1. Select a section of text from "The Human Nervous System" excerpt and create a detailed map.
2. Using the "Technologies of Mass-Production and Destruction" excerpt in Appendix C, create a "big picture" map as a way of seeing how the text is organized.
3. For one of the courses in which you are currently enrolled, make a concept map or chart on a section of text that you have annotated.

Question/Answer Strategy

Think back to the study guides that your high school teachers may have given you. These study guides were intended to help focus your thinking for a test, usually by posing a series of questions. The premise was that if you could answer the questions on the study guide, you would be able to do well on the test. The question/answer strategy uses a similar premise, only you are the active learner who is creating both the questions and the answers. You think about the important information in the text and lectures, pose questions that cover the material, and then answer each of the questions you posed.

Let's first examine the format of these questions. If you look at Figure 14.10, you'll see that the format probably looks different than what your previous teachers may have used. Using the question/answer strategy, you write your question on the left-hand side of the paper, and your answer right across from it on the right-hand side. Note also that the right-hand space where you answer the question is wider and longer than the left side where you write your question. This format should give you a not-so-subtle clue that the questions you pose should require more than a one-word answer!

When you are posing your questions, be sure that you write higher-level as well as memory-level questions. By higher level, we mean that the questions either begin with words such as *why* or *how* or encourage synthesis of the information to be learned. You will certainly write memory-level questions as well. Such questions typically begin with words such as *who, what,* and *when.* Most importantly, the questions you write should reflect the kinds of information that your professor expects you to learn.

Look at the two examples of the question/answer strategy presented in Figure 14.10. The examples, which are some questions written for the text excerpt "Cognition" found in Appendix A, show you the difference

FIGURE 14.10 *Example of the Question/Answer Strategy*

1. Why would a "wet suit" not be considered a prototype for the concept "clothing"? (What is a prototype?)	*1. A prototype is defined as the best or clearest example of a natural concept. Thus for the concept "clothing," a prototype might be "shirt" or "coat"—pieces of clothing that you might be more likely to mention. Because "wet suit" would not be mentioned very frequently when asked about the concept of clothing, it would not be considered a prototype.*
2. How are concepts represented? (What is a concept?)	
3. How are propositions related to thinking? (What is a proposition?)	

between writing primarily memory-level questions and having a mix of both. If you know that your professor is going to give you multiple-choice exams that have numerous application and synthesis questions, you would want to write questions such as those that are numbered. If, on the other hand, your professor simply expects you to memorize information, the questions posed in parentheses may be sufficient for your rehearsal. Also note that the questions you write using the question/answer strategy are probably much more focused than those you predicted during the prereading stage when you were unfamiliar with the important information in the text chapter. This is why active learners understand what the task is, as outlined in Chapter 10. If you don't know the task, not only will you have difficulty in selecting a strategy, but you will also run into problems focusing on the right information to include in your strategy.

Another factor you should note about the answers is that—like the information that you include in other written strategies—they are complete and precise. It's fine to abbreviate and write in phrases, but your question/answer strategy isn't going to be very effective if you leave out important information or include information that is wrong. You should also be sure to put the material in your own words, whenever possible. Remember what we said in Chapter 13 when we discussed annotation: You can remember information better when you put it in your own words rather than trying to memorize everything in the author's or professor's words.

When you study your question/answer strategy, fold your paper back so that just your questions are showing. Ask yourself a question, or get your roommate, family member, or study partner to ask it. Then answer it by saying the information out loud. If you are asking yourself the question, check to see how much of the material you remembered correctly. If someone is asking you the questions, tell her to be sure you are answering fully and accurately. If your answer matches what you wrote, repeat the process with the next question. If your answer was incomplete or wrong, read the correct answer several times and try to say it again before moving on to the next question, or have your study partner read the correct answer to you. In addition, because the questions on the exam will most certainly be in random order, don't always begin with the first question you wrote and work your way through to the end. You can start with the last question, do every other question, or use some other pattern.

14.4

SOMETHING TO THINK AND WRITE ABOUT

Thinking Critically

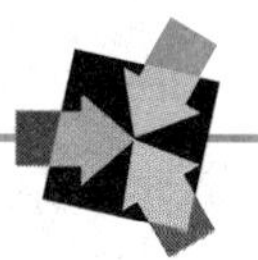

Write five additional higher-level questions that cover the "Cognition" excerpt in Appendix A. Answer your questions completely and precisely. Compare your questions with those of a classmate, and evaluate their strengths and weaknesses.

	QUESTIONS	ANSWERS
1.		
2.		
3.		
4.		
5.		

Construct a set of questions/answers for a chapter in a course in which you are currently enrolled. Be sure to ask some higher-level questions that begin with the words *how* and *why*.

Time Lines

You can use the strategies discussed above in a variety of studying situations with a little modification. Time lines, on the other hand, are appropriate in much more restricted situations. Basically, you can use time lines when it is important to know chronology—the order something happened over a period of time. For example, you might use time lines in a history course when it's important to know the chronology of the Vietnam conflict, in an art class when you need to be able to compare and contrast major movements in Asian art with those of Western art, or in a geology course when you're expected to know the evolution of the earth's crust over millions of years. Hence, you can use time lines in many different disciplines, but they do have a very specific function.

Time lines are flexible in that they can be constructed in a variety of ways. Look at the example in Figure 14.11. This is a time line combined

FIGURE 14.11 *Example of a Time Line Chart*

TIMELINE: EUROPE AND THE UNITED STATES 1900–1990s

	Political	Social	Cultural
1900	▮ Boer War (1899–1902) ▮ Germany enters arms race with Britain (1900) ▮ Labour Party founded in Britain (1900) ▮ Russo-Japanese War (1904–5) ▮ Old Age Pensions in Britain (1909)	▮ Guglielmo Marconi transmits signal across the Atlantic (1901) ▮ Wright brothers make first powered air flight (1903) ▮ Boy Scout movement founded (1907) ▮ Henry Ford begins assembly-line manufacture of motorcars (1909) ▮ Robert Peary reaches North Pole (1909)	▮ Jean-Paul Sartre (1905–81) ▮ Dmitri Shostakovitch (1906–57) ▮ Cubist painters (Pablo Picasso, Georges Braque) exhibit in Paris (1907–10) ▮ *Der Rosenkavalier* by Richard Strauss (1909–10)
1910	▮ World War I (1914–18) ▮ Treaty of Versailles (1919) ▮ Benito Mussolini founds Fascist Movement (1919)	▮ Roald Amundsen reaches South Pole (1911) ▮ *Titanic* sinks (1912) ▮ Igor Sikorsky builds first four-engined airplane (1913) ▮ Panama Canal opened (1914) ▮ Birth control clinic opens in New York (1916)	▮ Marcel Proust publishes *À la recherche du temps perdu* (1913–27) ▮ Igor Stravinksy's *Rite of Spring* performed (1913) ▮ Sigmund Freud's *Totem and Taboo* published (1913) ▮ Benjamin Britten (1913–76) ▮ Albert Camus (1913–60) ▮ Albert Einstein publishes *General Theory of Relativity* (1915) ▮ D.W. Griffith's *Birth of a Nation* (1915) ▮ Dadaism founded (1915)
1920	▮ League of Nations meets (1920) ▮ Adolf Hitler founds National Socialist (Nazi) Party (1923) ▮ Locarno Conference (1925) ▮ Germany becomes member of League of Nations (1926) ▮ Kellogg-Briand Pact (1928)	▮ General strike in Britain (1926) ▮ Alexander Fleming discovers penicillin (1928) ▮ US stock market collapses (1929), leading to worldwide recession	▮ John Logie Baird invents television (1925) ▮ *The Jazz Singer*, first talking picture (1927) ▮ *Plane Crazy*, first Mickey Mouse cartoon (1928)
1930	▮ Hitler becomes chancellor and Germany withdraws from League of Nations (1933) ▮ Hitler denounces Treaty of Versailles and ▮ Germany re-arms (1935) ▮ Spanish Civil War (1936–9) ▮ Edward VIII of Britain abdicates (1938) ▮ World War II (1939–45)	▮ Prohibition in US ends (1933) ▮ Robert Watson-Watt develops radar system (1935) ▮ Persecution of Jews begins in Germany (1935) ▮ Sikorsky builds first successful helicopter (1939)	▮ *King Kong* (1933) ▮ Carl Jung publishes *Modern Man in Search of a Soul* (1933) ▮ Elvis Presley (1935–77) ▮ *Gone with the Wind* (1939)
1940	▮ Nuremberg Trials (1946) ▮ War in Indochina between French and nationalists led by Ho Chi Minh (1946–54) ▮ Marshall Aid program (1947) ▮ NATO formed (1949) ▮ France recognizes independence of Cambodia and Vietnam (1949)	▮ Frank Whittle invents the jet engine (1941)	▮ *Citizen Kane* (1941) ▮ Abstract Expressionist movement in painting develops in USA (after 1945) ▮ George Orwell publishes *Nineteen Eighty-Four* (1949) ▮ Simone de Beauvoir writes *Le Deuxième sexe* (1949)

From *The World's History: Combined Edition* by Spodek, © 1998. Reprinted by permission of Prentice-Hall, Inc., Upper Saddle River, NJ.

with a chart that can be found in the excerpt titled "Technologies of Mass-Production and Destruction" in Appendix C. Note that this time line is divided by decades and that it looks at political, social, and cultural events that occurred during each decade. Much more common are time lines like the one in Figure 14.12, which simply shows the key events that occurred during World War II.

As you can perhaps tell by looking at the two time lines, in the majority of studying situations, time lines should be supplemented with

FIGURE 14.12 *Example of a Time Line List*

WORLD WAR II—KEY EVENTS

July 7, 1937	Japanese troops invade China
September 1939	Nazi-Soviet Pact: Germany invades Poland. Britain and France declare war. Poland partitioned between Germany and Russia
Mar–Apr 1940	German forces conquer Denmark, Norway, the Netherlands, and Belgium
May–June	Italy declares war on Britain and France; German forces conquer France
June 21, 1941	German forces invade USSR
Dec 7	Japanese bomb US Navy, Pearl Harbor
Jan-Mar 1942	Indonesia, Malaya, Burma and the Philippines are conquered by Japan
April 1942	US planes bomb Tokyo
June	US Navy defeats Japanese at the Battle of the Midway
1942–43	End of Axis resistance in North Africa; Soviet victory in Battle of Stalingrad
1943–44	Red Army slowly pushes Wehrmacht back to Germany
June 6, 1944	Allies land in Normandy (D-Day)
Feb 1945	Yalta conference: Churchill, Roosevelt, and Stalin discuss post-war settlement
May 7, 1945	Germany surrenders
August 6	US drops atom bomb on Hiroshima, Japan, and then on Nagasaki
August 14	Japan surrenders

other strategies such as CARDS, concept maps, or charts. For example, if you were doing a time line portraying the major events of World War II (Figure 14.12), it would indicate the chronology of the war—which events happened when. But that would be insufficient knowledge to have when preparing for an exam. You would need to know *why* Japanese troops invaded China, *what* the Nazi-Soviet Pact was, and *what* factors led to the Japanese decision to bomb Pearl Harbor. This information cannot be gleaned from the time line alone.

When you are studying your time lines, use only your dates as the cue. Talk through the important events, laws, battles, etc., that occurred on that date. At the same time, use your other strategies to talk through the nature of each of the events, thinking about cause and effect or how one event influenced another, when appropriate. Use the newspaper reporter's questions—who, what, where, when, why, and how—to be certain that you are completely and precisely describing each event. In addition, it's important to understand how events are related, so be sure that you see the big picture as well. When you are studying the chronology of a topic such as World War I or II, it's always important to see the big picture first, then break the information into smaller segments for learning, and finally return to the big picture once more to see how the pieces fit together.

14.5

SOMETHING TO WRITE ABOUT AND DISCUSS

Thinking Critically

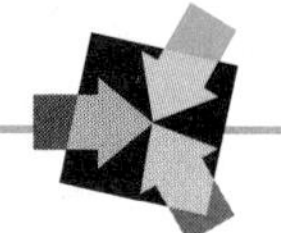

- Using another section of the "Technologies of Mass-Production and Destruction" excerpt in Appendix C, construct a time line. Then create another strategy that you would use in conjunction with your time line that would give you additional information.
- If you are enrolled in a course in which a portion of the information would lend itself to creating a time line, construct one.

Verbal Rehearsal Strategies

Verbal rehearsal strategies are those that involve talk in some way—talking to yourself, out loud, or to a study partner. Although you might think it odd to talk to yourself as you study and learn, saying information—even to yourself—is a powerful tool because it is a form of active learning that keeps you connected with the information. Talking and listening as you study helps you use other senses as well, and the more senses you use when you study, the easier learning will be. We will discuss two different verbal strategies: reciprocal questioning and talk-throughs. Each of these strategies is a form of verbal summarization and is generally used along with written strategies. Before reading the remainder of this section, however, read the *Research into Practice* segment that follows. This research examined the effectiveness of verbal rehearsals.

Research into Practice

Verbal Rehearsal Improves Student Performance*

In this study, the researchers examined the effect that verbal rehearsal strategies had on college students' test performance. The participants in the experimental group of this study read and studied a text excerpt and then learned about verbal rehearsal and how verbal rehearsals should be carried out. They also heard examples of good verbal rehearsals, or what the researchers called "elaborative rehearsal." When students engage in elaborative rehearsal strategies, they go beyond the text information and respond to the text on a personal level by thinking of personal examples

* Source: Simpson, M. L., Olejnik, S. Yu-Wen Tam, A., & Supattathum, S. (1994). Elaborative verbal rehearsals and college students' cognitive performance. *Journal of Educational Psychology* 86: 267–278.

and applications. In the second phase of the study, they constructed their own verbal rehearsal, practiced it, and tape-recorded it. Then they answered both multiple-choice and essay questions over their reading.

The students in the control group also learned about verbal rehearsals, but they were left to their own devices as to how to carry out good verbal rehearsals. They did not hear examples of good verbal rehearsals, nor were they taught elaborative rehearsal strategies.

The researchers found a strong relationship between test performance and the use of elaborative verbal rehearsal strategies. In addition, the relationship between verbal rehearsal and test performance was stronger for the essay portion of the test than for the multiple-choice portion.

The results of this study are important to college students for several reasons. First, the study clearly shows that verbal rehearsal, particularly elaborative verbal rehearsal, works. Students who actively rehearse the information by saying it out loud and who personalize perform better than students who have weak verbal rehearsals and do little or no elaboration. Second, this study also indicates the importance of selecting task-appropriate strategies. There was a stronger relationship between the essay scores and verbal rehearsal than there was between the multiple-choice scores and verbal rehearsal, indicating that when you have an essay task, it might be in your best interest to engage in at least some verbal rehearsing.

Reciprocal Questioning

Reciprocal questioning involves two learners: one who takes the role of the teacher, and one who takes the role of the student. The "teacher" asks a question from one of the written strategies described above, from text annotations, or from lecture notes. Most should be questions that elicit higher-level or critical thinking rather than those that promote memorization and one-word answers. Then the "student" answers the question completely and precisely. The teacher checks the student's answer against the written strategy. If the student has answered the question correctly, the teacher asks the next question. If the question was not answered adequately, the teacher answers the question correctly and the two discuss the correct answer. This poorly answered question is then included in a review pile, and the question is asked again at the end of the study session.

After all of the questions have been asked and answered and, if necessary, reviewed, the two switch roles—the "student" becomes the teacher and asks the questions, and the "teacher" becomes the student and answers them. The new teacher should be sure that he or she asks the questions in a different order and adds some new questions.

FIGURE 14.13 *Examples of Good and Poor Questions*

Good Questions	Poor Questions
1. How did health and food technology facilitate population growth between the 1920s and the 1990s?	1. What did China do to discourage couples from having large families?
2. In what kind of countries might birth rates drop below death rates? Why might a drop in birth rates occur?	2. What was the "green revolution"?
3. Explain three different reasons why there have been demographic shifts.	3. Name a third-world country.

Figure 14.13 gives you an idea of the difference between good and poor questions. These questions are about the section called Demographic Shifts from the excerpt titled "Technologies of Mass-Production and Destruction" found in Appendix C. Notice that most of the questions in the Poor column begin with the word *what* and require a one-word answer or simple memorization. The questions in the Good column are *why* and *how* questions that require critical thinking, synthesis, and analysis. Remember that active learners write more of these *why* and *how* questions, especially if the task requires it.

Reciprocal questioning can be a powerful strategy for several reasons. First, it brings another sense into play. You have read the information using the visual sense, you have written important concepts down in an organized fashion using the kinesthetic sense, and you are now hearing the information using the auditory sense. As we said earlier, anytime you can use more than one of your senses in learning, you are more likely to remember. Second, because there are two of you involved in reciprocal questioning, you have two different perspectives. The old adage "Two heads are better than one" is true in this situation. One person may be very strong in understanding concept A and the other very knowledgeable about concept B. Thus, pulling the ideas of two people together generally makes for clearer, more precise learning for both. Third, because you hear the answers to questions in another person's voice rather than just your own, you can begin to phrase the information in ways other than how it is stated in the text. Because professors rarely write questions that come exactly from the text, it's important to put information in your own words so that you will recognize it in a slightly different form on the test. When you have two people putting it in their own words, you have yet another perspective of how the information might be phrased.

Finally, reciprocal questioning helps you monitor your learning. When you are asked a question and then provide the answer, you get immediate feedback about your knowledge on that particular topic. That helps you monitor what concepts you understand and what concepts you need to further work on.

14.6 SOMETHING TO THINK ABOUT AND DISCUSS

Thinking Critically

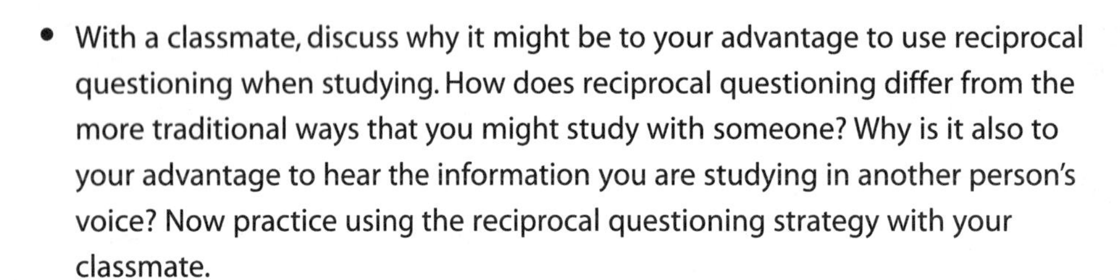

- With a classmate, discuss why it might be to your advantage to use reciprocal questioning when studying. How does reciprocal questioning differ from the more traditional ways that you might study with someone? Why is it also to your advantage to hear the information you are studying in another person's voice? Now practice using the reciprocal questioning strategy with your classmate.

Talk-Throughs

As the name of this strategy suggests, talk-throughs involve saying the information (talking it through) to yourself, either silently or out loud, to monitor your learning. When you talk through the concepts, you become both the student and the teacher who were described above in the reciprocal questioning strategy. But rather than having someone ask you questions or ask you to explain concepts, you fill both roles. Start by making a talk-through list on an index card, or if you have many concepts to learn, use a piece of notebook paper. As seen in Figure 14.14, a talk-through card simply lists, in an organized fashion, the concepts you need to learn and remember. Notice that the supporting ideas are indented so that it is easy to see which ideas are connected in some way. For example, on this talk-through card, it is easy to see that there are two main elements of thought covered in the subheadings "Concepts" and "Reasoning," taken from the "Cognition" excerpt in Appendix A. Note also that, in this case, the text's heading and subheadings are the basis for organizing the talk-through card and that these headings are further supplemented with key terms. Although this is not always the case, headings and subheadings are a good place to start because they give you the overall big picture of the chapter. (This idea was discussed in greater detail in Chapter 12.)

After you have made your talk-through card, begin rehearsal by saying what you know about the first major concept. Talk it through, if necessary, looking back at your written strategies, including text annotations and lecture notes. After you have said the information silently or out loud, it is a good idea to go back to your strategy and read over the

FIGURE 14.14

Example of a Talk-Through Card

Elements of thought

- *Concepts*
  - *Artificial concepts*
  - *Natural concepts*
    - *Prototypes*
  - *Concept representations*
    - *Schemas*
    - *Self-schemas*
  - *Relations between concepts*
    - *Propositions*
  - *Mental images*
- *Reasoning*
  - *Formal reasoning*
  - *Everyday reasoning*
  - *Reasoning errors*
    - *Moods*

information again to be sure that you are complete and precise. As you learn each piece of information, also be sure that you can make connections between the major concepts and the supporting details. Explain to yourself how the pieces fit together. Don't forget to think about how the major concepts are related, keeping that big picture in mind.

14.7

SOMETHING TO WRITE ABOUT AND DISCUSS

Thinking Critically

On the lines that follow, construct a talk-through card as you prepare for your next exam in one of your courses. Make sure that you organize the information so that you can see which are the major concepts and which are smaller concepts that are linked in some way to the major concepts. Then have a classmate evaluate your talk-through card. After you know the concepts fairly well, use the reciprocal teaching strategy in your final preparations for the exam.

____

____

____

____

____

____

____

Strategy Selection

As we stated earlier, the strategies you select depend on a variety of factors: the task your professor asks you to do, the course for which you are studying, and how you learn best. For example, you would use different strategies in a history course that requires you to answer essay and short-answer questions than you would in a psychology course that requires you to answer higher-level, multiple-choice questions. If you tend to be a visual learner, you would probably use more concept mapping and charting than you would reciprocal teaching. Even when you could use the same strategy for several different courses, how you use the strategy—the procedural knowledge of the strategy—would be different. As an example, let's say that you are taking Professor A's biology course. He requires you to memorize the terms that are presented in the text and the lectures and to know the results of your biology labs. For this task, you might choose to use CARDS, as described earlier in the chapter. You would write your definitions on the backs of the index cards, self-test, and be ready to take the test. You could do the same with your lab results. Your roommate, however, is in Professor B's biology course—same course, even the same text. But Professor B expects more than memorization. She wants her students to synthesize the information, to understand how it is connected, and to be able to recognize examples. Your roommate might still elect to use CARDS, but hers would have to contain more than just definitions. In addition, your roommate would have to be sure that she uses the organizing term in the upper right-hand corner to group like terms so that she could see the connections between concepts. Thus, the same strategy can be modified in any number of ways, depending on the task. Figure 14.15 summarizes the rehearsal strategies presented in this chapter and suggests when they might be most effective. But remember: Active learners can modify strategies so that they can be used in situations other than those outlined in Figure 14.15.

The ability to modify strategies is called strategy flexibility. Flexibility involves not only the ability to use a given strategy in a variety of situations but also the ability to change or modify the strategy in a way it will work for you. All strategies can be modified. Many times, active learners can be very creative in how they modify strategies to suit their own needs. We have had students who use their CARDS to make maps, combine maps and time lines, and integrate time lines and CARDS. Many students use their CARDS as a basis for conducting talk-throughs and incorporate their lecture notes and lab results in their charts. When students are flexible with their strategies, there is no end to the potential they have for using the strategies in a variety of situations.

FIGURE 14.15 *Summary of Rehearsal Strategies*

Rehearsal Strategies	Use In	Types of Questions
CARDS	Hard sciences, foreign languages, mathematics, statistics; any course where you have to learn many new terms	Best with objective questions; can be modified for use with either memory-level or higher-level questions
Concept maps and charts	Hard sciences, social sciences, history; if you are a visual learner; when you need to see relationships	Can be used for both objective and essay questions; best for higher-level questions that require you to see the big picture
Questions/answers	All courses	Best for objective test questions unless you plan to modify to predict essay questions
Time lines	History, art history, music history, anthropology; any course where you need to know chronology	Memory-level questions; can supplement this strategy with others such as concept maps, charts, or CARDS
Reciprocal questioning	All courses	All types of questions but works well when rehearsing answers to higher-level questions
Talk-throughs	All courses	All types of questions; helps you concentrate on key concepts rather than small details

In this chapter, we have given you a variety of rehearsal strategies you can modify and use in many different learning situations. These strategies are important to use after you have previewed your text and read and annotated your text and lecture notes. Rehearsal strategies help you to further reduce and consolidate the information to be learned, store the information in memory, and of course retrieve it at test time. Rehearsal strategies also help you see the relationships between and among ideas as well as assist you in monitoring your learning. To pull together the ideas presented in this chapter, read and respond to the *Real College* scenario that follows.

REAL COLLEGE: *Conrad's Confusion*

Read the following scenario and then respond to the questions based on what you learned in this chapter.

Conrad is a first-year college student who is pretty nervous about doing well in his courses. He is particularly unhappy with his ability to see the big picture in some of his courses and is surprised that his classes seem to require him to use different types of strategies in order to do well. In high school, Conrad simply read the parts of his texts that answered questions on study guides that most of his teachers gave. He would memorize this information and do well on just about all of his tests. But in college, four of his professors expect him to conceptualize information. He has to go beyond just the definition of terms in biology, and his history professor has told the class that they would need "to put information in an historical perspective." In his literature course, he has to think about how character development and use of language relate to the plot in the short stories they are studying. His introductory computer course requires running a series of programs so it involves both memorization and application. To make a long story short, Conrad doesn't even know where to start studying for these courses. In high school, he used to put lots of information on index cards and sometimes would make complex outlines, but he doesn't even know what other study strategies to consider now.

What would your advice to Conrad be? He is currently on a scholarship, and it is important for him to keep his grades high so he can continue to get this scholarship.

____

____

____

____

____

____

____

____

____

____

FOLLOW-UP ACTIVITIES

1. Think for a moment about how you learn best. Do you seem to learn better through reading information, through listening, or by writing things down? Or do you learn best when you use a combination of reading, listening, and writing strategies? Once you can determine how you learn best, studying may be more efficient and effective. Some campuses have places that will help you determine your learning style. If you think that your studying could be improved by having more knowledge about how you learn best, you might try your campus Learning Center or perhaps your Counseling Center.
2. Try out the strategies explained in this chapter in your classes. Keep track of which strategies seem to work best for you in which situations. In addition, modify the strategies to suit your own characteristics as a learner and the tasks your professors ask you to do.

Networking

- If you have your own computer or have access to one, try to create concept maps and charts using the computer. Most word processing programs make it easy to construct graphics so you can have fun and be creative in the way you do these rehearsal strategies.

Reviewing Strategies
Hanging In There

Read this chapter to answer the following questions:

What is the difference between rehearsal and review?

Why is it important to use your talk-through card to review?

How do you form study groups that will promote learning?

Why is it important to have a specific study plan?

What principles of reviewing improve memory?

STUDY TIP

Reviewing more than triples how much you remember. Therefore, spend time every day reviewing for each of your classes.

By now you have probably come to the conclusion that studying is hard work, especially if you want to be successful in college. Active learners engage in activities before, during, and after both reading and lectures as a way of keeping the information from their courses fresh in their mind. Rehearsing, which we discussed in the last chapter, and reviewing, which is presented in this chapter, are both done after reading or taking lecture notes. Rehearsal enables you to learn the information. It not only helps you store the concepts you'll need to learn, but it also helps you to retrieve the material at test time. Reviewing, on the other hand, is a way of making sure that the important information has been learned in such a way that it is complete, organized, and precise. By reviewing daily, you remember about three times as much as when you do not review. Thus, there is a tremendous payoff in review.

Before reading the rest of this chapter, read the *Research into Practice* section. This study examined both the quality and quantity of study time of undergraduate college students.

Research into Practice

Quality Study Time Pays Off*

The researchers who conducted this study investigated the general common belief that the more students study, the better their grades will be. They hypothesized that it wasn't the amount of time that students studied but their patterns of study that made the difference. For example, they wanted to know if students who used appropriate learning strategies or organized, conceptualized, and reviewed information performed better than those who didn't, even when study times were equivalent. All 113 undergraduate students who participated in the study kept a studying log over a ten-week quarter. Students wrote in their logs the amount of time they spent studying as well as the kinds of reading, organizing, rehearsing, and reviewing strategies they used as they studied for an educational psychology course.

What the researchers found, although not alarming, is important because the results clearly indicated it was what students did with their time that made the difference in performance. Both high performers and low performers studied approximately the same amounts of time. However, students who performed well in the course spent almost four times as much time engaged in what the researchers called "organizing activities"—summarizing, integrating, associating, generating examples —as the low performers did. In addition, the better students spent about fifty-six minutes per week reviewing, while poor students spent only forty-four minutes. Students who did not do well spent almost all of their study time in reading, rereading, and overall skimming.

The results of this study suggest that students who actively interacted with the material did significantly better in the course than those who did not. So remember, it's just not the amount of time spent in studying that matters . . . it's the active rehearsal and reviewing strategies that make the difference in performance.

The Nuts and Bolts of Reviewing

As we stated above, rehearsing and reviewing are different. It is usually best to rehearse, when you have large blocks of time. Remember that when you rehearse you write, say, and listen to the information until you know it very well. You look for connections between ideas and

* Source: Dickinson, D. J., & O'Connell, D. Q. (1990). Effect of quality and quantity of study on student grades. *Journal of Educational Research* 83: 227–231.

understand how concepts are related. By the time you get to the point at which you are reviewing, your purpose is different. You know the material after you have rehearsed it. Reviewing ensures that the information will stay fixed in your memory.

You can use reviewing at various times during the studying process. For example, think back to Chapter 11 when we talked about lecture notes. We emphasized the importance of reviewing notes daily. Getting to class ten minutes early and using those ten minutes to read over your notes is a form of reviewing. In this case, reviewing refreshes your memory of what went on in the last class and prepares your mind to receive new information, making it easier to connect ideas. But the kind of reviewing that we will be primarily focusing on in this chapter is generally done as a final phase of studying and test preparation. You review by self-testing to monitor your learning and gain a better understanding of what information you know very well and what information requires further study through additional rehearsal.

15.1 SELF-EVALUATION

Think about the types of review you currently engage in. Answer yes or no for each of the following questions.

YES	NO	
☐	☐	Do you review on a daily basis?
☐	☐	Do you review when you have small pockets of time?
☐	☐	Do you review several days before an exam?
☐	☐	Do you review more than once before an exam?
☐	☐	Do you review at the beginning of each study session?
☐	☐	Do you review at the end of each study session?
☐	☐	Do you review with classmates?
☐	☐	Do you review by self-questioning?

If you answered yes to most of these questions, you are probably on the right track and doing what you need to in order to complete the studying process. Read the remainder of the chapter to see what additional reviewing strategies you might use. However, if you answered no to several of these questions, you might want to rethink how you review as you read the remainder of this chapter.

Using Your Talk-Through Card for Reviewing

In the last chapter on rehearsal, we discussed how to make and use a talk-through card. Talk-through cards simply list the concepts you want to rehearse and learn as you study the material. Remember that you start with the first concept on the card, rehearse by reading the information through a couple of times, and then see whether you can say it without looking at your notes or rehearsal strategies. As you work through your list of key points, you think about connections and relationships between ideas. By the end of your study session, you should have learned at least a portion of the major concepts on your talk-through card. You repeat this same procedure with other concepts in other study sessions until you know and understand each one. This is rehearsal.

But you can use that same talk-through card to review. A day or two before the exam, take out the talk-through card that you used as a guideline to rehearse. Because it lists key points with a cursory organization of the supporting material, it can also serve as a review card. Simply start with the first concept and completely and accurately talk through the key points. If you know all the information related to that concept, check it off and go on to the next. If you have trouble remembering the material, return to your annotations or rehearsal strategies and say the information again. Keep in mind that if rehearsal has been done properly, reviewing should just be a matter of keeping the information retrievable in your memory and seeing which concepts are still giving you problems. Hopefully, you will remember most of the important information and see links between concepts when you are reviewing. By the time you get to the reviewing stage, the information should be stored in your memory. You are simply checking to see that you remember it and will be able to retrieve it at test time.

15.2 SOMETHING TO WRITE ABOUT AND DISCUSS

In the space that follows, create a talk-through card for a test that you will be having soon. (Or you could use the talk-through card you created in Chapter 14.) Use this card as an organizing tool when you rehearse and to review from as the exam comes closer. After the exam, discuss with your classmates how well this strategy worked for you.

1. *What were the advantages and disadvantages? What might you do differently the next time you make a talk-through card?*

____

____

____

2. *Make a talk-through card for one of your courses. List the concepts that you want to rehearse and review for the next test in this course.*

Making a Specific Study Plan

We have talked in other chapters about the importance of planning. Rather than having a catch-as-catch-can approach to test preparation, you should think about how much time you will spend studying and what you will do during those study sessions. It's particularly important to structure specific study and review sessions as the time for the exam draws closer. That's why we suggest that you develop a specific study plan for each exam you have to take. Initially at least, we believe it's important for students to actually write out a plan and clip it in their daily planner. Because a well-thought-out plan is very specific, it goes beyond the space provided in regular daily planners. Some students get to the point at which they have a study plan in their heads and know what they are going to do in each study session just by writing a few notes in their normal daily planners. It has been our experience, however, that most students benefit from creating a more structured plan.

You construct your study plan about a week or so before the exam. First, you think about your goals by asking yourself a series of questions:

- What grade do I want to earn on the exam?
- How much time do I need to invest in order to make this grade?
- Where will I find the extra time? Will I have to give up other activities in order to carve out time to study?
- What kind of exam is it? Multiple-choice? Essay? What kinds of problems do I usually have when I take tests of this nature?

- Do I know the balance of items? Are there more text or lecture questions? Is this a memorization task, or will I be expected to answer higher-level questions?
- What kinds of rehearsal strategies will work best for this exam? Will I need to begin by reformatting or constructing any strategies that I have already made?

After you have answered these questions, you are then ready to construct an SSP—a **S**pecific **S**tudy **P**lan. As shown in Figure 15.1, an SSP outlines what you will do in each particular study session. It shows what rehearsal or review strategies you will use, what concepts you will study, and approximately how long each study session will last. For example, in the SSP in Figure 15.1 it's easy to see that this student has three study sessions (1, 2, and 3) in which she will study alone and two specific sessions set aside just to review with her classmates (4 and 6). One session (5) is set aside just for self-testing as a way of getting a handle on which concepts may still be problematic. Also note that each study session begins with a review of information that was rehearsed in the previous session. Each session should also end with a review of what was learned in the current session. Thus, several different types of reviewing are going on for each SSP session.

As you construct your SSP and think about the time you will need to rehearse and review the material, remember from the principles discussed in Chapter 4 that you should always allow more time than you think you will need. Recall that some concepts are easier to learn than others. If you block out two hours for a study session to learn a set of concepts and it takes you only an hour and a half, you have gained a half-hour in which you can do something else. But if you set aside the same two hours and it actually ends up taking you three hours to feel comfortable with the concepts, you have lost an hour. Thus, it's important to have some flexibility in your schedule that allows for additional time should you need it. As we discussed in Chapter 4, you don't want to have your time scheduled so tightly that it doesn't allow for a little additional study time, particularly before an exam.

When you complete each study session, check it off and note how long it actually took you and any specific problems you had that you might need to return to in your next session.

FIGURE 15.1 *Example SSP for an Exam Covering Both Text Chapters and Lecture Notes*

Session	What to Do?	What to Use?	Problems?
#1 Sunday pm: 4:00–7:00	Study all concepts related to "Learning."	CARDS, concept maps, lecture notes	
#2 Monday pm: 4:40–6:30	Review "Learning." Study all concepts related to "Memory."	CARDS, concept maps, lecture notes	
#3 Tuesday pm: 7:00–9:30	Review "Learning" and "Memory." Study all concepts related to "Cognition."	CARDS, concept maps, lecture notes	
#4 Wednesday pm: 7:30–9:00	Review with study group.	Questions/answers, reciprocal questioning	
#5 Thursday am: 9:00–10:30	Self-test.	Questions/answers, talk-through card	
#6 Thursday pm: 7:30–9:00	Review with study group.	Talk-through card, oral questions/answers	

EXAM FRIDAY!

Did you exceed the amount of time you allotted, or did you need less time? This will help you as you develop an SSP for the next exam in this course.

Another thing to note about the SSP is that it sets aside time to do three different types of review. First, you begin each session with a review of what you previously learned. Using your talk-through card as a guide, say what you remember from the earlier study session. If there's material that is still giving you problems, begin the current study session with it. The second type of reviewing comes at the end of each session when you review only those concepts you concentrated on in the current session. This type of review serves as a monitoring device to let you know what you actually remember from the session. If you start this review and find that you are having problems, you can return to those concepts immediately and rehearse some more. This is the point at which you discover whether you will need to devote more time to the study session than you originally planned.

The last type of review comes a day or two before the test. At this time, you want to monitor your understanding of all the concepts you will be tested over. Concentrate what little time you have left on the material you understand least. Many students make the mistake of spending equal amounts of time on everything before an exam, even information they know fairly well. Learn from their mistakes! The closer the exam, the more you want to concentrate on concepts you don't know well.

Setting some goals for yourself and making an SSP for each exam you must take helps you stay on track with both rehearsal and reviewing. Note that it is important to focus on learning specific concepts, not on the amount of time you actually have allotted for studying. For example, if you were studying for the test outlined in the SSP in Figure 15.1, you would want to learn all of the information related to the concept "Learning" in your first study session. It is usually ineffective to go over all the information in every study session. Students who plan around time rather than around mastery of the information can easily go into a testing situation unprepared.

15.3 SOMETHING TO WRITE ABOUT AND DISCUSS

For the next exam in one of your classes, set goals by answering the following goal-related questions. Then construct an SSP. Remember to set aside time in your SSP for rehearsal and review. Also, remember to begin and end each study session with review.

My goals and SSP for _______________ test.

1. *What grade do I want to earn on the exam?* _______________

2. *How much time do I need to invest in order to make this grade?* _______________

3. *Where will I find the extra time? Will I have to give up other activities in order to carve out time to study?*

   ____

4. *What kind of exam is it? Multiple-choice? Essay? What kinds of problems do I usually have when I take tests of this nature?*

____

5. *Do I know the balance of items? Are there more text or lecture questions? Is this a memorization task, or will I be expected to answer higher-level questions?*

____

6. *What kinds of rehearsal strategies will work best for this exam? Will I need to begin by reformatting or constructing any strategies that I have already made?*

____

____

Session	What I'll Do	Strategies I'll Use	Problems
1.			
2.			
3.			
4.			

Forming Study Groups

One of the most powerful ways to review is by forming a study group. Some students will form study groups that meet on a weekly basis to talk about and review what went on in class that week. Other students like to use study groups just before an exam as a way of reviewing and perhaps even getting a new or different perspective on what they have learned. Either way, study groups can have big advantages.

Perhaps the biggest advantage of being part of a study group is that it allows you to listen to information in another person's voice, thus providing insights that you may not have thought of. In a traditional course, you listen to your professor's interpretation of the information during lectures, and you read the text for another interpretation. Through these two sources, you come up with your own interpretation or meaning. You have listened, read, and written down material, so you have used several of your senses. All of this interaction should help you gain a greater degree of understanding of the material. It stands to reason, then, that by listening to and interacting with others who are also trying to understand the course information, you would gain a deeper understanding, be able to remember the concepts better, and subsequently do better on the exams.

It's important to think about the characteristics of *good* study groups. Just meeting with one or several people does not necessarily make a study group! Good study groups have the following characteristics:

- ***Everyone comes to the study group prepared.***
  Study groups do not take the place of studying on your own. Everyone should come to the group prepared to orally review the information, pose possible test questions, and voice questions about material they don't understand. If study group members have to spend all their time trying to teach a large portion of the course material to someone who didn't even attempt to learn it on her own, most members will not benefit. Note that in the SSP in Figure 15.1, three study sessions come before getting together with the study group.

- ***Everyone comes prepared to talk through a difficult idea with the group.***
  It helps everyone in the group if you choose something that is giving you a bit of trouble or something that you may have some questions about. As you are reviewing your understanding of the concept, others who may understand it better than you should be encouraged to

offer additional explanations. If you shy away from discussing information you don't know very well, it defeats the purpose of the group.

- ***Members of the study group should be classmates, but not necessarily friends.***
  Everyone knows what can happen when friends get together to study: Everything goes fine for the first few minutes, but it's too easy to get off track and wind up having a gab session or, worse yet, no study session at all. It's much better to have serious students, who all have the goal of doing well, in your study group rather than just recruiting your friends. That's not to say that studying with friends will never work; it's simply harder to study with friends than it is with classmates working toward a common goal.

- ***Meet at a place that is conducive to studying.***
  Campus libraries often have study rooms set aside for just this purpose. Such rooms are generally small and soundproof so that normal conversation and discussion can be carried out with ease. If your library doesn't have study rooms, residence halls often have common areas equipped with study rooms. Empty classrooms can also work well. If your only alternative is to study in someone's room or at someone's home or apartment, remind yourself what the purpose of the session is—to review the course material for a test, not to socialize.

- ***Have a goal in mind and structure your study group based on your goals.***
  When you initially form a study group, you should have a more specific goal than to get together and study. Most groups meet at regular times. We know of a study group in a statistics course that meets weekly to review the important ideas presented that week; then it also meets a couple of times right before the exam to review what they know and to predict possible test questions. Groups that have a game plan in mind before they come together are generally the most successful. Along those lines, if you're really serious about having a good study group, it doesn't hurt to set some ground rules right from the beginning to prevent difficulties later on. For example, what will happen if someone comes to the group without doing any preparation on his own?

Almost everyone can benefit from belonging to a study group at one time or another, but study groups work particularly well for students who learn better auditorily and through discussion, and in some courses, that may be problematic. We don't know of any student who is in a study group for *every* class, but those who learn best by listening generally belong to more study groups than those who learn best through reading and writing. Similarly, students who usually study alone often use study groups when they are taking a particularly difficult course for which it helps to have the opinions and input of others.

15.4

SOMETHING TO THINK ABOUT AND DISCUSS

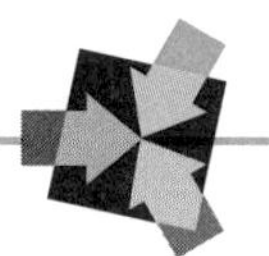

Thinking Critically

Think about both the advantages and disadvantages of forming and belonging to a study group. If you belonged to study groups in the past, how did they work? If you have not been part of a study group, for what classes would they be most beneficial? Why?

Improving Your Memory through Reviewing

At the beginning of this chapter, we stated that by reviewing information you can remember almost three times as much as if you did not review. You can maximize the amount you remember, thereby improving your memory, if you keep in mind five basic reviewing principles:

1. *Organize.*
Research indicates that people tend to remember information the way they have organized it. Thus, the first step you should take as you begin to rehearse and review course material is to be sure that it is organized, and therefore stored, in an easily retrievable way. Decide how the concepts can be best organized and then learn them in that way. Remember, you don't have to organize the material in the same way the text does or even in the same way your professor does. Create an organization that will work for you.

2. *Use images and other mnemonics.*
The word *mnemonics* comes from the Greek word for "mindful," and mnemonics are memory devices—little tricks you can use to help you remember specific kinds of information. Even if you are unfamiliar with the term *mnemonics*, you have probably used them without even knowing it. For example, you may have learned the rhyme "use *i* before *e* except after *c* or in words sounding like *a*, as in neighbor and weigh." This mnemonic is known by practically every elementary schoolchild. You can use mnemonics to learn a list by taking the first letter of each item you are trying to memorize and making them spell something. Your mnemonic device doesn't have to make sense to anyone but you. In fact,

the more outrageous the memory device, the easier it generally is to remember. For example, if you wanted to remember the parts of the forebrain as presented in the excerpt titled "The Human Nervous System," you might use this mnemonic: 4brain = TLC. This mnemonic works if you are familiar with the letters TLC being used together, as in ***t***ender ***l***oving ***c***are. In this case, TLC stands for ***t***halamus, ***l***imbic (system), and ***c***erebral (cortex). You could then create other mnemonics that would help you remember the parts of the midbrain and the hindbrain or the functions each of these portions serves.

Forming images is another powerful way to help you remember when you review. Like other mnemonics, images can be very personal and don't have to make sense to anyone except the person forming the images. Images work best when the information you are trying to learn is concrete rather than abstract. In other words, it is difficult to make images for concepts such as courage, democracy, or freedom, and it is much easier to make images for ideas such as cell division, presidential elections, or chamber music. Images work well because they give you both verbal and visual labels for things. A simple example may help you understand this idea. The three letters d-o-g together form a very familiar word—dog. Few people would have trouble understanding this word when they saw it in print. But what would happen if you asked each person who read that word to tell you his or her image of a dog? Would everyone describe *dog* in the same way? Of course not. Your image of a dog would be based on some experience you have, whether it's a dog you currently own or one that bit you when you were a child.

3. ***Say it rather than reread it.***
We have stated more than once that rehearsal is a much better way to learn information than rereading. In the first place, few students have time to reread large portions of text. Second, when students reread, they pick up very little additional information. When you say the information, however, you tend to summarize the key points in your own words. Verbalizing information is particularly important as you review. If you ask yourself questions (or get someone else to ask them) and then answer the questions, you will remember considerably more than if you simply tried to reread the material.

4. ***Have several review sessions.***
Research indicates that students who try to read, rehearse, and review in a short time frame do not do as well as those who spread their study out over time, even when the amount of time engaged in learning is about the same. (Think back to what the researchers described in the *Research into Practice* section earlier in the chapter found.) Thus, we

would expect the student who spent five hours studying spread out over a period of three days prior to the exam to do better on an exam than the student who studied five hours the night before the exam. Students who space their learning and use several study sessions tend to get less tired and can concentrate better during studying, thus improving the amount they can recall on test day.

5. *Overlearn.*
We add this suggestion to make you aware of the difference between "kinda" knowing something and overlearning it to the point at which it is almost automatic. When you have overlearned something, you know it so well that you don't even have to think about it. We have all overlearned some things as schoolchildren—the Pledge of Allegiance, "The Star-Spangled Banner," nursery rhymes, the lyrics to popular music. At a sporting event, for example, we stand to sing the national anthem without seemingly having to do much to recall the lyrics. If you could just remember the information for your biology or anthropology exam in the same way! The reason you can remember some information so easily is that you have been exposed to it over and over and over again. You know it so well that it is almost second nature to you. Contrast that with the feeling you have when you have studied but know that you do not know the information very well. If you feel as though you "kinda" know the material, you are probably not going to do very well on an exam. By reviewing course information from test to test, you will become more familiar with it. Although you probably will not have overlearned the concepts to the point at which they are second nature to you, reviewing will give you a greater sense of knowing—somewhere in between "kinda" knowing and overlearning.

In this chapter, we have stressed the importance of reviewing as a final step in the active learning process. Reviewing can be done alone or with study groups or partners. Whichever way you choose to review, keep in mind the importance of self-testing as a way to monitor your learning. Make an SSP and stick to it; make a conscious effort to work on improving your memory.

In the *Real College* scenario that follows, see if you can help Enrico solve his problems. This scenario is a little different from those in previous chapters in that we ask you to begin to pull together some of the studying issues we have been discussing in *Active Learning.*

REAL COLLEGE: *Enrico's Excuses*

Read the following scenario and then respond to the questions based on what you learned in this chapter.

By his own admission, Enrico is a slacker! In fact, his e-mail nickname is eslacker. He has been fairly lucky so far in that at least he isn't failing any of his classes. He puts in the minimum amount of work possible to try to maintain what he calls "average" performance—no less than a D in any course for Enrico! But all of this is starting to wear on him; on top of that, he's running out of excuses for his parents ... and he's running out of time. The semester is now two-thirds of the way over, and he finds himself worried and anxious that he might actually fail his courses this term.

Enrico uses every excuse in the book for not following a study regimen: "There's lots of time left." "I have a photographic memory so I don't have to study and review." "I'll study over the weekend when I have more time." "I don't like this course and the professor is so boring. I'll do better next term when I can take something I like." "I work best under pressure. That's why I study at the last minute." He's even told professors that "The dog ate my homework"; at 3:00 in the afternoon, he once told a professor that he missed class because "My alarm clock didn't go off."

Enrico has decided to TRY to turn over a new leaf. His roommate encouraged him to make an appointment with the campus Learning Center where someone might be able to help him move from making excuses into taking some positive action to get back on track. Reluctantly, he made an appointment with someone at the Center and actually showed up—a little late, but he did make it!

Given what you read about Enrico, put yourself in the place of the person in the Learning Center assigned to help him. What kind of advice would you give Enrico if it were your job to help him get his studying life together? What strategies would you tell him to use so that he could get on a studying cycle? In particular, how might you encourage him to use daily reviewing as a way of promoting active learning? What quick-start tips might help Enrico see the light?

____

____

____

____

____

____

FOLLOW-UP ACTIVITIES

1. Try forming a review group for one of your classes, especially one that might be difficult for you. Remember that this group can meet throughout the term to review lecture notes or difficult topics from the text or lecture. Reviewing, like rehearsing, is an ongoing process.
2. Try out some of the memory devices such as imagery or mnemonics. Which memory aids work best for you? Why?
3. Try to get in the habit of making an SSP about a week before each of your exams. It helps you to set goals for yourself and to keep you on task.

Networking

- Try to set up an on-line review session prior to an exam in one of your classes. You and a classmate can review by sending questions to one another via e-mail. Each of you can answer questions posed by the other and provide feedback as to the completeness and accuracy of your answers.

Characteristics of Texts

In Part V, you will learn how the characteristics of the text influence active learning. Chapter 16 shows you how to modify your learning strategies based on the kind of text you are reading.

Chapter 17 introduces becoming a flexible reader. It presents strategies for increasing your reading rate and discusses some common habits that may slow your reading.

Before you read the chapters in Part V, please respond to the following statements. Read each statement and decide whether you agree or disagree with it.

Keep your responses in mind as you read the chapters in Part V. When you have finished reading Part V, revisit this page. How are your responses similar to or different from what is introduced in the chapters?

BEFORE			AFTER	
Agree	Disagree		Agree	Disagree
☐	☐	*1. I try to use the same learning strategies in all of my courses.*	☐	☐
☐	☐	*2. Some textbooks are more user-friendly than others.*	☐	☐
☐	☐	*3. Learning from a history textbook requires a different approach from learning from a mathematics textbook.*	☐	☐
☐	☐	*4. When I don't understand what I am reading, I slow down and read it again.*	☐	☐
☐	☐	*5. It takes me longer to read one textbook page than a magazine article of the same length.*	☐	☐
☐	☐	*6. When I read, I say the words to myself.*	☐	☐

Strategy Modification
All Texts (and Courses) Are Not the Same

Read this chapter to answer the following questions:

How do your courses differ from each other?

How do your textbooks differ from each other?

How can you modify your strategies to suit different courses and texts?

STUDY TIP

Choose your strategies for learning based on the type of course and type of tests you will experience.

As you have probably noticed by now, all of your courses are not the same. Obviously, the content is not the same in your history class and your chemistry class, but have you noticed that the ways in which your classes are organized and structured also differ? Some of your classes may involve taking lots of lecture notes, and others may involve class discussion; you may have a lab class in addition to a lecture class, or you may have a lecture, lab, and discussion all in one course! Additionally, the textbooks are often vastly different. In fact, you may have noticed that some of your textbooks are not even especially well written! For some courses, your "texts" consist of several sources (e.g., textbooks, newspapers, original source documents, lab manuals, and computer printouts). Because your class structure and text sources can be so wide-ranging, you will find different types of assessments, depending on the course. You may have essay or multiple-choice tests, you may have to write journals or papers, or you may be required to complete any number of different tasks. When you begin to study for your courses, you will base your decision of which strategies to choose on the type of class, type of text, and type of assessment. So in order to prepare you for the variety of tasks you need to do, we will examine discipline-specific differences in college courses.

In this chapter, we will discuss the different kinds of situations you might find in different courses, such as mathematics, science, humanities, and social sciences. Before reading the rest of the chapter, read the *Research into Practice* section.

Research into Practice

Academic Task Demands*

In this study, Dr. Simpson conducted a survey of the academic demands placed on first- and second-year college students in their core courses. She wanted to find out answers to several questions including: What are college students expected to do in order to succeed in their college courses? What are the differences in the academic demands across disciplines?

Dr. Simpson found that students are often asked to write responses to short-answer and essay questions, but that college faculty believe students' answers to these questions are often incomplete. Therefore, students need to know how to predict possible test questions and how to answer essay questions completely and accurately. She also found that students need specific strategies, depending on the discipline. For example, in the sciences, students need strategies for learning process-related material.

In interviews with students who had completed an elective "Learning to Learn" course that taught strategies for learning across disciplines, Dr. Simpson found a major difference among students with high and low grades in their courses. Students with higher grades were able to remember the strategies they learned by name (such as annotation, charting, or predicting test questions—some of the same strategies you have learned in this text). They spoke about how and when they used these strategies. They also talked about how they modified the strategies to suit their needs. Students with lower grades could not remember the strategy names, nor did they talk about their use in any of their courses.

This study is important because it shows that students need different strategies, depending on the content of a course and the tasks required for it. The results of the faculty survey, which indicated the faculty perception that student responses to short-answer and essay test questions

* Source: Simpson, M. L. (1996). Conducting reality checks to improve students' strategic learning. *Journal of Adolescent & Adult Literacy* 40: 102–109.

are often incomplete, are also important for college students to consider when faced with those tasks. Overall, the results of this study show that students who use effective strategies for learning earned higher grades than students who did not.

16.1 SELF-ASSESSMENT

Complete the following chart for each of your courses this term. Keep your answers to these questions about how you prepare for class in mind as you read the rest of the chapter.

	Course:	Course:	Course:	Course:	Course:
I read the text before class.	☐	☐	☐	☐	☐
I read the text after class.	☐	☐	☐	☐	☐
My class lecture follows the text.	☐	☐	☐	☐	☐
I am responsible for reading multiple texts for this course.	☐	☐	☐	☐	☐
I try to study in the same way for each course.	☐	☐	☐	☐	☐

Textbook Characteristics

Saying that you can read each of your textbooks in the same way for each of your courses is like saying you can read *People* magazine in the same way as you read Shakespeare! Obviously, you have to adjust your reading to the type of course and textbook you are using. As you encounter different college textbooks, you will notice some basic differences, depending on the content area. Textbooks in the humanities are different from textbooks in the social sciences or physical sciences. In the next section, we will examine how textbooks in several content areas are organized, and we will suggest some strategies for reading each type of textbook. Before reading the next section, complete the self-assessment to examine how you currently prepare for your courses.

Mathematics Courses

Mathematics Textbooks Reading a mathematics textbook is not like reading a novel or another textbook. Mathematics textbooks tend to use few words in order to keep ideas clearly outlined, so you must understand almost every sentence. You will be expected to understand abstract relationships and theories as you read about them. Mathematics texts tend to present new concepts, formulas, diagrams, and practice problems sequentially, which means they build on one another. So learning mathematics is cumulative. The concepts you are learning this week are based on the concepts you have already mastered. For example, you never would have been able to learn how to divide fractions if you did not know the basic rules of whole-number division.

You will find that mathematics textbooks are not very repetitive—so every concept counts! With little chance of picking up missed information by reading further in the text, you must be sure you have mastered each concept before moving on to a new one.

Study Strategies for Mathematics Courses In general, mathematics courses in college are based on problem solving. In addition to what we generally think of as mathematics courses, computer science, engineering, statistics, chemistry, and physics are also math-based courses. Whether you are in a class of ten or three hundred, you will be asked to apply mathematics principles and formulas in a variety of situations. Sometimes mathematics courses are discussion-based, but often they are lecture-based, with the instructor explaining new concepts and the student taking copious notes. Many times mathematics instructors focus lectures on solving problems on the board.

To approach reading in mathematics, it is a good idea to preview the text before class. If you find that you can read and understand the chapter before the lecture, that's even better, but many students find that they comprehend mathematics texts better after listening to the lecture and seeing some problems worked as examples in class. When you preview the text, note the concepts and formulas that are covered as well as any new terminology so you will have some background information before listening in class. When you are in class, take good notes and ask questions. The more information and examples you have in your notes, the better it will be as you read the text.

After class, read the text. It's best to read the chapter as soon after class as possible so that you will remember all of the key points and ideas discussed in class. Take your time as you read. Annotate key words, formulas, definitions, and symbols in the margins to help you remember them. Note the symbols used in your text because they have very specific

meanings and must be used correctly when working math problems. For example, to understand *ab*::*cd*, you must first understand that :: is the symbol for "is proportional to."

Math work cannot be neglected. Plan to spend some time each night reading or working problems. As you read, work out the problems in your text. After reading examples, cover up the answer to the sample problem to work it out for yourself. It is also important to write down questions about concepts you need to have clarified so you can ask them during the next class period, before the class moves on to a new concept. Try to create your own problems and solve them for additional practice. If you find that you are experiencing difficulty understanding your textbook, you may find it helpful to use another math book (you can probably find one in the library) as a reference book to help clarify confusing points. As we pointed out in Chapter 14, you might try verbalizing the problems. Talking the information through by putting symbols into words, for example, can let you know where your understanding is breaking down.

16.2 SOMETHING TO WRITE AND THINK ABOUT

1. *What mathematics courses are you taking this term? (If you are not taking a mathematics course this term but have recently taken one, answer the questions based on that course.)*

____

____

2. *How is your math course similar to or different from mathematics courses described above? (Think about whether the class has lecture, discussion, or lab, and consider the type of exams given.)*

   Similarities: ______________________________

   ____

   Differences: ______________________________

   ____

3. *Which of the following components are contained in your textbook:*
   - ☐ New terminology (vocabulary words specific to the content)
   - ☐ New principles or theories described
   - ☐ Chronological format (concepts organized by date)
   - ☐ Sequential format (concepts built on one another)
   - ☐ Topical format (concepts organized by topic)

4. *What kind of background knowledge, if any, does the text assume you have?*

   ____

   ____

5. *Which of the strategies presented in this book are the most effective for learning in this course? Why?*

   ____

   ____

Science Courses

Science Textbooks Science courses can be divided into two categories—math-based science courses and text-based science courses. Each category will have vastly different texts. Texts for math-based science courses, such as chemistry or physics, will contain formulas like your mathematics texts, but they will also contain important diagrams explaining science processes.

Text-based science courses, such as biology, agriculture, forestry, botany, astronomy, and geology, are often more similar to humanities courses than mathematics courses. There is usually little mathematics involved; instead, you will be required to read, understand, and apply science processes discussed in the text. Often these courses include a lab in which you experience hands-on application of scientific principles.

In science textbooks, you will find many new terms and definitions. Usually those new terms will be used later in the text to define other terms, so if you don't understand the term when it is introduced, you will have trouble understanding future reading. Science textbooks also discuss proven principles and theories in terms of their relationship to each other. So it's important to be aware of and understand how the theories connect.

Study Strategies for Science Courses Because of the amount of new terminology involved in learning science, it's important for you to read your science textbooks before class. In this way, you will already be familiar with the terms and concepts discussed in the text and be able to build your understanding of the concept as you listen in class. It is also a good idea to connect the concepts discussed in class with concepts described in your text by comparing your lecture notes to your text annotation each night.

As with your math courses, science concepts are usually presented sequentially, which means they build on each other, so if you don't understand the concepts presented early on, you will have difficulty learning later concepts. As we have stressed throughout this book, your best defense is to test yourself as you read to make sure you fully understand each concept. Adopt a scientific approach, and ask yourself questions such as:

- Is this concept or phenomenon a theory, or has it been proven?
- What other theories is this concept related to?
- How does this phenomenon work? What is the scientific process involved?
- Why does this phenomenon occur?
- What does it show us?

Making a concept map of key terms and concepts so that you can see how the ideas relate is another helpful strategy. When you preview each chapter, begin a concept map for the ideas contained in the chapter. As you read, fill in your concept map with the important scientific processes. Or you may want to make CARDS on the concepts and new terminology. However, in order to be effective, you must do more than just memorize the terms; spread out your CARDS to show the hierarchy of terms or the order of the scientific process. This way, you will be connecting the ideas together.

Science texts often contain diagrams or charts to explain concepts. Because science exams usually contain questions about the concepts

FIGURE 16.1

Science Diagram

From *Life on Earth* by Audesirk/Audesirk, © 1997. Reprinted by permission of Prentice-Hall, Inc., Upper Saddle River, NJ.

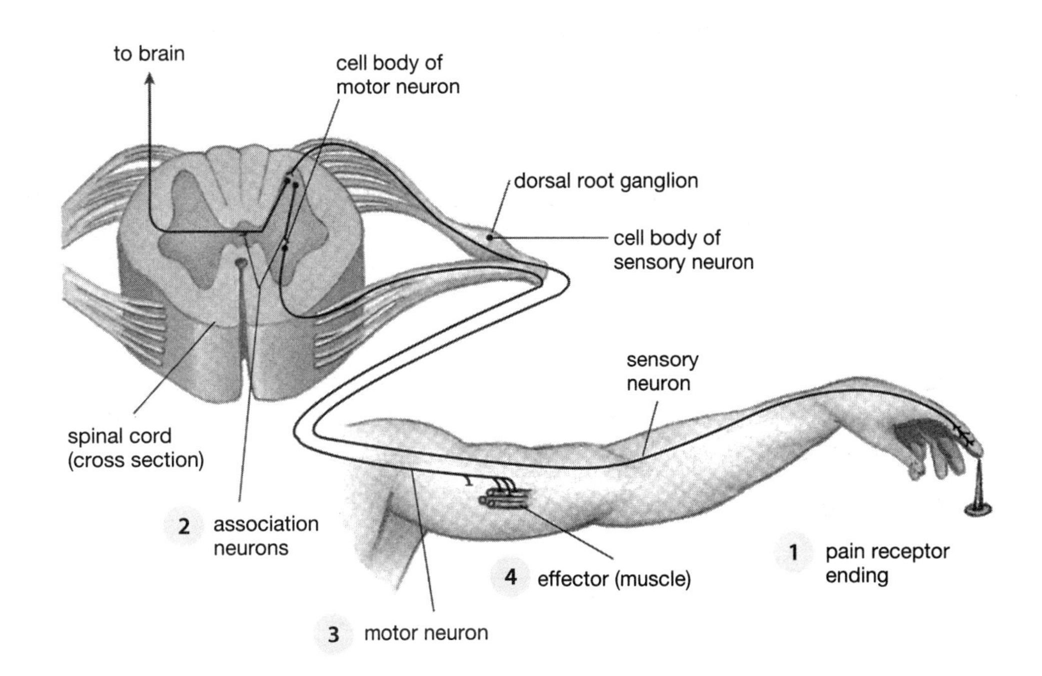

described in diagrams or charts, you must be able to read and understand each one. As you read your text, annotate the diagrams and take the time to learn what they are depicting. A good self-testing strategy to make sure you fully understand the concept is to cover up the words in the diagram and try to talk through the information. If you can explain how the concept works, you've got it! In addition, although exams in your science classes may consist of multiple-choice, essay, or short-answer questions, many of your test questions will require you to apply science concepts to new situations. To answer these questions, you must understand and be able to describe each science concept. If you find that you cannot, reread your annotations and your lecture notes to be sure you understand the key points.

In Figure 16.1, the diagram illustrates how the human body reacts to pain. If you were going to take an exam about this concept, you would need to be able to talk through the entire sequence of events in the order they occur. To help you remember the sequence, as you annotate the diagram, think about a personal experience of pain, perhaps the first time you touched a hot stove. What reaction did your body have? How does your experience relate to the diagram? By relating the science process to what you already know, you will be better able to understand and remember the concept.

16.3

SOMETHING TO WRITE AND THINK ABOUT

1. *What science courses are you taking this term? (If you are not taking a science course this term but have recently taken one, answer the questions based on that course.)*

   ____

   ____

2. *How is your science course similar to or different from the science courses described above? (Think about whether the class has lecture, discussion, or lab, and consider the type of exams given.)*

   Similarities: ______________________________

   ____

   Differences: ______________________________

   ____

3. *Which of the following components are contained in your textbook:*

   ☐ New terminology (vocabulary words specific to the content)

   ☐ New principles or theories described

   ☐ Chronological format (concepts organized by date)

   ☐ Sequential format (concepts built on one another)

   ☐ Topical format (concepts organized by topic)

4. *What kind of background knowledge, if any, does the text assume you have?*

   ____

   ____

5. *Which of the strategies presented in this book are the most effective for learning in this course? Why?*

   ____

   ____

Humanities Courses

Humanities Textbooks Humanities courses focus on all areas of human endeavor—invention, relationships, creation—just about any area you can think of is represented in the humanities. Initially, many students think that humanities texts are easier to read than the texts in more fact-based courses like math or science, but humanities courses are challenging because they require students to read, interpret, analyze, and evaluate the text. In general, humanities textbooks do not introduce much new content vocabulary, but you may encounter unfamiliar use of words or dialects in your reading. Topics in humanities textbooks are often presented chronologically, as in a literature textbook that is arranged by the year each story, poem, and play was written. However, sometimes they are organized topically, as in a philosophy textbook organized by themes. Humanities textbooks are usually not sequential nor do the concepts build on one another, so you should be able to read any chapter in your humanities texts and understand it without reading the previous chapters. Unlike science courses where you look for how concepts are related, in humanities courses you will look for similarities and differences between themes, metaphors, ideology, and philosophy. Therefore, strategies help you think critically about what you are reading.

Study Strategies for Humanities Courses

Humanities courses include literature, philosophy, drama, music, art, and many more. In humanities courses, you are often asked to read from a variety of sources, including novels, plays, and poetry, as well as from a textbook. You also may be required to attend plays, musical events, or other cultural activities in addition to class lectures.

Because many humanities courses are discussion-based, it's important to read the text before attending class. As you read, you should focus on analyzing and interpreting the information. Ask yourself questions such as, Why did the author choose to write this? What is the significance of what I am reading? What themes or metaphors are being used?

In class, it is usually important to take notes about what your classmates are discussing because professors often create exam questions based on class discussion. However, some students write down only what the professor is saying and don't seem to understand the importance of discussion in their humanities courses. As mentioned in Chapter 11, you should attempt to capture discussion in your notes when you are in class.

In addition to reading before class and taking good notes during class, you should connect the reading to class discussions during your review after class. This review may entail annotating your text about themes, metaphors, symbolism, or issues discussed in class; marking important passages or quotations; or connecting themes across readings. Because humanities courses often involve writing papers or taking essay exams, it is always a good idea to keep track of ideas for possible paper topics as you are reading as well as try to predict essay questions after listening to the class discussion.

16.4

SOMETHING TO WRITE AND THINK ABOUT

1. *What humanities courses are you taking this term? (If you are not taking a humanities course this term but have recently taken one, answer the questions based on that course.)*

   ____

   ____

2. *How is your humanities course similar to or different from the humanities courses described above? (Think about whether the class has lecture, discussion, or lab, and consider the type of exams given.)*

   Similarities: ______________________________

   ____

   Differences: ______________________________

   ____

3. *Which of the following components are contained in your textbook:*

   ☐ New terminology (vocabulary words specific to the content)

   ☐ New principles or theories described

   ☐ Chronological format (concepts organized by date)

   ☐ Sequential format (concepts built on one another)

   ☐ Topical format (concepts organized by topic)

4. *What kind of background knowledge, if any, does the text assume you have?*

   ____

   ____

5. *Which of the strategies presented in this book are the most effective for learning in this course? Why?*

   ____

   ____

Social Science Courses

Social Science Textbooks Social science textbooks are usually concerned with what happens in a society. The social sciences involve the study of people in terms of political, economic, social, interpersonal, and cultural aspects of society. These texts are often filled with terms that may seem familiar but have a specialized meaning. For example, the word *class* would have very different meanings in a sociology course than it would in an education course. Social science texts usually present ideas in either chronological order or topical form. For example, a history textbook usually discusses events in the order they occur in time (chronologically), but sociology texts often discuss ideas by topic.

Sections of text are often highlighted in a text box or some other way in social science texts. In high school, you probably used the same tactic whenever you saw a text box—you skipped it. However, in college texts these boxes often contain important information that is not contained in the rest of the text. Sometimes they are supporting articles, or they are examples of a principle outlined in the text, or they are the original documents mentioned in the chapter. But no matter what they contain, follow this general rule: READ THE TEXT BOXES. You may find that many of your exam questions come from information found in the text boxes. Professors are aware that students tend to skip text boxes and want to make sure students pay attention to the important information contained in the boxes, so they base test items on them.

In your social science courses, you will be asked to read and understand many new concepts, so you will need strategies to help you organize large amounts of information.

Study Strategies for Social Science Courses Social science courses include psychology, sociology, education, anthropology, history, political science, economics, and more. Students sometimes experience difficulty in social science courses because they try to memorize facts, forgetting that because the social sciences are based on theories, there are few facts. Also, social science texts often deal with large time spans, making it hard to simply memorize facts. A history class could cover several thousand years all in one semester!

As with your humanities courses, you should read your social science textbooks before you attend class so you are ready for class discussion or lecture. As you read, annotate both the text and any diagrams or other typographical aids. Identify comparisons or contrasts between ideas, because they often make their way into social science exams. In addition, note possible test questions.

Because you will need to be able to see trends, their influence on historical events, and parallels with current events, you will need to use strategies that help you identify relationships between ideas. Charting is a good way to keep track of these relationships between concepts. Often students lose track of the big picture in their social science courses and get bogged down in the details. By charting the information, you will be able to see how all the ideas fit together into a larger concept. You will also be able to track trends or discover principles about the information. Another good strategy is to create a time line to help you remember the sequence of important events. But remember that most social science courses will involve more than just memorizing names and dates, so use your time line to help you see the big picture as well.

16.5 SOMETHING TO WRITE AND THINK ABOUT

1. *What social science courses are you taking this term? (If you are not taking a social science course this term but have recently taken one, answer the questions based on that course.)*

   ____

   ____

2. *How is your social science course similar to or different from the social science courses described above? (Think about whether the class has lecture, discussion, or lab, and consider the type of exams given.)*

   Similarities: ______________________________

   ____

   Differences: ______________________________

   ____

3. *Which of the following components are contained in your textbook:*
   - ☐ New terminology (vocabulary words specific to the content)
   - ☐ New principles or theories described
   - ☐ Chronological format (concepts organized by date)
   - ☐ Sequential format (concepts built on one another)
   - ☐ Topical format (concepts organized by topic)

4. *What kind of background knowledge, if any, does the text assume you have?*

   ____

   ____

5. *Which of the strategies presented in this book are the most effective for learning in this course? Why?*

   ____

   ____

REAL COLLEGE: *Kim's Courses*

Read the following scenario and then respond to the questions based on what you learned in this chapter.

Kim is taking five courses this term: biology, political science, American literature, statistics, and music appreciation. So far, she has approached learning in each course the same way. She goes to class, listens to the lecture, and then reads the assigned chapters in the textbook. She tries to read the text the night of the lecture, but many times she does not get to the reading until right before the exam.

She is doing well in her music appreciation course but is having trouble in all of the other classes. In American literature, the professor expects the class to discuss the novels and does not hold a lecture at all. Because she would rather listen to the professor before reading, Kim usually doesn't have much to contribute to the discussion. Kim does not take any notes in this class and feels that she doesn't really understand what she is supposed to be getting out of the reading. She has failed her first essay exam because the professor said that she was not reading critically enough.

In her biology class, the professor seems to lecture at one hundred miles per hour! It seems as if he introduces twenty new concepts in every class. Kim finds that she has trouble taking good notes because she never knows what the professor is talking about. She knows that something needs to change, but she isn't sure what she needs to do.

Statistics presents a whole other problem for Kim. She didn't understand what was going on from the first day of lecture. Now that they are about fifteen chapters into the textbook, she is completely lost and does not know what to do. They only have two exams in statistics; a midterm and a final. Kim is nervous about taking the midterm, which is in two weeks.

In political science, Kim has so many reading assignments that she has trouble keeping track of them all. The class has reading assignments from the textbook and the newspaper; they are also reading two full-length biographies, and sometimes the professor brings additional readings to class. They are also required to watch the national news each night because they are supposed to be connecting everything they read to current political events. Kim is not sure how to go about connecting all of the different readings to current events.

Using what you know about text and course characteristics, how would you suggest Kim approach learning in the courses that are presenting difficulties for her this term?

- American literature: ______________________________

____

- Biology: ______________________________

____

- Statistics: ______________________________

____

- Political science: ______________________________

____

FOLLOW-UP ACTIVITY

Keep track of how you approach learning in each of your courses this term: When are you reading the text? What strategies are you using to learn? How effective is your approach? Make modifications to your strategy based on the information presented in this chapter.

Networking

- Many web pages cover college learning in a variety of content areas. To find out more about how to approach learning, find some resources using the following key words: studying mathematics, science learning, studying humanities, etc. It may help to start out by looking up a Learning Center to find some of these resources. Find and report to the class on some additional strategies for learning in all your courses.

Becoming Flexible
Varying Your Reading Rate

Read this chapter to answer the following questions:

What does it mean to be a flexible reader?

How can you increase your reading speed?

What are some habits that may slow your reading?

What does the word *flexible* mean to you? You might think of a gymnast who is able to perform amazing physical feats. Or you might think about a choice (e.g., "What do you want to do?" "Whatever. I'm flexible"). No matter the context, being flexible means that one can adapt to the situation. You don't often hear the word *flexible* used in learning situations, but you should begin to think about being a flexible learner. Flexible learners adapt their approach to learning based on the four factors that impact learning discussed in this text: your characteristics as a learner, the task, the study strategies to be used, and the materials with which you must interact.

Becoming a flexible reader is most closely tied to the fourth factor, the kind of text you are reading. In this chapter, we will discuss what it means to become a flexible reader and how to adjust your reading speed to suit your purpose. Before reading the rest of the chapter, consider the *Research into Practice* section, which discusses college students' reading rates.

STUDY TIP

Push yourself to increase your reading speed to save yourself some valuable time.

Research into Practice

Reading Rate*

In this article, O'Reilly and Walker examined studies of *reading rate,* or how fast students read, to examine the methods used to improve reading speed. These studies have found that the average speed for processing most types of texts with good comprehension is between 200 and 400 words per minute (WPM). However, when college students read at speeds below 200 WPM, their comprehension of the text may drop because when students read at 200 WPM or slower, they are using inefficient strategies for reading. Often they are reading word by word, which makes it difficult to comprehend text at the sentence level and beyond.

College reading programs have used many types of methods to increase student reading rates, including computer eye training and other methods for increasing eye movement. However, O'Reilly and Walker point out that these methods may not be effective for one of two reasons. Students often read slowly either because they have trouble understanding vocabulary or because they have difficulty relating new information to what they already know. Therefore, training their eyes to move faster only solves part of the problem.

One of the most effective ways to increase reading rate is to read, read, and read some more! The more exposure students have to reading, the more their vocabularies will improve, as well as their ability to process text quickly.

This study is important for college students because it points out a variety of reasons why students read slowly, and it realistically evaluates current strategies for improving reading rate.

Flexible Reading

A flexible reader knows that it is unrealistic to attempt to read everything at the same speed. In other words, you cannot expect to read your chemistry textbook at the same speed at which you read the local newspaper. Your reading rate will vary depending on three factors:

1. ***The difficulty of the material to be read.*** The easier the material, the faster you will be able to read.
2. ***Your background knowledge about the topic.*** The more you know about a topic, the faster you can read it.

* Source: O'Reilly, R. P., & Walker, J. E. (1990). An analysis of reading rates in college students. *Reading Research and Instruction* 29: 1–11.

3. ***Your interest in the topic.*** The more interest you have in the material, the faster your rate.

The average adult reads about 200 words per minute; the average college student reads about 250 words per minute. Given the amount of reading that is required in college, it is to your advantage to increase your reading rate without sacrificing comprehension. When you were learning to read difficult material in elementary school, your teacher probably advised you to slow down. Many college students follow the same advice to this very day when they read something difficult. However, if you are already reading at a slow rate and slow yourself down even further, you actually might be making it harder to comprehend the text.

If a student is attempting to read the sentence, "The boy went to the store to get a loaf of bread and a gallon of milk" and is reading too slowly, he would read the sentence as individual words instead of phrases:

> The/ boy /went/ to/ the/ store/ to/ get/ a/ loaf/ of/ bread/ and/ a/ gallon/ of/ milk.

A reader who reads individual words will have a more difficult time with comprehension because he must first recognize each of the individual words; then he must put the words together into meaningful phrases and put those phrases together into a sentence. By then, a good deal of time has passed (in reading terms) and a lot of comprehension is lost. In this case, slowing down is *decreasing* the ability to comprehend the information.

Should you ever slow down when reading difficult material? Well, yes and no. You should slow down to the point of comprehension, but you should not read too slowly. To find out about your reading rate, read the passage in the *Self-Assessment.* Then read the rest of the chapter to find out some common habits that can slow your reading and some strategies to help increase your rate and your comprehension.

17.1 SELF-ASSESSMENT

Read the following article to assess your reading rate. Use a stopwatch or a watch with a second hand to keep track of your time. When you have completed the reading, record your time; then answer the comprehension questions. Use the formula following the passage to determine your reading rate. Time yourself only for reading the passage, not for answering the comprehension questions.

It's Party Time

Amid a national epidemic of sometimes deadly binge drinking, many campuses are experimenting with ways to dry out.

By Claudia Kalb

Michael Tindle is a frat brother, a tennis player and a music fan, the kind of guy who enjoys college as much for its social life as its academics. But Tindle is also the kind of guy who has little love for rowdy drinking games and drunken roommates. So last year, when he entered the University of Michigan, he decided to live in a "substance-free" residence hall. The rules: no alcohol, no smoking. At first, Tindle, who is 19, worried that he would feel out of place. "I thought it would be all computer nerds who don't have any kind of social life," he says. But there were plenty of "regular people" just like him.

As social drinking turns toxic on campuses, students like Tindle are looking for ways to stay dry and many schools are re-examining their alcohol policies. A national survey conducted by the Harvard School of Public Health found that 44 percent of U.S. college students binge-drink, downing five or more drinks in one sitting. The effects range from dangerous—falling down a staircase or losing consciousness—to deadly. Experts estimate that 50 students die from alcohol poisoning or in alcohol-related accidents each year. "Regardless of selectivity or prestige, whether Ivy League, Pac-10 or small liberal-arts college down the road, it's a problem at all of them," says George Dowdall, a coauthor of the Harvard study and an associate dean at Saint Joseph's University in Philadelphia.

Students aren't just having beer or wine; they're mixing hard liquors together. And they're using tubes and funnels to pour it down. "In the past, drinking was more a means to an end—to feel comfortable in a social situation," says William DeJong, director of the Higher Education Center for Alcohol and Other Drug Prevention in Newton, Mass. "Now, it's drinking for the sake of drinking to oblivion."

Ninety-five percent of violent crime on college campuses is alcohol-related, according to the National Center on Addiction and Substance Abuse at Columbia University. And alcohol is implicated in everything from academic problems to sexually transmitted diseases and rape. Last year heavy drinking led to riots on campuses from the University of New Hampshire to Washington State University, as students clashed with police over their "right to party."

But the times may be changing. Last fall a string of alcohol-related deaths at MIT, the University of Virginia and Louisiana State University jolted many students, parents and college administrators into action. Schools that receive federal funds are required by law to have an Alcohol and Other Drug (AOD) policy—but in the past, many have been lax. Now administrators are stepping up and expanding their programs. MIT recently instituted a system of citations and fines for illegal drinking and is preparing to hire an administrator to oversee alcohol abuse. Many schools now provide substance-free housing. The University of Michigan, at the forefront of this trend, offered 500 substance-free slots in 1989. Today, thanks to their popularity, 2,600 places are available. "Students tell us that they view it as a way to opt out of the worst parts of a campus alcohol culture," says university spokesman Alan Levy. Other schools organize dry social events. At Holy Cross in Worcester, Mass., students congregate for "mocktails" and munchies or play midnight basketball. And at the five-college consortium of Amherst, Hampshire, Mount Holyoke, Smith and the University of Massachusetts, a joint Web site, dubbed Chilipeppers: Hot Without the Sauce, lists communitywide activities where the drinks are everything but alcoholic.

Some schools choose more unorthodox approaches. At Salisbury State University in Maryland, the task force on alcohol abuse decided to create—not disband—a campus pub. Prohibiting alcohol "doesn't seem to us to be practical or philosophically make a lot of sense," says Prof. Jerry Miller, chair of the task force. "Students are going to drink. Our commitment is to encourage people to drink responsibly." Penalties for underage drinking in the pub are severe—a year's probation or loss of housing. Last year the University of Arizona ran a message on posters and in school newspapers: "64 percent of U of A students have four or fewer drinks when they party." The point: to acknowledge the drinking, but encourage moderation. Since the school adopted this direct approach in 1995, the school's binge-drinking rate has dropped from 43 percent to 31 percent.

Even fraternities, which have long played a major part in college drinking, are looking for solutions. The Harvard survey found that 86 percent of fraternity brothers and 80 percent of sorority sisters binge-drink. But those numbers could be shrinking. Three days after a Phi Gamma Delta pledge died of alcohol poisoning at MIT, the fraternity's national organization announced plans to ban alcohol from all of its college houses by the year 2000. Other national fraternities—including Phi Delta Theta and Sigma Nu—have made similar plans. And more are likely to follow; earlier this year the National Interfraternity Conference, which represents dozens of fraternities nationwide, adopted a unanimous resolution "strongly" encouraging its members to provide alcohol-free facilities and to rededicate themselves to core frat values like leadership and community service.

Experts say prospective students concerned about alcohol abuse should spend a night or two in a dorm and go to a couple of parties—both on and off campus. Talk to both school and town police and ask how often they're breaking up raucous parties or making underage drinking arrests. Visit the local hospital emergency room and find out how many intoxicated students are treated in a given week. Remember that when it comes down to it, you are a consumer. Think hard about attending a school that claims to have no drinking problem at all. The best colleges and universities acknowledge that alcohol abuse is a part of college life—and they're doing everything they can to combat it.

With Julie Weingarden in Detroit
Newsweek, Fall 1998

Comprehension check: Answer the following questions without looking back at the passage.

1. *Which of the following is NOT an approach used by colleges to cope with binge drinking?*
   (a) Issuing fines and citations for illegal drinking
   (b) Expelling binge drinkers
   (c) Creating substance-free housing
   (d) Opening a campus pub

2. *The Harvard School of Public Health found that ______ percent of U.S. college students drink five or more drinks in one sitting.*
   (a) 64
   (b) 54
   (c) 44
   (d) 34

3. *Alcohol has been found to be related to the following problems on college campuses:*

   (a) Academic problems

   (b) Violent crimes

   (c) Riots

   (d) All of the above

4. *After a fraternity pledge died from binge drinking, the fraternity plans to ______ by the year 2000.*

   (a) Ban alcohol

   (b) Disband

   (c) Ban fraternity parties

   (d) Promote leadership

5. *This article suggests that binge drinking will:*

   (a) Decline significantly

   (b) Remain the same

   (c) Increase significantly

   (d) Decline a little

Number of Words	**Your Time**	**Reading Rate** (number of words ÷ time)	**Comprehension Score**
971			%
	Use decimals for fractions of a minute. (e.g., If it took you 3 minutes and 45 seconds, your time would be 3.75 minutes.)		Answers: 1. (b), 2. (c), 3. (d), 4. (a), 5. (d)

Habits That Slow Reading

Many students may have one of several habits that slow their rate of reading speed. Because these habits were developed when they were children, they may not even be aware of them. As you read the following sections, think about your own reading habits.

Backtracking

A person who reads the same words over and over is backtracking. Think about the example sentence used earlier about the boy going to the store. A person who backtracks would read the sentence as

> The boy went to the store/ went to the store/ store/ to get a loaf of bread/ loaf of bread/ and a gallon of milk.

This person is reading words in the same line several times, which can dramatically slow both reading and comprehension. Students backtrack when they are not confident they have understood the reading or when they are daydreaming and not concentrating on what they are reading. However, once backtracking becomes a habit, students tend to do it no matter what they read, which is why it is one of the toughest habits to break.

In order to stop backtracking, you must convince yourself that you understand the information as you read. It is one thing to consciously realize that you do not understand a sentence and need to go back and reread it. However, most people who backtrack do not even realize they are doing it. One good way to stop this habit is to follow along with a pen or your finger as you read. You won't be able to backtrack unconsciously if you are following your finger, and it will help keep your eyes moving steadily forward. Or if you know you backtrack, be sure to take time to preread. Having an idea about where the chapter is headed will help your concentration and, therefore, may also help your tendency to backtrack.

Subvocalization

A person who says the words to herself as she reads is subvocalizing. People who subvocalize may move their lips, or they may say the words under their breath. When you were learning to read, you probably learned to sound out the words, and the teacher often asked you to read aloud. Later, when you began to read silently, you were still saying the words in your head. If you have never stopped "saying" the words, you are probably subvocalizing. Subvocalization dramatically slows reading rates because you can say only about 200 words per minute, but you can read and comprehend at much faster rates.

Luckily, this is a fairly easy habit to break. If you find that you move your lips as you read, put your finger over your lips, and when you feel they are moving, will yourself to stop. If you are saying the words under your breath, put your hand on your throat as you read. You will feel a vibration if you are subvocalizing, and again you can will yourself to stop. Some students have said that humming while reading helped them stop subvocalizing.

Fixations

Each time your eye focuses on a word, it is called a fixation. Fixating is also a habit left over from when you first learned to read. In elementary school, you learned to recognize letters and then words one at a time, which made you fixate often. In fact, you probably stopped at every word. However, effective readers do not fixate on every word; instead,

they read groups of words in a single fixation. A person who fixates too often would read the sentence as

> The/ boy /went/ to/ the/ store/ to/ get/ a/ loaf/ of/ bread/ and/ a/ gallon/ of/ milk.

This person is stopping on each word. To break the habit of fixating too often, a student needs to learn how to include more information in each fixation.

One way to break the habit of too many fixations is to use the key word method. In this strategy, you don't waste your time reading words like "the" or "and." Instead, you focus on more meaningful words. As you fixate on key words, your eyes tend to include the words like "the" without having to fixate on them. A person using the key word strategy often would read the sentence as

> The boy **went**/ to the **store**/ to get a loaf of **bread**/ and a gallon of **milk**.

Experiment with this method to see how many times you must fixate in order to get the main idea of a sentence and to prove to yourself that you can comprehend without focusing on every word.

Another strategy to reduce fixation is phrase word reading. Using this strategy, you go through the passage and stop in the middle of each phrase. When you stop, your eye takes in the entire phrase. It is different from the key word strategy because you are not looking for specific words; rather, you are taking in larger chunks of information at a time. A person using the phrase word strategy would read the sentence as

> The **boy went**/ **to the store**/ to get a **loaf of bread**/ and a **gallon of milk**.

Some students learn best using the key word strategy, but others say they comprehend better using the phrase word strategy. Try out both strategies to see which one works best for you.

17.2 SOMETHING TO THINK ABOUT AND DISCUSS

How often do you fixate? Try this experiment with a partner to determine the number of fixations you make per line:

1. Punch a small hole in a sheet of paper with typed paragraphs on it.
2. Hold the blank side of the paper close to your eye so you can see through it.
3. Have your partner read the paragraphs contained on the sheet of paper and watch her eyes.
4. Count the number of fixations (times she stops) per line.

5. Change places with your partner and repeat, having your partner count your fixations.
6. Discuss the habits that may be slowing your reading and your partner's reading.

Increasing Your Reading Speed

Many companies advertise speed-reading programs that cost several hundred to several thousand dollars! These offers are sometimes unrealistic when they claim one can read at a thousand words per minute or finish a novel in less than one hour. However, you can increase your reading speed, and sometimes even double it, without spending big bucks. All you need is something interesting to read and some time each day to push yourself to read faster.

The purpose of pushing yourself to read faster is to increase your overall reading speed. When you practice reading faster, you should not use your textbooks or even novels assigned for class. You cannot expect to be able to speed-read a difficult textbook filled with new concepts and comprehend all the information. Likewise, if you speed-read a novel in your literature class, you will be missing the language that makes the novel a great work. You may grasp the basic plot but little else. When you are practicing reading faster, use a piece of text you find enjoyable—a newspaper article, a magazine article, a novel you are reading for pleasure—but do *not* use material that you will be tested over.

Keys to Reading Faster

- ***Choose high-interest material.*** It is best to push yourself to read faster with material that you are familiar with and enjoy reading. For example, if you like to read mystery novels, choose one to use for pushed reading.
- ***Practice every day.*** To increase your reading rate, you will need to push yourself to read faster every day for ten to fifteen minutes. Use your local or school newspaper or anything else that will sustain your interest for that amount of time. You might want to choose three or four shorter articles and take a short break after each one.
- ***Read at slightly-faster-than-comfortable speeds.*** As you read, push yourself to read slightly faster than you usually do. You should feel a little uncomfortable reading at this speed and feel that you would prefer to slow down, but you should also sense that you understand what you are reading.

KEYS TO READING FASTER

- *Choose high-interest material.*
- *Practice every day.*
- *Read at slightly-faster-than-comfortable speeds.*
- *Check your comprehension.*
- *Try to read at the same time each day.*
- *Don't give up.*

- ***Check your comprehension.*** Increasing your reading rate while losing comprehension provides no benefit. Therefore, you need to check your comprehension of the material you are reading. However, because you are changing a habit, it is okay to have comprehension of only 70 percent to 80 percent of what you read during pushed reading. If you are having 100 percent comprehension, you can probably read faster! To check your comprehension, try to summarize the information. Did you identify all of the key ideas? What about important details and examples? If you find you are not comprehending the information, slow down a bit. Don't worry that you are only understanding 70 percent to 80 percent. Remember, you are not pushing yourself on material you will be tested over, so you do not need to have 100 percent comprehension.
- ***Try to read at the same time each day.*** Finding fifteen minutes to read every day should not be much of a problem; in order to keep an accurate record of your improvement, you should try to find the time when you are most alert and read at that same time every day.
- ***Don't give up.*** This is a slow but steady process. You may make some great improvements one week and then see little change the next. Don't worry about the fluctuations in your rate, as long as you are seeing an overall increase in your reading rate. However, if you find that you have gone several weeks without any improvement, make a conscious effort to push yourself even faster when you read.

17.3 MONITORING YOUR LEARNING

Practice pushing yourself to read faster using the strategies you have learned. Remember to read at a slightly-faster-than-comfortable pace. Use a stopwatch or a watch with a second hand to keep track of your time. When you have completed the reading, record your time and then answer the comprehension questions. Use the formula following the passage to determine your reading rate. Time yourself only for reading the passage, not for answering the comprehension questions.

Living Hand to Mouth

New research shows that gestures often help speakers access words from their memory banks.

By Sharon Begley

When Robert Krauss was a boy, 50 years ago, his grandfather told him a story about two men walking down a street one cold winter's day. One man babbled incessantly, while his companion, frigid hands stuffed in his pockets, merely nodded here and there. Finally, the talker asked, "Shmuel, why aren't you saying anything?" To which the friend replied, "I forgot my gloves."

As a boy, Krauss was hard put to understand how someone could be struck dumb by having his hands stilled. But now, as a professor of psychology at Columbia University, he has made the role of gestures in speech a focus of his research. When Krauss started, the conventional scientific wisdom was that gestures are a visual language that conveys meaning—a pointed finger means "you," a hand brushed sideways means "over there." But since some gestures, such as chopping the air in rhythm with one's sentences, are clearly meaningless, there is an emerging consensus that gestures serve another function, says Krauss: "They help people retrieve elusive words from their memory."

A slew of recent and upcoming papers pinpoint how talking with your hands can unlock what Krauss calls "lexical memory." One study, for instance, finds that speakers gesture more when they try to define words that have a strong spatial component—like "under" or "adjacent"—than when defining words that are more abstract, like "thought" or "evil." And doctors notice that stroke patients whose brain lesion impairs their ability to name objects gesture more, "as if they are trying everything they can to come up with a word," says Krauss. Even people who don't think they're gesturing may be. Krauss attached electrodes to people's arms to measure the activation of their muscles—a little clench that doesn't blossom into a full gesture. Then he asked them to come up with words that fit a definition he supplied. "You get more muscle activation when you try to access a word like 'castanets,' which has a connotation of movement, than when you try to access an abstract word like 'mercy'," he finds.

If gesticulating is like wielding a key to the door of lexical memory, then someone who can't use his hands should have more trouble unlocking the door. That is just what a new study in the *American Journal of Psychology* finds. In the experiment, volunteers held onto a bar to keep their hands still; when Donna Frick-Horbury of Appalachian State University in North Carolina read them definitions ("an ancient instrument used for calculations"), the subjects more often failed to think of the word ("abacus"), or took longer to do it, than when they could gesture freely. "Many subjects would actually make motions of using an abacus before coming up with the word," says psychologist Robert Guttentag of the University of North Carolina at Greensboro, who oversaw the study.

Such findings provide a clue to how our word memory works. Many doors in the brain seem to open onto memories. Just as a whiff of turmeric may unleash a recollection of Grandma's kitchen, so gesturing may open a door to a word with a spatial or movement connotation, says neuroscientist Brian Butterworth of University College, London. This theory "makes sense," says memory expert Daniel Schacter of Harvard University, "because we know that the more elaborately a memory is encoded"—with vision, smell and movement, for instance— "the easier it is to access."

Not everyone talks with his hands. At the extremes, some people gesture 40 times more than others, Krauss finds. An anthropology study in 1940s New York found that Italian and Jewish immigrants gestured a lot; Jews tended to keep their gestures small, while Italians were more expansive. Krauss suspects that the differences reflect the rhythmicity of languages: the more rhythmic, the more gestures. But something even more interesting may be going on. "How much people gesture may reflect a difference in how they think," says Krauss. "People who gesture a lot may conceptualize things in spatial terms. For instance, rather than thinking of 'comprehension' as a purely abstract concept, they may think of it as physically grasping something. And some people may conceive of 'freedom' not only as political, but also in more spatial terms," such as "without boundaries," which lends itself to gesture. The more an abstract word has physical counterparts, the more helpful gesturing would be. Next time you're tongue-tied, then, try hand-waving.

Newsweek, November 2, 1998

Comprehension check: Answer the following questions without looking back at the passage.

1. *Robert Krauss's research has found:*
   (a) Gestures are a visual language that conveys meaning.
   (b) Gestures have very little meaning.
   (c) Gestures help to retrieve words from memory.
   (d) Gestures make people able to communicate.

2. *In Krauss's experiment with defining words, people:*
   (a) Remembered words more quickly when they were able to gesture
   (b) Were not aware they were using gestures
   (c) Were not able to remember the words
   (d) Made gestures instead of saying the words

3. *Research on gestures has found:*
   (a) All people gesture when they talk.
   (b) Older people gesture more than younger people.
   (c) Only immigrants gesture.
   (d) Gestures are related to how people think.

4. *According to Krauss, a person would gesture more when trying to define the word ______.*
   (a) Good
   (b) Above
   (c) Pretty
   (d) Green

5. *Overall, this article suggests:*
   (a) All people should gesture when they speak.
   (b) If you are not allowed to gesture, you will not be able to access words.
   (c) Gesturing helps people access words from their memories.
   (d) People store thoughts as gestures in their memory.

Number of Words	**Your Time**	**Reading Rate** (number of words ÷ time)	**Comprehension Score**
749			%

Use decimals for fractions of a minute. (e.g., If it took you 3 minutes and 15 seconds, your time would be 3.25 minutes.)

Answers:
1. (c), 2. (a), 3. (d), 4. (b), 5. (d)

(Most college students will have a reading rate between 250 WPM and 500 WPM on this passage. Your comprehension should be 70% to 80%.)

How Fast Should You Read?

Students often ask us how quickly they should read. However, this is not an easy question to answer because the rate at which you read depends on your purpose for reading and the type of material you are reading. Your goal is to be flexible in your reading and to choose a rate depending on your purpose. For example, you should be able to read a magazine or novel at a faster rate than a textbook.

In general, you should always strive to read faster than 200 WPM because lower speeds can inhibit your comprehension. Otherwise, we are hesitant to give you exact numbers because the rate at which you "should" read depends on three factors:

1. Your Current Reading Rate

It would make no sense to tell a student to read at 400 WPM if she is currently reading at 225 WPM with 70 percent comprehension. Instead, we would tell that student to use the pushed reading strategy described in this chapter to help increase her overall reading rate without sacrificing comprehension.

2. Your Purpose for Reading

Slowest speeds: If you are reading to write a paper about a topic or to prepare for an exam, you will read at fairly slow speeds. This includes reading difficult texts, poetry, technical manuals, textbooks, or literature with which you must take time to notice and savor the language.

Moderate speeds: If your purpose is to read for pleasure or for general information, you will be able to read more quickly. This type of reading includes novels, newspapers, magazines, and other reading for enjoyment.

Fastest speeds: If you are scanning material for specific information, you will be able to read at faster rates. This type of reading includes dictionaries, catalogs, phone books, and other reference books.

3. Your Task

If you will be tested over the material, take more time to really understand it. It makes no sense to rush through your history text if you are not getting all the information. If you are reading for pleasure, there may be times when you want to read slowly to enjoy your book and times when you want to use pushed reading to increase your rate. Be sure to leave yourself some time for both.

Using the pushed reading strategy should help you increase your rate no matter what you read.

REAL COLLEGE: *Rudy's Reading Rate*

Read the following scenario and then respond to the questions based on what you learned in this chapter.

Rudy is a first-year student at a small college. His goal is to finish his degree in computer science in three years, so he is taking eighteen to twenty-one credit hours each term. However, he is overwhelmed by the amount of reading he has to do for each of his classes. He has to read technical reports and manuals for his computer science courses; novels, poetry, and plays in his English class; a very difficult textbook in his physics class; and a textbook and newspaper in his political science course. He knows that his problem is that he reads too slowly. Ever since grade school, he has always been the last one to finish his reading and the last one to turn in an exam. He is sure that if he could just learn to read faster, he would do better in school. He has signed up for a speed-reading course in which he spends a lot of time using computer eye-movement programs, but he does not feel comfortable reading with that equipment and does not think it is helping. He generally tries to read everything as fast as he can but finds that he gets tired quickly and can't keep it up. He also finds that he really doesn't understand what he is reading in some of his courses.

Using what you know about increasing reading rate and the habits that slow down reading, give Rudy some advice on how to go about increasing his reading speed.

____

____

____

____

____

____

____

____

____

____

____

FOLLOW-UP ACTIVITY

As you work on increasing your reading rate, keep track of your speed and your comprehension in a journal. You should notice a steady increase in your rate over a period of time. Eventually, you will find that your comprehension is reaching 100 percent at higher speeds. You can then decide whether to continue to increase your reading rate.

Networking

- Thousands of sites on the Internet publish short stories or magazine articles. Find some stories that interest you on the web, and use them for your reading-rate practice. You might want to check out *Newsweek* or your favorite newspaper as a starting point. Then find some sites about topics that interest you to find material for your pushed reading. If you find that you read more slowly on the computer, as many people do, print out the stories you find before using them to increase your reading speed.

Pulling Everything Together

In Part VI, we pull together all of the different strategies you have learned. In Chapter 18, you will learn strategies for preparing for and taking objective exams. We also introduce some general test-taking strategies.

Chapter 19 discusses strategies for preparing for and taking essay exams. You will also learn about taking specialized exams, such as open-book or take-home exams.

In Chapter 20, we revisit the four factors that influence learning. We sum up the key points discussed in the text and answer some common questions students have about active learning and studying in college.

Before you read the chapters in Part VI, please respond to the following statements. Read each statement and decide whether you agree or disagree with it.

Keep your responses in mind as you read the chapters in Part VI. When you have finished reading Part VI, revisit this page. How are your responses similar to or different from what is introduced in the chapters?

BEFORE			AFTER	
Agree	**Disagree**		**Agree**	**Disagree**
☐	☐	***1. Taking a multiple-choice test is easy because all I have to do is recognize the correct answer.***	☐	☐
☐	☐	***2. To study for an objective test, I memorize all the key terms.***	☐	☐
☐	☐	***3. It is best to spread out studying time over several days.***	☐	☐
☐	☐	***4. Essay tests are easier than objective tests because I can fake my way through answers I don't know.***	☐	☐
☐	☐	***5. One of the best ways to prepare for essay exams is to try to predict essay questions.***	☐	☐
☐	☐	***6. To become an active learner, I should choose one strategy that works and stick with it.***	☐	☐

Preparing for Objective Exams

Read this chapter to answer the following questions:

What exam preparation strategies work in almost all situations?

How should you prepare for objective exams?

STUDY TIP

When you go into a testing situation, have a plan. And be sure to watch your time. You do not want to run out of time before you run out of test!

Because we believe that preparing to take an exam begins on the day you begin to read about and listen to topics on which you will be tested, we almost feel as though having a special chapter on exam preparation goes against the philosophy of this book. That is, active learners are in a constant state of getting ready to take an exam! They have a difficult time distinguishing when previewing, reading, and taking lecture notes turn into the rehearsal and review that go into test preparation. That said, we also know that many activities that occur as test time gets closer might be more appropriately labeled test preparation strategies.

Before you continue reading this chapter, however, read the *Research into Practice* segment that follows. In this article, Dr. Michael Pressley and his colleagues attempt to answer the following question: What can be done to make exam preparation easier? They synthesize what the literature says about why college students find exam preparation so difficult. Following *Research into Practice,* we discuss some general test preparation strategies and then present strategies specifically designed for objective tests.

Research into Practice

Why Does It Have to Be So Difficult?*

In this article, Dr. Pressley and his colleagues acknowledged that preparing to take an exam is a difficult task for a number of reasons. First, there is the problem of inconsiderate texts. (Remember that we talked about inconsiderate texts in Chapter 12.) When texts are inconsiderate, it is often difficult to select important ideas or make connections. Then there is the problem of inadequate teaching. Professors who are poor lecturers can be challenging to take good notes from, and they may not even clearly outline the task. Sometimes students themselves are at fault. They may not be active readers, and they may lack the strategies necessary to learn the information in an effective and efficient way. Moreover, students often have deficiencies in background knowledge that hinder them from acquiring new information, or they may simply not activate the knowledge they possess. A whole host of other problems can come from the learner, such as the lack of monitoring skills and knowing task-appropriate test-taking strategies. Finally, there is the problem of low motivation.

But what can be done by professors to help make it easier for students to prepare for exams? Pressley and his colleagues made several suggestions, based on a synthesis of earlier research. First, texts can be made more considerate in three ways: Write texts in which it's easy both to see connections by using text signals and to identify the main points; in addition, illustrations that overlap with the text's meaning help improve memory and create interest. Professors can make the test preparation task easier by lecturing in an organized fashion and by matching the speed of the presentation with the difficulty of the material. Students need to learn how to be active and involved readers. Pressley and his colleagues stated that "One of the worst myths we have encountered in education is that learning to read is something accomplished in elementary grades. There is no compelling evidence that teens use diverse strategies … [that are] associated with expert reading."

The synthesis in this article offers a good explanation as to why even the best and the brightest students can have problems in test preparation with specific courses. It seems as though at least three things need to work in concert: The text should be considerate; the professor should be an organized lecturer who is sensitive to the students' level and the diffi-

* Source: Pressley, M., Yokoi, L., van Meter, P., Van Etten, S., & Freebern, G. (1997). Some of the reasons why preparing for exams is so hard: What can be done to make it easier? *Educational Psychology Review* 9: 1–38.

culty of the course material; and the students should have adequate background knowledge, be able to monitor their skills, and use task-appropriate strategies.

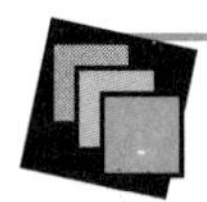

General Test Preparation Strategies

Although this chapter will focus on the specific strategies you can use primarily in preparation for objective exams, there are some general test preparation guidelines that apply to almost any type of exam. We will address these general strategies first because there are some "quick starters" that can get you moving in the right direction.

In general, you should:

QUICK START: TEST PREPARATION TIPS

- *Start early.*
- *Break up the work.*
- *Stay healthy.*
- *Self-test.*
- *Study with a classmate.*
- *Look at old exams.*
- *Talk to students who have taken the course.*

- ***Start early.*** Be sure that you have completed your text reading at least several days before the test. Remember that reading and studying are not the same thing. All your reading should be completed *before* you begin studying. Because you are starting early, you will also be able to distribute your study time over several days rather than trying to cram it all into one or two days before the exam. Spending a total of 10 hours studying spread over 5 days is much more effective than trying to spend 10 hours studying the day before, or even 5 hours a day for 2 days before the test.
- ***Break up the work.*** If you begin studying several days in advance, you will be able to break up the information you have to study into chunks of major concepts. In other words, don't sit down to study with the idea in mind that you will study every chapter and every page of notes. Study sessions such as this encourage passive interaction with the material. Study groups of information that seem to fit together, or at least identify which concepts you want to learn in a particular study session. If you have twenty key concepts to learn, learn five a day for four days. Stick with it until you learn those concepts. This helps you stay more focused on the task at hand.
- ***Stay healthy.*** It's especially important as you are studying for exams to keep health issues in mind. Eat right and get enough sleep. Try to stay in a studying routine rather than staying up all night cramming. Eat regular meals and exercise (if that is part of your normal routine). As part of staying healthy, it's also important to monitor your emotional health by evaluating your stress level. When you get too stressed out, it influences other aspects of your performance and becomes a vicious cycle. We find that in peak exam periods, such as

around mid-terms and finals, more students get colds, the flu, and other maladies, perhaps because they are ignoring a healthy lifestyle.

- ***Self-test.*** It's important to have a firm understanding of what you know and what you don't know. Self-testing, a form of monitoring that we have discussed on more than one occasion in this text, is the only way you can be sure you truly know information. Remember that self-testing involves asking yourself questions about the material, saying the information to yourself or to someone else accurately and precisely, and then checking to see whether you are correct. Self-testing is not just reading over your notes or textbook.
- ***Study with a classmate.*** Unless you absolutely hate studying with someone else, studying with another serious-minded student has great benefits regardless of what kind of test you will have. Getting ideas and explanations from others and being able to look at things from a different perspective are all advantages of studying with a classmate. As discussed in Chapter 15, it works best if this person is not someone you generally socialize with. In addition, you might want to think of studying with another person only once, a couple of days before the exam. One of the most successful models for studying with another is for both individuals to study on their own and then get together to ask each other questions a day or two before the exam. Both parties can then find out which concepts they know very well and which ones they need to spend more time on.
- ***Look at old exams; talk to others who have previously had the class.*** We mentioned this idea in Chapter 10, but it merits repeating here. Finding out as much information about the test as possible, whether it's from looking at old exams or by talking to others, is simply a

smart thing to do. It's not cheating; it's being an informed consumer, so to speak. If professors let students keep their exams, you can be fairly certain they will not be giving that same test again. But it's probably also a safe bet that the kinds of questions asked will be similar. When talking with students who have already taken the class and had the professor, it's a good rule of thumb to find out specifics about the level of questions and grading. Do test items tend to focus on higher-level questions or on memorization? Does the professor ever curve grades? What kind of match is there between the text, the lectures, and the exam? By collecting this type of information, you can better focus your attention on the way the concepts will be tested.

Many of these general tips are commonsense. But they are tips that students often overlook as they get caught up in exam preparation. In the next section, we will focus more specifically on preparing for and taking objective exams.

18.1 SELF-EVALUATION

1. *Think about how you currently prepare for exams. If you were going to have a couple of tests next week, what would you do, in general, to get ready? List what you would do below. Because this is a self-evaluation activity, be honest!*

   ____

   ____

   ____

   ____

   ____

2. *Do you prepare for all of your exams (both objective and essay) in the same way? If you don't, how do you adjust your studying based on the type of test?*

   ____

   ____

   ____

   ____

   ____

Preparing for and Taking Objectives Exams

Preparing for Objective Exams

Objective exams consist of several different kinds of questions. The most commonly used types are multiple-choice and true/false questions, but matching and fill-in-the-blanks are also objective-type questions. Another name for these types of items is *recognition items* because all of the information is there; your task is to recognize it. For example, in the case of multiple-choice questions, you have to recognize which answer out of the four or five choices is correct. For a true/false question, you have to recognize whether the statement is true or false. These items are considered objective because there is (or should be) clearly one correct answer, if the test is well written. In other words, in a multiple-choice question, only one of the answers should be correct. Moreover, if you studied and really know the information, the correct answer should be obvious to you.

STUDYING FOR OBJECTIVE EXAMS

- *Make a jot list of key points.*
- *Organize this information around broad concepts.*
- *Begin each study session with a review.*
- *Rehearse and self-test.*
- *Concentrate on areas of weakness.*

Because of the precise knowledge required to answer objective items, it is extremely important that two key factors guide your preparation: (1) organizing information and (2) thinking about the information in the way your professor expects. Let's think about organization first. In Chapter 10, we talked about the importance of understanding the task. As an example, let's say that you are in an introductory-level psychology course. Every two to three weeks, you have a 50-item objective test—always all multiple-choice items. In any given testing period, you have about 30 pages of lecture notes and 3 or 4 chapters of information to study. Where do you begin? We have found that the best place to start when you know you will have an objective test is to make a jot list of all the key concepts from texts and lectures. Figure 18.1 shows what this jot list might look like for a psychology course that includes the "Cognition" excerpt from Appendix A. Notice that the jot list is not particularly formal. Rather, it simply serves to force you to think about the concepts before you begin to study. Unless you make a conscious effort to jot down these concepts, you may leave out important information or simply gloss over concepts that you should spend a significant amount of time on.

Once you have made your jot list, then you can go about organizing the information to study. A savvy student has all the rehearsal strategies related to the overriding concept together. (Let's use the psychology concept "learning" as an example.) She also knows which sections of lecture notes go with this concept. She begins to look for overlap between the text and lectures and focuses her studying on the *concept of learning* rather than on just her text information one time and the lecture notes

FIGURE 18.1 Jot List for a Multiple-Choice Psychology Exam (Test is over Chapters 5, 6, and 7).

CHAPTER 5—Learning

Classical conditioning
- Pavlov
- basic principles
- exceptions
- principles into action

Operant conditioning
- basic principles
- reinforcement
- punishment
- shaping
- a cognitive perspective

Observational learning
- basic principles
- aggression
- applications

CHAPTER 6—Memory

Information processing
- types

Memory systems
- STM
- LTM

Levels of processing

Retrieval cues

Forgetting
- why
- decay
- interference
- repression
- intentional

Memory distortion
- construction
- eye witness testimony

Biological basis

CHAPTER 7—Cognition

Thinking (basic elements)

Concepts
- propositions
- images
- reasoning

Animal cognition

Making decisions
- framing
- bad decisions
- naturalistic

Problem solving
- methods for
- metacognition
- factors that interfere with

Artificial intelligence

Language
- nature of
- development of

at another. When you are studying for objective exams, the key is to focus each study session on a couple of broad concepts, such as "learning" or "memory" in psychology, rather than simply try to read through everything you have to learn for the entire test. In other words, one night you might study all the material related to learning, the next night memory, and the third night cognition. Following this procedure encourages you to think actively and critically.

Using your jot list as a guide, each study session begins with a brief review of what you learned in the last session. Then rehearse and self-test the material from the next broad concept. Your study schedule might look something like the plan in Figure 18.2. Note that each study session begins with a review and that after you have covered all the material, you end with a self-testing session where you identify specific areas of weak-

FIGURE 18.2 *Study Cycle for Friday's Psychology Exam*

SESSION 1 —	Monday
Focus:	Learning
4:30–5:00	Organize all information
5:00–6:00	Study: Classical conditioning and operant conditioning
6:00–6:45	Eat dinner
7:00–8:00	Review: Classical and operant conditioning
	Study: Observations
SESSION 2 —	**Tuesday**
Focus:	Memory
10:00–10:30	Review topic of learning
10:30–11:30	Study: Information processing and memory processes
11:30–12:00	Lunch
3:00–4:00	Study: Forgetting, memory distortion, and biology of memory
4:00–4:30	Review: Memory
SESSION 3 —	**Wednesday**
Focus:	Cognition
4:30–5:00	Review: Information from sessions 1 and 2
5:00–6:00	Study: Basic elements of thinking, animal cognition, and making decisions
6:00–6:45	Eat dinner
7:00–9:00	Study: Problem solving and language
	Review and self-test: All three chapters

ness. You concentrate on these areas of weakness as you and your study partner question each other in one final study session before the exam. On the morning of the exam, you would simply talk through the couple of ideas that were still giving you difficulty.

Organizing, in terms of both how you will group the concepts to be learned and how you will structure your study sessions, is crucial to performing well on objective tests. However, organizing won't help you much if you aren't sure about the level of thinking required. On essay tests (which we'll talk about in the next chapter), you can pretty much count on having to think critically and to analyze and synthesize information. But on objective exams, many students make the mistake of believing that the test questions are designed solely to see if they have memorized information. That is, they think the questions don't go beyond asking for facts. Students who fall into this trap can experience grave difficulty and often don't do well. As we discussed in Chapter 10, it's important to know the kind of thinking that your professor expects. If she expects you to memorize the facts and most of the questions are factual in nature, you would study in one way. However, if she asks for application, synthesis, and examples, as well as other types of higher-level questions, you would study another way.

To clarify this point, let's look at several example questions. Each of these questions is based on one of the appendixes' excerpts. The first example in each pair of questions is a memory-level task; the second is a higher-level question. The correct response is starred.

Set A (based on "Cognition")

1. An **artificial concept** is:
   a. A clear-cut example
   b. Defined by a set of properties*
   c. Fuzzy and unclear
   d. Something that depends on probability
2. Which of the following statements is an example of an **artificial concept**?
   a. An apple is a fruit.*
   b. A pickle is a vegetable.
   c. Horse racing is a sport.
   d. All of the above are artificial concepts.
   e. None of the above are artificial concepts.

Set B (based on "Technologies of Mass-Production and Destruction")

1. According to demographers, the *best* way to reduce population growth is to:
   a. Provide free birth control
   b. Restrict families to having only one child
   c. Improve health measures*
   d. Increase the food supply
2. Which of the following conditions *best* explains why couples in poorer countries might decide to reduce the number of children they have?
   a. Free birth control is provided.
   b. Health conditions improve the likelihood that babies will live into adulthood.*
   c. Families receive money for having fewer children.
   d. Governments pass laws that restrict the number of children couples can have.

Set C (based on "The Human Nervous System")

1. Which of the following are the functional parts of the forebrain?
   a. Cerebrum, thalamus, cerebral cortex
   b. Limbic system, cerebral cortex, reticular formation
   c. Medulla, cerebrum, cerebral cortex
   d. Thalamus, limbic system, cerebral cortex*

2. A dysfunctional hypothalamus might result in:
   a. The display of inappropriate emotions
   b. Excessive thirst
   c. Increased body temperature
   d. All of the above*
   e. b and c only

It is fairly easy to see the differences in these two types of questions. The first question in each group is very straightforward and requires little interpretation or thinking beyond the memory level. Studying for an objective test that asked this type of question would be a relatively easy task: Identify the key terms and ideas, and memorize a definition, component parts, and the like. But think about the problem you might have if you simply memorized information and then had an exam that asked questions like the second one in each pair. You would have a much more difficult time because you had thought about the information in an incorrect way. If you have only memorized when the task is to somehow go beyond memorization, taking the test will be a struggle.

The point here is that you need to be clear about the professor's expectations and the way he or she tests. As we mentioned earlier, look at old exams, talk to students who have taken a class with the professor, and/or ask the professor yourself. Whatever you do, have an accurate picture of the kind of test you will have. Then as you are doing your rehearsal, review, and self-testing, you can frame your studying accordingly: Sometimes it's as easy as learning some examples that illustrate a particular definition; sometimes it's synthesizing a complex theory; and sometimes it's trying to look at the information from a different point of view.

18.2

SOMETHING TO WRITE ABOUT AND DISCUSS

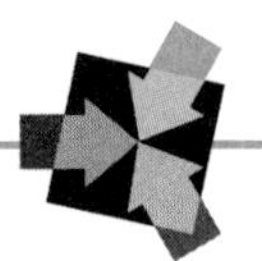

Thinking Critically

One way to get a feel for the difference between thinking about the information in a factual way and in a more conceptual, higher-level way is to rewrite questions. Each question below is written as a factual question. First, circle the correct answer to the question that is posed. Then, in the space provided, rewrite the question so that it is a more difficult, higher-level question. All of the questions are based on the "Cognition" excerpt in Appendix A, so be sure to refer to it as you rewrite your questions. Finally, discuss your questions with a classmate.

1. *Which of the following* best *explains what "concepts" are?*
   (a) People, places, and things
   (b) Mental categories that are similar to each other
   (c) Ideas that do not have specific defining features
   (d) Ideas that can stand as independent assertions

Rewrite a higher-level question about "concepts": ______________________

____

____

____

2. *Blessing and Ross (1966) used verbal protocol analysis to determine:*
   (a) How much mental imagery children used during reading
   (b) Whether children reached valid conclusions through cognitive reasoning
   (c) How experienced problem solvers differed from inexperienced ones
   (d) Thinking processes used during social interactions

   Rewrite a higher-level question about the Blessing and Ross study: ______________________

   ____

   ____

   ____

3. *Reasoning based on two propositions called premises is what kind of reasoning?*
   (a) Imaginal
   (b) Everyday
   (c) Confirmation
   (d) Syllogistic

   Rewrite a higher-level question about this type of reasoning: ______________________

   ____

   ____

   ____

Taking Objective Exams

You have studied, you feel good about what you know, and you are *absolutely ready* to take this exam. Well, you're almost ready! The last thing you need to think about is a game plan. A sports analogy fits well here. The basketball team members have studied the playbook, looked at films of themselves and the opponent, and are mentally ready to play this game. They are pumped and psyched! But if they don't have a game plan or fail to follow the game plan provided by the coaches, all their work may not result in a win. Any athletic team going into a game needs a game plan to follow—some sort of strategy for winning the game.

A testing situation for you is just like game day for the basketball team. You have prepared, you are mentally ready to take the test, and you want to do well. Now you have to follow through with your game plan for taking the test. To plan your strategy, it helps to ask yourself some questions before you get into the testing situation:

- How will I work through the test? For example, will I simply start with the first item and answer the questions in consecutive order?
- What will I do when I come across an item I'm not sure of? Will I skip it and come back to it later, or will I mark something before going on to the next item?
- How will I choose an answer when I absolutely can't even make an educated guess? For example, will I mark all true/false questions that I don't know with either true or false?
- What will I do if I am running out of time and still have several questions to answer?

It's important to think about how you approach an exam before you are actually in a testing situation. Sometimes your game plan might go awry, but it's always better to go in with an approach in mind. We suggest the following guidelines that might help you out in the testing situation:

- ***Get to class early.*** Leave home early enough so that you don't have to rush. When you rush, you tend to get anxious, especially on an exam day. Once you get to class, get out your pen and anything else you might need. Relax and take a couple of deep breaths. Give yourself some positive reinforcement by saying something such as, "I studied," "I know this stuff," or "I know I should do well on this exam."

TAKING OBJECTIVE TESTS
- *Get to class early.*
- *Look through the exam.*
- *Find a question you know.*
- *Eliminate answers.*
- *Use information from other items.*
- *Use all the allotted time.*
- *If you have to guess, guess and move on.*

- ***When you get your exam, take a minute or so to look through it.*** See how many items there are so that you know how to divide up your time. Read the directions so you know what you are required to do.

- ***Find a question you know.*** Read the first item. If you don't know the answer, leave it blank and go on to the next item. Do this with each item until you find one that you are certain of. We believe that it is good advice to do the items you know first; then come back and spend more time on those you are unsure of. The only problem this seems to create is that students sometimes make mistakes on their answer sheet by putting an answer in the wrong place. Therefore, if you are going to skip around on the test, you need to make sure that your answer goes on the corresponding place on your answer sheet.

- ***Eliminate answers whenever possible.*** On a multiple-choice question, you might be able to eliminate two answer choices immediately, but the other two alternatives might both be plausible. If this occurs, you at least have a 50/50 chance of choosing correctly. That beats a 25 percent chance when you haven't eliminated any of the choices.

- ***Use information in other items on the exam to help you with items you don't know.*** Once you have gone through the entire test, you can often pick up information from one question that will help you answer another. That's why it's a good idea to go through and answer the items you know first.

- ***Use all the allotted time.*** Many students fail to use the entire class period to take their exam and end up making careless mistakes, such as leaving items blank when they could have guessed. Even when you have answered every question, it's best to go through the test one more time just to be sure. Remember, it's easy to mark a wrong answer when you actually know the correct answer. Going back and rereading each item and making sure you are satisfied with the answer you selected can often gain you several points.

- ***When faced with a situation in which you have to guess, make a selection and move on.*** Go with your gut selection; don't change your mind unless you have found information later in the test that helps you remember an idea related to the question. On a multiple-choice exam, for example, some students will select the same answer choice for every question they don't know. For true/false questions, you might answer all true or all false for items on which you guess. Whatever you do, however, never leave objective test items blank unless you are penalized for guessing. Leaving items blank can only cause you to lose points.

18.3 SOMETHING TO THINK ABOUT AND DISCUSS

Think back to your last experience of preparing for and taking an objective test. How did you prepare for this test? Did you have a game plan? Were you satisfied with your performance? Did you change the way you studied for subsequent tests? If so, how? After you have thought about these questions, talk them over with a classmate. Compare and contrast your responses with those of your classmates.

REAL COLLEGE: *Terrence's Tactics*

Read the following scenario and then respond to the questions based on what you learned in this chapter.

In high school, Terrence was always a model student. He wasn't one of those kids who waited until the morning of a test to try to cram as much information as possible into his brain. Terrence usually started a day or two before his scheduled exams and reviewed the study guides that most of his teachers gave him. An hour or so of reading over this information typically resulted in a good test grade for him.

Now, early in his first semester of college, Terrence finds that these tactics aren't working so well for him. He earned a D on his first anthropology exam, and things don't look all that promising for the multiple-choice test in psychology he has in a few days. It's not that he doesn't have the time; he just doesn't know what to do!

His professors don't seem to be much help at all. Gone are the study guides that once made studying easy. Gone are the kind of tests he had in high school that simply asked him to memorize facts from class lectures. And gone are the frequent tests that were so common in high school. In anthropology, he only has two more tests and a small paper. Terrence knows that he has to do something to get back on track.

For the impending psychology test, at least he has kept up with his reading ... well almost. And he does know what the task is: He is responsible for five text chapters, all of his lecture notes, and two outside readings that focus on psychological research. And he knows that he will have around fifty multiple-choice questions, most of which the professor said would be example and application questions. There are another ten matching items where he will have to match researchers with important research they carried out.

What advice would you give Terrence about how he should get back on track? What general advice would you give Terrence for studying for objective exams? Specifically, how might he have to change his studying strategies as he goes from anthropology to psychology?

____

____

____

____

____

____

FOLLOW-UP ACTIVITIES

1. One of the most important things you can do to improve your readiness for objective exams is to monitor your learning through self-testing. Remember that when you self-test, you try to answer questions without looking at the information. You put the information to be learned in your own words and say it to yourself or a study partner. When studying for your next objective exam, make a particular effort to self-test. Evaluate your confidence level on test day once you have self-tested.
2. Create a study plan for your next objective test. What concepts will you concentrate on for each study session? How will you know when you understand and can remember all the information? How will you review?

Networking

- Have you ever tried studying with a study partner on-line? If not, you might pair up with another student in class and ask each other questions via e-mail. Each of you could respond to one another's questions and evaluate the responses. In addition, having an e-mail contact in class is a good way to get assistance if you need it. For example, if you are having problems understanding a concept in your text or one that was presented in class, you could e-mail your study partner. Maybe he or she could help you out.

Preparing for and Taking Essay and Specialty Exams

Read this chapter to answer the following questions:

How should you prepare for essay exams?

What kind of study plan should you have for essay exams?

How should you study for special types of exams such as take-home or open-book exams?

Preparing for essay exams involves different strategies than preparing for objective exams. This often comes as a shock, especially to first-year college students who may have had little experience with essay exams in high school, or if they have had essay exams, they prepared for them the same way they prepared for objective exams. As a general rule, essay preparation requires a different type of approach, a different way of thinking, and a different way of organizing.

When we use the term *essay exam,* we are referring to any type of question for which you have to write an extended response. In this instance, the term *essay* would include a traditional multiparagraph answer to a rather broad question; short-answer questions that may require you to write a paragraph or two in response to a more narrowly focused question; and identification items that require you to define a term, explain the significance of something, or write several sentences describing a person, place, event, et cetera. Sometimes these types of exams are referred to as *recall* tests because you are asked to recall all of the pertinent information from memory. Unlike recognition questions, which we discussed in the last chapter (e.g., multiple-choice, true/false), that ask you to

STUDY TIP

Preparing for essay exams involves predicting reasonable questions and then practicing how you would answer them.

recognize the correct information, recall questions require you to remember the information on your own. In other words, either you know it or you don't; obviously, you can't guess!

Because essay-type questions require you to engage in different kinds of cognitive activities, a different studying approach is also called for. Read the following *Research into Practice* section, which introduces you to a strategy called PORPE—**P**redict, **O**rganize, **R**ehearse, **P**ractice, and **E**valuate—that was devised by Dr. Michele Simpson and her colleagues.

Research into Practice

PORPE—A Good Way to Study for Essay Exams*

The focus of this study, "An Initial Validation of a Study Strategy System," was to see if students who were taught to use an exam preparation strategy known as PORPE did better on both immediate and delayed multiple-choice and essay tests than students who did not use this strategy. A group of college students were taught over a three-week time frame to **P**redict, **O**rganize, **R**ehearse, **P**ractice, and **E**valuate as a way of preparing for exams. Another group was taught how to generate and answer questions as a way of studying so that their performance could be compared with students using PORPE. Although the researchers designed PORPE to help students prepare for essay exams, one of the most interesting findings of this study was that it also seemed to help students prepare for multiple-choice exams. The group taught to use PORPE outperformed the question/answer group on both multiple-choice and essay questions and in both immediate and delayed recall conditions. Immediate recall occurred right after students used the PORPE procedure to study the psychology information, and delayed recall occurred when they were given another exam a week after they had studied. In addition, students who were taught to use PORPE wrote essay answers that were more organized and cohesive. Although this research was conducted using only content from the discipline of psychology, the authors predicted that PORPE could be used effectively in many other content areas.

The results of this study are important for college students because few students have an organized way to study for essay exams. One of the interesting implications of this study is that it shows the importance of predicting broad essay questions. Students who were in the question/answer group generated a series of questions and then answered those

* Source Simpson, M. L., Hayes, C. G., Stahl, N., Connor, R. T., & Weaver, D. (1988). An initial validation of a study strategy system. *Journal of Reading Behavior* 20: 149–180.

questions, whereas students in the PORPE group were taught how to predict more global questions and then to support their answers with more detailed information from the passage they had read. In other words, those in the PORPE group learned how to focus on the big picture first and then use the factual information as support. On the other hand, those in the question/answer group concentrated on the details without ever seeing how everything was connected. Seeing those connections proved to be particularly important when students were asked to answer essay questions.

Let's first focus on preparing for traditional essay and short-answer questions since your preparation for these two types of questions would be almost identical.

PORPE

PORPE
- *Predict*
- *Organize*
- *Rehearse*
- *Practice*
- *Evaluate*

PORPE is a strategy specifically designed to help you prepare for essay or short-answer exams. As when studying for objective exams, you have completed your reading, you have constructed useful study strategies, and you have an organized set of lecture notes from which to study. Now you are ready to totally focus on preparing for the specific exam. By using PORPE, you have a structured and organized way to prepare for recall exams (see Figure 19.1). As we explain each step of PORPE, we have included an example based on a predicted essay question from the "Cognition" excerpt taken from Appendix A.

STEP 1: Predict.

(Predict several days before the test.) The first thing you need to do is to predict some broad questions that your professor might ask you. Generally, the fewer the number of questions you are required to answer, the broader the questions asked. If your professor says that the test

FIGURE 19.1 *PORPE Time Line*

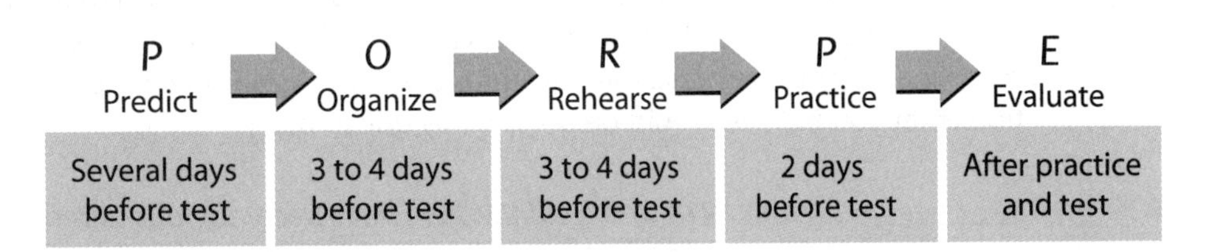

FIGURE 19.2 *Example of Step 1: Predict.*

Step 1: Predict. Predict a question that you think might be asked on the exam.	Q: Thinking involves three basic components. Explain each component, and also explain how the three components are related and interact to produce what we call thinking.

consists of two questions, they will probably be much broader than if she said you would have to answer five questions.

The better predictor you are, the better you will do on the exam. But predicting questions can be a tricky business. It has been our experience that when students begin to use this strategy, they predict questions that are either far too broad or way too narrow. For example, predicting a question such as "Discuss the presidency of Theodore Roosevelt" would be too broad; a question such as "What was the Fair Deal?" would be too specific for an essay question.

The other factor you should keep in mind when predicting is that rarely will your specific question be precisely what the professor asks. But if you become a good predictor, there will be considerable overlap between what you predict and the actual questions on the test. Figure 19.2 shows an example of a good essay prediction for the text excerpt, "Cognition," taken from Appendix A.

19.1 SOMETHING TO WRITE ABOUT AND DISCUSS

Thinking Critically

The following questions are predictions for the excerpt titled "Technologies of Mass-Production and Destruction" found in Appendix C. You have probably interacted with this chapter excerpt in other previous activities in *Active Learning.* Go back and skim the annotations for this chapter excerpt. Then, for each of the questions, decide whether the question is too broad (B), is too narrow (N), or would make a good (G) essay question for this chapter excerpt. Then explain the reasoning behind your decision. Finally, try to rephrase the questions that you thought were too broad into questions that you believe would be good essay questions.

_________ 1. *From 1914 to the 1990s, there have been obvious demographic shifts. Discuss the factors contributing to these shifts and the effects they have had technologically.*

Reasoning: ______________________________

____

____

________ 2. *How has life changed as a result of twentieth-century technology?*

Reasoning: ______________________________

____

____

________ 3. *Compare and contrast the weapons used in World War I with those used in World War II.*

Reasoning: ______________________________

____

____

________ 4. *What effect did the worldwide depression during the 1920s have on politics?*

Reasoning: ______________________________

____

____

________ 5. *What influences did technological advances have on the progression and expansion of World War II?*

Reasoning: ______________________________

____

____

STEP 2: Organize.

(Organize three or four days before the test.) After you have predicted several questions, you need to organize the information. Most students like to use an outline as a way of organizing so they can see the key points they want to make and the support they want to provide for each key point. Other organizing strategies, such as concept maps, also work well (see Chapter 14). When you are organizing the material, you have to think about both key generalizations and information to support those generalizations. You also want to make your overall exam outline or jot list as comprehensive as possible because you will use it as a guide to flesh out a more detailed outline for each essay question you predict.

If you put garbage in, garbage will come out, so to speak! Therefore, spend some time organizing your thoughts so that you will study worthwhile material … not garbage. Figure 18.1 (see page 304) indicates what a jot list might look like for a psychology essay exam.

As you become more focused and predict specific questions, your outline should be more comprehensive and detailed. To fill in your outline, use information that you included in your text annotations (Chapter 13) and rehearsal strategies (Chapter 14), as well as what you have annotated in your lecture notes (Chapter 11). Be sure that you draw from both text and lectures as well as any other sources for which you are responsible. And be sure to do a detailed outline for each of the questions you predicted. Figure 19.3 shows what an outline would look like for the essay question we predicted in Step 1 of PORPE.

FIGURE 19.3 *Example of Step 2: Organize*

Step 2: Organize.

In an organized fashion, write down the ideas you want to include in your essay.

3 COMPONENTS OF THINKING

1. Concepts—mental categories that are similar, (e.g., fruit is a concept)
   a. Artificial concepts—clearly defined by a set of rules (e.g., vegetables)
   b. Natural concepts—not hard and fast or clearly defined (e.g., Is a pickle a vegetable? Is chess a sport?)
      - Based on prototypes—best or clearest examples of a concepts (e.g., a prototype of "art" would be paintings or sculptures rather than a neon light show)
   c. Represented in several ways—by features, visual images, or schemas (cognitive frameworks about our own representation of the world)
2. Propositions—sentences that relate concepts to each other and can stand as separate assertions; thinking involves forming and considering propositions (e.g., in the proposition "Politicians are often self-serving," there are two propositions—politicians and self-serving)
3. Images—when we form an image, we think about it by scanning the image in our memory; an image not like the real object; serve important purposes since people use images to understand and to increase their own motivation
4. How concepts, propositions, and images interact—all 3 contribute to enabling us to think; concepts allow us to group things so that we can access information more quickly; propositions use concepts to enable us to actively manipulate concepts internally and are based to a certain extent on experiences; images enable us to think about information from a perspective other than verbally

STEP 3: Rehearse.

(Rehearse several times for each question, beginning three or four days before the test.) Now it's time to commit the information in your outline to memory. Read the question you predicted. Then read through your outline slowly and deliberately. "Listen" to what you are saying. Does it make sense? Do you have enough support? Do the ideas flow? After you have read through the outline several times, ask yourself the question again. This time, try answering it without looking at the outline. Check off the information you remember. Reread the information you don't remember, and say it several times to yourself. Be sure that you are rehearsing the concepts accurately and precisely (see Figure 19.4). Whenever you're not sure of something, immediately return to your outline and read that part through again; if you are really experiencing problems, you might need to check your text or lecture notes to clarify or add support. Then try to restate the answer to that portion of the question. Always keep in mind that when you rehearse, it's important to also engage in the self-testing part. Just reading through your outline several times will give you a false sense of security.

FIGURE 19.4 Example of Step 3: Rehearse

Step 3: Rehearse.

Say the information you organized in Step 2 over several times until you know it.

STEP 4: Practice.

(Practice two days before the test.) You have predicted, organized, and rehearsed. Now it's time to practice writing out an answer to one of your questions. Do it under the same conditions that you will be expected to

FIGURE 19.5 *Example of Step 4: Practice.*

Step 4: Practice. Under timed conditions, practice writing out the answer to the essay you predicted. Be sure your essay is organized.

Introductory paragraph	Thinking involves three basic components: concepts, propositions, and images. These components are strongly related to one another and interact. Without this interaction, thinking would be impossible.	
Generalization; Transition	The first component of thinking is concepts. Concepts are mental categories for things, events, or ideas that are, in some way, similar to one another. For example, fruit would be a concept since all fruits have certain characteristics in common. There are, however, two distinct kinds of concepts: artificial concepts and natural concepts. Artificial concepts have a clearly defined set of rules. Broccoli, for example, is clearly a vegetable because it has definite characteristics that make it easy to identify. Natural concepts, on the other hand, are not so clearly defined. Classifying chess as a sport and pickles as vegetables would be examples of natural concepts since these classifications are more fuzzy and make you stop and think. Artificial concepts tend to be based on prototypes or the best and clearest examples of a particular concept. Thus, while shirts and slacks are clearly clothing, the word wetsuit isn't as clearly defined.	Examples and support
Generalization; Examples and support	The second component of thinking is propositions. Propositions are sentences that relate concepts to each other and can also stand as separate assertions. Thinking involves the forming and considering of propositions. For example, when we hear a statement such as "Politicians are often self-serving," we evaluate two concepts: politicians and self-serving. Based on your experience, you may agree or disagree with this statement. It is clear, then, that we use concepts to formulate and consider propositions, and that this process enables us to think.	
Generalization; Explanation	The third and final component is images. Images are pictures in our mind that are representations of real concepts or propositions. Images are important to understanding since it gives us another way to think about information. Not only do we have the words that represent concepts and that help us form propositions, but we also can have images to represent them. Having two ways to think about information increases our comprehension as well as our motivation.	
Conclusion	All three components enable us to think. Concepts allow us to group ideas or objects together so that we can get at and retrieve information more quickly. Because concepts are represented in several ways—by features, images, or schemas—we can easily formulate or evaluate propositions. Moreover, propositions use concepts to enable us to actively manipulate concepts internally. Without these three components, thinking would be virtually impossible.	

write in your class. For example, if you are required to answer two essay questions in an hour-long class period, you would want to take only 25 minutes to practice one of your questions. That would leave 25 minutes to write the second question and 10 minutes to go back and proof your work.

In addition to writing under timed conditions, you should also construct your answer so that it is organized the same way that you will organize it in class. Write in complete sentences, include appropriate examples, and be sure to have an introduction and a conclusion. (We will talk about organizing your writing a little later in the chapter.) Figure 19.5 shows an example of an essay answer for the question we predicted in Step 1.

STEP 5: Evaluate.

(Evaluate immediately after practicing.) Now comes the most difficult part—evaluating your own writing. After you have finished practicing, read what you have written. After you have finished reading your practice essay, get out your outline and any other strategies you have been using to study from, and check for accuracy and completeness. Ask yourself the following questions:

- Is my introduction clear and focused?
- Are my generalizations complete and precise?
- Are my examples and supporting information accurate and complete?
- Do I have a conclusion that relates back to my introduction and overall thesis?

Figure 19.6 shows an evaluation of the question we predicted in Step 1.

Once you have honestly answered these questions, you can go back and do some rethinking and reorganizing (if necessary). It may be that you need to spend a little more time rehearsing your outline, or you may need to back up a bit further and organize your essay somewhat differently. You may even want to show your essay to your professor so that

FIGURE 19.6 Example of Step 5: Evaluate

Step 5: Evaluation. Answer the following questions:	Is my introduction clear and focused?	YES
	Are my generalizations clear and focused?	YES
	Are my examples and supporting information accurate and complete?	YES
	Do I have a conclusion that relates back to my introduction and overall thesis?	YES

she can provide you with feedback about how you are doing. You may also want to take it to the Writing Center, if there is one on your campus, if you need help organizing your response. But until you have actually attempted to write the entire essay out, you won't know where your problems are.

19.2 SOMETHING TO THINK AND WRITE ABOUT

Thinking Critically

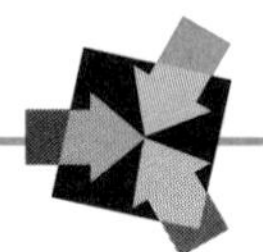

In a paragraph or two, discuss what you believe are the differences between preparing to take an objective exam and an essay exam.

____

____

____

____

____

____

Taking the Essay Test

When you are in the actual test-taking situation, keep these three important factors in mind: (1) how much time you are allotted to write each answer; (2) how you will structure each answer within that allotted amount of time; and (3) the guidelines your professor provided about how he or she will evaluate or grade your essay. Each of these factors has a bearing on how you will spend your in-class essay-writing time.

Time Allotted for Writing

Time is usually your biggest enemy when answering essay or short-answer questions. That's why it's important to keep an eye on the clock. When you are deciding on the approach you are going to take during the exam—your game plan—think carefully about how you will divide up your time. For example, if you have one essay question and five fairly comprehensive identification items to write on, would it be best to spend half your time on the essay and the other half on the identifications? Or would it be better to spend more time on the essay and less time on the ids? It's all give-and-take, but decide how you will divide your time among the tasks and then stick to it. It's a good rule of thumb to begin with what you know best and feel the most comfortable with. If you know the answers to all the identifications and feel a bit shaky about how best to approach the essay, start with the ids and then use the remaining time to do the best job you can on the essay. Always save some time to go back and read through your responses, however. You don't want your professor to be pulling the exam from your hands as you frantically attempt to write down your last thoughts. If you practice your essay writing under timed conditions as we discussed earlier, you should be able to comfortably complete your writing within the allotted time.

Structuring Your Essay

It has been our experience that few professors provide students with guidance on how they want essay or short-answer questions structured. As a result, many students will write a paragraph to answer an essay question and a sentence or two to answer a short-answer item. Usually, when professors ask you to write an essay, they want extended comment. That is, they want you to write considerably more than a paragraph! When you think of an essay, you should plan on writing at least an introductory paragraph, several paragraphs that discuss specific points you think are important to answering the question, and then a concluding paragraph. Short-answer questions, as a general rule, are a paragraph or two long and tend to be somewhat less structured than an essay.

If your professor tells you exactly how she wants you to structure your essay, *follow exactly what she says.* However, if your professor does not provide you with any guidance, the following structure is generally accepted in most disciplines. As you read this section, refer to the sample essay in Figure 19.5, and look at the different sections that are highlighted for you.

- Write an introductory paragraph that outlines your thesis and indicates that you understand what the question is asking. By thesis we mean the overall focus of your essay or the argument you will be making. If the question has multiple parts, be sure that your thesis somehow pulls in *all* the parts. The first paragraph need not be long and involved. Rather, it should be clear and concise and should give the reader a picture of what your overall point will be.

- Each of the next several paragraphs should begin with a generalization about one of the key points you want to make. For example, if the question asks you to discuss political, economic, and social issues, you would write three paragraphs, one dealing with each of these three issues. For each generalization, you should provide support in the form of events, names, dates, people, examples, and so forth—specific information that supports your broad generalization. Each paragraph should deal with only one key point and should provide a generalization and support for that point. Be careful about including several broad generalizations in the same paragraph. By the same token, don't just write down a bunch of facts without tying them together with generalizations. Unlike objective tests where we encourage you to guess, follow the "When in doubt, leave it out" suggestion for essay exams. If you have included wrong information in your essay, your professor has no alternative but to take points off. If, however, your essay is sound and you have made numerous good points, you might get few or no points taken off if you happen to leave out a piece of information because you weren't sure if it was correct or not. In addition, whenever possible, have smooth transitions from one idea to the next by using words such as *first, second, third; furthermore; in addition to;* and *moreover.*

- Finally, end your essay with a concluding paragraph that ties together the points you want to make. Again, the conclusion doesn't have to be lengthy, but you should end with a short paragraph that returns to your thesis and pulls together the most important ideas related to that thesis.

Few professors would oppose this structure, so if your professor does not provide guidance about format, this one will rarely (if ever) get you into trouble. But some professors spend quite a bit of class time explaining how they want the essay formatted. If your professor does a good job of explaining what she expects, be sure to get down as much information as you can about what she wants; then when you practice your essay, use that model.

Evaluation Guidelines

Now comes the tricky part! How do you write essays within the allotted time frame, have an acceptable structure, and manage to keep the mechanics and grammar errors down to a minimum? That's why it becomes very important to know, before you go into the exam situation, how strict your professor will be in taking off points for mechanics, grammar, and usage. If your professor doesn't say anything about those expectations in class, be sure to raise your hand and ask. Most professors fall somewhere in the middle: They do not expect perfection, but they will probably deduct points on a paper that has so many errors that it is difficult to read and understand. Moreover, most professors understand that you are writing under the gun, and that spelling and grammar errors occur more easily when you are under time pressures. On the other hand, we know professors who not only expect near-perfect structure and content but also expect an essay that is error-free. The bottom line is to know what your professor expects and then do your best to balance time, structure/content, and grammar/spelling issues.

A Word about Identification Items

Identification items ask you to write what you know about specific events, people, laws, dates, and so forth. They differ somewhat from essay or short-answer questions in that they are more focused and usually require only a few sentences of explanation. Sometimes, you can even write phrases rather than entire sentences when answering identification questions.

The problem with identification tests is twofold. First, there are usually numerous options for the professor to choose from. In history, for example, where identification questions are common, every chapter or lecture is filled with material that could be included on a test. How do you decide which terms are the most important to study? A good place to begin is with your text. If your text provides a listing of key terms or if there is a chapter summary, making sure you can identify what is in either of those sources is usually your best starting point. Match up those terms with what your professor has spent time on during lectures. Look for overlap because identification items usually focus on material that has been addressed in a lecture or has been pointed out in the text. We have found that professors will often only mention a person or event in passing during lectures and then expect you to find out more from your text reading. This information often ends up as identification items on exams.

Second, there's the problem of knowing the kind of information your professor expects you to include in an identification answer. Most of the time, professors will want you to include more than just definitional information. They may want you to discuss the significance, provide an example, or explain how it relates to some other issue or idea. Whatever the expectations, be sure you know what they are. If your professor expects you to define and give an example and you only define, you will only receive half credit, no matter how good your definition is.

Specialized Exams

We conclude this chapter by briefly discussing how to prepare for specialized exams. Specialized exams are those that may not happen as frequently in your college career, but you need to know how to prepare for them when they do come along. We will discuss three types of specialized exams: (1) problem-solving exams, the most common of the specialized exams; (2) open-book exams; and (3) take-home exams.

Problem-Solving Exams

Several types of courses require you to solve problems—mathematics courses might be the most common, but courses in the sciences (such as physics and chemistry) also are included in this category. Because many students fall into the trap of studying for exams of this nature by doing the same problems over and over again, we thought it was important to provide some additional suggestions for studying in courses that require you to solve problems.

Working problems as a way of studying for this type of test is certainly not a bad idea and should be part of your studying routine. Note that we said *part of.* However, if all you do is sit down and work the same set of problems over and over again, you will probably not do very well. The important thing to remember is that you have to think about and conceptualize what you are doing. If you just do the problems in rote fashion time and time again, you aren't really learning the material. You know that you won't get those exact same problems on the exam, so you have to think about the concepts underlying the problems. That's why we suggest that you talk through your problems. As you do a problem, think about and verbalize what you are doing. If you can't talk through problems as you solve them, it's a pretty strong indication that you don't understand the concept. This holds true in math, statistics, and physics.

Let's look at an example and talk through some of the thinking that would make it easier to solve this problem. Thinking about math problems, especially word problems, in this manner also lets you know if you understand the reasoning behind your method of solving the problem.

The Problem. Susan begins a 20-mile race at 7:00 a.m., running at an average speed of 10 mph. One hour later, her brother leaves the starting line on a motorbike and follows her route at the rate of 40 mph. At what time does he catch up to her?

The Question. What is the problem asking for? I am supposed to solve this problem to find out what time he catches up with her so I'll need to make sure that the answer I come up with is reflected as time.

The Solution.

- ***Visualize the problem.*** This diagram shows that when Susan's brother overtakes her, they have both traveled the same distance.

  Susan > > > > > > > > > > > > >|
  Her brother > > > > > > > > > > > > >|

- ***What is the basic idea behind the problem?*** Both are traveling at a constant rate of speed so we would think about the basic equation as:

$$\begin{aligned} \text{Distance} &= (\text{Rate})(\text{Time}) \\ d &= rt \end{aligned}$$

- ***Explain the variables.***

  Let t = number of hours Susan runs until her brother catches her
  Then $t - 1$ = number of hours Susan's brother rides until he catches up (he leaves 1 hour later so he travels 1 hour less)

- ***Write and solve the equation.***

$$\begin{aligned} 10t &= 40(t-1) \\ 10t &= 40t - 40 \\ -30t &= -40 \\ t &= \frac{-40}{-30} = \frac{4}{3} = \text{1-1/3 hours} = \text{1 hour and 20 minutes} \end{aligned}$$

The Answer. Remember that the question asked for time. Susan's brother caught her 1 hour and 20 minutes after she began the race. Therefore, he would catch up with her at 8:20 a.m. If you wrote 1 hour and 20 minutes as your answer, you would not receive credit because you did not answer the question that was asked.

Another strategy is to make up a test for yourself with the types of problems you will be tested on. When most professors assign problems to work on, they won't usually ask you to do them all. Put some of the problems they don't ask you to do on note cards; then work them as a way of seeing whether you understand the concepts. After you have worked through the problems, shuffle the note cards and work on them again in a different order, concentrating on those that gave you problems. If you need to, return to your text, the problems that were gone over in class, or your lecture notes for help.

Finally, for courses in which you must solve problems, if you find yourself having difficulty with the homework or not understanding how to do particular problems, *get help early!* Courses such as mathematics, physics, and chemistry tend to be arranged sequentially; the ideas build on one another. If you miss or don't understand something presented in week two of the term, chances are you are going to have trouble with what is presented after that. Likewise, if you think you are "mathematically challenged," you should arrange to be part of a study group, get a tutor, or make regular appointments to speak with your professor right at the beginning of the term. And don't forget to use e-mail if your professor has that option available. We've known students who have received e-mail responses from an insomniac professor in the wee hours of the morning!

Open-Book Exams

Open-book exams allow you access to your text, and sometimes even your notes, during the examination period. Unlike take-home exams, open-book exams are generally given in the usual class period, which means you take them under timed conditions. This type of exam is often given in literature courses so that students can have access to specific pieces of text that they have been asked to read and interact with.

When students are told they will have an open-book exam, they will often smile and breathe a sigh of relief. We have even heard students say that they didn't have to study because they were having an open-book test. Nothing could be further from the truth. It takes just as much effort to prepare for this type of test as it does to prepare for a more traditional objective or essay test.

Organization is the key to preparing for open-book exams. If you are getting ready for an open-book literature exam, for example, and you know you are going to be able to use your text to write on two essay questions, first you have to go through the usual preparation step of predicting, organizing, rehearsing, practicing, and evaluating. But you have to put extra time into organizing. You would want to mark quotations that you might use to support points you want to make or pull specific examples from the readings. You will need to have the information you deem important marked in some way so that it is easy to find. For example, you can tab important passages or pages in your text with adhesive notes. Because you are in a timed situation, you can't waste time trying to find a particular passage or example in your book. You must know where things are and have the information organized so that you can get at it quickly.

Take-Home Exams

Take-home exams allow you to have access to your text and notes and put no time restrictions on the amount of time you can spend taking the test. The professor gives you the test questions, along with some basic instructions, usually to remind you that you can't get outside assistance to answer the questions. Some professors may even have you sign an academic honesty pledge. When professors give take-home exams, they generally expect a very high level of proficiency and thinking. For example, if they give you an essay exam as a take-home, they would expect your writing to display synthesis, analysis, and critical thought. They would expect a tremendous amount of support, and a paper virtually free of grammatical and spelling errors. Therefore, you usually have to spend a considerable amount of time working on take-home exams. What looks like something that is in your favor can turn out to be a more difficult task than taking an in-class test.

Professors can give take-homes in many ways. Some give out the questions a week or so in advance and expect you to work on the questions a little at a time. Others give you the exam only a day or so before it is due so if you haven't been keeping up with the course reading or haven't been attending class, you will have a difficult time doing a good job on the test. The point we want to make is that even if you know you will have take-home exams in a course, it is extremely important for you to keep up. Do your reading, attend class, construct rehearsal strategies, and continue to review. Keep up with the course the same as you would if you have to take more traditional exams. Then, when you get your take-home exam from your instructor, you will be ready to organize all the information and spend less actual time taking the test.

A personal experience about take-home exams is a good reminder of just how difficult tests such as these can be. As a graduate student, one of the authors took an advanced course in tests and measurements in which the professor gave take-home tests—just two of them—a mid-term and a final. The professor distributed the take-home mid-term on a Thursday; it was due on the following Tuesday. The author really didn't look at the exam until Friday afternoon, thinking she would work on some of the easier questions and save the more difficult ones for the weekend. The test was *only* twenty-five multiple-choice questions. How hard could it be? She started reading the questions and was certain that the professor had given out the wrong test. She didn't know the answers to *any* of these questions, even when using her book and notes. She could feel her heart beating fast, and she broke out in a cold sweat. PANIC! Where had she been for the last seven weeks? Then she went back to the beginning of the test again and read the first item very carefully. Something clicked … well … sort of. She vaguely remembered something like that being discussed in class. She looked in her book and notes again. Then it hit her. Every question on this exam required students to make connections between pieces of information. Every question had two or three steps before you could get to the point where you could figure out the right answer. It was the most difficult test she had taken or would ever take. The point here is that take-home tests can be extremely difficult and require you to think about the course information in a different way. In sum, there's no such thing as a free lunch!

REAL COLLEGE: *Inez's Intentions (Gone awry!)*

Read the following scenario and then respond to the questions based on what you learned in this chapter.

Inez had good intentions. She really did! And her semester was going quite well … up until this point. Inez had, shall we say, some academic difficulties during her first semester in college, but she had learned from her mistakes, and so far so good. But now it was time for the real test. She knew that an exam was rapidly approaching in Dr. Jameson's history course, and she was scared! Today was Thursday and this test was the following Tuesday. She had done an admirable job of keeping up in her courses this semester, except for Dr. Jameson's, and she had even intended to stay on top of things in history. But somehow, she fell a little behind. Okay, a lot behind. Now it was time for the first of only two exams in the course, and she faced the prospect of returning to the academic black hole called probation. To top it off, Dr. Jameson's exams had the reputation of being lethal. The most difficult thing was that half the exam consisted of thirty multiple-choice questions; the other half was one essay question. That meant that she had to study in two different ways for the same test, and she hadn't even completed the reading assignments yet. And to make things even worse, she knew that numerous questions would come from the text and that she would have to pull text-related information into her essay. Professor Jameson had already been very explicit about that in class.

Given the amount of time she has left to study and the kind of exam she will have, what recommendations would you give to Inez? How should she prepare for and go about taking her history exam so she can maximize her grade? If Inez had followed her intentions, what should she have done to prevent her problems?

____

____

____

____

____

____

____

____

____

FOLLOW-UP ACTIVITIES

1. Think about the most difficult test you have had so far in your college career. What made this test difficult? How did you study for the test? Do you feel that you could have done better if you had studied differently? Looking back on the exam, how might you have prepared differently?
2. For your next essay exam, try using the PORPE procedure and evaluate its effectiveness.

Networking

- If you have been working with a classmate this term in a course that requires you to write essay exams, you might try sending your study partner a copy of a practice essay over e-mail. Have your study partner critique your essay by evaluating its strengths and weaknesses. You can do the same for your study partner.

Winding Down and Summing Up

Read this chapter to answer the following questions:

How do learner characteristics influence studying?

How does task knowledge influence studying?

How does strategy selection influence studying?

How do text characteristics influence studying?

How do all four of these factors interact?

In this text, we have portrayed studying and learning in college as hard work: hard work but not impossible work. We have encouraged you to try out strategies and suggestions and to modify them based on your own needs. We know that not every idea presented in this book will work for everyone. However, if we helped you get on the right track or improve some of your studying behaviors, we will have done our job. Our goal has been to help you get on and stay on a strong academic footing.

In this last chapter, we will revisit the four factors that influence learning and pull together the most important concepts presented in the text. For the four factors—characteristics of the learner, identifying the task, identifying the strategies, and characteristics of the text—we will briefly review why each is important. Then we will answer some questions that students often ask us. You might try answering each of the questions yourself before you read our response. We will also show you why it is crucial to view studying and learning in a cyclical manner and to consider the four factors that influence learning as you plan your studying for each of your courses.

STUDY TIP

Becoming an active learner takes time and practice. The key is to be a student who learns efficiently as well as effectively.

Active Learning: The Four Factors Revisited

To be an active learner, you must remember that learning involves much more than thinking of yourself as an empty vessel waiting to be filled with knowledge! Active learners are involved learners. They understand that learning is a process in which students, professors, and texts all interact in numerous and complex ways. These interactions are portrayed clearly in the four factors we have discussed throughout this text. Before you read the remainder of the chapter, however, read the *Research into Practice* section. In this article, Dr. Barry Zimmerman discusses the characteristics of self-regulation (or active learning) during studying. Although he states the processes involved in active learning a bit differently than we have in this text, what he is saying should sound familiar to you.

Research into Practice

The Characteristics of Active Learners*

In his research, Dr. Zimmerman identified 10 self-regulatory processes that were similar among people with four different areas of expertise: writers, athletes, musicians, and students. Dr. Zimmerman found that those who regulate their learning or other activities engage in goal setting, setting both short-term and long-term goals. Second, they analyze the task and then identify methods for carrying out the task. Zimmerman found that self-regulated students used between fifteen and twenty different strategies during studying. Third, they engaged in the process of imagery, creating and remembering images to help them learn. Fourth, they self-instructed, meaning they self-tested as a guide to knowing their level of understanding. Fifth, they used time-management strategies, allocating time in order to meet their goals. Sixth, those who were self-regulated engaged in self-monitoring to track their progress. Seventh, they self-evaluated, setting standards for themselves and, in the case of students, checking over their work before handing it in. Eighth, they had self-consequences and rewarded or punished themselves for successes and failures. Ninth, they engaged in the self-regulatory process of environmental structuring, choosing or creating effective places for learning. Finally, they used help-seeking behaviors by getting assistance when they experienced problems learning information.

* Source: Zimmerman, B. J. (1998). Academic studying and the development of personal skill: A self-regulatory perspective. *Educational Psychologist* 33: 73–86.

The processes that Dr. Zimmerman found common among individuals, regardless of their areas of expertise, are the same processes we have stressed in this text. When strategies and processes have been researched and found to be effective, students recognize their importance. When you engage in these kinds of activities, research indicates that you have a big payoff in performance!

20.1

SOMETHING TO WRITE ABOUT AND DISCUSS

Thinking Critically

Think about the 10 self-regulatory processes discussed in the *Research into Practice* section. For each one, write down something you are currently doing in one or more of your classes that would suggest you are engaged in this process.

1. *Goal setting:* ______________________________

____

____

2. *Task strategies:* ______________________________

____

____

3. *Imagery:* ______________________________

____

____

4. *Self-instruction:* ______________________________

____

____

5. *Time management:* ______________________________

____

____

6. *Self-monitoring:* ______________________________

____

____

7. *Self-evaluation:* ____

____

____

8. *Self-consequences:* ____

____

____

9. *Environmental structuring:* ____

____

____

10. *Seeking help:* ____

____

____

Characteristics of the Learner

The first factor you need to consider on your way to active learning is you the student and the characteristics you bring to the learning situation. In Chapters 4 through 8, we discussed these characteristics in detail and stressed that, in some way, each plays a role in determining your level of success in college.

Common Questions and Answers about Learner Characteristics

Q. I have good intentions and want to learn to manage my time. I even go so far as to make schedules and turn down fun things to stay home and study. But somehow I always get distracted and manage not to accomplish much in my allotted studying time. Any suggestions for doing better?

REMINDERS ABOUT LEARNER CHARACTERISTICS

- *Motivation is the "academic glue" that holds your learning experience together.*
- *Attitudes and interests influence how active a learner you are.*
- *Organizing your life goes a long way toward getting on the right academic track.*
- *Your beliefs about learning influence how you study.*

A. Rather than trying to change everything about managing your time, try little things. Take a first step. For example, if you come home from class with good intentions to study but take a nap instead, change your routine. Rather than going home or back to the residence hall, try going to the library to study. In the beginning, you don't have to do it every day. Try it just a couple of times a week. Then change something else about your schedule. Keep making minor adjustments until you are satisfied.

A. Take an honest look at your "body clock." If you are attempting to read, study, or review at times when you are tired or need some downtime, you will be easily distracted even if you have good intentions. Think about when you are most alert. Plan your studying around those times. Then use your downtimes to watch TV, visit with friends, take a brief nap, or do chores. Save the best times for academic work.

Q. Unfortunately, I never developed many interests when I was in high school, and I found almost all my classes boring. Now that I am in college, not much has changed. I have little interest in anything that I take, and therefore, I have a difficult time motivating myself to keep up with my work. I see other students around me excited about learning things like history or anthropology. None of it does anything for me. What can I do to either develop some interests or at least motivate myself to study information that does not interest me?

A. Developing interests sometimes is simply a matter of maturing. Many students don't find out what they are interested in until they are well through their first couple of years of college. It's quite common, as evidenced by the many students who have undeclared majors well into their sophomore year. The point is not to be too hard on yourself because of your lack of interests early in your college career. But this doesn't solve the problems of boredom and lack of motivation. Maybe your boredom and poor motivation stem from something other than your lack of interest. Take a look at your attitude about college in general. Do you want to stay in college, or is there something else you would rather be doing at this point in your life? If you really want to be in college, you can motivate yourself and maybe even develop some interests. Join a campus organization. Spend some time with others who seem to have lots of interests. Some of it may rub off! If you come to the conclusion that college isn't for you at this point and have an alternative plan in mind, explore that option as well. Many students find that after leaving college for a semester or two, they really want to return and end up doing very well. The bottom line here is to know yourself.

Q. I am a returning student who has been out of school for six years. I finished high school and really didn't want to go on to college. I work in a dead-end job; I have a small child and numerous other responsibilities. My spouse also goes to school part-time. We both have a strong desire to get a degree, but the demands on my time are such that it's difficult to get everything done. How can I organize my life so that I still have time for my family and so that I can complete my education?

A. Juggling a family, school, and normal daily survival is a difficult task indeed. But it is not impossible. Older students return to college all the time, and a vast majority of them are very successful. Because nontraditional students really want to be in school, they find support systems to help them out. If you have family close by, they can be very supportive in helping out with child care or by running errands. If not, seek out other individuals in similar situations and pool your resources. Above all, keep in mind that it is a temporary situation; it will not be like this forever.

A. Another suggestion is to plan family time first; then plan school and studying time around that. When one of the authors was a graduate student, she made sure that all day Sunday was family time and rarely began studying in the evenings until her daughter was in bed around 9:00. It was difficult, but not impossible.

20.2 SOMETHING TO THINK ABOUT AND DISCUSS

Do you have any other questions related to characteristics of the learner? Jot down a question and then discuss it with your classmates.

___

___

___

Identifying the Task

In Part III of this text, we discussed the second factor that influences learning and studying: the importance of determining just what it is your professor expects you to do. Remember that task identification involves more than simply knowing what kind of test you will take or that you are required to write a paper.

Common Questions and Answers about Task

Q. I had just figured out what the task was in my sociology class when the class switched professors. We have three different professors in this class, each of whom teaches for five weeks. From what I understand, they all make up their own tests, so I'm going to have to try and figure out three different sets of expectations. I don't think it's very fair to teach a course this way, do you?

REMINDERS ABOUT TASK

- *Task involves knowing the level of questions you will be asked or the criteria used to evaluate your paper or project.*
- *If you understand the task expected of you, you should be able to clearly articulate it.*
- *You have to understand the task before you can select the most appropriate study strategies.*
- *Most professors don't change the task in the middle of the term, so once you figure out the task, it usually remains consistent.*

A. Whether you think it's fair is not the point. This is the way this particular course is taught. The fact that every professor in the department doesn't give the same exams is the real problem here. And you are right when you say that you have to figure out three sets of expectations. A situation such as this is certainly more difficult than having only one professor. However, you can do several things to maximize your task knowledge. First, and very important, talk to students who have taken the course before you. See if they can remember how the three professors differed and how they constructed their tests. Second, don't be shy. When a new professor starts his five-week segment, ask him within the first day or two to talk a little about how he tests. If you or someone in your class approaches this idea in the appropriate manner, the professor will probably respond to your questions. Third, if you feel too shy about asking in class, make an appointment to talk with your professor after class; better yet, send him an e-mail outlining your concerns. You might say or write something like this: "Professor Jones tended to ask questions phrased like *x*. He was interested in the class being able to compare and contrast different theories and to conceptualize information. Because of the way he tested and lectured, I studied for Professor Jones's class by doing these things.... Would I be on the right track if I did the same sorts of things for you? What would you suggest I do differently? Can I look at a copy of an old exam to get an idea of how you ask test questions?"

Q. I know this doesn't happen very often, but what do you do if a professor constantly changes the task without telling you?

A. This is a tough one! We gave an example in Chapter 10 about the professor who had given objective tests in the form of multiple-choice items all term and then switched to fill-in-the-blanks for the final exam. Students had no idea he was going to do this, and many of them were rightfully upset. In this situation (it occurred at the end of the semester), there was little they could do. But if you find the professor's expectations are inconsistent, the best thing to do is to talk with him. Make an appointment, go to his office, and explain your concerns. Be sure that you have specific examples of the inconsistencies or changes. Tell him how you have been studying and how you find it difficult to use a consistent approach to studying when the task is always different. Then ask him for some suggestions. Some professors may not even realize they are changing the task unless students bring it to their attention.

Q. I'm in a class where I can't even begin to figure out what it is I'm supposed to do. The professor is very intimidating. Just about everyone in the class is scared to ask a question or to see her during her office hours. Lots of students either have dropped the class or don't even come. The professor seems to think it's great "to get all the dead weight out of this class." I'm hanging in there, but I don't know why. What can I do?

A. As odd as this might sound, you have to make an appointment to talk with this professor. As we discussed earlier, go with a set of prepared questions, written out, so that you won't forget the questions you have to ask her. Try to have a "what have I got to lose" attitude because if you don't go to see this professor, you're not going to do very well at all. Could you do worse by trying to talk with her? Don't whine, however! Ask your questions, and then ask for any suggestions she might have. Another piece of good advice—do this sooner rather than later. Failing a couple of tests while you struggle with what to do next is rarely a good idea.

20.3 SOMETHING TO THINK ABOUT AND DISCUSS

What additional questions do you have about task? Write down at least one question and then discuss it with your classmates.

____

____

____

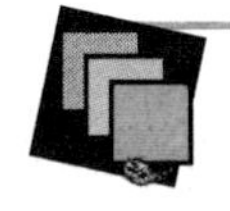

Identifying the Strategies

Once you understand yourself as a learner, can maintain motivation and time-management skills, and understand the tasks in your courses, selecting the strategies is perhaps the easiest part. But there is one caveat—you have to know some strategies from which to select. We have said many times that trying to make one or two strategies fit every learning situation will not work in most academic situations. Because students learn differently and tasks differ from course to course, it is imperative to know a variety of strategies.

Common Questions and Answers about Strategies

Q. When I was in high school, I really never had to use any study strategies. I didn't even have to read my textbooks. Now that I'm in college, I'm overwhelmed because I really don't know where to begin. I

REMINDERS ABOUT STRATEGIES

- *It's important to have declarative (knowing what), procedural (knowing how), and conditional (knowing when and why) knowledge about strategies.*
- *Once you learn a variety of strategies, it's also important for you to modify them to suit your own characteristics as a learner and the tasks you must complete.*
- *Strategy selection does not occur in isolation.*

manage my time fairly well, but I feel as if I could be doing things much more efficiently. I really have very little confidence in myself as a learner. What can I do?

A. Many students arrive at college having had similar experiences. As we said in Chapter 1, there are differences between the way you learned in high school and the way you learn in college. Learning in college generally requires being a more active, involved, and independent learner. Being active requires that you think as you read and study. You have to see the big picture, tear apart this big picture into smaller pieces for learning, and then take the all-important next step of putting the ideas back together in an organized fashion. That's why it's important to develop a studying cycle. You preview, read and annotate, rehearse, and review. It's not a matter of just reading over your text and lecture notes, hoping that something will sink in through osmosis! You have to be involved. One way to tell what information you have learned in a reading or study session is to talk it through right at the end. How much of what you read or studied can you remember? You don't have to remember everything, but if you walk away from a two-hour session and can't remember anything, you have wasted your time. In fact, we believe that it's important to stop often as you read and study to think about what you are learning and to regroup as you go along. Once you have success finding a study cycle that works for you, you will gain much more confidence in yourself as a learner and will see an improvement in your performance.

Q. It seems to me that it takes up too much time to follow a studying cycle, especially if I have to preview, annotate my text, construct strategies, rehearse, and then review. I also have to study my lecture notes. How can I do all this and still have time to socialize with my friends?

A. Think back to what we said in Chapter 4 about getting organized. Try the 40-hour rule. Devote 40 hours a week to being a student. Just 40 hours! That's less than 2 full days, and it includes class time as well. If you are in class 15 hours a week, that leaves you 25 hours to devote to your studying cycle. Remember, active students don't have the same cycle for every class, nor do they distribute their studying time equally among all of their classes. For example, your studying cycle in chemistry class would be different from that of your English literature class. Again, it all relates back to the task that your professor expects you to accomplish. If the task in chemistry is primarily one of solving problems and your task in English literature is to interpret what you are reading, your approaches to each will be quite different. The key is to have a cycle, to make adjustments and modifications to the strategies, and to give adequate time (40 hours) each week to being a student. You'll still have lots of time to party!

Q. Even good students have to cram at some point or another. I have found myself in situations where I have no choice but to cram. Once I was really sick, and another time there was a family emergency. In both cases, my studying time was dramatically cut. How should I maximize my study efforts when time is a factor?

A. This question is very difficult to respond to. The best advice we can give is to take different approaches, depending on the task. For example, if you have a 300-page novel to read for a literature course, there is no way you will be able to get through it and prepare for an examination in a day or so. You can only hope that there is a good critical essay on the novel or that someone in your class is willing to talk about the book with you. You might always make your case to your professor to see if other arrangements can be made. In another situation, you might handle it differently. Let's say that you have about half of your psychology reading done and then you get hit with a bad case of strep throat. You are too sick to die! By the time you are well enough to return to class, the test is only two days away. No makeup tests are allowed. In this scenario, it would be important to: (a) Get a classmate's notes to photocopy; (b) think about your first exam, decide whether it was based more on the text or more on the lectures, and use your time accordingly; (c) concentrate your studying efforts on reading over the notes several times and using them to test yourself if the test is based more on lecture; (d) rely on summaries, visual aids, and heavy previewing to get you through if the test is text-based. If the course is a science, concentrate more on diagrams and other visuals. If there are questions or problems at the end of the chapter, work them. If the course is a humanities or social science course, concentrate more on the summaries and heavy pre-reading. Supplement this information with the lecture notes.

20.4 SOMETHING TO THINK ABOUT AND DISCUSS

What additional questions do you have about strategies? Write down at least one question and discuss it with your classmates.

____

____

____

Characteristics of the Text

The final piece of the studying and learning puzzle that we presented is the characteristics of the different texts with which you will interact. Remember that text is not just textbooks, although they are the most common type. Lecture notes, documentaries, films, slides, and, of course, what you read from the computer are texts as well.

Common Questions and Answers about Text Characteristics

Q. I like parts of the split-page method of note taking but not all of it. Is it all right just to use the parts that work for me?

REMINDERS ABOUT TEXT

- *Text organization varies, so be sure you understand how your text is organized.*
- *Different text organization requires you to approach texts differently.*
- *Because lecture notes are also texts, it's important to determine whether your professor lectures inductively or deductively.*
- *Reading texts too slowly can interfere with text comprehension.*

A. Lots of students take pretty good notes even before they learn the split-page method. In fact, many students take notes in a very structured outline form, and it works well for them. We always suggest that students adopt the parts of strategies or techniques that suit the task and their own characteristics as learners, so using only part of the method is fine. But we strongly suggest that you use the two-inch margin for annotations or questions regardless of how you decide to write down information in the body of your notes. The annotations or questions allow you to self-test, which is an important part of test preparation. Without self-testing, you are never really sure how well you know and understand the material.

Q. One of my professors puts her notes on-line. Do I have to take notes in class if I can get the professor's notes right off the web? It seems foolish to me to go to all that work if I don't have to.

A. We believe that it's very important to have ownership of your notes. By ownership we mean that you have been in class, listened to the lecture, and taken the notes yourself. Students who merely copy someone else's notes or, worse yet, simply print them off the web have no such ownership. We're not saying that professors' notes shouldn't be used. On the contrary, they can be a very valuable check to see whether you are on target in getting the lecture information down correctly. But we believe that you should use them in addition to, not in place of, your own notes. Another problem we have found with web notes is that they are often taken by another student in the class and are really not the professor's notes. We know of one time when the student whose notes were put on the web made only a C in the course. You would certainly want to do better than that! A final comment about professors' notes: It has been our experience that when professors put their notes on the web, it is usually in brief outline form. If you find this to be the case, be sure to fill in the ideas as the professor lectures. We believe that in most cases it's best to simply use the professor's notes as a guide and take your own notes since there is rarely enough room to take all the notes you need on the paper you have printed out from your professor's web site.

Q. The textbook for my botany class doesn't seem to be very well written. I don't think the problem is simply that I don't understand the concepts but rather that the author didn't write in an organized way. Is there something I can do to help myself make sense of this text?

A. If your textbook isn't very well organized (and quite a few aren't), it's up to you to try to create an organization that makes sense. In instances like this, it's particularly important for you to preview each chapter to see if you can figure out why the author's organization doesn't work for you. Once you have figured out the problem, you can then annotate your text in a way that makes more sense to you—in a way that enables you to see the connections between and among ideas.

20.5 SOMETHING TO THINK ABOUT AND DISCUSS

What questions do you have about text characteristics? Write down at least one question and discuss it with your classmates.

____

____

____

____

REAL COLLEGE: *Paul's Plan*

Read the following scenario and then respond to the questions based on what you learned in this chapter.

Paul has just finished his first semester of college. He didn't do too badly—his grade point average was a 2.5—but he didn't blow the top off either. Paul became increasingly frustrated as the term went on. He felt as though he was studying hard and putting in long hours—certainly more than he ever put in during high school. For all his efforts, he believed he should have earned a 4.0, not a 2.5.

Paul will be under a considerable amount of pressure next semester because he must raise his average to a 3.0 or lose his scholarship. He has registered to take a second-semester French course, introductory biology (which will also have a 1-hour lab), calculus, and history. He made a B in his first French class and is generally good in mathematics-related courses, but he's somewhat concerned about the biology and the history. He's not very interested in either one, and he knows that the history course requires a lot of reading. Biology requires considerable reading too, but it's a different type of reading than history. In addition, he knows that he'll be taking very different types of tests in each of these classes, making it mandatory that he prepare for these tasks differently.

Using what you have learned about the four factors that influence learning and what it takes to be an active learner, outline a plan of action for Paul for next semester. Keep in mind that he needs to think of his own characteristics as a learner, the tasks, and the characteristics of the texts as he selects the strategies to use in his courses.

FOLLOW-UP ACTIVITIES

1. The fact that you have made it to the last chapter in this book probably means that you are also nearing the end of a term. First, evaluate your performance this term by thinking about the things you did right. What kinds of studying behaviors seemed to work for you? Did you modify the way you studied over the course of the term?
2. Now think about some of things you would like to change so that you can be a more efficient, effective, and active learner next term.

Networking

- As you are registering for courses for next term, be sure to jot down the name of the professor who is teaching the course if the name is not on your printed schedule. Then try to find something on the web about this professor and course. Many professors have their own web pages, and these web pages can provide a wealth of information about a course. You might even think about looking at course web pages before you register as a way of getting an idea of task, reading load, and other expectations.

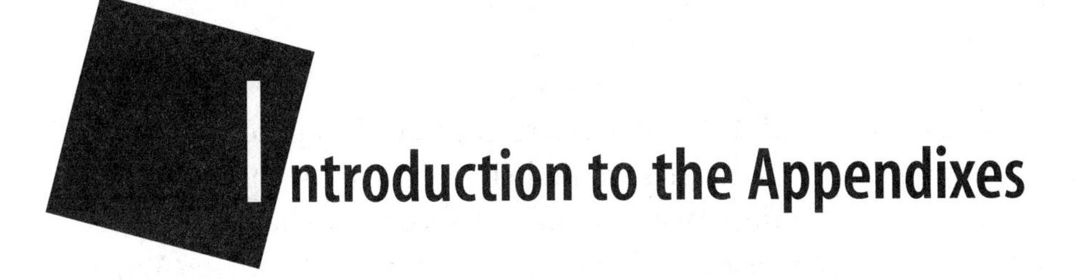

Introduction to the Appendixes

The three appendixes in *Active Learning* are included for you to practice the strategies that are presented throughout the text. The appendixes offer text from three disciplines: psychology, biology, and history. Practicing on these text excepts first, and then modifying the strategies to the texts in your own classes, is the best way to make the book's strategies your own.

You will notice as you look through and begin to interact with the text of the appendixes that we have maintained, as much as possible, the look of the original text. In some cases, however, we did not have permission to reprint certain visual aids such as diagrams, photographs, and maps. In such instances, there are blank spaces. Feel free to annotate, construct concept maps of key information, or predict and answer questions in these spaces.

Appendix A, Cognition, focuses on how the mind processes information—how we come to understand ideas and how we go about making decisions. Many new terms are introduced, and theories about how we process information are explained in this chapter.

Appendix B, The Human Nervous System, describes the complexity of the nervous system. The chapter discusses the system's two major components: the central nervous system and the peripheral nervous system. The brain and the mind are also discussed. This chapter excerpt also introduces many new terms that you will need to understand how to fit together. In other words, it will be important to see the big picture of the nervous system not just to memorize the numerous terms. You should also note that this chapter, like most scientific text, is very dense—there is a lot of information packed into very few pages.

Appendix C, Technologies of Mass-Production and Destruction, examines the growth of technology, particularly the production of goods and services and the production of tools for war. After prereading this chapter, it should be clear that the strategies you select to learn the information presented here will be different than those used for the other appendixes. Although the material is not particularly dense, such as that in the biology chapter, a considerable amount of information is presented. This is evidenced by the length of time covered by this chapter—1914–45.

As you interact with these text excerpts, you will want to ask yourself these questions: What strategies would help me learn the information presented? What do I find easy and difficult about this chapter and about the discipline in general? How would I preread? Annotate? What rehearsal strategies are the most appropriate? How should I review? What should my studying schedule look like? For the most part, the way you will answer these questions will be different for each excerpt just as they would be for any other classes you are taking.

As you apply the strategies to the text excerpts, you should develop a strong repertoire of strategies that can be modified and honed to compliment your own characteristics as a learner, the tasks you are asked to carry out, and the texts with which you interact. Remember—modification and flexibility are the keys to being an active learner in college.

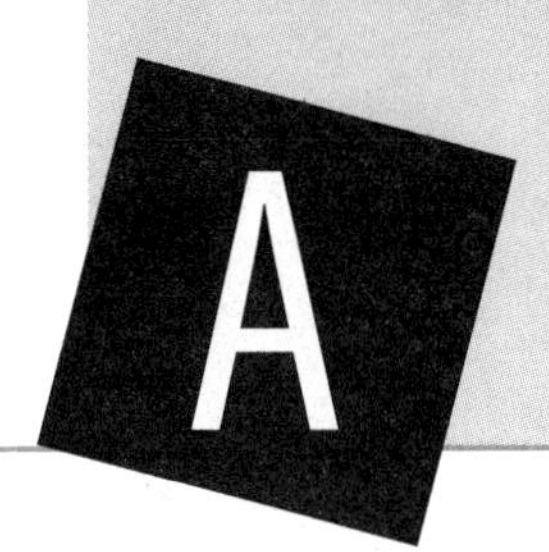

Excerpt from a Psychology Text

Cognition

Thinking, Deciding, Communicating

Why is it that some people are great thinkers, while others are merely average? What happens in the brain during thought? Will computers ever become as smart as people? Do animals think? These and related questions have to do with **cognition**—a general term used to describe thinking and many other aspects of our higher mental processes. Where cognition is concerned, thinking and reasoning are only part of the picture. Have you ever agonized over an important decision, carefully weighing the advantages and disadvantages of potential alternatives? In all probability you have, perhaps in terms of selecting a college, choosing a major, or deciding between courses of action. To make the right decision you probably *thought* long and hard about the various alternatives; you tried to *reason* your way to a conclusion about their relative merits; and finally you made

Cognition: The mental activities associated with thought, knowledge, and memory.

some sort of *decision*. We perform these activities many times each day, and in a variety of contexts. It is on these and related issues that we'll focus in the present chapter.

We'll begin our discussion by examining the nature of *thinking*, an activity that involves the manipulation of mental representations of various features of the external world. Thinking includes *reasoning*—mental activity through which we transform available information in order to reach conclusions. We'll also look at an intriguing question that would definitely *not* have been included in this book twenty years ago: Do animals think? Next, we'll turn to *decision making*, the process of choosing between two or more alternatives on the basis of information about them. Here we'll explore different factors that influence the decision-making process. Third, we'll examine several aspects of *problem solving*, which typically involves processing information in various ways in order to move toward desired goals. Finally, we'll examine an aspect of cognition that provides the basis for much of the activity occurring in each of the processes listed so far: *language*. It is through language that we can share the results of our own cognition with others and receive similar input from them. We'll also consider new evidence suggesting the possibility that other species may also possess several basic elements of language.

Have you ever agonized over an important decision, carefully weighing the advantages and disadvantages of potential alternatives?

One additional point: As we'll soon see, our abilities to think, reason, make decisions, and use language are impressive in many respects. But they are far from perfect. As is true for memory, our cognitive activities are subject to many forms of error: When we think, reason, make decisions, solve problems, and use language, we do not always do so in ways that would appear completely rational to an outside observer (Hawkins & Hastie, 1990; Johnson-Laird, Byrne, & Tabossi, 1989). As we examine each aspect of cognition, therefore, I'll call attention to these potential sources of distortion, because understanding the nature of such errors can shed important light on the nature of the cognitive processes they affect (Smith & Kida, 1991).

Thinking: *Forming Concepts and Reasoning to Conclusions*

What are you thinking about right now? If you've answered the question, then it's safe to say that at least to some extent you are thinking about the words on this page. But perhaps you are also thinking about a snack, the movie you saw last night, the argument you had with a friend this morning—the list could be endless. At any given moment in time, consciousness contains a rapidly shifting pattern of diverse thoughts, impressions, and feelings. In order to try to understand this complex and ever changing pattern, psychologists have often adopted two main strategies. First, they have focused on the basic elements of thought—how, precisely, aspects of the external world are represented in our thinking. Second, they have sought to determine the manner in which we *reason*—how we attempt to process available information cognitively in order to reach specific conclusions.

Basic Elements of Thought: Concepts, Propositions, Images

What, precisely, does thinking involve? In other words, what are the basic elements of thought? While no conclusive answer currently exists, it appears that our thoughts consist largely of three basic components: *concepts, propositions,* and *images.*

Concepts: Categories for Understanding Experience What do the following objects have in common: a country home, a skyscraper, a grass hut? Although they all look different, you probably have no difficulty in replying—they are all buildings. Now, how about these items: a Ford Explorer, the space shuttle *Discovery,* an elevator? Perhaps it takes you a bit longer to answer, but soon you realize that they are all vehicles (see Figure 7.1). The items in each of these groups look different from one another, yet in a sense you perceive—and think about—them as similar, at least in certain respects. The reason you find the task of answering these questions relatively simple is that you already possess well-developed concepts for both groups of items.

Concepts: Mental categories for objects or events that are similar to one another in certain respects.

Concepts are mental categories for objects, events, experiences, or ideas that are similar to one another in one or more respects. Concepts play a central role in our task of understanding the world around us and representing it mentally. For example, imagine that in conversation a friend uses the term *zip drive.* You've never heard it before, so you ask what she means. When she replies, "It's a speedy, high-capacity portable hard drive useful for backing up files on your computer and transferring large numbers of computer files from one computer to another," you're home free. You already have a concept for "hard drive" and immediately place this new term in that category. Now you can think about it quite efficiently: You know that it stores large numbers of computer files, that it is portable, and that it can help accomplish

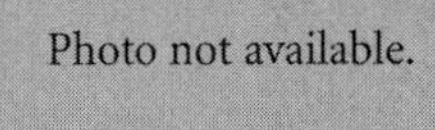

FIGURE 7.1

Concepts: Mental Categories for Diverse but Related Objects

What do these objects have in common? You probably have no difficulty labeling them "vehicles." This is because you already have well-developed concepts for such items.

certain tasks, such as helping you to avoid losing information in the event of a computer crash. In this and countless other situations, concepts allow us to represent a lot of information about diverse objects, events, or ideas in a highly efficient manner.

Artificial and Natural Concepts Is a tomato a fruit or a vegetable? Many people would answer, "a vegetable." Botanists, however, classify it as a fruit, because it contains seeds and its structure is definitely more like that of apples and pears than those of potatoes or spinach. This fact illustrates the important distinction between what psychologists term artificial (or logical) concepts and natural concepts. **Artificial concepts** can be clearly defined by a set of rules or properties. Thus, a tomato is a fruit because it possesses the properties established by botanists for this category. Similarly, as you learned in geometry, a figure can be considered to be a triangle only if it has three sides whose angles add to 180 degrees, and can be a square only if all four sides are of equal length and all four angles are 90 degrees. Such artificial concepts are very useful in many areas of mathematics and science.

In contrast, **natural concepts** have no fixed or readily specified set of defining features. They are fuzzy around the edges. Yet they more accurately reflect the state of the natural world, which rarely offers us the luxury of hard-and-fast, clearly defined concepts. For example, consider the following questions:

Is chess a sport?

Is a pickle a vegetable?

Is a psychologist a scientist?

Is someone who helps a terminally ill person commit suicide a murderer?

As you can readily see, these all relate to common concepts: sport, vegetable, science, crime. But what specific attributes are necessary for inclusion in each concept? If you find yourself puzzled, don't be surprised; the boundaries of natural concepts are somewhat indistinct.

Such natural concepts are often based on **prototypes**—the best or clearest examples (Rosch, 1975). Prototypes emerge from our experience with the external world, and new items that might potentially fit within their category are then compared with them. The more attributes new items share with an existing prototype, the more likely they are to be included within the concept. For example, consider the following natural concepts: *clothing, art.* For clothing, most people think of items like shirts, pants, or shoes. They are far less likely to mention wet suits, mink coats, or coats of armor. Similarly, for art, most people think of paintings, drawings, and sculptures. Fewer think of artwork such as the light show at Disney World.

In determining whether a specific item fits within a natural concept, then, we seem to adopt a *probabilistic* strategy. The more similar an object or event is to others already in the category, especially to the prototype for the category, the more likely we are to include the new item within the concept. In everyday situations, therefore, concept membership is not an all-or-nothing decision; rather, it is graded, and items are recognized as fitting within a category to a greater or lesser degree (Medin & Ross, 1992).

Artificial Concepts: Concepts that can be clearly defined by a set of rules or properties.

Natural Concepts: Concepts that are not based on a precise set of attributes or properties, do not have clear-cut boundaries, and are often defined by prototypes.

Prototypes: The best or clearest examples of various objects or stimuli in the physical world.

Concepts: How They Are Represented That concepts exist is obvious. But how are they represented in consciousness? No firm answer to this question exists, but several possibilities have been suggested. First, concepts may be represented in terms of their features or attributes. As natural concepts are formed, the attributes associated with them may be stored in memory. Then, when we encounter a new item, we compare its attributes with the ones we have already learned about. The closer the match, the more likely we are to include the item within the concept.

Visual Images: Mental pictures or representations of objects or events.

Propositions: Sentences that relate one concept to another and can stand as separate assertions.

A second possibility is that natural concepts are represented, at least in part, through **visual images:** mental pictures of objects or events in the external world. When considering whether chess is a sport, did you conjure up an image of two players bending intently over the board while an audience looked on? If so, you can readily see how visual images may play a role in the representation of natural concepts. I'll have more to say about the role of such images in thought later in this discussion.

Finally, it is important to note that concepts are closely related to *schemas,* cognitive frameworks that represent our knowledge of and assumptions about the world (see Chapter 6). Like schemas, natural concepts are acquired through experience and also represent information about the world in an efficient summary form. However, schemas appear to be more complex than concepts; each schema contains a broad range of information and may include a number of distinct concepts. For example, each of us possesses a *self-schema,* a mental framework holding a wealth of information about our own traits, characteristics, and expectations. This framework, in turn, may contain many different concepts, such as intelligence, attractiveness, health, and so on. Some of these are natural concepts; so the possibility exists that natural concepts are represented, at least in part, through their links to schemas and other broad cognitive frameworks.

To sum up, concepts may be represented in the mind in several ways. Whatever their precise form, concepts certainly play an important role in thinking and in our efforts to make sense out of a complex and ever changing external world.

Propositions: Relations between Concepts Thinking is not a passive process; it involves active manipulation of internal representations of the external world. As we have already seen, the representations that are mentally manipulated are often concepts. Frequently, thinking involves relating one concept to another, or one feature of a concept to the entire concept. Because we possess highly developed language skills, these cognitive actions take the form of **propositions**—sentences that relate one concept to another and can stand as separate assertions. For example, consider the following propositions:

Politicians are often self-serving.

This is a very interesting book.

Frozen yogurt is not as sweet as ice cream.

Concepts play a key role in each: *politicians* and *self-serving* in the first; *book* and *interesting* in the second; *frozen yogurt, sweet,* and *ice cream* in the third. Moreover, each sentence indicates some kind of relationship between the concepts or between the concepts and one or more of their features. For example, for many people a self-serving tendency is one feature of the concept *politician.* Research evidence indicates that much of our thinking involves the formulation and consideration of such propositions. Thus, propositions can be considered one of the basic elements of thought.

Images: Mental Pictures of the World Look at the drawing in Figure 7.2. Now cover it up with a piece of paper and answer the following questions:

1. Was there a flag? If so, in what direction was it fluttering?
2. Was there a tiller (handle) attached to the rudder?
3. Was there a porthole? On which side of the boat?

FIGURE 7.2

Mental Scanning of Visual Images

When shown a drawing such as this one and then asked questions about it, most people take longer to estimate the distance between the flag and the rudder than between the flag and the porthole.

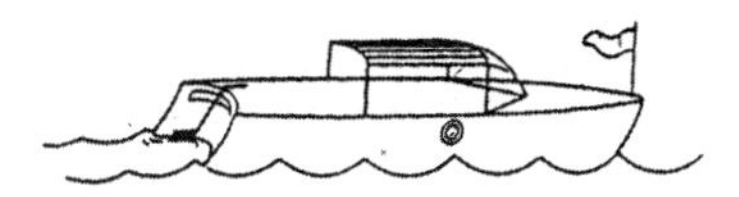

(**Source:** Based on an illustration used by Kosslyn, 1980.)

You probably answered all of these questions quite easily. But how? If you are like most people, you formed a visual image of the boat. Then, when asked about the flag, you focused on that part of your image. Next, you were asked to think about the rudder, at the opposite end of the boat. Did you simply jump to that end of the boat, or did you scan the entire image? Research findings indicate that you probably scanned the entire image: After being asked about some feature near the front of the boat, most people take longer to answer a question about a feature near the back than to respond concerning a feature somewhere in the middle (Kosslyn, 1980). Such findings suggest that once we form a mental image, we think about it by scanning it visually just as we would if it actually existed. Other findings support this conclusion. For example, when asked to estimate distances between locations on a familiar university campus, the farther apart the places indicated, the longer people take to make their estimates (Baum & Jonides, 1979).

Other findings, however, indicate that our use of visual images in thinking is not precisely like that of actual vision (Pylyshyn, 1981). In one study, for example, participants were asked to imagine carrying either a cannonball or a balloon along a familiar route (Intons-Peterson & Roskos-Ewoldsen, 1988). Not surprisingly, the participants took longer to complete their imaginary journeys when carrying the heavy object. So perhaps we don't simply "read" the visual images we generate; if we did, participants in this study should have been able to move through the imagined route equally fast in both conditions. The fact that they could not indicates that visual images are embedded in our knowledge about the world, and are interpreted in light of such knowledge rather than simply scanned.

Key Questions

- What are concepts?
- What is the difference between artificial and natural concepts?
- What are propositions and images?
- What is verbal protocol analysis?

Whatever the precise mechanisms through which they are used, mental images serve important purposes in the thinking process. People report using images for understanding verbal instructions, by converting the words into mental pictures of actions; for increasing motivation, by imagining successful performance; and for enhancing their own moods, by visualizing positive events or scenes (Kosslyn et al., 1991). Clearly, then, visual images constitute another basic element of thinking.

For more information on how psychologists study various aspects of thinking, please see the Research Methods section below.

RESEARCH METHODS

How Psychologists Study Cognitive Processes

People think—that's obvious. But how do psychologists measure *what* someone is thinking? After all, it is difficult to assess cognition directly. For example, what goes on in your mind as you grapple with a tough decision? What mental processes are involved when you try to determine the meaning behind a warm smile from an attractive person you'd like to meet? Or how do the cognitive processes of expert problem solvers differ from those of persons who are less skilled in this regard? Issues like these have led to the development of techniques that help psychologists understand the nature of various cognitive processes—such as thinking and memory—by measuring performance on tasks thought to involve these processes. One widely used cognitive assessment tool is *reaction time*—the amount of time it takes a person to react to a particular stimulus; an example would be pressing a computer key as quickly as possible each time a randomly occurring STOP sign icon appears on a computer screen. By varying the requirements of a cognitive task, such as the task's difficulty or the number of mental steps involved, psychologists can use differences in reaction time, or in the number or types of errors people commit, to make inferences regarding the nature of the underlying mental processes involved.

Perhaps the most interesting technique for studying cognitive processes, however, is **verbal protocol analy-**

sis. Participants in studies using this technique are asked to give continuous verbal reports, or to "think aloud," while making a decision or solving a problem (Ericsson & Simon, 1993). Verbal protocol analysis can provide information difficult to obtain by other means—most importantly, information about the types of knowledge people access while performing a particular task. This technique has the advantage of providing an ongoing record of the thinking *process,* rather than a single measure obtained at the end of the process (Crutcher, 1994; Payne, 1994).

How is the information obtained through the use of verbal protocols analyzed? By combining data obtained from many participants, psychologists are able to pinpoint meaningful patterns in the verbal protocol data. For example, researchers might note instances in which certain types of thoughts seem to occur consistently at a certain point as people attempt to solve a difficult problem. Or participants might be asked to report their thoughts while imagining themselves in a social situation; for example, at a party where two people they know are talking about them (Davison, Navarre, & Vogel, 1995). In the party example, analysis of the participants' reports might reveal important differences in responses based on age, gender, or other characteristics of interest to the researchers.

Verbal protocols can also be broken down into shorter segments to reveal the mental processes that underlie certain parts of a task. Research examining the "think-aloud" procedure has shown that the information obtained is typically consistent with the results obtained through the use of other well-known cognitive assessment techniques, such as reaction time or error data (Ericsson & Simon, 1993).

In one recent study, Blessing and Ross (1996) used verbal protocol analysis to examine ways in which experienced problem solvers differ from less-skilled problem solvers. One way in which expert and novice problem solvers are known to differ is the extent to which they rely on the surface content and deep structures of word problems (Chi, Feltovich, & Glaser, 1981). *Surface Structure* refers to the specific descriptions used to convey word problems, whereas *deep structure* refers to the underlying principles or mathematical equations needed to solve them. Some evidence indicates that experts do not focus on the context in which a problem is presented, but instead concentrate on discovering the problem's deep structure. In contrast, novices do not search for deep structure, but instead spend their time examining the problem's surface content.

Despite these findings, Blessing and Ross (1996) hypothesized that the experts do not ignore the suface structure of a problem altogether, but rather use this information—when relevant—as a clue to the type of problem it is and its solution. To test this possibility, the researchers asked experts (highly skilled math students) to solve word problems and to think aloud as they solved each one. Three versions of each problem were constructed so that the surface content was either appropriate, neutral, or inappropriate with respect to the problem's deep structure. Consistent with the researchers' predictions, participants spent the *least* amount of time solving problems whose surface structure matched its deep structure.

Even more interesting, however, were the results of the think-aloud protocol. These results indicated that participants presented with the "matching" version of each problem stated either the correct answer or the key equation(s) necessary to solve it almost immediately after reading the problem. In contrast, participants who solved the other ("neutral" or "nonmatching") versions of the same problem did not solve the problem in the same way. Because the clues provided by their problems' specific descriptions were *not* appropriate to the problems' deep structure, these participants were forced to translate each sentence of their word problem sequentially; as a result, it took them longer to solve the problem.

To summarize, these results illustrate the usefulness of verbal protocol analysis. Please note, however, that the think-aloud approach is not without its problems (Payne, 1994). First, as you might expect, verbal protocol analysis can be extremely time-consuming. Second, data obtained via this technique may reflect what participants believe they "should" be saying rather than the true underlying cognitive processes involved in a task. Finally, critics point out that asking participants to verbalize their thoughts may fundamentally alter the mental processes of interest. Still, the use of verbal protocol analysis, in conjunction with other well-established methods, can provide an important window into the inner workings of the mind.

Reasoning: Transforming Information to Reach Conclusions

One task we often face in everyday life is **reasoning:** drawing conclusions from available information. More formally, in reasoning we make cognitive transformations of appropriate information in order to reach specific conclusions (Galotti, 1989). How do we perform this task? And to what extent are we successful at it—in other words, how likely are the conclusions we reach to be accurate or valid?

Verbal Protocol Analysis: A technique for studying cognitive processes in which participants are asked to talk aloud while making a decision or solving a problem.

Reasoning: Cognitive activity that transforms information in order to reach specific conclusions.

Formal versus Everyday Reasoning First, it's important to draw a distinction between *formal reasoning* and what might be described as *everyday reasoning*. In formal reasoning, all the required information is supplied, the problem to be solved is straightforward, there is typically only one correct answer, and the reasoning we apply follows a specific method. One important type of formal reasoning is **syllogistic reasoning**—reasoning in which conclusions are based on two propositions called premises. For example, consider the following syllogism:

Premise: All people who are churchgoers are honest.

Premise: All politicians are churchgoers.

Conclusion: Therefore, all politicians are honest.

Is the conclusion correct? According to the rules of formal reasoning, it is. But you may find it hard to accept—and the reason for the problem should be obvious. At least one of the premises is incorrect: there is no strong evidence that all politicians attend church. This simple example illustrates an important point: Formal reasoning can provide a powerful tool for processing complex information, but *only* when its initial premises are correct.

In contrast to formal reasoning, *everyday reasoning* involves the kind of thinking we do in our daily lives: planning, making commitments, evaluating arguments. In such reasoning some of the premises are implicit, or unstated. Others may not be supplied at all. The problems involved often have several possible answers, which may vary in quality or effectiveness; and the problems themselves are not self-contained—they relate to other issues and questions of daily life (Hilton, 1995). For example, imagine that you have a problem with your next-door neighbor. You and your neighbor share a driveway leading to your garages. It is narrow, so only one car at a time can pass. Lately, your neighbor has taken to parking her car midway down the driveway, next to her side door. This prevents you from putting your own car in your garage. You begin to reason about this situation in order to understand why your neighbor is doing this. One potential premise might be "She has been quite ill lately"; a second might be "People who are ill are weak and don't want to walk a lot." These could lead to the conclusion "Although she is a nice person, she is too ill to be considerate." Other premises, however, are also possible: "She has been quite ill lately" coupled with "But she has gotten a lot better" and "People who look as healthy as she does don't mind walking." Your conclusion then might be quite different: "She is using her recent illness as an excuse for being irresponsible."

Notice that in this situation, the premises are not specified for you, as in syllogisms; you must generate them for yourself. And many different premises are possible. The ones you choose will probably depend on numerous factors, including your recent experiences with other neighbors, with people who are ill, and so on. Finally, when you do reach a conclusion, it is not easy to determine whether it is correct or whether others, too, might be accurate.

Everyday reasoning, then, is far more complex and far less definite than formal syllogistic reasoning. Since it is the kind we usually perform, however, it is worthy of careful attention.

Reasoning: Some Basic Sources of Error How good are we at reasoning? Unfortunately, not as good as you might guess. Several factors, working together, seem to reduce our ability to reason effectively.

Syllogistic Reasoning: A type of formal reasoning in which two premises are used as the basis for deriving logical conclusions.

The Role of Mood States You may not be surprised to learn that the way we feel—our current moods or emotions—can dramatically reduce our ability to reason effectively (Forgas, 1995). Most of us have experienced situations in which we've lost our cool—and, unfortunately, our ability to reason effectively as well. You may be surprised to learn, however, that *positive* moods can also reduce our ability to reason effectively. In one recent study, Oaksford and colleagues (1996) used brief film clips to induce either positive, negative, or neutral moods in the study participants. Following the mood induction, all participants in the study attempted to solve a difficult analytical task. Interestingly, the participants in the positive mood condition required significantly *more* trials to solve the problem than participants in the other groups. How do we account for these results? Apparently, inducing positive mood states makes more, and more diffuse, memories available to us—definitely an asset if the task at hand requires a creative solution. Solving analytical tasks like the one used in this study, however, relies less on long-term memory retrieval and more on the ability to work through the discrete steps necessary to solve the problem. In short, a positive mood state does not guarantee that our ability to reason effectively will be enhanced. (See Chapter 10 for additional information on the effects of mood on cognitive processes.)

The Role of Beliefs Reasoning is often influenced by emotion-laden beliefs. For example, imagine that a person with deeply held convictions against the death penalty listens to a speech favoring capital punishment. Suppose that the arguments presented by the speaker contain premises the listener can't readily refute, and thus point to the conclusion that the death penalty is justified for the purpose of preventing further social evil. Yet the listener totally rejects this conclusion. Why? Because of his or her passionate beliefs and convictions against the death penalty, the listener may alter the meaning of the speaker's premises or "remember" things the speaker never really said. This, of course, serves to weaken the speaker's conclusion. Such effects can arise in many ways. Whatever your views on this particular issue, the general principle remains the same: When powerful beliefs come face to face with logical arguments, it is often the latter that give way. We'll consider the powerful effects of emotion again in Chapter 10.

The Social Context Social context can also exert powerful effects on reasoning (Hilton, 1995). To illustrate this, consider the following example: While entering a restaurant—one you've never tried before—you ask a couple who are leaving, "How was it?" If they reply, "It was great!" what do you conclude? After all, the couple did not comment directly on the quality of the food, the service, or the atmosphere inside the restaurant. However, from a variety of contextual variables—the tantalizing aromas emanating from the restaurant, the fact that many people are eating there, the unmistakable look of satisfaction on the couple's faces (or on the faces of other people leaving the restaurant), and the enthusiasm in their voices—you probably conclude that your chances of experiencing a delightful meal are good. But this may not be sound reasoning. Clearly, aspects of the social context contribute significantly to the accuracy of the conclusions we reach. We'll consider some of these factors again in Chapter 16.

The Confirmation Bias: Searching for Positive Evidence To illustrate another source of error in reasoning, let's consider our anti–death penalty person once again. Suppose that over several weeks he or she encounters numerous magazine articles; some report evidence confirming the usefulness of the death penalty, while others report evidence indicating that capital punishment is ineffective in terms of deterring crime. As you can readily guess, the individual will probably remember more of the articles that support the anti–death penalty view. In fact, there is a good chance that this person will read only these articles, or will read these articles more carefully

Confirmation Bias: The tendency to pay attention primarily to information that confirms existing views or beliefs.

Hindsight Effect: The tendency to assume that we would have been better at predicting actual events than is really true.

than the ones arguing in favor of capital punishment. To the extent that this happens, it demonstrates the **confirmation bias**—our strong tendency to test conclusions or hypotheses by examining only, or primarily, evidence that confirms our initial views (Baron, 1988; Klayman & Ha, 1987). Because of the confirmation bias, individuals often become firmly locked into their conclusions; after all, when this bias operates, it prevents people from even considering information that might call their premises, and thus their conclusions, into question (see Figure 7.3).

WEB

Hindsight: The "I knew it all along" Effect Revisited Have you ever heard the old saying "Hindsight is better than foresight"? What it means is that after specific events occur, we often have the impression that we could have predicted or actually did predict them. This is known in psychology as the **hindsight effect:** the tendency to judge events as more predictable after their occurrence than in foresight (Fischoff, 1975).

A dramatic real-life illustration of this effect was provided by the launch of the Hubble space telescope in the spring of 1990. Shortly after the telescope reached orbit, it was discovered to have a serious defect. Within a few days of this discovery, several officials stated that they had known all along that this might happen; in fact, the problem resulted from a failure to conduct certain tests of the telescope that they had personally recommended. Were these individuals correct? Existing evidence on the hindsight effect casts considerable doubt on this possibility. In many studies, conducted in widely different contexts, learning that an event occurred causes individuals to assume that they could have predicted it more accurately than is really the case (Christensen-Szalanski & Willham, 1991; Mitchell, Russo, & Pennington, 1989).

Can anything be done to counteract the hindsight effect? There are several possibilities. For example, if individuals are asked to explain a reported outcome along with other possible outcomes that did *not* occur, they are better able to recall their actual views before learning of the event, and this reduces the hindsight effect (Davies, 1987; Slovic, Fischoff, & Lichtenstein, 1977). Other people may also reduce the hindsight effect by calling attention to the fact that they too were surprised by the event and that it was indeed truly difficult to predict (Mazursky & Ofir, 1996; Wasserman, Lempert, & Hastie, 1991). In sum, it does appear that we can combat our strong tendency to assume that we are better at predicting events than is truly justified. And to the extent that we avoid tendencies to flawed thinking, our ability to reason effectively may be enhanced. Please refer to the **Ideas to Take with You** feature for tips to help you reason more effectively.

FIGURE 7.3

The Confirmation Bias

The confirmation bias leads individuals to test conclusions or hypotheses by examining primarily—or only—evidence consistent with their initial views. As a result, these views may be maintained regardless of the weight of opposing evidence.

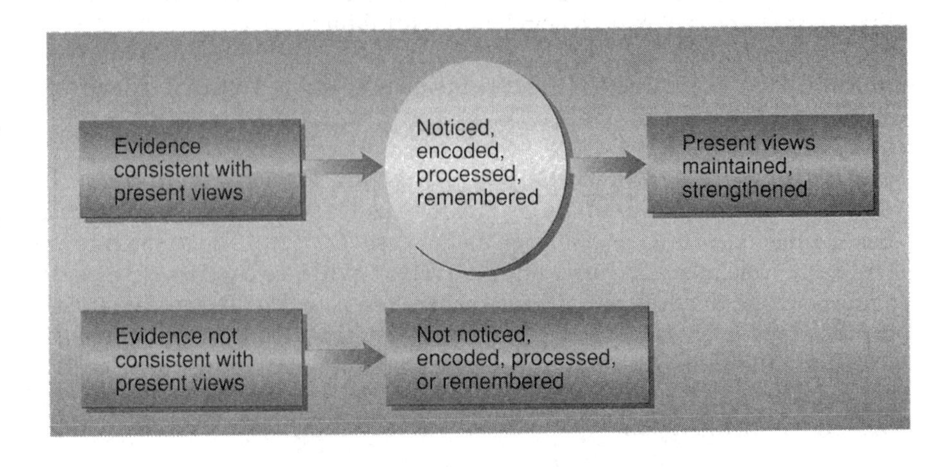

Ideas to Take with You

How to Reason Effectively

Each day we face a succession of events that require the use of our wits—in other words, our ability to reason. Several factors can greatly reduce our ability to reason effectively, however, thereby placing us at risk for making bad decisions. To reduce the chances that you'll fall prey to one or more of these factors, consider the following suggestions.

MOOD STATES: Feeling Too Good or Too Bad Can Spell Trouble

Most people's mood states fluctuate over time—that's normal. When it comes to reasoning, however, extremes in emotional states can be bad news. Losing your cool, for instance, can result in decisions you may regret later. Yet, being in a good mood also has its advantages and disadvantages. Performance on creative tasks seems to be enhanced by a positive mood state, but performance on analytic tasks is diminished. So beware of making important decisions or trying to solve difficult problems when you are unhappy or angry—or when you're walking on air.

Photo not available.

PERSONAL BELIEFS: Try to Focus on the Facts

Personal beliefs can cause us to ignore or overreact to a point of view on an issue about which we feel strongly. Protect yourself from this potential source of error by asking yourself whether you are responding to the facts—or to your personal beliefs.

THE SOCIAL CONTEXT: Filling in the Gaps

Social conventions can cause our reasoning to go astray because of our tendency to view all information through the filter of our personal experience. For example, we may interpret a message quite differently depending on who said it, how we choose to interpret the intended meaning, and the setting in which we hear the message.

Photo not available.

THE CONFIRMATION BIAS: Failure to Consider Alternative Views

The confirmation bias is our tendency to pay attention primarily—or exclusively—to information that supports our own preexisting attitudes or opinions. To combat this tendency, seek out information from all points of view, and then carefully weigh the merits of each argument.

Photo not available.

Excerpt from a Biology Text

From *Life on Earth*, by Audesirk/Audesirk, © 1997. Reprinted by permission of Prentice-Hall, Inc., Upper Saddle River, NJ.

The Human Nervous System

The human nervous system may be divided into two parts: central and peripheral. The **central nervous system** consists of a **brain** and a **spinal cord** that extends down the dorsal part of the torso. The **peripheral nervous system** consists of nerves connecting the central nervous system to the rest of the body (Fig. 26-7).

The Peripheral Nervous System Links the Central Nervous System to the Body

The peripheral nervous system consists of **peripheral nerves** that link the brain and spinal cord to the rest of the body, including the muscles, the sensory organs, and the organs of the digestive, respiratory, excretory, and circulatory systems. Within the peripheral nerves are axons of sensory neurons that bring sensory information *to* the central nervous system from all parts of the body. Peripheral nerves also contain the axons of motor neurons that carry signals *from* the central nervous system to the organs and muscles.

The motor portion of the peripheral nervous system can be subdivided into two parts: the **somatic nervous system** and the **autonomic nervous system.** Motor neurons of the somatic nervous system synapse on skeletal muscles and control voluntary movement. Their cell bodies are located in the gray matter of the spinal cord (see Fig. 26-9), and their axons go directly to the muscles they control.

Motor neurons of the autonomic nervous system control involuntary responses. They synapse on the heart, smooth muscle, and glands. The autonomic nervous system is controlled both by the medulla and the hypothalamus of the brain, described later in the chapter. It consists of two divisions, the **sympathetic nervous system** and the **parasympathetic nervous system** (Fig. 26-8). The two divisions of the autonomic nervous system generally make synaptic contacts with the same organs but usually produce opposite effects.

The sympathetic nervous system acts on organs in ways that prepare the body for stressful or highly energetic activity, such as fighting, escaping, or giving a speech. During such "fight-or-flight" activities, the sympathetic nervous system curtails activity of the digestive tract, redirecting some of its blood supply to be used by the muscles of arms and legs. Heart rate accelerates. The pupils of the eyes open wider, admitting more light, and the air passages in the lungs expand, accommodating more air. The parasympathetic nervous system, in contrast, dominates during maintenance activities that can be carried on at leisure, often called "rest and rumination." Under its control, the digestive tract becomes active, heart rate slows, and air passages in the lungs constrict.

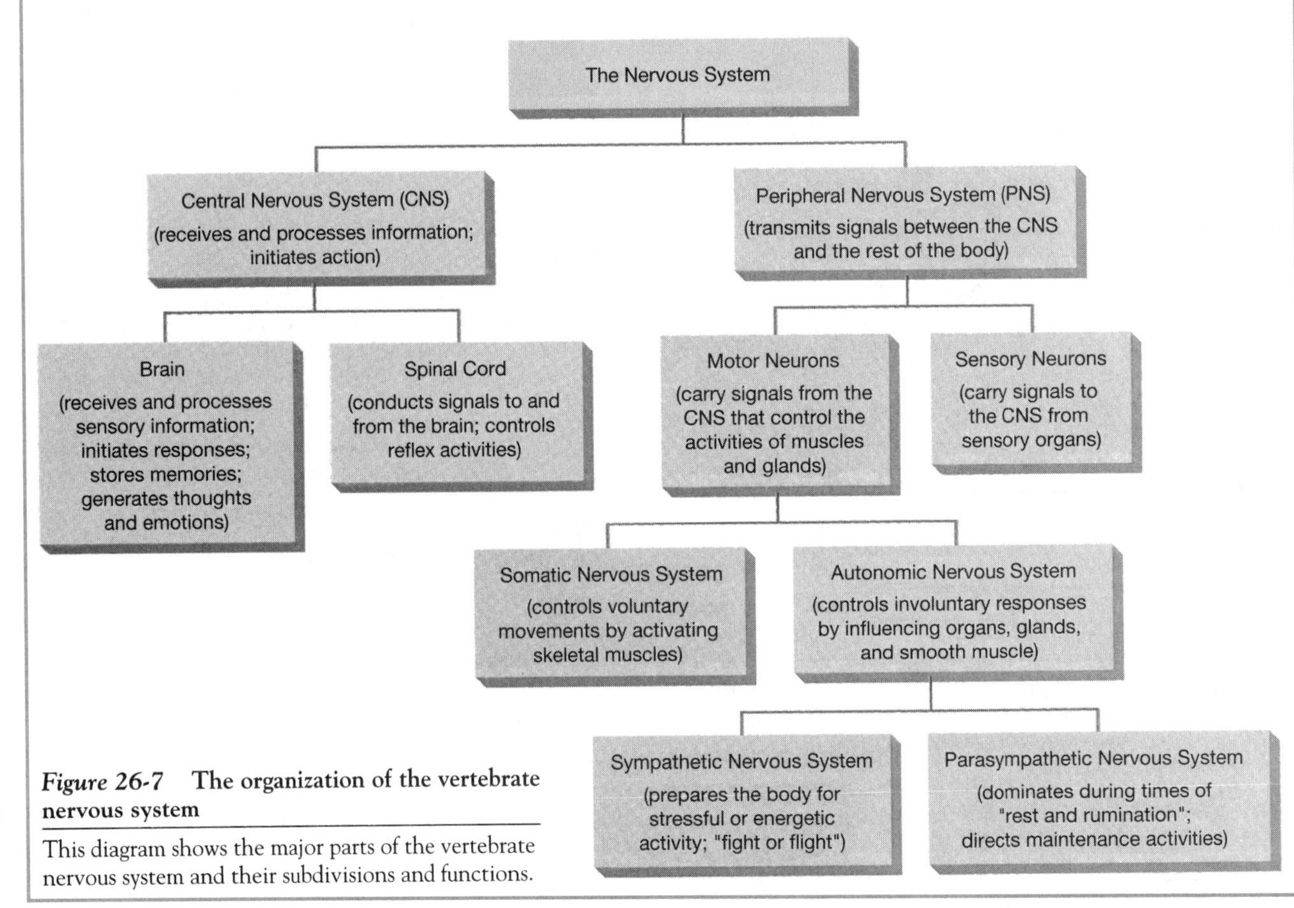

Figure 26-7 **The organization of the vertebrate nervous system**

This diagram shows the major parts of the vertebrate nervous system and their subdivisions and functions.

Two differences in the organization of the sympathetic and parasympathetic nervous systems are evident in Figure 26-8. First, parasympathetic axons are found in nerves that originate from two separate locations, the brain (midbrain and medulla) and the base of the spinal cord. In contrast, sympathetic axons are found in nerves that originate from the middle and lower portions of the spinal cord. Second, in both the sympathetic and parasympathetic divisions, there are two neurons that carry messages in sequence from the central nervous system to each target organ, but they synapse at different locations. In the sympathetic nervous system, the synapse occurs in ganglia (ganglia—singular, **ganglion**—are clusters of neurons) that are near the spinal cord. In the parasympathetic nervous system, the synapse occurs in smaller ganglia located at or very near each target organ.

The Central Nervous System Consists of the Spinal Cord and Brain

The central nervous system consists of the brain and spinal cord. It is the integrating portion of the nervous system, where sensory information is received and processed, thoughts are generated, and responses are directed. The central nervous system consists primarily of association neurons—somewhere between 10 and 100 billion of them!

The brain and spinal cord are protected in three ways. The first line of defense is a bony armor, consisting of the skull that surrounds the brain and the vertebral column that protects the spinal cord. Beneath the bones lies a triple layer of connective tissue called **meninges** (see Fig. 26-12). Between the layers of the meninges, a clear lymph-like liquid, the **cerebrospinal fluid,** cushions the brain and spinal cord.

The Spinal Cord Is a Cable of Axons Protected by the Backbone

The spinal cord is a neural cable about as thick as your little finger that extends from the base of the brain to the hips, protected by the bones of the vertebral column (Fig. 26-9). Between the vertebrae, nerves called dorsal roots, carrying axons of sensory neurons, and ventral roots, carrying axons of motor neurons, arise from the dorsal and ventral portions of the spinal cord, respectively; these merge to form the peripheral nerves of the spinal cord, which are part of the peripheral nervous system. In the center of the spinal cord are neuron cell bodies, which form a butterfly-shaped area of **gray matter.** These are surrounded by bundles of axons called **white matter** owing to their white insulating myelin coating (see Fig. 26-9). The spinal cord relays signals between the brain and the rest of the body, and it contains the neural circuitry for certain behaviors, including reflexes.

To illustrate some of the functions of the parts of the spinal cord, let's examine a simple spinal reflex, the pain-withdrawal reflex, which involves neurons of both the central nervous system and the peripheral nervous system (Fig. 26-10; see also Fig. 26-6). The cell bodies of the sensory neurons from the skin (in this case signaling pain) are found just outside the spinal cord in a row of ganglia. Each of these **dorsal root ganglia** is located on a spinal nerve and nestled close to the vertebral column. Both association and motor neuron cell bodies are found in the gray mat-

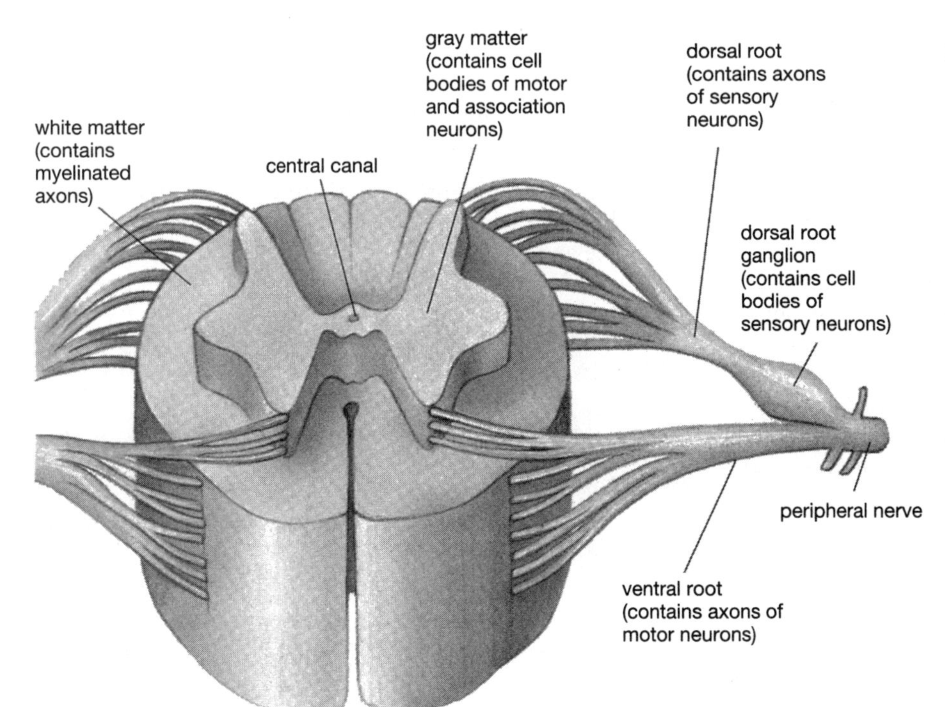

Figure 26-9 **The spinal cord**

The spinal cord runs from the base of the brain to the hips, protected by the vertebrae of the spine. Peripheral nerves emerge from between the vertebrae. A cross section of the spinal cord reveals an outer region of myelinated axons (white matter) traveling to and from the brain, surrounding an inner, butterfly-shaped region of dendrites and the cell bodies of association and motor neurons (gray matter). The cell bodies of the sensory neurons are located outside the cord in the dorsal root ganglion.

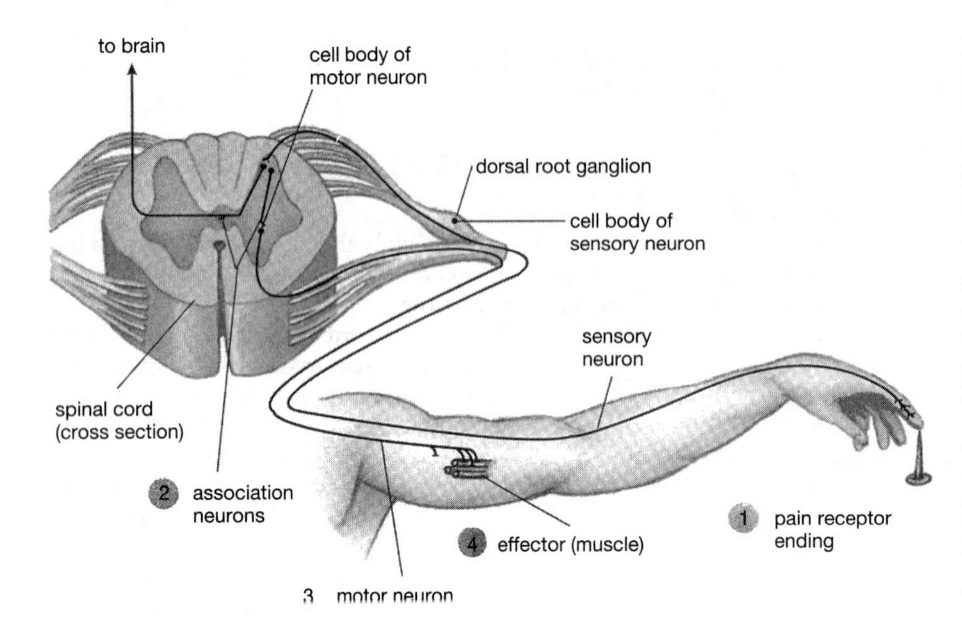

Figure 26-10 **The vertebrate pain-withdrawal reflex**

This simple reflex circuit includes one each of the four elements of a neural pathway. The sensory neuron has pain-sensitive endings in the skin ① and a long fiber leading to the spinal cord. The sensory neuron stimulates an association neuron in the spinal cord ②, which in turn stimulates a motor neuron, also in the cord. The axon of the motor neuron ③ carries action potentials to muscles ④, causing them to contract and withdraw the body part from the damaging stimulus. Note that the sensory neuron also makes a synapse on other association neurons not directly involved in the reflex, which carry signals to the brain, informing it of the danger below.

ter in the center of the spinal cord. The axons in the surrounding white matter communicate with the brain. Association neurons for the pain-withdrawal reflex, for example, not only synapse on motor neurons but also have axons extending up to the brain. Signals carried along these axons alert the brain to the painful event. The brain, in turn, sends impulses down axons in the white matter to cells in the gray matter. These signals can modify spinal reflexes. With sufficient motivation, you can suppress the pain-withdrawal reflex; to rescue a child from a burning building, for example, you could reach into the flames.

In addition to simple reflexes, the entire program for operating some fairly complex activities also resides within the spinal cord. All the neurons and interconnections needed to walk and run, for example, are found within the cord. In these cases, the role of the brain is to initiate and guide the activity of spinal neurons. The advantage of this semi-independent arrangement is probably an increase in speed and coordination, since messages do not have to travel all the way up the cord to the brain and back down again (in the case of walking) merely to swing forward one of your legs. The motor neurons of the spinal cord also control the muscles involved in conscious, voluntary activities such as eating, writing, or playing tennis. Axons of the brain cells directing these activities carry signals down the cord and stimulate the appropriate motor cells.

The Brain Consists of Several Parts Specialized for Specific Functions

All vertebrate brains have the same general structure, with major modifications corresponding to life-style and intelligence. Embryologically, the vertebrate brain begins as a simple tube, which soon develops into three parts: the hindbrain, midbrain, and forebrain (Fig. 26-11). It is believed that in the earliest vertebrates, these three anatomical divisions were also functional divisions: The **hindbrain** governed automatic behaviors such as breathing and heart rate, the **midbrain** controlled vision, and the **forebrain** dealt largely with the sense of smell. In nonmammalian vertebrates, these three divisions remain prominent. However, in mammals, and particularly in humans, the brain regions are significantly modified. Some have been reduced in size, and others, especially the forebrain, greatly enlarged.

The Hindbrain Includes the Medulla, Pons, and Cerebellum

In humans, the hindbrain is represented by the medulla, the pons, and the cerebellum (Fig. 26-12). In both structure and function, the **medulla** is very much like an enlarged extension of the spinal cord. Like the spinal cord, the medulla has neuron cell bodies at its center, sur-

Figure 26-11 **The embryonic vertebrate brain**

The embryonic vertebrate brain shows three distinct regions: the forebrain, midbrain, and hindbrain. This basic structure persists in all adult brains.

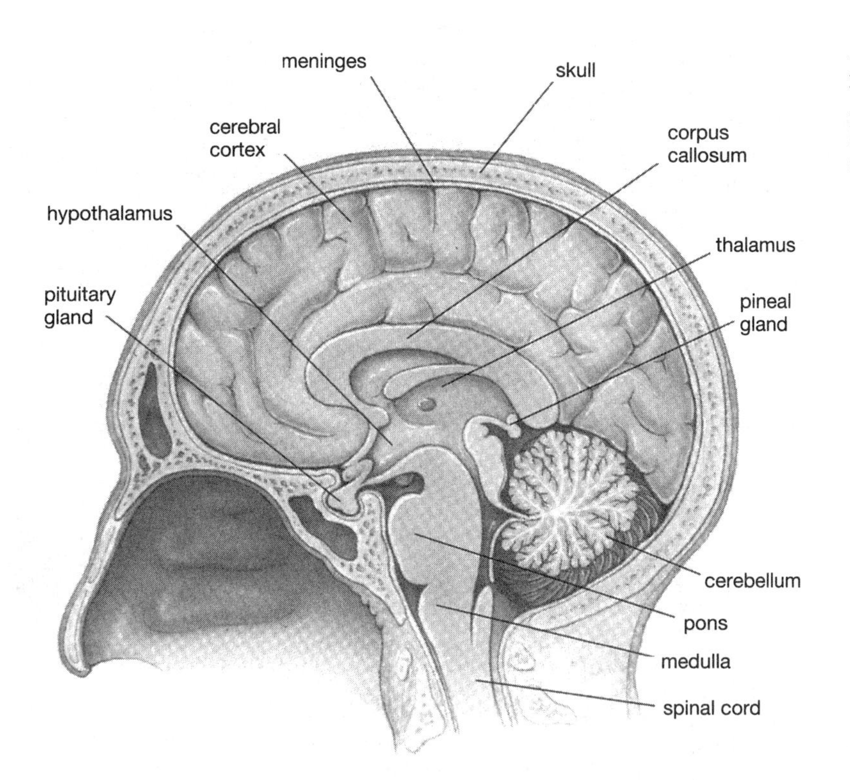

Figure 26-12 **The human brain**

A section taken through the midline of the human brain reveals some of its major structures.

rounded by a layer of myelin-covered axons. The medulla controls several automatic functions, such as breathing, heart rate, blood pressure, and swallowing. Certain neurons in the **pons,** located above the medulla, appear to influence transitions between sleep and wakefulness and between stages of sleep. Others influence the rate and pattern of breathing. The **cerebellum** is crucially important in coordinating movements of the body. It receives information from command centers in the higher, conscious areas of the brain that control movement and also from position sensors in muscles and joints. By comparing what the command centers ordered with information from the position sensors, the cerebellum guides smooth, accurate motions and body position. Not surprisingly, the cerebellum is largest in animals whose activities require fine coordination. It is best developed in birds, who engage in the complex activity of flight.

The Midbrain Contains the Reticular Formation

The midbrain is extremely reduced in humans, but an important relay center, the **reticular formation,** passes through it (Fig. 26-13). The neurons of the reticular formation extend all the way from the central core of the medulla, through the pons, the midbrain, and on into lower regions of the forebrain. It receives input from virtually every sense and every part of the body and from many areas of the brain as well. The reticular formation plays a role in sleep and arousal, emotion, muscle tone, and certain movements and reflexes. It filters sensory inputs before they reach the conscious regions of the brain, although the selectivity of the filtering seems to be set by higher brain centers. Through a combination of genetically determined wiring and learning, the reticular formation "decides" which stimuli require attention. Important stimuli are forwarded to the conscious centers for processing,

Figure 26-13 **The reticular formation**

The human reticular formation (shown here in blue) is a diffuse network of neurons running through the lower regions of the brain from the medulla in the hindbrain, through the midbrain, and up into the thalamus and hypothalamus of the forebrain. It receives input from most of the senses and sends outputs to many higher brain centers, filtering the sensory information that reaches the conscious brain.

and unimportant stimuli are suppressed. The fact that a mother wakens upon hearing the faint cry of her infant but sleeps through loud traffic noise outside her window testifies to the effectiveness of the reticular formation in screening inputs to the brain and to the role of learning in determining the importance of sensory stimulation.

The Forebrain Includes the Thalamus, Limbic System, and Cerebral Cortex

The forebrain, also called the **cerebrum**, can be divided into three functional parts: the thalamus, the limbic system, and the cerebral cortex. In mammals, the cerebral cortex is much enlarged compared with that of fish, amphibians, and reptiles. This trend culminates in the human cerebral cortex, which is thrown into complex folds that increase its area (see Fig. 26-12).

The Thalamus The **thalamus** (see Figs. 26-12 and 26-13) carries sensory information to the limbic system and cerebrum. This information includes sensory input from auditory and visual pathways, from the skin, and from within the body. Inputs from the cerebellum and limbic system are also channeled through this busy thoroughfare. Very little information processing goes on in the thalamus.

The Limbic System Anatomically, the **limbic system** is a diverse group of structures located in an arc between the thalamus and the cerebrum (Fig. 26-14). These structures work together to produce our most basic and primitive emotions, drives, and behaviors, including fear, rage, tranquility, hunger, thirst, pleasure, and sexual responses. The limbic system includes the hypothalamus, portions of the thalamus, the amygdala, and the hippocampus.

The **hypothalamus** (literally "under the thalamus") contains many different clusters of neurons. Some of these are neurosecretory cells that release hormones (see Chapter 25). Through its hormone production and neural connections, the hypothalamus acts as a major coordinating center, controlling body temperature, hunger, the menstrual cycle, water balance, and the autonomic nervous system. In addition, stimulation of specific areas of the hypothalamus elicits emotions such as rage, fear, pleasure, and sexual arousal.

The **amygdala** is believed to be responsible for the production of appropriate behavioral responses to environmental stimuli. It receives input from many sources, including the auditory and visual areas of the cerebral cortex. Different clusters of neurons in the amygdala produce sensations of pleasure, punishment, or sexual arousal when stimulated. By stimulating different portions of the amygdala, researchers can either reduce or enhance aggressive behavior. Conscious humans whose amygdalas are electrically stimulated have reported feelings of rage or fear. Recent studies have revealed that damage to the human amygdala eliminates the person's ability both to feel fear and to recognize fearful facial expressions in other people.

Figure 26-14 **The limbic system**

The limbic system extends through several brain regions. It seems to be the center of most unconscious, emotional behaviors, such as love, hate, hunger, sex, and fear.

The shape of the **hippocampus** as it curves around the thalamus inspired its name, which is derived from the Greek word meaning "sea horse." As in the amygdala and hypothalamus, behaviors that reflect a variety of emotions, including rage and sexual arousal, can be elicited by stimulating portions of the hippocampus. The hippocampus also plays an important role in the formation of long-term memory and is thus required for learning, discussed in more detail later in this chapter.

The Cerebral Cortex In humans, by far the largest part of the brain is the **cerebral cortex**, the outer layer of the forebrain. The cerebral cortex and underlying parts of the forebrain are divided into two halves, called **cerebral hemispheres,** that communicate with each other by means of a large band of axons, the **corpus callosum**. The differences between the hemispheres is discussed a bit later in this chapter. The cerebral cortex is the most sophisticated information processing center known, and it is also the area of the brain that scientists know the least about. Roughly *50 to 100 billion* neurons are packed into this thin surface layer. To accommodate this profusion of cells, the cortex is thrown into folds, called **convolutions,** that greatly increase its area. In the cortex, cell bodies of neurons predominate, giving this outer layer of the brain a gray appearance. These neurons receive sensory information, process it, store some in memory for future use, and direct voluntary movements.

The cerebral cortex is divided into four regions based on anatomical criteria: the frontal, parietal, occipital, and temporal lobes (Fig. 26-15). Functionally, the cortex contains primary sensory areas where signals originating in sensory organs such as the eyes and ears are received and converted into subjective impressions, for example, light and sound. Nearby association areas interpret the sounds, as speech, for example, and the visual stimuli as recognizable objects. Association areas also link the stimuli with previous memories stored in the cortex and generate commands to produce speech. Primary sensory areas in the parietal lobe interpret sensations of touch originating in all parts of the body, which is "mapped" in an orderly sequence. In an adjacent region of the frontal lobe, primary motor areas generate commands for movements in corresponding areas of the body (Fig. 26-15). The association area of the frontal lobe protected by bones of the forehead seems to be involved in complex reasoning such as decision making, predicting the consequences of actions, controlling aggression (see Fig. E26-3), and planning for the future, as discussed later in the chapter. Damage to the cortex due to trauma, stroke, or a tumor results in specific deficits, such as problems with speech, difficulty reading, or the inability to sense or move specific parts of the body. Because brain cells cannot reproduce, once a brain region is destroyed it cannot be repaired or replaced, so these deficits are often permanent. Fortunately, however, in some cases diligent training can cause undamaged regions of the cortex to take control over and restore some of the lost functions.

Brain and Mind

Historically, people have always had difficulty reconciling the physical presence of a few pounds of grayish material in the skull with the range of thoughts, emotions, and memories of the human mind. This "mind-brain problem" has occupied generations of philosophers and, more recently, neurobiologists. Beginning with observations of patients with head injuries and progressing to sophisticated surgical, physiological, and biochemical experiments, the outlines of how the brain creates the mind are beginning to emerge. Here, we will be able to touch upon only a few of the more fascinating features.

The "Left Brain" and "Right Brain" Are Specialized for Different Functions

The human brain appears bilaterally symmetrical, particularly the cerebrum, which consists of two extremely similar-looking hemispheres. However, it has been known since

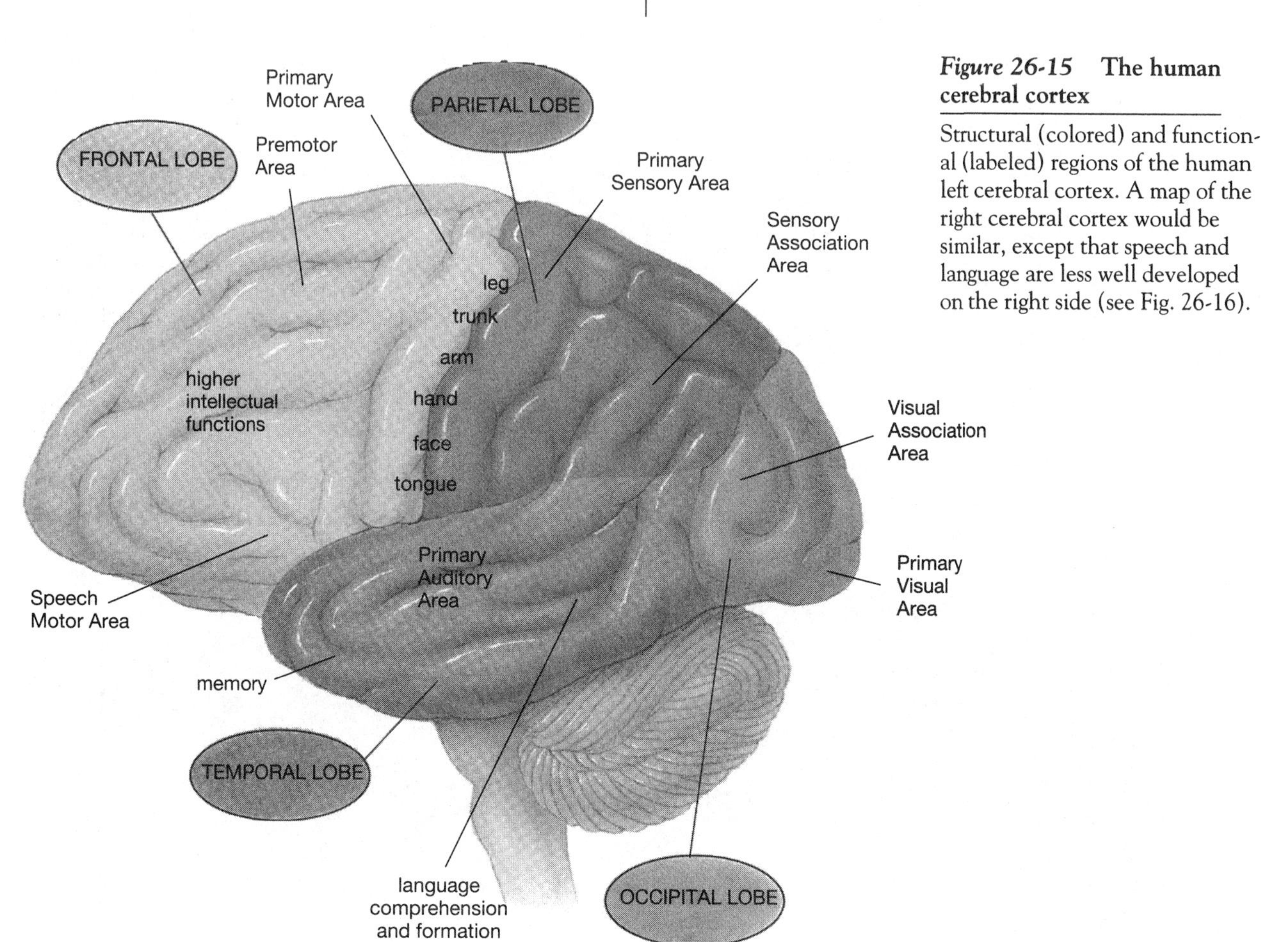

Figure 26-15 **The human cerebral cortex**

Structural (colored) and functional (labeled) regions of the human left cerebral cortex. A map of the right cerebral cortex would be similar, except that speech and language are less well developed on the right side (see Fig. 26-16).

the early 1900s that this symmetry does not extend to brain function. Much of what is known of the differences in hemisphere function comes from two sources: studies of accident victims with localized damage to one hemisphere and studies of patients who have had the corpus callosum (which connects the two hemispheres) severed. This surgical procedure was performed in rare cases of uncontrollable epilepsy to prevent the spread of seizures through the brain.

Studies based on selective damage to the left cerebral hemisphere had led to the belief that the right hemisphere was relatively retarded, lacking the ability to speak, write, recognize words, or reason. For example, people suffering damage to localized areas of the left hemisphere, but not the right, often became unable to speak, read, or understand spoken language. In addition, the left hemisphere for most people is superior in mathematical ability and in logical problem-solving tasks (Fig. 26-16).

Roger Sperry, of the California Institute of Technology, worked with people whose hemispheres had been surgically separated by cutting the corpus callosum. In his studies, Sperry made use of the knowledge that axons within each optic nerve follow a pathway that causes the left half of each visual field to be projected on the right cerebral hemisphere, and vice versa (Fig. 26-16). Through an ingenious device that projected different images onto the left and right visual fields (thus sending different signals to each hemisphere), he and other investigators have gained more insight into the roles of the two hemispheres. If he projected an image of a nude figure onto the left visual field only, the patients would blush and smile but would claim to have seen nothing, because the image had reached only the nonverbal right side of the brain! The same figure projected onto the right visual field was readily described verbally. These experiments, begun in the 1960s and refined since then, have revealed that the right side of the brain is actually superior to the left in several areas, including musical skills, artistic ability, recognition of faces, spatial visualization, and the ability to recognize

***Figure 26-16* Specialization of the two cerebral hemispheres**

In general, each hemisphere controls sensory and motor functions of the opposite side of the body. Further, the left side seems to predominate in rational and computational activities, whereas the right side governs creative and spatial abilities. Roger Sperry's split-brain experiments made use of the fact that images on the left half of the visual field are projected onto the right half of the retina and from there reach only the right visual cortex (orange), while the right half of the visual field is projected onto the left visual cortex (blue).

and express emotions. For his pioneering work, Sperry was awarded the Nobel Prize in 1981.

Recent experiments indicate that the left-right dichotomy is not as rigid as was once believed. Patients who have suffered a stroke that disrupted blood supply to the left hemisphere typically show symptoms such as loss of speaking ability. Frequently, however, training can partially overcome these speech or reading deficits, even though the left hemisphere itself has not recovered. This fact suggests that the right hemisphere has some latent language capabilities. Interestingly, female stroke victims recover some lost abilities more often than males, and females also have a larger corpus callosum. These findings suggest a sex difference in the degree of specialization of the two hemispheres and the extent of their interconnections. Further evidence of this difference has recently been provided by sensitive techniques that allow imaging of neural activity in the brains of normal subjects performing various mental tasks. When subjects were asked to compare word lists for rhyming words, a specific region of the left cortex of male subjects became active, but in females, similar areas in *both* left and right hemispheres were activated

The Mechanisms of Learning and Memory Are Poorly Understood

Although theories abound as to the cellular mechanisms of learning and memory, we are a long way from understanding these phenomena. In mammals, and particularly in humans, however, we do know a fair amount about two other aspects of learning and memory: the time course of learning and some of the brain sites involved in learning, memory storage, and recall.

Memory May Be Brief or Long Lasting

Experiments show that learning occurs in two phases: an initial **working memory** followed by **long-term memory.** For example, if you look up a number in the phone book, you will probably remember the number long enough to dial but forget it promptly thereafter. This is working memory. But if you call the number frequently, eventually you will remember the number more or less permanently. This is long-term memory.

Some working memory seems to be electrical in nature, involving the repeated activity of a particular neural circuit in the brain. As long as the circuit is active, the memory stays. If the brain is distracted by other thoughts, or if electrical activity is interrupted, such as by electroconvulsive shock or by a concussion, the memory disappears and cannot be retrieved no matter how hard you try. In other cases, working memory involves temporary biochemical changes within neurons of a circuit, with the result that synaptic connections between them are strengthened.

Long-term memory, on the other hand, seems to be structural—the result, perhaps, of persistent changes in the expression of certain genes. It may require the formation of new, permanent synaptic connections between specific neurons or the permanent strengthening of existing but weak synaptic connections, for example, by increasing the area of synaptic contacts. These new or strengthened synapses last indefinitely, and the long-term memory persists unless certain brain structures are destroyed. Working memory can be converted into long-term memory, apparently by the hippocampus, which processes new memories then transfers them to the cerebral cortex for permanent storage.

Learning, Memory, and Retrieval May Be Controlled by Separate Regions of the Brain

Learning, memory, and the retrieval of memory seem to be separate phenomena, controlled by separate areas of the brain. Ample evidence shows that the hippocampus (part of the limbic system) is involved in learning. For example, intense electrical activity occurs in the hippocampus during learning. Even more striking are the results of hippocampal damage. A person whose hippocampus is destroyed retains most of his or her memories but is unable to learn anything that occurs after the loss. One victim was still unable to recall his address or find his way home after 6 years at the same residence. He could be entertained indefinitely by reading the same magazine over and over, and people whom he saw regularly required reintroduction at each encounter. People with extensive hippocampal damage can recall events momentarily, but the memory rapidly fades, as does the memory of a dream upon awakening. This phenomenon has led to the hypothesis that the hippocampus is responsible for transferring information from working into long-term memory.

Retrieval, or recall, of established long-term memories is localized in another area of the brain, the outer **temporal lobes** of the cerebral hemispheres. In a famous series of experiments in the 1940s, neurosurgeon Wilder Penfield electrically stimulated the temporal lobes of conscious patients undergoing brain surgery. The patients did not merely recall memories but felt that they were experiencing the past events right there in the operating room!

The site of storage of complex long-term memories is much less clear. The psychologist Karl Lashley spent many years training rats and subsequently damaging parts of their brains in an effort to locate the site of the memory, but failed. None of the injuries could erase a memory completely. In 1950, a frustrated Lashley wrote: "I sometimes feel, in reviewing the evidence on the localization of the memory trace, that the necessary conclusion is that learning just is not possible."

Some researchers suggest that each memory is stored in numerous distinct places in the brain. Or perhaps memories are stored like a hologram image, both everywhere and nowhere at the same time: The memory is more precise if the whole brain is intact, but each "bit" (probably several thousands of neurons) of cerebral hemisphere can store an essentially complete memory. Further research might provide definitive answers, but for now, the storage site of memories remains an unsolved mystery.

Insights on How the Brain Creates the Mind Come from Diverse Sources

Humans have always been intensely interested in the workings of their own minds. But until about 100 years ago, the mind was more appropriately a subject for philosophers than for scientists, because the tools to study the brain did not yet exist. Through the first half of the twentieth century, the mind was treated by psychologists as a "black box" whose internal workings could be deduced only through the investigation of how past and present experiences were interpreted and influenced behavior. New discoveries, however, are rapidly changing our views of the workings of the brain.

During recent decades, we have begun to understand the neural bases of at least some psychological phenomena. Many forms of mental illness, such as schizophrenia, manic depression, and autism, once thought to be due to childhood trauma or inept parenting, are now recognized as the result of biochemical imbalances in the brain. Studies are revealing a strong heritability factor (and hence, a biological basis) for traits that were once considered entirely learned, such as shyness and alcoholism.

A striking illustration of how the physical structure of the brain is related to personality was unwittingly provided by Phineas Gage in 1848. An explosion propelled a large metal rod through his skull, removing his left temporal lobe (Fig. 26-17). He miraculously survived, but his personality changed radically. Before the accident, Phineas was conscientious, industrious, and well liked. After his recovery, he became impetuous, profane, and incapable of planning or working toward a goal. Subsequent research has implicated the frontal lobe in emotional expression, control of aggression, and the ability to work for delayed rewards. Other sites of damage have revealed additional anatomical specializations. One patient with very localized damage to the left frontal lobe of the cerebral cortex was unable to name fruits and vegetables (although he could name everything else). Describing this patient, one science writer quipped: "Does the brain have a produce section?" Similarly, damage to certain areas of the cortex on the underside of the brain results in a selective inability to recognize faces.

Photo not available.

In the past, much of our understanding of the human mind-brain connection came from the study of victims of brain damage such as that caused by a stroke, trauma, tumor, or surgical procedure. If the victim was cooperative, and if the case came to the attention of an interested researcher, tests were administered to define the change or loss of ability. Often, the exact extent of the damage remained unknown until revealed by autopsy.

Now new techniques, such as the PET and MRI scans, are permitting insight into the functioning of normal, as well as diseased, brains (see "Scientific Inquiry: Scanning the Brain"). These and increasingly sophisticated techniques of the future will create ever-larger windows into the "black box" that is the human brain. It is possible that the exact nature of consciousness will always remain obscure, but the next decades will see continued merging of the fields of psychology and neurophysiology, and a clearer understanding of how the human brain generates the human mind.

Excerpt from a History Text

18 CHAPTER

TECHNOLOGIES OF MASS-PRODUCTION AND DESTRUCTION

1914–1990s

"Our twentieth century was going to improve on others . . . A couple of problems weren't going to come up anymore: hunger, for example, and war, and so forth."

WISLAWA SZYMBORSKA

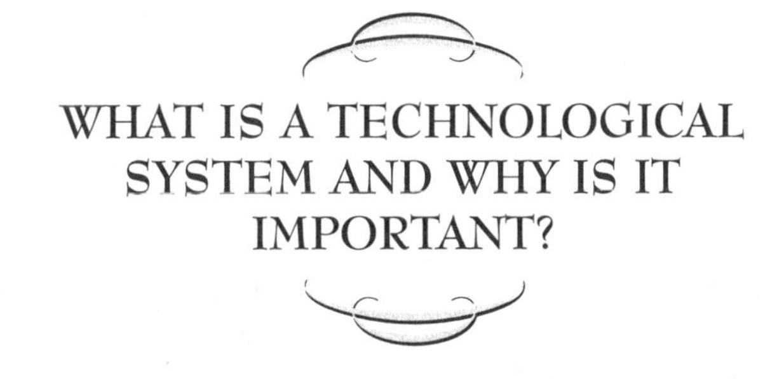

WHAT IS A TECHNOLOGICAL SYSTEM AND WHY IS IT IMPORTANT?

TECHNOLOGICAL SYSTEMS

In popular accounts of technology, inventions of the late nineteenth century, such as the incandescent light, the radio, the airplane, and the gasoline-driven automobile, occupy center stage, but these inventions were embedded within technological systems. Such systems involve far more than the so-called hardware, devices, machines and processes, and the transportation, communication, and information networks that interconnect them. Such systems consist also of people and organizations. An electric light-and-power system, for instance, may involve generators, motors, transmission lines, utility companies, manufacturing enterprises, and banks. Even a regulatory body may be co-opted into the system. (p. 3)

The technological enterprise has continued to grow as the most pervasive characteristic of the twentieth century. It has dramatically altered:

- the number, longevity, and health of the people who inhabit the globe;
- the size and organization of our families;
- the location, design, and equipment of our homes, neighborhoods, and workplaces;
- the nature and organization of the work we do and the training necessary to do it;
- the clothes we wear;
- our travel for business and pleasure;
- the quantities and varieties of food we eat as well as the regions of the globe from which they come;
- the forms of our recreation;
- the strategies and destructive potentials of the wars we wage;
- the complexity and structure of our economic, social, and governmental organizations; and
- the ecology, that is, the interaction of the life systems, of the earth.

DEMOGRAPHIC SHIFTS

Improvements in technology have changed our relationship to life and death, health and sickness. Biological and health advances have included new drugs such as sulfa-based medicines (1930s), penicillin and antibiotics (from the 1940s), hormonal and mood-altering chemicals (from the 1950s), and new methods of contraception, especially the birth control pill (1950s) which have changed sexual attitudes and practices around the globe.

Public health services, the fortunate linking of medical knowledge with government responsibility, have increased, especially in the provision of safe drinking water and sewage offtake (although not always and everywhere as quickly as new needs have arisen). An increasing variety of vaccines has eliminated the fear of many childhood diseases. Polio was tamed in the 1950s, and through the international activities of the World Health Organization in achieving the vaccination of virtually all humans in areas of the world infected with the disease in the 1960s and 1970s, smallpox, a disease of historically epidemic proportions, has been totally eradicated. The last known case was in Somalia in 1977. The once-feared smallpox virus lives today only in laboratory specimens kept for research purposes.

The progress of technology and its application often collided with other ecological constraints. For a time in the 1950s and 1960s, for example, the chemical insecticide DDT seemed to offer a weapon

TIMELINE: EUROPE AND THE UNITED STATES 1900–1990s

	Political	Social	Cultural
1900	▮ Boer War (1899–1902) ▮ Germany enters arms race with Britain (1900) ▮ Labour Party founded in Britain (1900) ▮ Russo-Japanese War (1904–5) ▮ Old Age Pensions in Britain (1909)	▮ Guglielmo Marconi transmits signal across the Atlantic (1901) ▮ Wright brothers make first powered air flight (1903) ▮ Boy Scout movement founded (1907) ▮ Henry Ford begins assembly-line manufacture of motorcars (1909) ▮ Robert Peary reaches North Pole (1909)	▮ Jean-Paul Sartre (1905–81) ▮ Dmitri Shostakovitch (1906–57) ▮ Cubist painters (Pablo Picasso, Georges Braque) exhibit in Paris (1907–10) ▮ *Der Rosenkavalier* by Richard Strauss (1909–10)
1910	▮ World War I (1914–18) ▮ Treaty of Versailles (1919) ▮ Benito Mussolini founds Fascist Movement (1919)	▮ Roald Amundsen reaches South Pole (1911) ▮ *Titanic* sinks (1912) ▮ Igor Sikorsky builds first four-engined airplane (1913) ▮ Panama Canal opened (1914) ▮ Birth control clinic opens in New York (1916)	▮ Marcel Proust publishes *À la recherche du temps perdu* (1913–27) ▮ Igor Stravinksy's *Rite of Spring* performed (1913) ▮ Sigmund Freud's *Totem and Taboo* published (1913) ▮ Benjamin Britten (1913–76) ▮ Albert Camus (1913–60) ▮ Albert Einstein publishes *General Theory of Relativity* (1915) ▮ D.W. Griffith's *Birth of a Nation* (1915) ▮ Dadaism founded (1915)
1920	▮ League of Nations meets (1920) ▮ Adolf Hitler founds National Socialist (Nazi) Party (1923) ▮ Locarno Conference (1925) ▮ Germany becomes member of League of Nations (1926) ▮ Kellogg-Briand Pact (1928)	▮ General strike in Britain (1926) ▮ Alexander Fleming discovers penicillin (1928) ▮ US stock market collapses (1929), leading to worldwide recession	▮ John Logie Baird invents television (1925) ▮ *The Jazz Singer*, first talking picture (1927) ▮ *Plane Crazy*, first Mickey Mouse cartoon (1928)
1930	▮ Hitler becomes chancellor and Germany withdraws from League of Nations (1933) ▮ Hitler denounces Treaty of Versailles and ▮ Germany re-arms (1935) ▮ Spanish Civil War (1936–9) ▮ Edward VIII of Britain abdicates (1938) ▮ World War II (1939–45)	▮ Prohibition in US ends (1933) ▮ Robert Watson-Watt develops radar system (1935) ▮ Persecution of Jews begins in Germany (1935) ▮ Sikorsky builds first successful helicopter (1939)	▮ *King Kong* (1933) ▮ Carl Jung publishes *Modern Man in Search of a Soul* (1933) ▮ Elvis Presley (1935–77) ▮ *Gone with the Wind* (1939)
1940	▮ Nuremberg Trials (1946) ▮ War in Indochina between French and nationalists led by Ho Chi Minh (1946–54) ▮ Marshall Aid program (1947) ▮ NATO formed (1949) ▮ France recognizes independence of Cambodia and Vietnam (1949)	▮ Frank Whittle invents the jet engine (1941)	▮ *Citizen Kane* (1941) ▮ Abstract Expressionist movement in painting develops in USA (after 1945) ▮ George Orwell publishes *Nineteen Eighty-Four* (1949) ▮ Simone de Beauvoir writes *Le Deuxième sexe* (1949)

against the malaria-bearing anopheles mosquito, but DDT proved toxic to humans and animal life and was generally banned from use. Quinine continued as the principal defense and treatment.

Food productivity multiplied. More land was brought under cultivation. New machinery, notably the tractor and combine, facilitated the opening of the American and Canadian Midwest, the Argentinian pampas, the steppe land of the Soviet Union, and the economically developing continent of Australia. By the end of the twentieth century, although some scientists questioned the wisdom of manipulating the basic designs of life, new biotechnology and genetic engineering were creating breakthroughs in kinds and totals of crop production. In 1997 scientists succeeded in cloning a sheep and were experimenting with producing blood in the bodies of animals that could be used for human transfusions. Scientists, clergy, ethicists, and political leaders continue to grapple with the implications of these discoveries.

In the developing nations of the **third world**, beginning in the 1960s, new seeds and fertilizers, engineered in part under the auspices of the philanthropic Rockefeller Foundation, increased the productivity of land under wheat cultivation by up to five times. Experimentation with additional crops, such as rice, is under way. Land that was

TIMELINE: EUROPE AND THE UNITED STATES 1900–1990s

	POLITICAL	SOCIAL	CULTURAL
1950	▮ Korean War (1950–53) ▮ Schuman Plan (1951): France, West Germany, Italy, Belgium, Netherlands, and Luxembourg agree on open market for coal and steel ▮ Greece and Turkey join NATO (1952) ▮ Geneva Conference (1954): Vietnam divided, with communist North under Ho Chi Minh ▮ SEATO formed (1954) to prevent spread of communism in Southeast Asia ▮ Warsaw Pact agreed (1955) ▮ Treaty of Rome (1957): Belgium, France, West Germany, Italy, Luxembourg and Netherlands establish EEC	▮ Joseph McCarthy heads inquiry into "un-American activities" (1950) ▮ Contraceptive pill becomes available (1952) ▮ Conquest of Everest (1953) ▮ Jonas Edward Salk develops vaccine against polio (1954) ▮ USSR launches *Sputnik I* (1957) ▮ US launches *Explorer I* (1958); space race begins	▮ *The Catcher in the Rye* by J.D. Salinger (1951) ▮ Theater of the Absurd movement, founded by Eugene Ionesco and Samuel Beckett (1953–60) ▮ Elvis Presley dominates rock music after release of *Heartbreak Hotel* (1956) ▮ Beginning of the Pop Art movement in the USA (after 1956)
1960	▮ Berlin Wall is built (1961) ▮ Fighting between Greeks and Turks in Cyprus (1964) ▮ US troops increasingly involved in Vietnam War (1964–8) ▮ Britain sends troops to Northern Ireland (1969)	▮ Crick, Wilkins, and Watson identify DNA molecular structure (1962) ▮ Rachel Carson writes *Silent Spring* (1963) attacking over-use of pesticides ▮ Neil Armstrong is first man on the moon (1969)	▮ Beatles pop group formed (1960) ▮ *2001: A Space Odyssey*, directed by Stanley Kubrick (1968)
1970	▮ Britain, Eire, and Denmark join EEC (1973) ▮ Coup in Portugal ends dictatorship of Premier Caetano (1974) ▮ Spanish dictator Franco dies; monarchy is restored (1975) ▮ Russian forces in Afghanistan (1979–89)	▮ Greenpeace founded (1971) ▮ John Paul II becomes first non-Italian pope for 450+ years (1978)	▮ *The Female Eunuch* by Germaine Greer (1970) ▮ *Sexual Politics* by Kate Millet (1970) ▮ *The Gulag Archipelago* by Alexander Solzhenitsyn (1975) ▮ *Star Wars*, directed by George Lucas (1977)
1980	▮ Falklands War (Britain v. Argentina; 1982) ▮ US invades Grenada (1983) ▮ Lockerbie air crash kills 270 people (1988) ▮ "Solidarity" in Poland (1989) ▮ Communist rule ends in Poland, Hungary, Czechoslovakia, Bulgaria, and East Germany (1989)	▮ *Voyager* spacecraft flies by Saturn (1980) ▮ AIDS virus identified (1983) ▮ Greenpeace vessel *Rainbow Warrior* sunk by French in South Pacific (1985) ▮ Stock market crashes in New York, Tokyo and London (1987) ▮ Piper Alpha oil rig in North Sea explodes, killing 166 (1988)	▮ *Gandhi*, directed by Richard Attenborough (1983) ▮ Live Aid raises money globally for famine relief (1985) ▮ *Bonfire of the Vanities* by Tom Wolfe (1987) ▮ *Satanic Verses* by Salman Rushdie (1988)
1990	▮ Soviet republics claim independence from Russia (1990) ▮ War in Yugoslavia (from 1991) ▮ Gulf War (1991) ▮ Bill Clinton elected president of USA (1992)	▮ Global warming threat recognized (1990) ▮ Internet system links 5 million users (1993) ▮ Bomb destroys federal building in Oklahoma City, killing 100+ people (1995)	▮ Euro Disney opened in Paris (1992) ▮ Aids quilt exhibited in Washington D.C. (1992) ▮ *Schindler's List*, directed by Steven Spielberg (1993)

already fully populated and under intense cultivation became increasingly productive.

For example, although India's population doubled between 1966 and 1991, the "green revolution" enabled the country to achieve self-sufficiency in food during those years. Distribution and equity, however, presented problems. Many critics noted the increasing income disparities created by the revolution in productivity. Wealthier farmers could most easily afford the new seeds and the additional fertilizer and irrigation water required to cultivate them. The green revolution made the rich richer as it increased productivity. Did it make the poor poorer? Survey results thus far are not conclusive.

New farm machinery reduced the need for labor, however, and rural population ratios dropped sharply—in America from 72 percent in 1900 to 36 percent in 1980; in Europe, quite similarly, from 70 percent to 36 percent; for the world as a whole from 84 percent to 62 percent. Farmers left the countryside in droves to search for urban jobs.

Developments in health and food technology facilitated a population explosion. More people were born and they lived longer. Life expectancy at birth in the USA rose from fifty-four years in 1920 to seventy-five years in 1990. In India it increased from thirty years at Independence in 1947 to fifty-four years in 1981 to sixty-two years in the 1990s. In

China it reached sixty-nine years and in Japan seventy-nine years in the 1990s. From 1900 to 1990, the population of the world multiplied three and one-half times from about 1.5 billion to approximately 5.3 billion, although the population growth around the globe was not uniform, as may be seen in the chart on p 439. The population *added* between 1980 and the year 2000 is predicted at 1.5 billion, almost the total population of the earth in 1900.

Demographers, seeking to explain the differential population growth, postulate two successive demographic shifts. First, as health conditions and food supply improved, death rates dropped while birth rates remained high and population increased. This has happened all over the world. Later, as parents saw that the mortality rates had fallen and that their children were likely to survive to adulthood, they chose to plan their family size through the use of contraception. Birth rates then dropped, as death rates had earlier. This second stage, of family planning, has occurred in the wealthier regions of the world, where death rates were lowest. In some of these countries, birth rates have actually dropped below death rates and the overall populations of some countries in Europe—Germany in the late twentieth century, France periodically—is actually declining. In poorer countries where death rates are still relatively high, however, the second stage of declining birth rates has not (yet) occurred, and population continues to rise. Demographers suggest, contrary to expectation, that the best way to reduce population growth is to improve health measures to help assure parents that their babies and children will live; then parents will plan fewer of them.

In addition to voluntary programs of birth control within individual families, many nations have undertaken official population policies. Many European countries, like France, in light of declining birth rates, have adopted policies that encourage more births by extending economic support to families with young children. On the other hand, many less wealthy and more crowded countries have promulgated policies to discourage large families. Most drastically, China since the 1980s has attempted to limit families to just one child. Implementation, however, has been difficult. A family wanting a male child, the usual preference, may break the law in attempting a second child if the first is a female, or may even kill a first-born female. In India, ruthless and thoughtless enforcement of rigid sterilization quotas by the government of Indira Gandhi cost her the 1977 elections. Government family planning programs have been restrained ever since. The powerful state and the individual family have clashed here over values and implementation; policies that may benefit the state and the society may not be regarded as beneficial by any individual family.

URBANIZATION AND MIGRATION

The growing population has been moving steadily into cities. We have seen (p. 416) that mechanization of agriculture is one of the factors pushing people away from the countryside. In addition, jobs in manufacture, bureaucracy, and service industries pull them to the cities. At the beginning of the century, urbanization was still linked to industrial growth; by the end of the century, the most rapidly growing cities, and, increasingly, the largest of them, are in the poorer, less industrialized areas of the world—for example, Mexico City and São Paulo each with about 20 million in 1990; Bombay and Calcutta in India and Buenos Aires, Argentina, each with about 11.5 million; and Manila, Cairo, and Jakarta, each with about 10 million.

In many of the richer countries, however, in a process termed **counterurbanization**, cities have turned inside out, and central city populations are actually declining. Poorer citizens remain in the center as the richer avail themselves of the new means of transportation and of communication via phone, fax and the World Wide Web to relocate to the suburbs. Businesses, too, recognizing a new freedom of movement, are leaving the central cities, partly to reduce their overhead costs. Multinational corporations cross international boundaries to relocate their factories, removing them from high-wage urban centers in the **first world** to new sites offering cheaper labor in the third.

Since the building of the first aircraft in 1903 by Wilbur and Orville Wright, and the first solo flight across the Atlantic in 1927 by Charles Lindbergh, international and intercontinental travel has become commonplace. Flights are taken for business and pleasure, and tourism has become one of the world's largest industries. In 1989, 38 million people visited the USA, spending $43 billion. Students, in particular, travel around the globe for formal and informal study and work opportunities.

In contrast, many others travel out of economic necessity and fear of repression—often on foot. Millions of political refugees from Vietnam, Afghanistan, Tibet, Iraq, Mozambique, Ethiopia, and numerous other African states, central America, and the USSR seek refuge and asylum in neighboring countries. "Guest workers," also by the millions, travel in search of jobs from southern Europe, North Africa, and Turkey to northern Europe; from the entire world to the oil-rich Persian Gulf areas; and, often illegally, from Latin America to the United States.

DOMESTIC CHANGE

Twentieth-century technology has transformed the quality of daily life as well as its location and density. The automobile, bus, truck, train, airplane, and jet affect transportation for almost all citizens of the world. The revolution in the means of communication—telegraph, telephone, copier, fax machine, modem, internet, radio, phonograph, various kinds of sound reproduction, photography, motion pictures, television, satellite transmission, and cable—have opened visions of the whole world to potentially all its citizens.

They have totally transformed work and play as well as the distribution of these activities in geographical space. Airconditioning has not only changed standards of comfort, but has opened many warmer areas of the world (including the southern United States) to increased immigration and development.

First developed after World War II, early computers were room-filling machines, designed to solve mathematical problems. Nowadays, they are found in homes and offices worldwide and are small enough to be easily portable. The computer has not only affected each one of the above revolutions in transportation and communication, but also has transformed data processing, office work, and the further development of both large-scale organizations and of science. With the advent of the World Wide Web it is now quite conceivable that future generations may never have to leave their homes to work, shop, bank and communicate with friends and family.

New technological systems such as the automated assembly line production of Henry Ford's automobile factories, the more recent introduction of robotics, and the management techniques of Frederick Taylor have changed the way we work and the efficiency of our production. Scientific research facilities have been established by private industry, like Bell Laboratories, by philanthropic corporations, like the Rockefeller Foundation, and, most of all, by national governments all over the world. They have changed our concept and mode of creativity. No longer needing to rely on experienced, gifted artisans tinkering in small shops, twentieth-century technology has systematized invention and promoted an increasing demand for ever more sophisticated and more expensive research facilities.

Synthetic fabrics and dyes have changed our wardrobes. Plastics have been the most important new, man-made material of the twentieth century and have replaced metals, rubber, and glass in innumerable uses. They have also increased the world's reliance on petroleum, a non-renewable fossil fuel, from which plastics are synthesized.

ENERGY

Twentieth-century technology has demanded ever-increasing supplies of inanimate energy. Among its most central symbols are the electric power generator, the internal-combustion engine, the hydroelectric dam, the oil well, and the nuclear reactor. Gaining access to energy resources has been a key issue for all countries. Some are richly endowed and begin with a large advantage. Others, such as Japan, have few energy resources and must find ways of seizing or buying them, or of tapping the natural energy of sun, wind and water, or of generating new forms of energy by unlocking the atom. Many countries of Western Europe have been seriously dependent on oil throughout the century, although they have other energy resources, especially coal, and are introducing new forms of more accessible energy. The United States, despite vast natural resources, has relied in large part on energy imports to build and support its economy.

Some countries, especially those in the Middle East, have fossil fuel energy resources (oil) far beyond their current needs. Because of the need for oil, the five countries in the world with the largest known crude oil reserves—Saudi Arabia, Iraq, the United Arab Emirates, Kuwait, and Iran—have all been subject to greater or lesser degrees of foreign competition for control and colonization.

They are even now at the center of international power struggles for control of that oil wealth. Since 1973, they have banded together with other oil-rich member states of the Organization of Petroleum Exporting Countries (OPEC) to gain better economic terms and more political power for their oil, restructuring the terms of world trade and power in the process. The **geo-politics** of oil supply and demand have therefore been critical issues in twentieth-century history (see p. 691).

Atomic power was first developed for military uses, but it now also provides significant amounts of the world's commercial energy supply. Despite the ecological problems of safety and of nuclear waste disposal, the meltdown of the Russian nuclear reactor in Chernobyl, Ukraine, in 1986, and the near meltdown in 1979 of the American reactor at Three Mile Island in Pennsylvania, many countries continue to expand their nuclear generating capacities. In France, for example, 75 percent of electricity production is supplied by nuclear power.

The hunger for energy drives technological development and vice versa. The increasingly sophisticated technology generates increasing demands for investment capital and skilled personnel. These demands have forced increased educational requirements on labor forces everywhere, and sometimes have led to tensions and even violent competition among nations. The desire to be competitive technologically has, in part, fostered warfare; and much modern technology, in turn, is devoted to the design and production of arms.

WARFARE

Technology has altered our warfare and, conversely, military needs have driven technological development. The presence of new weapons systems has not, however, increased the feeling of human security, but rather has heightened a sense of insecurity, terror, and dread. Nuclear weapons and the delivery systems that make them a universal threat have left everyone, everywhere always aware of the possiblity—whether through intention or accident—of total destruction. Paradoxically, some would argue, the MAD (mutually assured destruction) balance of terror between the two superpowers of America and Russia kept them from war for four decades. Both countries have implemented encouraging, even startling, new programs for arms reductions, which have allayed at least some fears for the moment. Biological and chemical warfare also threaten unimaginable destruction, and the nations of the world negotiate to try to limit or ban them.

WORLD WAR

Two world wars dominated the first half of the twentieth century. Competition among nations over technological advances, productivity, and markets helped to instigate both conflicts. From the late eighteenth century, Britain's technological supremacy was unchallenged, and, from her position of industrial and military strength, she imposed a Pax Britannica, which kept the world safe from major war for more than half a century. By the turn of the century the United States had begun to catch up with, and even surpass, Britain, but distance and American isolationism muted the competition. As Germany also began to approach and surpass Britain in technological capacity, however, competition for industrial markets and prestige brought increasing tension.

WORLD WAR I 1914–18

This economic competition was embedded in still larger issues of nationalism, a powerful force in early twentieth-century Europe (see Chapter 17). People's reverence for their nation-states, and for their shared language, history, and ethnicity within those states, had become so passionate that they were willing to fight and die for them. Cynics argued that the masses of the population were being manipulated to the battle-front by industrialists in each country who stood to profit from war production, but the national feelings were powerful in themselves. Indeed they seemed strongest among smaller, newer states with little economic base in military production.

The more powerful nations also believed that their security could be strengthened by forming defensive alliances. In the closing decades of the nineteenth century these countries joined with their geographic or ideological neighbors to create a system of alliances which led in the early years of the twentieth century to a Europe divided into two potentially hostile camps—the Triple Alliance of Germany, Austria-Hungary, and Italy; and the Triple Entente of France, Russia, and Britain.

Build-up and Early Events of World War I

1882	Triple Alliance among Italy, Germany, and Austria-Hungary
1891–1905	German Schlieffen Plan
1894	Formation of Franco-Russian alliance
1898	Germany starts building a High Seas Fleet, generating Anglo-German naval armaments race
1902	Anglo-Japanese Alliance
1904	Anglo-French Entente
1906	British launch *Dreadnought*, first all-big-gun battleship
1907	Anglo-Russian Entente
1911	Moroccan Crisis; tension between Germany and France over Morocco
1914:	
June	Serbian nationalist assassinates Archduke Ferdinand, heir to the Austro-Hungarian throne
July	Austria invades Serbia; Russia mobilizes and Germany declares war on Russia and France
August	Germany invades Belgium on way to France; Britain declares war on Germany; Battle of Tannenburg: Russia defeated by Germany
September	Battle of the Marne: Allies halt German advance on Paris; Russia retreats from east Prussia; All German colonies in Africa in Allied hands
Oct–Nov	First battle of Ypres: Allies lose more than 100,000 men, but Germans fail to reach Channel ports; Trench warfare (lasts till end of war); Turkey enters war on side of the Central Powers

World War I (called the Great War until World War II surpassed it in magnitude) began on June 28, 1914 when a Serbian nationalist, eager to gain from the Austro-Hungarian empire certain territories with heavily Serbian populations, assassinated Archduke Ferdinand, heir to the Austro-Hungarian throne. A month later, Austria-Hungary declared war on Serbia, triggering a domino effect among other European powers and the Ottoman Empire. Under the system of alliances built up over the preceding three decades, countries now came to the aid of one another. Russia mobilized its armies to defend Serbia. Germany declared war on Russia and France, and invaded Belgium. Britain declared war on Germany.

In November, the Ottoman Empire joined Germany and the Austro-Hungarian Empire in an alliance called the Central Powers. The British, French, and Russians on the other side formed an alliance called the Allied Powers (Allies). At the start of the war, the Central Powers won early victories in Belgium and Poland but in September the German advance was stopped by the Allies at the first Battle of the Marne. Along the western front the opposing armies then continued to fight in two facing trenches which stretched 500 miles (805 km) from the English Channel to the border of Switzerland. On the eastern front Russian armies lost over a million men in combat against the combined German and Austrian forces.

The United States stayed neutral until 1917, selling weapons and material to both sides. In 1917, with Russia in collapse, Germany turned its attention to the western front. To choke off American supplies to the British and French, Germany began intensive submarine warfare against American shipping. Germany gambled that the Allies would collapse before the United States responded—and lost. When German submarines began sinking unarmed passenger ships the United States decided to aid the Allies. Once the United States entered the war in April 1917, providing supplies and troops, the Allies moved toward victory. The fighting finally ended with an armistice in November 1918.

The war introduced new weapons. The machine gun, first used extensively in this war, and the tank, invented in 1914, helped define the nature of World War I. Hundreds of thousands of soldiers dug into trenches on each side, faced each other with very little movement for months at a time and then charged in human waves, in which tens and even hundreds of thousands were slaughtered by machine guns. In addition, Germany introduced poison gas in World War I, leading to subsequent international bans against its use, although it continues to be stored in the armories of many nations. Submarine warfare and aerial bombardment, initiated at the end of World War I, also marked the military campaigns. None of the combatants had expected a war like this, so long and so deadly. By its end a total of 10 million soldiers and civilians had been killed.

The victory of the Allies—primarily Britain, France, and America—over the Central Powers—Germany, the Austro-Hungarian Empire, and the Ottoman Empire—seemed at first to promise lasting peace in a new world order in which colonialism would give way to the independence of all national groups. The American President Woodrow Wilson declared that the goal of the Allies was to "make the world safe for democracy." The voices of all peoples should be heard. Allied war aims, as expressed by Wilson, called for:

> A free, open-minded, and absolutely impartial adjustment of all colonial claims, based upon a strict observance of the principle that in determining all such questions of sovereignty the interests of the population concerned must have equal weight with the equitable claims of the Government whose title is to be determined. (cited in Hofstadter, pp. 224–5)

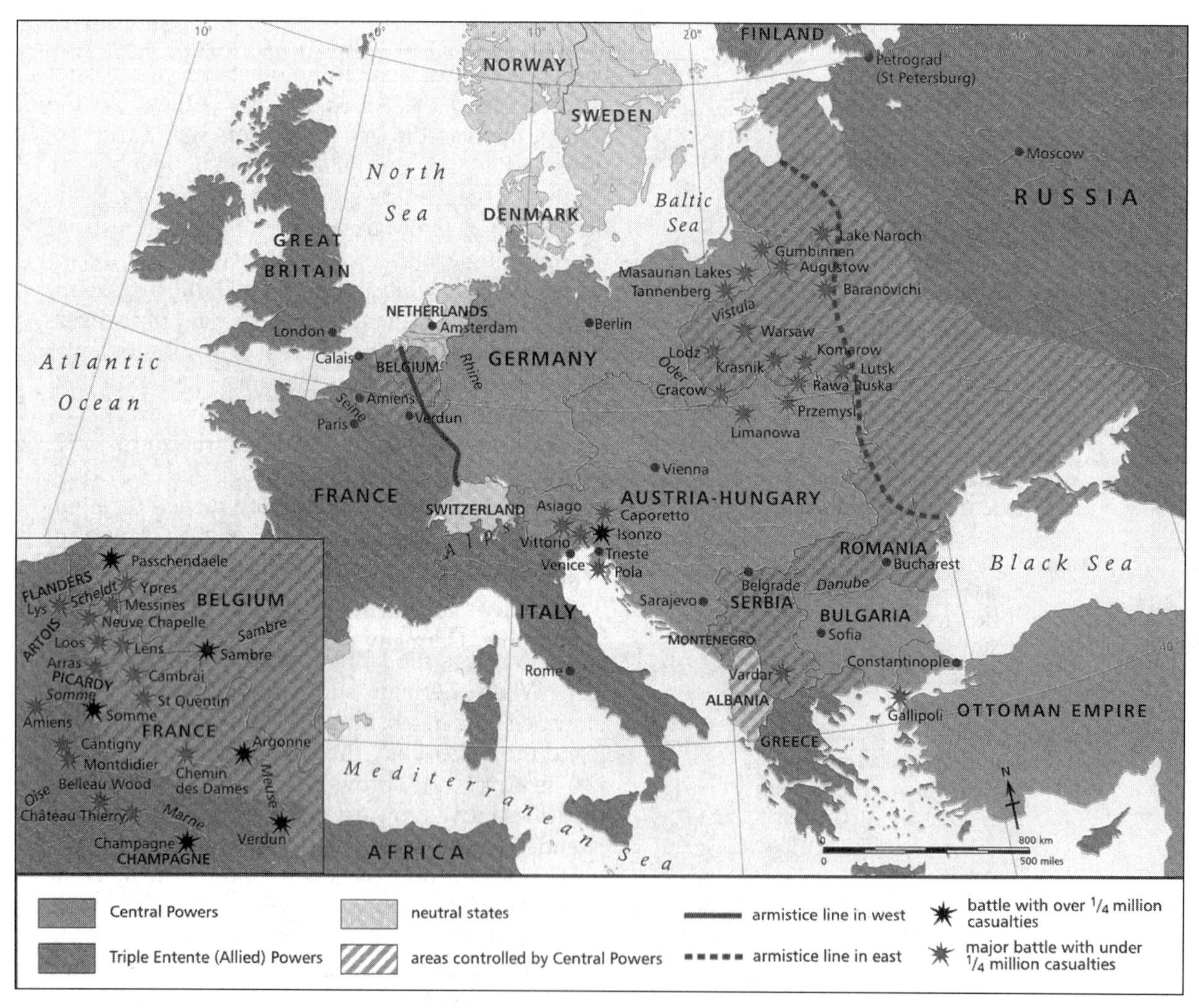

World War I European rivalries for political and economic superiority, within Europe and throughout its imperial holdings, erupted in 1914. A fragile system of alliances designed to contain the ambitions of Germany and Austria-Hungary (the Central Powers) collapsed, resulting in a conflict of horrific proportions. Turkey joined the Central Powers. In France and Italy a stalemate war of attrition developed, but in the east a war of thrust and counter-thrust caused enormous popular dissent and exhaustion, eventually bringing the collapse of the Turkish, Russian, and Austrian empires alike. In all, 10 million people died.

The Treaty of Versailles 1919

Many combatants came to the peace conference in Versailles, including Japan, an ally of Britain, that had seized Germany's possessions in East Asia during the war. Prince Faisal of Jordan represented Arabs who had contributed to victory over the Ottoman Empire. W.E.B. DuBois, an American scholar and political activist, called for social justice on behalf of the Pan-African Congress. In the end, the American, British, and French delegations were most critical to the post-war negotiations.

Two empires, the Austro-Hungarian and the Ottoman, were dissolved. Austria-Hungary was reduced and divided into two separate states. The Ottoman Empire disappeared; its core region in Anatolia and the city of Istanbul became the new nation of Turkey. From their former territories Poland, Czechoslovakia, and Yugoslavia were created; Romania and Greece were expanded. Syria and Lebanon were created as new proto-nations, temporarily **mandated** by the victors to France for tutelage until they could stand on their own independently; Palestine and Iraq were similarly created and mandated to Britain. The negotiators hoped the new borders would protect hostile ethnic groups from each other and from external domination. Legal safeguards for minorities were also enacted in new state constitutions.

Germany lost the region of Alsace-Lorraine to France, large areas in the east to Poland, and small areas to Czechoslovakia, Lithuania, Belgium, and Denmark. Germany was ordered to pay severe **reparations**, although in practice these were later negotiated to more realistic levels. Most gallingly for Germany, it was forced to accept responsibility for causing all the loss and damage of the war. Germany left Versailles humiliated, resentful, but, despite the loss of lands and the financial reparations, potentially still very powerful.

Photo not available.

The League of Nations was founded by the European powers in 1920 in the hope of eliminating warfare and fostering international cooperation. But disillusionment soon followed. The League was crippled by two congenital defects. First, its principal sponsor, the United States, refused to join. The world's most powerful technological, industrial, financial, and military power, the United States withdrew back into the isolation of its ocean defenses.

Second, the League reneged on its promise to end European colonialism in Asia and Africa. On the contrary, the peace treaty written in Versailles in 1919 perpetuated and enlarged foreign colonial rule through the grant of mandatory powers to Britain and France over Middle Eastern lands conquered from the Ottoman Empire and to Britain and others over Chinese lands previously held by Germany. In India, the British fell short on their wartime promise to expand self-rule and instead restricted freedoms of the press and assembly. The League died completely when it failed to counter Italy's invasion of Ethiopia, Germany's re-armament, and the outbreak of the Spanish Civil War in 1936. The war in Spain, 1936–9, saw right-wing insurgent forces led by General Francisco Franco, supported by troops dispatched by Germany and Italy, overthrow the liberal constitutional government, which received little organized support from democratic countries. Many analysts saw this confrontation, which turned Spain into a dictatorship for a generation, as a dress rehearsal for World War II. President Woodrow Wilson's visionary goal of making the world safe for democracy was deferred indefinitely.

ECONOMIC DEPRESSION BETWEEN THE WARS 1920–39 AND THE EXPANSION OF THE WELFARE STATE

Worldwide economic depression in the 1920s further destabilized domestic and international politics. Depression is a severe economic downturn in production and consumption which continues over a significant period of time, at least several months. Depression was considered normal in a free market economy as the forces of supply and demand periodically fell out of step and then came back into line. But the Great Depression was far more extreme in its extent and duration. On October 24, 1929—"Black Thursday"—the New York stock exchange crashed, ending five years of relative prosperity and marking the beginning of a worldwide economic depression which would continue until the outbreak of World War II in 1939.

The United States had emerged from World War I as a creditor nation. The payment of reparations from the war had crippled the German economy and a less rigorous schedule of payments was negotiated. It depended on loans from several nations, especially the United States. With the crash of the stock market, however, American financiers called in these loans, undercutting the European economy. In addition, agriculture, which had produced at record levels during the war, had difficulty cutting back production, resulting in huge, unsold surpluses and a depression in agriculture. In times of such economic difficulty, each country, and especially the United States, acted to close its borders to imports so that it could sell its own products internally without competition. But as each country raised its barriers, international markets dwindled, increasing the depression.

Mass unemployment swept Britain, America and Germany. Latin American countries, notably Argentina, which had been approaching a European living standard, found their economies devastated, turned away from European economic connections, and sought to salvage what they could through domestic development (see pp. 756–7). Communist Russia, also standing somewhat apart from the world economy, had introduced centralized national planning in 1928, emphasizing heavy industrialization. Its economy flourished, mocking the capitalist economies locked in depression (see pp. 614–19).

In 1921 there had been 2 million unemployed in Britain. They collected unemployment insurance in accord with an act that had been passed a decade earlier. The government also implemented an old age pension system, medical aids, and subsidized housing. But the world depression increased this unemployment to almost 3 million. Unemployment payments multiplied, while tax collections dropped. The welfare state expanded and government remained stable, but the depression ground on.

America, the country most dedicated to private capitalism and "rugged individualism," and therefore most reluctant to expand government social

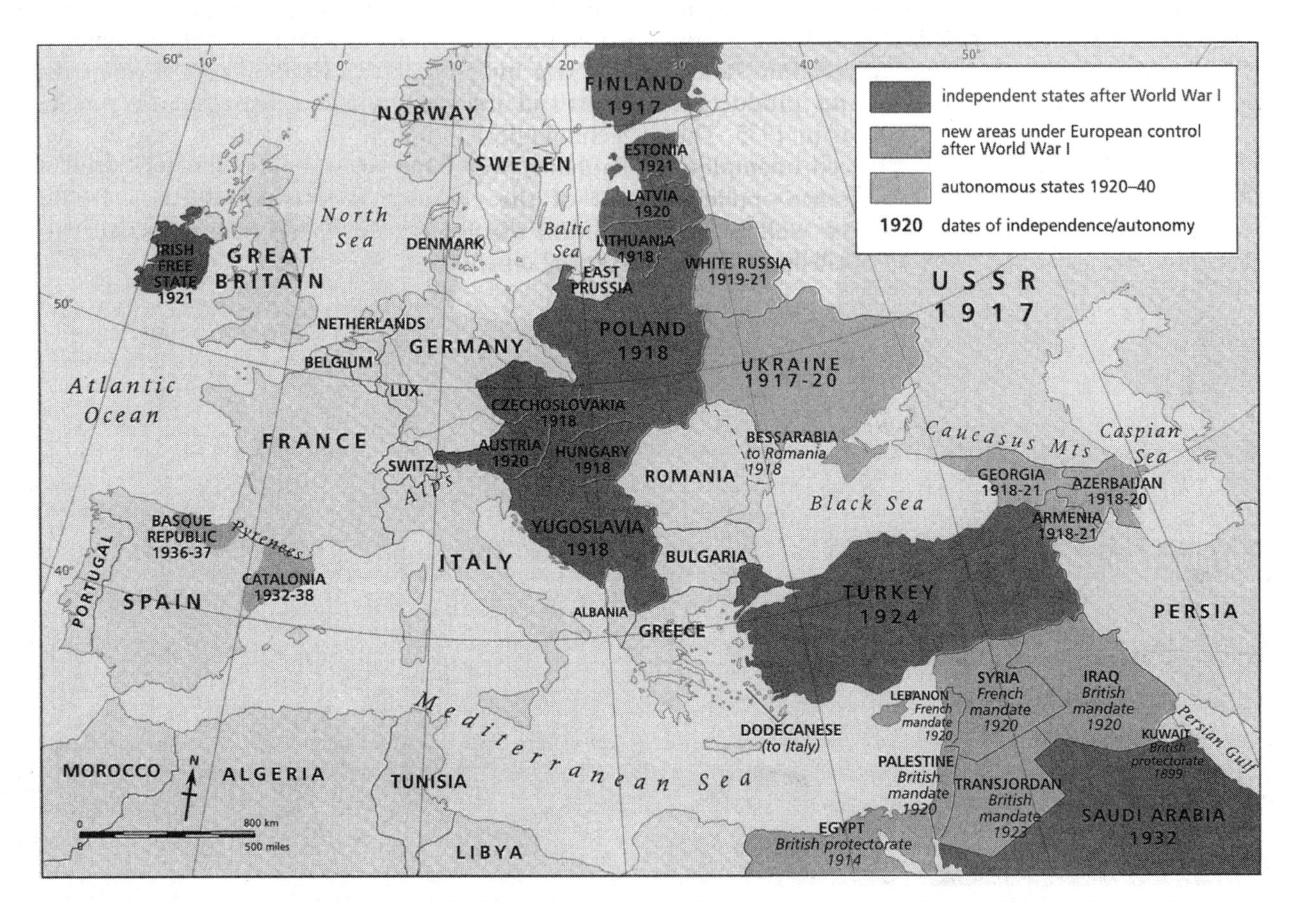

The new post-war nations In the wake of World War I, old empires fell and new states and colonies (called mandates and protectorates) were created. The Austro-Hungarian and Ottoman Empires were eradicated. A belt of nation states was established throughout Central and Eastern Europe; some had very brief lives and were soon annexed by Russia. The core of the Ottoman Empire became Turkey, while other segments were mandated to Britain and France as quasi-colonies.

welfare programs, saw national income drop by half between 1929 and 1932. Almost 14 million people were unemployed. Elected in 1932, in the midst of national despair, Democratic President Franklin Delano Roosevelt rallied the nation with charismatic optimism. Declaring that "The only thing we have to fear is fear itself," he immediately instituted social welfare programs as a means of preserving the capitalist foundation. He provided financial relief for the unemployed, public works projects to create construction jobs, subsidies to farmers to reduce production and eliminate surpluses, and federal support for low-cost housing and slum clearance. A Civilian Conservation Corps was established, ostensibly to promote conservation and reforestation, but mostly to provide some 3 million jobs to youth. The Tennessee Valley Authority created an immense hydroelectric program, combining flood control with rural electrification and regional economic development.

Roosevelt increased the regulation of business and promoted unions. The Securities and Exchange Commission, created in 1929, regulated the stock exchange. The National Recovery Administration encouraged regulation of prices and production until it was judged unconstitutional in 1935. The Social Security Act of 1935 introduced unemployment, old age, and disability insurance—policies already in place in Western Europe well before World War I. Child labor was abolished. Forty hours of work was set as the weekly norm. Minimum hourly wages were fixed. Union organization was encouraged and union membership grew from 4 million in 1929 to 9 million in 1940. The most capitalist of the major powers thus accepted the welfare state. Throughout the century, the scope of welfare expanded and contracted with different governments, philosophies of government, and budgetary conditions, but the principle that the state had a major role in protecting and advancing the welfare of its people persisted.

In Germany, the world depression followed on the heels of catastrophic inflation. In the 1920s the payment of very expensive war reparations wiped out the savings of the middle classes and amplified resentment over the punitive Versailles treaty, including its emphasis on German war guilt and insistence on Germany's disarmament. By 1924 industrial production had recovered but then the Depression wiped out the gains. The new government, located at Weimar, was perceived by many as a noble but weak and precarious experiment in constitutional democracy in a nation that had been led into war by a monarchy. Exciting new movements in art and architecture that were responsive to new technological potential for creativity, notably the Bauhaus, were threatened and ultimately driven out of the country. Anti-democratic forces and political ideologies triumphed over aesthetic and cultural creativity.

WORLD WAR II 1939–45

The strains of the 1930s ultimately triggered World War II. Germany, Italy, and Japan all sought to alleviate the suffering of the Depression by building up armaments and seeking new conquests. In Germany, Adolf Hitler (1889–1945) led a new party, the National Socialists, or Nazis. The party used strong-arm tactics to cow the opposition, but finally came to power legally on a platform of extreme nationalism, construction of public works, expansionism, and virulent anti-Semitism, all of which Hitler had spelled out in his manifesto, *Mein Kampf, "My Struggle."* Some business and military leaders supported him as a counter-weight to communism. As leader of the largest party in the German parliament in 1933, Hitler became Chancellor. He acted quickly to suppress all other parties, to revoke citizenship from Jews, and to arm Germany. He intensified each of these programs over the next few years and in 1936 he moved troops into the Rhineland (the region around the Rhine River) in violation of the Versailles Treaty. In 1938 Hitler invaded the German-speaking areas of Czechoslovakia. On September 1, 1939 he invaded Poland, and finally met resistance from the great powers who until this time had appeased his aggressions. Britain and France declared war.

In Italy, Benito Mussolini (1883–1945) had become prime minister in 1921 as leader of a party of 300,000 members who threatened to march on Rome if he were not appointed. His party was called fascist, meaning that it represented extreme nationalism, the power of the state over the individual, the supremacy of the leader over the party and nation, and a willingness to use intimidation and violence to achieve his goals:

> War alone brings up to its highest tension all human energy and puts the stamp of nobility upon the peoples who have the courage to meet it. ... Thus a doctrine which is founded upon this harmful postulate of peace is hostile to Fascism ... all the international leagues and societies ... as history will show, can be scattered to the winds when once strong national feeling is aroused by any motive. (Columbia College, p. 1151)

In 1935, preceding Hitler's moves, Mussolini invaded and took over Ethiopia while other nations sat by and did not act, not even by closing the Suez Canal to Italy's troops. Mussolini did not share Hitler's anti-Semitism, but in many other respects

WORLD WAR II—KEY EVENTS

July 7, 1937	Japanese troops invade China
September 1939	Nazi-Soviet Pact: Germany invades Poland. Britain and France declare war. Poland partitioned between Germany and Russia
Mar–Apr 1940	German forces conquer Denmark, Norway, the Netherlands, and Belgium
May–June	Italy declares war on Britain and France; German forces conquer France
June 21, 1941	German forces invade USSR
Dec 7	Japanese bomb US Navy, Pearl Harbor
Jan-Mar 1942	Indonesia, Malaya, Burma and the Philippines are conquered by Japan
April 1942	US planes bomb Tokyo
June	US Navy defeats Japanese at the Battle of the Midway
1942–43	End of Axis resistance in North Africa; Soviet victory in Battle of Stalingrad
1943–44	Red Army slowly pushes Wehrmacht back to Germany
June 6, 1944	Allies land in Normandy (D-Day)
Feb 1945	Yalta conference: Churchill, Roosevelt, and Stalin discuss post-war settlement
May 7, 1945	Germany surrenders
August 6	US drops atom bomb on Hiroshima, Japan, and then on Nagasaki
August 14	Japan surrenders

he was an appropriate junior partner in Hitler's aggressive plans. When civil war broke out in Spain in 1936, both Hitler and Mussolini sent assistance to the right-wing Nationalists. At this point their two nations formed an alliance called the Axis.

In East Asia, as we shall see in the next chapter, Japan also moved aggressively against its neighbor, China. Following the successes of the Meiji Restoration (see p. 564), Japan had become the strongest military power in East Asia, and had cultivated political philosophies to justify invading and taking over neighboring countries. Like Germany, it too had a rapidly rising population, reaching 62 million by 1928, and felt confined. Japan needed to import most of its raw materials but it was technologically more sophisticated than its neighbors. In 1931, Japanese military forces seized Manchuria. The Japanese government had forbidden this action, but acquiesced after the fact. The League of Nations condemned the invasion but imposed no real sanctions, and the condemnation moved Japan to ally with Germany and Italy. In 1937 Japan invaded China, and the Pacific War, as the Japanese call World War II, had begun (see p. 630). Japan became a member of the Axis powers from December 1941.

Until Germany's invasion of Poland the democratic nations which had been victorious in World War I had observed all these separate aggressions and done nothing. The League of Nations had collapsed in the wake of Italy's invasion of Ethiopia. England and France had acquiesced in all of Germany's earlier moves. America had retreated to isolation. These nations had not caused World War II, but by their inaction they had done nothing to prevent it. After their declaration of war, France

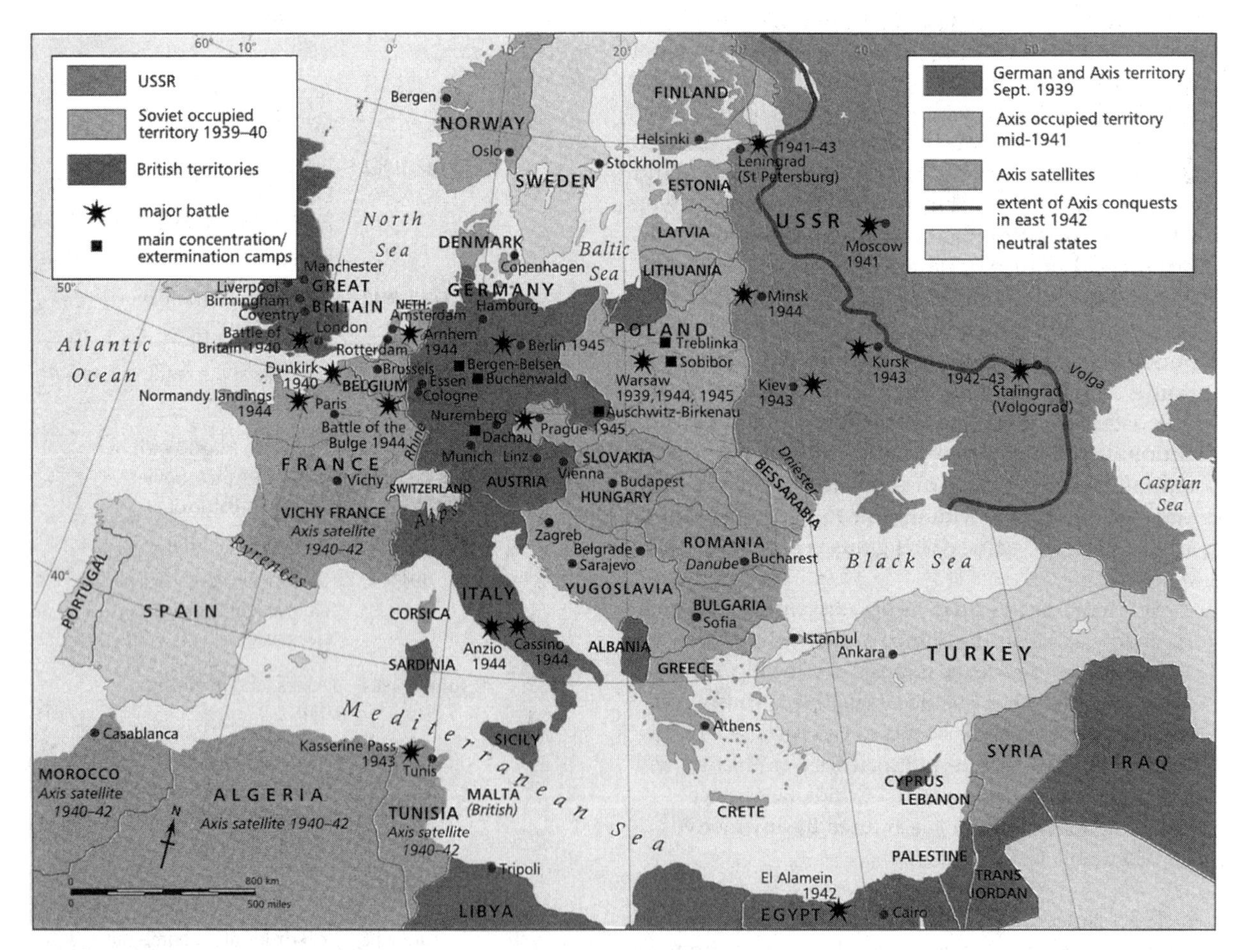

World War II in Europe Fighting began in 1939 with a "blitzkrieg," or lightning war, by Germany and her Italian ally. By late 1942 they controlled most of Europe. But Germany's invasion of Russia in 1941 brought the power of that huge state into opposition and enmeshed Germany into exhausting land war. Britain held out defensively and then began to fight back, especially after the United States entered the war, bringing in air power and material support. By early 1944, the tide had turned.

and Britain took no immediate military action against Germany and a brief period of "phony war" followed during the winter of 1939-40. In April 1940 Hitler again went on the offensive and Germany invaded Denmark and Norway. On May 10 it invaded Belgium and advanced into France. Allied forces were evacuated from France at the end of May and on June 22 the French signed an armistice with Germany. Germany now turned its attention to Britain, and heavy bombing of London and other strategic cities in England took place throughout the autumn.

From Europe the war spread to Africa and by 1942 Germany and its allies had conquered most of western and central Europe, almost half of European Russia and much of north Africa. Battles took place on sea, land, and in the air. As the war progressed the Grand Alliance of Britain, the Free French (an exile government based in London), and the Soviet Union slowly evolved. With the Japanese bombing of the American naval base in Pearl Harbor in December 1941, America entered the war sending combat forces to both Europe and the Pacific. America also joined the other powers of the Grand Alliance (and the larger coalition of twenty other countries) to defeat the Axis powers, and the war in Europe finally ended at the beginning of May 1945 with the fall of Berlin and the German collapse in Italy and on the Western Front. In the Pacific the United States dropped an atomic bomb on the city of Hiroshima, Japan, on August 6 and three days later another atomic bomb on the city of Nagasaki (see p. 634). On August 14 Japan surrendered and the Pacific war was also over.

World War II is called a "total war" because it involved more nations than had ever before engaged in armed combat and destroyed large numbers of both military and civilians. It is estimated that about 45 million people died—30 million of them civilians. The heaviest fighting was in the Soviet Union and it lost more people than any other country—around 20 million. Japan lost about 2 million people and Germany just over 4 million. Britain lost 400,000 people and the United States about 300,000. Over 6 million Jews died in Nazi concentration camps.

Technology in the War

World War II witnessed a dramatic increase in the use of technology—tanks, submarines, and aircraft—as well as the number of troops. Winston Churchill (1874–1965), prime minister of Britain, captured the significance of this increase in a broadcast to America. After commanding the Battle of Britain, in which the Royal Air Force, aided by the newly invented radar, defended Britain against the bombing runs of Germany's Luftwaffe (airforce), he requested equipment and technology: "Give us the tools and we shall finish the job."

The mobilization of so many personnel and so much equipment opened new visions of life. People who served overseas and who saw for the first time new modes of life, as well as death, were changed in the process. Most affected by the process were women. The demands of keeping factories running full blast during the war while putting millions of soldiers under arms required a larger labor force. During World War I millions of women began to work outside the home for pay, and the stereotypes of "men's work" and "women's work" started to erode. This experience contributed to the achievement of women's suffrage in the United States after World War I and in Western Europe after World War II. After World War I the majority of women did not remain in the workforce, but after World War II women continued in unprecedented numbers to work in industrial and unconventional jobs. The mobilization of women was, however, culturally specific: German and Japanese women were encouraged to continue to stay at home, despite the exigencies of war; women served actively in Russian factories; Britain conscripted some women in World War II.

Horrors of the War

Two horrors distinguished World War II from all others that came before. Massive warfare had been known before. So too had individual leaders setting out to conquer the known world, from Alexander and Genghis Khan to Napoleon. But the decision by the ruling National Socialist (Nazi) party of Germany to obliterate an entire people—the Jews—from the world, without any ostensible economic or territorial goal, and mobilizing the full resources of the state against the unarmed opponent to carry out the task, constituted a new goal, one executed by new technology.

Anti-Semitism was not new in Europe, but the Nazi program was unprecedented. First, it reversed the trend of acceptance and civic equality introduced a century and a half earlier by the French Revolution. Second, it targeted Jews as an ethnic or racial group rather than as a religion. This was not a policy for conversion or even for exile. Anyone with a Jewish grandparent was considered Jewish under Nazi laws and marked for death.

Although born of an Austrian father and raised in Vienna, Adolf Hitler, the leader of Germany, declared the "Aryan" Germans at the top and the Jews at the bottom of a hierarchy that included the British and other northern Europeans near the top, Poles and other Slavs in the middle, and Africans and other peoples of color near the bottom. Intending to exterminate these "lesser peoples," he built concentration camps where prisoners were used as slave labor before being gassed and cremated. Millions of Jews were brought to the camps by a railway network specially constructed for this

Photo not available.

purpose. Even in the closing days of the war, when Germany clearly had been defeated, Hitler ordered the trains and the crematoria to continue operations. By 1945, some 6 million Jews accompanied by millions from other "inferior" races, especially gypsies and Poles, joined also by homosexuals and handicapped people, had been murdered. The Holocaust, as this butchery was named, made World War II into a conflict of good versus evil even in the eyes of many Germans after the war. The moral crisis and the appalling devastation of the Holocaust are impossible to fully comprehend, but the writing of survivors such as Elie Wiesel (see p. 597) helps us to understand them. (See also the importance of the Holocaust experience in the founding of the State of Israel on p. 701.)

The atomic bombs dropped by America on Hiroshima and Nagasaki, Japan, introduced a new weapon ultimately capable of destroying all life on earth, changing both the nature of war and peace as well as humanity's conception of itself. At the first test of the bomb, as the fireball rose over the Alamogordo, New Mexico, testing grounds, J. Robert Oppenheimer, appalled architect of the bomb and director of the $2 billion Manhattan Project that produced it, quoted from the Hindu *Bhagavad Gita*: "I am become as death, the destroyer of worlds." Of the 245,000 people living in Hiroshima on 6 August, 75,000 died that day, perhaps another 100,000 thereafter, while still others suffered various kinds of radiation poisoning and genetic deformation. Three days later, a second bomb was dropped on Nagasaki, and on 14 August Japan submitted its unconditional surrender. Today, despite years of continuing efforts towards arms control, there are tens of thousands of nuclear bombs and warheads on missiles, submarines, and airplanes capable of destroying human life many times over.

In retrospect, debate has raged over the wisdom and purpose of using the atomic bomb to end the war in the Pacific. Critics see the act as racist, pointing out that this weapon was not used in Europe (although the bomb was not prepared by the time

Germany surrendered in May, 1945). Cynics suggest that its real purpose had less to do with defeating Japan than with demonstrating American power to Russia on the eve of the Cold War (see p. 602). Those who justify the use of the bomb suggest that losses of life on both sides would have been higher had the Allies invaded Japan's home islands instead. The casualties in the battles for Pacific Islands had been in the hundreds of thousands, and war in Japan itself might cost a million more Allied troops and even more Japanese. The use of the bomb certainly saved Allied lives, and even may have saved Japanese lives. Finally, they argue, in a war of such scope and brutality, combatants inevitably use the weapons that are available.

Some of the war technology had by-products of use to civilians as well. Radar, which Britain developed to protect its island kingdom from Germany in the Battle of Britain, 1940, was valuable in commercial aviation. Nuclear energy could be employed under careful supervision for peaceful uses in power generation and medicine. Drugs, such as sulfa and penicillin, entered the civilian pharmacopeia. But the technology of warfare drew the lion's share of the scientific and technological budgets of many nations, including the largest industrial powers, the USA and USSR, and of many developing countries, as well.

Following World War II, the temporary alliance between the United States, Britain, and France on the one hand and the Soviet Union on the other completely shattered. A period of "cold war" began (see p. 602), ending only in 1991 with the break-up of the Soviet Union (see Chapter 19). The division of Europe between the western, democratic, capitalist or mixed-economy states and the eastern states under communist governments ended. A new re-unification of Europe had already begun in the late 1980s as many of the USSR's satellite states in eastern Europe became independent. In 1990 East and West Germany were reunified. As the Cold War had siphoned enormous amounts of money and creative energy into military concerns, so the end of the Cold War promised to make more funds and energies available for peaceful uses.

Photo not available.

Index